Traveling in Time and Space

Traveling in Time and Space

A personal encounter with Jesus

Written and illustrated by Diane Marie Taylor

Writers Club Press

San Jose   New York   Lincoln   Shanghai

Traveling in Time and Space
A personal encounter with Jesus

Writers Club Press
an imprint of iUniverse, Inc.

For information address:
iUniverse, Inc.
5220 S. 16th St., Suite 200
Lincoln, NE 68512
www.iuniverse.com

ISBN: 0-595-20526-7

Printed in the United States of America

This book is dedicated to the people of the future.

Reach for the unknown and find God
Reach for God and find the unknown
God's laughter bubbles into stars

CONTENTS

Part III

ACKNOWLEDGEMENTS

I would like to acknowledge all the writers, scientists, and spiritual thinkers who have written the many books I read through the years. Without this great source of material and knowledge I might not have grown so securely in spirit and insight. I give thanks to these thousands of writers for their beliefs, ideas, and speculations, but I also want to give special mention to the authors whose ideas helped me write this book: Courtney Brown, Zecharia Sitchin, Donald Spoto, Whitley Strieber, and Fred Wolf. And of course, Y, the highly evolved friend who I choose not to name at this time.

INTRODUCTION

I have been traveling somewhere for as long as I can remember, Infrequently, to be sure, because sometimes a number of years would go by before I would be 'gone traveling' again. Suddenly I would be standing on greener grass staring at a bluer sky; then, just as suddenly I would be back home again. As a general rule, I usually popped in and popped out again within seconds, never sure where I had gone or why.

The first time that I can remember traveling was as a child. I remember flying in my cousin's pink chenille bathrobe. I sat down in it, wrapped the arms around my waist, folded the flaps over my legs and feet and off I went. I flew off the second floor balcony, swerved left and down towards the cracked, concrete driveway, skimmed a turning curl near the red brick house next door, back towards the alley, then up. I towered over the rooftops and trees of River Rouge, Michigan, flying higher and higher up into the dark star-blue sky. I can still see Jefferson to the Rouge River, the bridge and nearby streets. I vaguely remember one dark night watching from above as a man stumbled, one side of the alley to the other, searching and rummaging in the trash containers. But most of those early memories are hazy or forgotten because they happened so long ago; besides; it was all just a dream, wasn't it?

I had always assumed that flying in a dream was just that, a dream, until a few years ago, when I began to travel to other places, within and without of dreams. These travels are of two kinds: voluntary and involuntary. I make a deliberate effort to travel to some places but other places I visit, popping in to and out of, whether I want to go or not, are obviously involuntary. Of the two kinds, involuntary traveling seems the most intriguing because, though infrequent, it leads to the most interesting and complex speculations, any one of which is ripe with new ideas about where, how, and why. Even so, it seems that I can never pull in enough information to complete the picture, or learn the reason or rational that underlies the travel. But heaven has given me a promise, "You will understand one day." And, finally I do, and so will you by the end of this book.

Jesus is my constant companion throughout this book and initiated many of the later travels so it is natural that I look to him for answers, which usually come to me in

hints rather than direct statements, puzzles rather than answers, but when Jesus does speak, I try to keep his words as accurate as possible. But please remember that my writing is done after the fact, not during his visit. My memory is imperfect therefore my writing is also imperfect.

At first, when I began this book I had a few facts and a vast number of speculations as if I were a miner holding a large sieve under a faucet of running water waiting for gold to appear and just as silly. But ultimately, I find that gold nuggets have appeared, and are scattered throughout in abundance. Therefore, this book is a process, a process of learning and instruction for myself and you, the reader. I find at its end that I am a new and different person, that my faith has remained solid, that my questions, if not answered completely to my satisfaction, have at least matured, and that my love for Jesus is still pure and unshakable. So I ask you to please come, go with me to wondrous places vivid with speculations and promises, places in a heaven for our time.

Traveling in Time and Space is comprised of three books. After writing each book I thought I was finished, it turned out I was not because Jesus requested that I write a new book, again and again. I am writing one now. And I never know in which direction he will lead me. Each book or part is set up differently and goes in a different direction.

I wrote most of the introduction for the first book after I completed it, I didn't know at the time that I would be adding two more books but its information still holds true for the whole Travel book. The second book is comprised of new travels to a single specific place, a short explanation is included in the first chapter. For the third book, Jesus suggested that I leave the notes as I wrote them. I have done as he instructed and only changed and edited for readability and accuracy. This third section resembles a diary than a book. Actually, I don't consider the Travel book mine in the usual sense, it belongs to Jesus because he as authored much of it. I will say this: I promise you that I have stayed true to his words and statements as much as I possibly know how.

Part I

AUDIENCE WITH GOD

On this trip I didn't pop in and out; instead, I was invited, lifted and flown to my destination. Two angels transported me to an audience with God. It happened like this: I sat down on the bed crossing my legs in preparation for meditation, when suddenly two invisible forces took hold of the outside of my shoulders. [1] One angel on each side lifted me, swiftly and easily, through the dark star filled heavens until I was set down on my feet in front of a near blinding, searing, golden light. The angels left me standing there, in terror and alone, in front of this swirling, golden maelstrom that filled all space with God's might.

I felt my insides squeeze, my guts wither and dry as if beneath a hot desert sun. Feeling abject shame and fear, I begged my body to crunch down or curl into a fetal position to hide, but could not, my body refused to obey. So I stood, it seemed forever, looking into a vast, swirling yellow mist. Finally, after long minutes of intrigue, I thought I saw a figure behind gold waves and swirls, a body, "a face?" a directional focus in which to direct my fright and anxieties.

Impatient and fearful, I gathered up enough courage to speak calling out to the billowing, mighty force in front of me, "We need heaven! We need justice!" Then cringing inside at my audacity under this vast universal chamber sky, I felt a true smallness and worthlessness of being, I was an ant watching a huge boot descend from above, I was a fallen moth with fire blackened wings, I was a little person exhausted from terror. It was

---

[1] They didn't grab me under the armpits like in my painting, in fact, the whole painting looks opposite to what I actually saw because what I witnessed is indescribable.

then that a powerful, male voice vibrated and thundered through all of space, "Heaven is not what you think!" "There will be justice!"

After God's voice answered me, I literally fell back onto my bed. Suddenly I was back in my sitting position, back into myself, so to speak, more quickly than I had ascended. I had fallen back to earth like a discarded piece of tissue wrapping paper, cut bow dangling, war torn and changed. I had been abruptly flung back to earth, my house, my bed— dismissed. I had the sensation of having fallen from a great height—no angels carried me home.

Shook-up, I got out of bed and went downstairs. I needed a cigarette (I still smoked back then) and a cup of hot coffee badly. Swirling questions and thoughts kept me awake all that night. I didn't know how to feel. I wasn't sure if I felt like a damp piece of ragged, dirty cloths or a new, polished copper penny. I had a hard time adjusting to what had just happened. I kept asking myself, "Why me? Why did God speak to me? God! Really God?"

The next day, I was still in a quandary of amazement; I don't think, to this day that I have completely recovered my equilibrium from that visit. I doubt that I will ever solve all the arguments still spewing around inside my head. I know I will never forget and I will never be the same. Will I ever stop asking myself why and what God meant? I have come up with some theories, and bit by bit, with the help of Jesus, I am slowly searching out answers. My mentor, Jesus Christ, who is also a friend, companion, guru, master, Lord, teacher, and lover is slowly directing me through these many questions and answers. I will share my experiences with you as I learn and explore.

NEXUS

Just recently, in the fall of 97, I abruptly and involuntarily traveled to a place I call Nexus because it looked like a hundred mobius strips tied together into a knotted center with people riding roads up and down, around, going ever-which-way. One minute I was sitting with my head back, arms on lap, sigh of quiet pleasure, a cup of tea on the table, peace and joy intended, relaxed in my chair, when, suddenly, I was somewhere else. I stood inside a vast amphitheater, a glass bubble filled with the bustle of people going about their business with, it seemed to me, a quiet, determined energy. Overhead, I saw a deep blue/black star-specked sky. Star light shined down and reflected off the moving figures, coating them in dull, washed-out hues; star people riding the multiple road-ways or escalators that spread upwards and outwards in every direction, some leaving, some coming my way, up, down, and across. Most people wore cloaks with hoods the color of star-washed sepia, pale pinks, or somber greens. I watched figures disappear into the sky at the top and others appear; seemingly, out of nowhere.

No one looked my way or took any notice of me as I stood there gawking. Perhaps no one would have ever noticed me if it hadn't been for a young lady who almost walked into me. She stopped, startled by my presence.

"Why! You're from Earth!" she exclaimed.

Her voice held a hint of amusement as her face smiled at me. Her light, beautiful, skin shone radiant while her eyes sparked in ripples of amused light. Hood slung far back on her head, light blond hair askew, one bare arm reached out of a large over-cuff towards me. Just then, at the part where she would have touched my arm or I would have gathered up the nerve to ask, "Who are you?" or "Where am I?" I popped back into my chair.

Stunned, I sat there for a few unbelievable moments before I could pull myself back together. I needed to think about what had just happened.

What had happened? The questions kept circling around in my head, "Where did I go." "Who was that lady" "Why did I leave from there so quickly" Fear, I think, is what sent me back into my chair, fear because the place was just too strange. But, I shouldn't have been so upset; this kind of sudden, involuntary travel has happened to me before, many times in fact, but the vivid abruptness of each trip makes me gasp anew, as if I needed to catch my breath from underwater. Each time it happens I feel a new born shock that it could, I feel stymied, empty, unfinished. And my biggest question is not, "Where did I go," so much as it is, "Why can't I stay longer."

No answer, of course. So, I am left to wonder if it is fear of strange places that pull me back into my chair or is it inexperience or a dislike of new adventure? Am I too timid to travel? I don't believe any of this for a minute; I am not afraid of strange places or new adventures, so why can't I stay longer?

Well, more questions than I can ever answer roll through my mind: Who was the lady? Why could she speak English? Why did she startle at my presence? Where did I go? Could I stay longer next time? When I try to sort out the questions or try to answer them, I keep getting farther into nowhere.

Was the lady startled because I was from earth, or because a chance meeting with an Earthling is infrequent? I wondered if her English was spoken inside my mind or if it could be a universal language, not likely. Were the other figures human? She certainly looked and acted human. Could the visual setting have been taken from my mind so that I saw only what I could 'put together' or 'was programmed to see'? I have learned through the years that we can only see what we are accustomed to seeing. Could it have been a dream? "No," it was too vivid; besides I was wide-awake.

My visit to Nexus seemed to take only a minute to begin and end. It was so short that I've had to re-play the event in my mind so I could describe it. Which leads me to ask, "If the visit was so short, just what part of myself actually went to Nexus, my body, my mind or both? A minute of time hardly allowed for my actual, one hundred and thirty five plus pounds of body to leave, go to some place in space or time or somewhere beyond Earth then travel back again to drop back into my easy chair.

However I want to play with questions and answers, I did experience some kind of dislocation in space/time; so, I surmise that it must have been a type of out-of-body experience. I say a type of OBE because in the usual out-of-body experience you have the feeling of being in two places at once, in fact, you can see your body down below, sitting or laying, as you float above it tied by a silver cord. When I traveled to Nexus, I had no sensation of my body moving apart from my mind or of being in two places at once. I felt whole and together, despite being a little shook up. What I felt was immediate, sudden, and involuntary. There was no forethought of where I would like to go or how; my soul/mind just popped into Nexus and out again.

I have learned since I went to Nexus that I don't stay long in one place, not because I am too timid or afraid, but because I need to take these awe inspiring bits of knowledge in small doses so I don't get culture shock. I need much more information to decide what exactly is happening when I travel. One event that may hint towards an answer is something my mentor, guide, and Lord, Jesus Christ, told me after he took me to revisit Nexus (at my request). He told me that I couldn't go up one of the roadways or escalators because "it would take me too far," and that, "I wasn't ready, yet." I am not sure if he was referring to my mental inability or my lack of knowledge or my cultural ineptitude. Although I haven't rode to the top of Nexus yet, once I was carried up to an audience with God.

CHRIST MENTOR

Jesus Christ's love is a light that surrounds the earth, a lacy, air-net, shimmering with light that grows, strand-by-strand, prayer-by-prayer, and lover-by-lover. His love multiplies like lace on a loom each silver thread, each flowery string connecting one person to another, each to every other and back to Christ. This all-encompassing web of emotional light swirling around our world is creating and expanding itself all the time. I sometimes compare it to the World Wide Web, flowing with energetic output and input, switches turned on but never off.

At first the global internet doesn't seem a good analogy to spiritual love, but ideas aggregate to one another, theories coalesce, old definitions squander limits without new input and modern ideas. I find that modern scientific thinking can enhance religious ideas rather than hinder. New terms can pull us away from old-fashioned thinking. Jesus can indeed be made of light energy and, just as strange; God can easily permeate the substance of the universe through the new ideas in relativity or quantum physics. All of us whether saints, prophets or just ordinary people are made of electrons and mostly empty space. We all interface and take part in the dance of the universe.

I often imagine Jesus' time as computer time. Then it would be as nothing to appear at two places at once and talk to a lot of people, to be on earth and photo-imaging Saturn at the same time. Computers can. A Science Fiction book I read once had Einstein reborn in a computer; he could speak to many people at a time because he lived in nanoseconds while we dragged out our lives in normal slow time. I am not saying Jesus is a computer; my point is that, modern terms can help us imagine his attributes, to make them more visible to us. And, just as many industrial machines would have looked amazing to someone long ago, it may be that God's 'machines' look like unfathomable magic to us. I always worry about using up Jesus' time, but he assures me that I needn't worry, that I am not using up any of his time. Somehow, by a mechanism I can't understand, he can be with me and with you at the same time. Somehow he can be at my side as mentor and guide, and yours too.

Every one who wants to mind-travel should have a guide or mentor. A mentor can introduce us into new areas of interest and enhance our understanding of where to go and what to do. Usually, our mentor will act as leader when we are afraid to venture further than we have gone before. Also, we usually get a sense of kinetic energy and power from a mentor that restores balance to our psyche. Lastly, we need our mentor to shore up our belief in our own powers of vision and love. Love can be a hard idea to grasp and keep. The idea that it is love which allows us free movement and joining throughout the universe must be felt to be believed and then reinforced time after time through imagination. Some people may catch on sooner than others, I did not. Sometimes I still grope forward blindly. At times, I've acted so infantile, I was and still feel shamed by my behavior but I will tell you about it anyway so you can see Jesus' love.

One night I was so distressed I kept screaming in a rage to Jesus, angels or anyone within my voice range. I stormed up and out into the blackness of space, assumed a fetal position, and then pulled blackness around myself like a cloak. I wanted dark, emptiness, aloneness. He spoke my name and I cried the more lashing out my anger and hopelessness; "Why, Why, Why"? I screamed at Jesus. Finely, temper tantrum over, feeling wrenched and wrung dry, I opened the dark, silent shell and let his softness envelop me. I know my behavior was childish and belittling. I know believe me; it embarrasses me still to write it. But my scream of hurt and pain can serve a purpose, it can show you Jesus' reaction of understanding and tolerance. It points out his love even when we don't disserve it. Jesus long enduring love is what helps us heal our wounds and keep moving through life. I've learned that heaven can help our feelings but often heaven can't or prefers not to change the circumstances that cause the pain.

My reputation is what I was screaming about. A number of lies had been going around about me for years. A specific lie seemed to be more alive than I was and usually got where I was going before me. I couldn't understand why Jesus didn't stop this lie from hurting me. It seemed as if all heaven ever did was soothe my wounds, a great gift unless you are at the end of tolerance like I seemed to be. Truthfully, I couldn't have survived my sanity without Heaven's soothing help; I realized this at the time but I wanted a real fix up, a real solution, real involvement from heaven. This lie had hounded me for years, no matter where I went, school, social, and even church I was treated like some kind of monster. I couldn't get a boyfriend because this lie arrived before I did. My own family even avoided me for long time because of it. Words to the contrary did not dispel anyone's belief. It got so bad that, at times, I wished I could die. I felt like a modern day Job but without the good ending.

Now that the pain is over, more or less, I have learned that there was some purpose to all the horrible madness I endured, I needed to build up a tough hide against gossip. Instead of worrying what other people say about me, I need to get active and forget about gossip and untruths. Besides, most people don't realize the pain they are causing or that I know. Often, I can mentally see people as they discuss me from miles away, though I can't always understand what is said, nor is what they say always hurtful. It is easy to talk about other people and I try to catch myself before I begin because it hurts deeply to be slandered or gossiped about. The pain can be mind destroying, especially if it is deliberate and slanderous. Jesus was referring to my mental anguish when he told me "many people never make it this far." I assume he meant that many people are driven to commit suicide. We all have lessons that we need to learn in life, I just hope and pray yours isn't as tortuous as mine was. I already feel sorrow for your pain, your puzzlement, and your agony because spiritual growth is always painful. Remember, your pain may serve a purpose as mine has. It may be the thorn that caused me to finally write this book, the impetus that got me moving further towards heaven. Whatever you do, don't give up, let Jesus be your guide.

Many religions require mentors or guides as a step towards the deeper, hidden mysteries. It was while reading about the Sufis that my hunger for a mentor grew into uncontrollable proportions. I thought that I couldn't continue my spiritual growth without some kind of help but despaired of getting it. Lack of money, as usual, was my limiting factor. Nothing in life is free and neither are some religions, I realized when I wanted to take a TM (Transcendental Meditation) class; or the time I desired to go on a retreat to shore up my faith; both were far beyond my means. I was afraid that my spiritual growth was stopped cold. I needn't have worried because Jesus stepped in to fill the gap.

He was suddenly 'there' beside me. What did I feel? It was many years ago but I imagine that I felt then as I feel now when Jesus is suddenly 'there' beside me. I feel expanded into his realm, I sense a deep reciprocal love pour between us, and most of all, I perceive his presence with a certainty and truthfulness that is hard to define. He gives off an aura of wisdom and lordship. Let me add here that even though we all have our inner voices, our conscience, and I certainly have mine, even though there are other speakers out there, gurus, saints, and angels at various places, even though some messengers speak falsely, when Jesus stands beside me, I do not doubt it is Jesus. It is only later, after he has left that my doubts surface. It is then that I question if that was Jesus or an imitation. Doubts always plague me because I have a great tendency toward mistrust, but then his smile will reassure me, his message comfort me, and my soul will know him. I've told Jesus of these doubts I experience after he has gone, he told me, "You always know."

So He stepped in and took up the role as my mentor, which at first, may seem unbelievable, but isn't because he is there for all of us when we pray. I am proud to have Jesus as a guide. In the past he was there when I needed him, too. I would pray and often feel a flow of inner peace and harmony as his answer. But this was different, more personal and true-Jesus as my guide? In all these years, the strangeness and startlement of it hasn't lessened, sometimes I still think I am a little crazy but Jesus assures me that he is he. Every once in a while, quite often at first, I'd gather up the nerve to ask again, "Are you really Jesus, the one who died for us?"

This is not as stupid a question as it seems because there are many people 'up there' and none of them have names, that I know of, only personality or "character." This means that when you travel you are flying almost blind because you have no referents. You tend to feel lost in a topsy-turvy topological landscape, a maze of nameless people and places. What is in a name? I didn't realize how dependent I was on such a simple reference like a name. It's like trying to think with labels or write without capitals. I don't know how I am perceived 'up there' because no one has ever asked me my name nor have I asked them for theirs. Just by meeting a person you can feel that he or she is enlightened or holy. One man I saw, obviously a great teacher, was sitting in front of red curtains, with his legs crossed in a yoga position, speaking to a group of initiates. He looked up at me as we arrived and smiled, none of his initiates turned to look at us. Another person I met wore a beard and long robe and showed me a glowing, silver book saying that I would learn many things from it. No, names are not needed here, which brings up another point, there is no way of knowing if a person is alive (on earth alive) or not (alive there but dead on earth). Alive or dead, the definition hardly matters because when standing in the presence of a great, holy person, all referents pale.

Usual referents don't apply to Jesus Christ either; we can throw away our measuring sticks when Jesus is nearby. With Jesus as my guide my knowledge increased quickly. He took me to visit people and places I would have never thought of alone. These visits never lasted longer than a minute or two but always had some meaning beyond my comprehension at the time. Often Jesus would ask me where I wanted to visit, he'd take my hand and off we'd go. I usually chose exotic places off world.

The first time we went to Mars, I was awe struck even though I couldn't see anything through the sand storm that was raging. As we stood against a vertical rock-face, sand blew past us turning even the close rock-face hazy, plus it was very dark so we couldn't see much. We both reached out our hands and touched the rock` I felt a thrill jolt through me from the excitement of it. Then we were gone. I remember my trip to Mars with Jesus whenever I begin to feel sorry for myself for the worldly adventures I am missing. Who else can say they've been to Mars?

One time I asked Jesus to take me to his favorite place on Earth. We went to Palestine. We walked past streets filled with people from his time, over small, lush hills, past open caves and near a large body of water. We stood for a minute on a hill filled with small trees and looked over the countryside; it was beautifully green. I didn't know it would be so green there. "It's not as green now, is it?" I said to him. "No," His smile held a sadness that wasn't there before. We left and went to visit other places.

It seemed to me that our relationship grew as time went on, I mean in the sense that he became more visual. I now realized that I could speak directly to Jesus and, more importantly, occasionally, though always with minimal words, he would answer. Now I thought I could get some real answers from him about the universe and our place in it. Nothing, of course, should be too easy, and getting solid answers was not.

The usual answer to any question, what is the purpose of the universe? Why is there pain? What are we here for? Are we evolving, getting better? Is heaven out there or in here or is heaven in the future or now? But, when I asked questions that were answerable, relating to human concerns, I would receive a lesson by experiencing it first hand.

I have always had a soft spot of special love and concern in my heart for young children, often to the exclusion of other people. One day a female voice, Mary's, said, "You are all children." At that time, the phrase didn't make enough sense to really hit me in the guts. Sure we all know we are all children in some ways but we are not helpless and innocent like a very young child. "I don't understand," I said to Jesus. He smiled and said, "You will." A short time later, someone I knew, call her Sue, did something so infantile and believed in this infantile act so strongly, even though all the people around knew how immature it was, that my psyche got hit with a good dose of reality. It caused me to take another look around at people and see through new eyes our little plays for attention, our trite excuses, and our extravagant wants. Then I felt Jesus smile as I replayed Mary's words, "You are all children," I see this often now in all of us, myself most of all. Our childishness, small hidden needs and drives have become obvious, yet we keep on struggling to grow too. I think that in heaven's eyes, we are like infants, each of us at a different stage of development. There may be as many different levels of spiritual development as there are people on earth. Imagine how wise a person could become if they had a hundred more years of health and learning to grow on. Could this be why Jesus is so tolerant? Perhaps, he thinks we all belong in kindergarten. He laughed when I told him this, yes Jesus does laugh often. This lesson wasn't earth shattering; it was only a small bit of understanding, a little step toward growth. Small events happen all the time, it was Mary's words that made the event stick to memory, to further my own development, just one small step towards that elusive, unreachable goal - wisdom.

This is how heaven teaches. Most of you already know this through your own experience with prayer that Jesus teaches by hints, coincidences, and miracles. We usually can feel his acceptance or displeasure at our thoughts or actions. Jesus speaks to other people too, I am not the only one, it is just that I feel the urge and need to write what I learn down. Jesus is constantly teaching and encouraging everyone's spiritual growth. We have all felt him, we have all known him. He is as close to us as we permit him to be.

I should explain something about my relationship with Jesus; I don't ask Jesus too many questions because it is hardly my place to grill Jesus, who is Lord. Who am I to demand answers to questions that mankind has been asking since the Greeks began philosophizing back in 600 BC. In fact, I found, to my consternation, that it is almost impossible to know what questions should be asked. Like a child who asks why the sun is yellow, we ask about only what we can understand, the answer of which may be completely inappropriate or even unanswerable.

Imagine, if you will, trying to explain to someone a hundred years ago even a small segment of your modern life. How could you explain that you go to work and use a machine that can do addition hundred times faster and better than the human brain or that you drive to work at sixty miles per hour, or put your cloths in a machine and they come out clean and then dry. What questions would they ask of you and how could you answer any of their questions intelligently? You could not. You would need to reduce the answer to fit the questioner, just as heaven must reduce answers to us. I imagine I have perplexed heaven with some of my questions over the years. To get real answers, I think, we will need to learn to ask the right questions.

I just now realized that I needed to make a declaration! I never intend or mean to imply in my writings or words anything opposite to Christian belief. Even so, I don't wish to involve myself in the usual theological questions and answers. I don't care who Jesus is by definition. Jesus can be God, the Son of God, the Trinity, a great religious genius or just a prophet. He is who he is. He is Lord. He is there for me. He teaches me. He loves me. What more do I need to know? As my mentor, he has taken me places and showed me events that helped me grow spiritually. More than this I don't need to know.

He as told me I could refer to him as Lord. I usually call him Jesus but think of him as Lord or Jesus Christ. Besides, if I ponder too much on just who Jesus is, I begin to feel insecure and inhibited. This is not what my growth is about; I need be myself with him, outgoing, curious, friendly, and loving. Above all, I need to keep the fires of imagination burning because that is the secret door through which all knowledge gropes.

I've noticed that Jesus has been giving me more direct answers since I began writing this book. In fact, it is Jesus who encourages me when I despair of ever finishing it. I like to think that this book will somehow be an asset to people at some future time that they will find it on some dusty shelf and take it into their heart. When I told Jesus that I was going to write this book, he liked the idea. Perhaps because of this, I've noticed I can't write anything that is directly contrary to what Jesus means. I don't mean that what I am writing is the whole absolute, truth, I mean that it can not be in any way an un-truth; a statement incompatible to Jesus and Heaven. There is a subtle difference between the two states of truth. My memory is fallible and imperfect; I have forgotten specific details about my travels with Jesus because some happened years ago and they are so numerous that I might bore you with too many details. Sometimes all I remember is the questions. Just recently, Jesus improved my peace of mind by answering a few of my many questions.

TALKS AND TRAVELS WITH JESUS

Jesus, just recently, sat down next to me on the couch. His behavior floored me because it was totally unprecedented and unusual; Jesus had never sat down with me before or answered any of my specific questions with specific answers. I felt so flabbergasted that I didn't have questions ready to mind; so, the first question I asked him was silly. I asked if he felt like he was real and solid or does he feel like subtle, insubstantial matter. I apologize for this first question but it is one I'd been wanting to know for a quite a while because his closeness and there ness has, at times, thrown me into a quandary of disbelief and uncertainty. I often asked him, "How can you be so 'there', are you inside or outside? While we sat together, I also asked Him if he had a body somewhere else? Was he just a projection?

He didn't answer all the questions but only the first by explaining, "Yes," that he does have a body and that he felt real and solid as he sat and talked to me. I think this meant that his reality is more real than ours. I also asked him about the difference between other earth people I have met up there, and the people from heaven, the angels and saints. I wondered if I'd met many people visiting from Earth and "how can I tell who is who?"

"Yes," he said, "it was as I thought, there are some people who live on earth who send their minds out and I have met a few." He also explained that I could tell if a person were from Earth or Heaven by the length of time they could stay. We from Earth are still inept at moving around in space and time. He explained further that I would not meet nor could I meet and know everyone who is there. "But," He added, "There are not very many from earth."

"There are not enough?" I asked. He answered saying that more people need to send their minds out to him. He included the instruction that they would also need to prepare themselves for travel and that a most important requirement would be his guidance.

Then I asked him what I should call other people that I meet who are not from Earth, he answered that I'd think of something. He meant that I, myself, would think of something to call the people I meet 'there.' Finally I asked him, "What should I call you?" He answered, "Lord." At this I almost wept from the emotional embrace of love as his words surrounded me. Many times I have cried real tears from the sheer joy of being close to him.

Hesitating, at first, I asked him why he loved me. It seemed to me that I'd been receiving the best end of our relationship; I didn't feel worthy to be his close friend. "I am hardly a great person," I explained to him, "I am not in Africa or North Korea feeding the hungry children, I am not even doing anything great for the neighborhood children. I am not worth much of anything to anybody." He smiled and said, "You have always loved me." Then he was gone.

I sat amazed wondering what he meant. Did he mean that in different lifetimes I loved him as I grew older, did he mean I loved him even as a child, or did he mean that in some other place and time I loved him. No answer. Not from him or myself. It is remarks like this that keep my head spinning and, I need to admit, my mind searching for elusive answers in the mystery of our relationship with God and the universe.

One day while I was wondering if I should write this book and why, Jesus explained to me that, "it is time for people to believe a new paradigm." He meant that it was time for people to look off the earth, to reach outside of ourselves, to join and visit with other living beings beyond. As a comparison, we could use America the melting pot and extrapolate this idea into the universe, we need to intermingle with other minds who are not on earth.

"Does that mean that we will soon be allowed to join them?" I asked.

"Yes!" was his answer, "Yes!" His yes was exciting.

Imagine how interesting a meeting between people on Earth and people from other places in the universe would be. I have met an odd assortment of people for a few seconds, here and there, when I traveled with Jesus; but not many because I didn't stay long in any one place. He has taken me by the hand (often I see his hand but the rest of him is indistinct and hard to see in detail) and led me to diverse places in the universe. I'll try to describe a few of the more memorable places for you, but keep in mind that these images were as much felt as seen. Also, each place had an atmosphere different from what we are used to on Earth; so much so that it was often hard for me to see what I was looking at.

The first time I met some people in space, it was with a background of stars, this may have been because it was easier to focus on just a few people than a whole scene full of unknown fauna or life. Then later, after I become more accustomed to traveling, I met people living on other worlds.

One world I remember most vividly because it felt like a song. We stood near greenery of different heights and looked through it into the far distance at high ribbon and bow towers that seemed to float rather than stand against the sky, (on closer inspection this proved false). As we walked closer we met people that were so tall and thin they towered over us. They were beautiful and pleasant with singing laughter; this may be why I remember their world as like music. I can't remember what clothing they wore only their smiles and tinkle bell voices. Their city, if that is what it was, felt spacious and fluttery, pastel buildings set wide apart, reaching up high and floating like notes on a flute, musical graffiti linking one tall tower to the next against a pale blue sky. This was my impression - all pleasantness and beauty, if their world had any discord, I wasn't there long enough to see or feel it. I don't know the reason Jesus took me there, he didn't say, but perhaps he wanted to show me that a real world could resemble paradise. Our world may resemble paradise one day too.

In February of this year, 1998, Jesus showed me the future. I was meditating, not in any trance or under hypnosis, just quietly sending my mind outwards. I could see Jesus as a soft, white blur in space. He put out his hand and led me to a future that was very different from the present time because it was less mechanical, people used mental imagery to activate and move items as well as themselves. I met a young male initiate lifting, or rather, trying to lift a large item off the table with his mind.

He turned and said to us as we walked into the room from outside, "This is extremely hard to do." The object, whatever it was, dropped back onto the table as he spoke.

Perhaps it would clarify what I describe, or fail to describe, if you remember that feelings are the determinant factor in this state of being. It felt right to be led here by Jesus; nevertheless, I had a hard time focusing on what he wanted me to see, and this unfocus affected me even though I had been to this same spot once before. I remembered the same multi-colored glass buildings far in the background and the same simple, white buildings close up but from a different angle.

The room that the young man had been in was bare and sparsely furnished, all I could see clearly was a wood table. There may have been counters against one wall. Everything else in the room seemed pale or light in color. To be honest, I can't remember what else was in the room. I got the impression of an unhurried pace and simplicity, as if there was all the time in the world to accomplish his goal. I could not see or define the item laying on the table that the young man was trying to mind-lift even though the table was sitting right in front of me. Shortly, we nodded and smiled at the young man as we turned and left.

Warm hazy sun light blinded me for a second as we walked out of the cool room into a small dirt clearing and then over to a grassy rock strewn hill. There, among the daises, weeds and wild grass, we sat and rested and talked. Thinking about what we had just seen, I asked Jesus if this setting in the future was something that he wanted or something he hoped would happen or was it, instead, a real unfolding of future events.

He answered with the words, "it is real" and a smile.

Did he mean it would be real or that it was real now? I don't know. Jesus conversations are usually short, sparse and infrequent, he speaks few words with much intent.

Jesus always seems tall, large and manly to me. He glows with an inner and outer light, which makes it hard to actually see specific details, but his eyes, clear as glass, sparkle with an inner mirth and wisdom. During his life, he was supposed to look dark like the other people from the Middle East at that time, and he does look dark, at times, with dark hair, but at other times he looks light, and sometimes almost invisible like a ghost. Thinking about it, we could ask ourselves, "Why should Jesus have limits to how he portrays himself? I can change what I am wearing at a whim when I am 'there'. I usually wear a white cloak or gown, as does Jesus, the angels, and almost every one else I have met in space/time. I have seen Jesus wear red but this frightened me because I often think it means foreboding events are on the way.

It may be important, but it is so hard to say exactly what Jesus looks like. Last night he looked and acted authoritative like a powerful king. He held out both his hands and put them onto mine, red wounds filled the palms of his hands, (not the wrists). I realize these were symbols, yet, he seemed larger than life and so much there that I felt an immense, overpowering love for him, a yearning and drawing towards his being that tares at my emotions.

I'll try but it is hard to describe his face even though I can still see it in my mind, this even though I am an artist. I think his hair was dark and he was wearing white with a red over-cloak. If eyes are the pathway into the soul, his have the depth of a universe behind them. More than this I can't say. Once when he held out his hand for me to take, it changed about three times from hairy to plump to old and then young and long fingered. Did he do this because he meant to, as a Koan to jolt me from my compliancy; another lesson to encourage my thinking process, he has done this often enough, or was this changing image a mental defect on my part, an inability to focus on his exact form? I don't know.

Mutability, though odd, is not important. All things are possible in the Universe. As I mentioned before, items 'there' are not set in concrete. It may be that I give Jesus a body from my imagination or, more likely, that he shows himself to me as he thinks I would want to see him at that time. Jesus says that soon I will see him and know exactly what he looks like, in detail. He doesn't mean that I will die. Perhaps he means that I will be able to write a description of him for this book? Usually when I am 'there', it is easy to change my looks or the cloths I wear, what takes skill is to stay changed. It also takes far too much mental power for me to stay or linger in a certain local, especially if it is strange looking and therefore hard to grasp. This changeability or mutability doesn't always apply. Nexus, I think, would be an exception to this rule as would the future time Jesus and I went to. I know it sounds crazy but there may be differences in the solidity of different places or in a place's changeability. I have been told that it is more difficult to influence matter on Earth than it is 'there', that is why we can't change our environment with only our minds, this is besides the fact that most of our mental abilities lay dormant and unused. I think imagination is the door to unlocking these mental abilities.

One Sunday morning during catholic Mass, I saw Jesus as a white blur moving around the church. He looked like a silver streak of light moving across the front of the church near the alter and then into a front pew. Then he semi-materialized beside me, kneeling, leaning forward with hands folded in prayer. He seemed very amused when he said, "you are the only one…" Then in a flash, he was gone. I couldn't hear all that he said but I think he meant that I was the only one who had seen him in church that day. But I am used to seeing people from heaven in church. I often sit with angels in church, they give me a sense of comrade and pleasure. I think angels fill all churches during Saturday and Sunday services, perhaps, they fill churches and mosques everywhere. I am not sure if it is true, but I think it is a beautiful idea.

What are angels anyway, you might want to ask. Well I did ask. "Angels are love beings," was the answer. This is their purpose in life; this is why they exist - to share their love. Some, as I have experienced, exist to serve God and none of us can doubt that they are needed in this universe. Some angels, actually they don't fit our definition of true angel but what they really are, I don't know, put on human clothing and culture then visit our cities and shopping malls disguised to look human. If you want some advise, always give to a person begging on the street, you never know when it might be an angel in disguise. If your mind is tuned in you might hear them speak to you, non-verbally. It is more a silent communication or subtle recognition than speech. This kind of spark can also flow between two spiritually minded people meeting unexpectedly, but an angel has a different flavor or essence. Now I am grasping at straws to explain something I've noticed but can't explain. Perhaps I should not try.

MY SPIRITUAL HISTORY

Hesitantly I pushed my mind outwards through one invisible barrier after another. Each barrier felt like a rubber sheet that accepted my form only so far, stretching, stretching to the breaking point, then out, back out into the black star driven sky. Further and further I traveled, through stars and nebula and dust, past worlds, suns, and galaxies; outward moved my imagination, my mind. This was the first time I tried to meditate; I had relaxed my body by starting at my toes moving up through my legs, torso, chest, then head, all this time ignoring the itch of impatience, my restlessness, my urge to quit. It was so stark and whisper silent out here. I loved the feeling of gliding faster than the speed of light, I laughed with the power of it as I watched stars fall past me. At one place I imagined a barrier of two angels with swords crossed in front of me to block the way. I tried to go around or over but could not. I tried pushing through but could not. I called to heaven for help, the angels stood their swords down and let me pass. Delightful. My imagination was running full tilt. I reached an area of black, lightless space. Ink black, the blackest black; no starlight in front of me. Then I watched as two red embers grew in size. Were they turning towards me? The red embers became larger and wider apart, coming closer? Curious I paused to watch. Suddenly, I know not from where, a hand of air pushed my face and turned it quickly away from the red lights. The force of contact felt like a slap when a parent punishes a child for crossing the street in front of a fast, moving automobile.

Gasping for air shaking all over. I didn't know whether to laugh or cry. I was home in my chair, in my living room, but where had I been? Fear at the sudden encounter with the unknown didn't leave me for many days after that. Meditation stayed off my list of pleasurable things to do for a while after that, but like any siren call, the mystery pulled me back; although, I've never been tempted to go back to that same dark place. At the time, I thought my meditation technique was wrong because I had learned from a book. Besides, it was only my imagination, wasn't it? But I was afraid. It had felt real, space felt real, and I felt contrite and censored.

Back in the 70s when TM (Transcendental Meditation) first became popular in the states, I desperately wanted to learn it but couldn't pay for it. So I fell back on my usual solution - I went to the library and found a book that would teach me how to meditate. I found books not only about TM but also on Hypnotism, Yoga, vivid dreaming, ESP, Out-of-body experiences, etc. In short, I read books on all the esoteric ideas that were floating around at the time. These ideas were a new avenue for me to explore and I absorbed them like a sponge. Not just esoteric ideas either, my reading list also included books about all the religions I could find, Buddhism, Taoism, Sufis Christian history, Hebrew history, etc. Then because I craved information, curiosity moved me towards the study of physics, quantum mechanics and every new idea that came my way. It seemed that I couldn't absorb enough knowledge. I think many people experienced and are still experiencing this same need, almost like a compulsion, to understand more about religion and how it fits in the world of today.

New Age books have sprung up to fill long shelves in the bookstores and some of them are very good. I read about channeling a few years ago but realized at once that I was not a channel even though Jesus and other people from heaven were communicating with me at that time. He agreed with me then, and even now that I am not a channel. Many people were on the same road as I was and many of us are still searching for that elusive ultimate, we know not what. Spirituality is probably one of those areas of knowledge that can never be fully satisfied even though we reach peaks now and then and think we have achieved it all. In fact, most of us go through a holier than thou stage at some point in our new-arrived at- spirituality where we try to shove our new found light on every one we meet. Thankfully this is usually of short duration. Some spiritual searchers have assimilated themselves further into their religion, others into the New Age philosophy, while others, like me, can't stick to any specific idea but keep searching further and further looking for meanings beneath meanings.

In my new combination, I've discovered all the old Gods doing new tricks. In other words, the people of heaven have caught up with science - actually our science has yet to catch up with theirs. I have found that God, who is removed from our science, permeates and is absorbed in theirs. God's science is our magic. This is one of those old ideas that fit the facts. If you read your Bible over again with new eyes you'll find chariots landing, people traveling or leaving Earth, God talking to people and teaching them how to raise crops, even in the New Testament Jesus saw Satan fall to Earth like lightning, the list goes on and on—as Spock would say—fascinating. Yet, even with all the reading, learning and instruction from Jesus, I had to face an indisputable fact - I was still like a child when it came to understanding Heaven, earth and in between.

I used to ask a lot of questions but then I realized that I was behaving like a young child who is always asking trite questions like 'why is snow white?' or 'what makes dirt dirty? How could any guide answer such juvenile questions? Questions like "Who are you?" Why can't I see you? Do you love God? Where are you? Why are we here? What is our purpose? Now I seldom ask Jesus broad, unanswerable questions, I wait and let him tell me what he wants me to know. He deserves the respect of intelligent questions. Now I ask fewer questions because I've learned that, not only are facts unimportant but also I realized that I don't know the right questions to ask. None of us do. We are all asking the wrong questions.

With experience, I hope to learn how to ask the right questions. For instance, it is our nature to want to know a person's name but 'out there' names are not important. It would be wrong to ask who a person is because who the person is shines and advertises itself to you; their character and soul give them meaning. This threw me off kilter for many years and, at times, still does. If you know a persons soul, you know the person. Opening a soul opens a book. Even knowing all this, I still worry about being lied to, I worry that I am being led down a primrose path to distraction by the one who mimics Christ. Jesus assures me that this isn't a valid worry because as he says, "I always know."

Everything I've done in the last twenty years, with few exceptions, has been based on my need to know and understand God. My craving to learn about heaven and its population has filled my days. There have been times when the emotional turmoil of not understanding almost tore me apart. I felt like a starving person who could not be satisfied because they never had enough food. Every event, every experience, every turn of the screw was fodder for my understanding of God. Everything became food to digest, ideas to turn inside out, visions to play with to check if they fit.

I wanted to learn if God was made of matter and if so, where he resided in the universe. Future events dispelled this need, my visit with God. Besides, I now realize that the universe is much too strange for us to decipher. God is too strange for us to decipher too. It isn't that some things are forever beyond our understanding; it is more that we are still too immature to ask the right questions

Imagination, the tendency to believe, faith in the impossible, and an open mind-set are all important traits when looking for heaven, but not absolutely necessary because Jesus can do the seeming impossible. He will pull people to him by reinforcing their faith and love even though they resist. I base this statement of my own experience many years ago when Jesus called me but I didn't know it yet. Still, the mind-set of the person is important. If you don't believe, it probably won't happen quickly. It's like extrasensory perception it helps to believe. You need to believe in heaven before you can see it or visit it, (this may or may not apply after death).

I remember a few "miracles" Jesus sent me without my knowing. They were tailor-made to fit my disposition, my type of thinking and my specific problems at that time. Once after I had a wild fight with my husband, I became ashamed and realized how low I had fallen when I watched two Jehovah Witnesses going door to door with calm, sweet smiles on their face. I thought to myself "they must have something I don't." How could they stay calm in this trashed out Detroit city of many

ruined lives. That my own life was heading downhill was becoming glar-
ingly obvious. They must have a message that they believe in very strongly.
It was their example more than anything that sent me back into the
Catholic religion. I became a foster mother to underprivileged children,
began reading the Bible, and began praying to Jesus for help. The importance of catholic mass remains central to me but I don't base my spirituality on it. My spirituality has its base in my talks and travels with Jesus.

Meditation began in me a yearning to understand God that was so
overwhelming and powerful that it has not dissipated to this day. Jesus
knows and encourages this yearning in me and all of us. His love has
encouraged and shaped my education throughout these many years
through study, life experiences, and direct teaching. I don't know why
Jesus is willing to guide me except that he is calling all people to him however they are willing to come. I believe strongly in open-mindedness, that
an open mind can accept knew paradigms with less stress. My love of
Science Fiction has sent me over the edge in that department, at times, but
Jesus smiles tolerantly at some of my more outlandish ideas. Some are not
so outlandish at all. The universe is filled with abundant life forms, probably some we can't imagine.

Information about my spiritual learning would not be complete without a few words on evil. I regret that I need to bring the subject up; it
repels me and makes me shudder; still, even Christ can't make disappear
all the evil in the world, as I can't avoid the subject of it.

Odd that you can be in heaven and hell at the same time. It's like the
line of a poem I wrote once, "Hell is just an eye-blink away." During those
tremulous years of pain when my name was being smeared with lies and
innuendoes, I lived each day as if in a minefield, my emotions subject to
exploding vibes every time I walked into a room. It didn't matter where I
went, anyplace could serve as a battleground for heartache: college classes,
church events, new jobs, singles groups, social events, even neighbors and
sometimes family. This battle has never let up, though now I can shrug it
off more easily.

Just the other night when I arrived at a new club and social event, I saw that my reputation had preceded me, the only difference was that I didn't let it hurt me as much as it used to. But the lie has definitely made huge dents in my work and life in general. With Jesus helping me throughout this ordeal, I have accepted it as well as I can. Who among us hasn't been severely tested? The amazing thing about the whole situation is that I not only survived the slings and arrows thrown at my back but I have grown stronger and tougher because of them. Take heart, you can too. Jesus has implied that my newfound strength will help me through the next phase—whatever it may be.

The last ten years have been very hard on me. There were times that I felt so traumatized I felt like I'd been thrown into hell. This in spite of heaven's help. It was Jesus who pulled me out again. He tells me now that it was something I needed to go through, that I was tested and also that I needed to work the problem out on my own. I don't understand why I needed to hurt so allconsumingly. Perhaps my problem was that I cared too much about what people thought of me. It might be that I needed to learn to shrug off slander, gossip and rumors as having little worth. All this is unimportant but leads to the description of some strange events that happened to me.

One night, a number of years ago, I was laying in bed sending my thoughts out trying to mind-touch and pray for a sick person. It was my habit to visit sick people or people imprisoned and ask the angels to help them. A dark, tall man who seemed to be made of half-shadow stood beside me and said, "I have found you. Let me look into your soul." Then he suddenly grabbed hold of my soul. I know this because I blacked out for a short time. When I came to, I was badly frightened. I wondered if I had somehow called him to me. How did he find me? And, more importantly, what did my soul show him? His action proved that he had no respect for my feelings. He took me and used me. I felt violated as if I had been raped—mind raped.

Mind rape—I've seen him again and again wearing different faces, he could look like a handsome blond man or look dark and angry. He can put on someone else's face. I have seen him at different times walking or at night before going to sleep. I can't tell you how I know it is him, but he has looked at me and smirked to my face. Thankfully, I haven't seen him for a few years and hope to never see him again.

One time he was exceedingly angry with me and the three small beings who came to me early one night and told me, "you saved us." He was standing there on the other side of my bedroom as they spoke, and he was livid with anger. So much so, that I became terrified and afraid even though I knew he was not solid matter and couldn't hurt me physically. Fearful for these small beings who had came to me under great duress or wayward circumstances, I could do nothing for them but cringe beneath the bed covers. I could only imagine what kind of effort it took them to appear before me like that. To this day, I still have no idea of what they were talking about. If I knew what I could do to save them, I would do it again. I would do it countless times until every one of these small beings were saved. If only I knew what I had done to help them, or what I will do in the future.

Once I had a dream with that evil man in it. He was very dark and angry because I had gone up into his space platform and smashed a lot of long incubators with frozen people lying inside them. Glass, water, and bodies spilled down and washed all over the floor as I yelled, "These are mine," because they were earth people. This had been just a dream; nevertheless, I awoke proud of what I had done. I don't remember the small beings any place in the dream so I still can't place their gratitude, yet.

I wish I had been dreaming when I saw a person change from one form into another one day. Perhaps it was because I was under a lot of stress from my ongoing unemployment. It happened during the day, outside in bright sunlight. I had just finished putting in an application for a job, which I didn't get; I was having a hard time holding on to work. As I was walking past a group of nurses, feeling terrible and angry, one of the nurses looked directly at me, and changed her face into a different shape then changed her hair to look exactly like the actress in Stephen King's "Misery." She smirked at me, and then changed herself back into her former self. I know that this couldn't actually have happened because the other nurses were still standing and talking to one another. It must have been a scene played out just for me, only inside my own mind. Was I going nuts? I stood there for a moment unmoving. I couldn't believe my eyes. Then as I walked to my car I remembered the smiling, daring smirk on the face. Could it have been him? I felt terrified and afraid, even in mortal danger from his hate. Even though I knew it was a false vision, I also knew it was a message sent to me, a warning. A warning about what? I still don't know why I saw this person change but wish I hadn't, especially because it happened again a few times. I don't know if the purpose was to drive me insane or not, I came very close to going over the edge. I had no one to turn to, who could I tell something like this to. My only recourse was prayer, meditation and Jesus' love. It was at times like this when I felt most deeply afraid that Jesus stood by me in comfort like in the poem "Footsteps in the sand." His arms would envelop me in love.

Our psychic sensitivity is increased after trauma. Mine was tremendously heightened after my husband's death. Once I saw the figures on face cards, the number and suite, shine through the back of the cards my partner was holding in their hand. I jumped up and quit the game, frightened. Another time, I was able to predict, to myself, the next call at Bingo because it lit up before it was called. This exceptional sight hasn't happened to me since that time, perhaps because I rejected it so strongly, for some reason I was afraid of this ability. This was a period in my life when deja vu seemed to be an every day occurrence. Many people have these same experiences and I wonder if theirs increased after a traumatic period like mine did. My senses stayed at a high peak of activity for a very long time after my husband died.

His death, in the early eighty's, was the start of my nightmares. I kept having severe nightmares so bad I couldn't sleep. It seemed that a dream would start out beautiful then suddenly change into a horror flick. In fact, I didn't need to be asleep. One night I was awake and laying in bed thinking when a large dirty-white cloud reached down and grabbed my leg. A male's voice came out of it saying, "Its nice here, come on." The voice and cloud both tried to suck me into its void and might have if I hadn't kept pulling away. This was so frightening I shudder to remember it. A few times, in my dreams, I woke up in a grave with many other dead people, we were all piled together, one on top of another, black blood mixed with black dirt. Is it any wonder the nightmares chased me into another marriage, in the hopes that a bed partner would chase the nightmares away. It did, for good. I never have nightmares now, though the effect lasted longer than the marriage.

Some happenings were not evil but just strange. Like the time I popped to another place where a man and women were sitting and talking together. He was wearing black and she was wearing white against a background that was all white. He seemed greatly perturbed that I had suddenly showed up in their space. "You shouldn't be here," was what he said in a stern voice. I popped out again.

Once I visited a jeweled cave with someone who was not my mentor. He beckoned me to visit with him. He wanted to show me all the treasured splendor that was his. The jewels were so large and splendid I couldn't take it all in. They were every color of the rainbow and shone with a pure luminosity that lit up that dark chamber. I didn't stay because I was afraid that it was too rich for my taste. Was this visit something that we would call wrong or evil? I am not sure. There must be many odd and different places that would try our understanding, though not necessarily evil. We can always hope they are dreams.

Mind Scenes

It is early afternoon in the eighty's, I am walking from the front door into the dinning room setting a grocery bag on the table, suddenly, I am no longer there. I am standing on the deck of a large wooden sailing ship as it rides the ocean waves. The sky is a clear vivid blue, the ship is old and worn, a wall is on my right, a chest-high side railing on the other, the smell of water permeates the air. Standing in front of me is an older, hefty, solid man with balding gray hair. Mouth open, he stares at me in wide-eyed shock, my face must have mirrored his own. Suddenly, I am back at my dinning room table, holding on to its edge, the day continues just as any other day.

This morning, January 22, 1998, while leisurely struggling with the need to wake-up, I suddenly discovered myself looking down at a strange dark haired man wearing a white fleece sheepskin jacket with dark cloth arms. He was lying on his left arm that was bent beneath his face at an odd angle. I sensed trauma or pain; then, as I watched, he began moving as if struggling to get up. Then, just as suddenly as it had changed before, my view now reversed; I was laying in my own bed looking at the wall, dazed in the half-stupor of near-sleep, feeling the warm covers pulled up against my chin.

Fully awake now, I lay there thinking about the event I had just dreamed or witnessed. What had happened? Must I assume that it was only a dream? It didn't feel like a dream, but unlike my visit to the ship, I was laying in bed when it happened. Also, I couldn't find any reference in my life to what I had seen. I don't think I've ever seen a jacket made out of plump, white, sheep hair. As far as I could tell, no movie, book, or television show had such a scene; besides, I seldom watch TV or go to the movies. If there was a reference in my life somewhere, it must be from book, but, if so, I have not found it.

What part of my mind processed those oddly vivid details and for what purpose? I am left to wonder if it could have been a real event that I'd watched. I believe the visit to the ship was real but what about dreams? Had I floated off into time or space to visit this specific trauma after it happened, his near death, perhaps. Did I watch him until he got up for some special reason? I wondered if it had been an actual memory in a past life or myself in a different life occurring now—what is time, anyway? Or, was I sharing an oneness with someone else who was watching the man during his trauma. This is really stretching reality, I know, but understanding and believing in what we may at first dismiss as imaginary is the theme for this book. I notice these snippets of events all the time. They may be considered dream fragments but why dream of someone wearing a sheepskin jacket? The list of speculations could be endless. I don't doubt that a large number of people experience similar dream fragments but most of us choose not to talk or write about them.

As unusual as I believe this dream visit or scene was; I deliberately avoid including items like this in my definition of travel. It wouldn't be accurate to include these episodes because I am not as sure if they are real. In contrast, my sudden, involuntary trip to the ship seemed very real but I don't know why. Dreams are events we can't readily explain. I may believe them to be a form of travel or memory but I don't ask so much of you. Also, meditation shouldn't be confused with dreaming because it has a different quality than a half-awake dream. It is a self-induced change of the mental frame of mind into stillness or a deliberate chain of steady thought-ideas.

We all know that a daydream is a made-up scene usually with ourselves as hero or Lotto winner but what is a real dream? I know many books have been written on the different types of dreams and some of the symbols that define dream action. We've all had similar dreams where we get lost in school or loose something of great value, but what about this kind of dream.

There was this old woman, wild and untamed who was living with my family. She was lost so I went looking for her. I went into an old folks home and a gray-haired lady with a round face said she had seen her on another street. I took a taxi to look for her. When I found the lady I was looking for near an old brick wall of a hospital beneath a clock tower, she paid the taxi fare home. She acted glad to see me but she kept turning her head in every direction and talking nonsense all the way. It was a dark and rainy night so we were wearing tweed coats for warmth. The old lady used a silver walking cane as she climbed out of the taxi.

It played like a normal dream with jumbled up events and topsy-turvy scenes; nevertheless, theme-wise, it had an odd texture. What was I doing in England during the first or second world war chasing after a senile old lady? Is the possibility worth consideration that even in our wildest dreams we can remember or visit other places and times? Could we dare think our dreams as having some bases of truth in them? Are some dreams a replay of real time lived in space/time? I had a dream ten years ago I'll never forget - I was shooting at something while tethered on the side of a black, metallic ship in deep space. I can still see the dark ship glinting starlight as I changed position with my gun; my whole family had just been killed. I felt so sorrowful about their deaths that when I woke up from the dream, I still felt as though I'd just suffered a great loss. According to some scientific theories, past and future may be intermingled onto one space/time. I wonder if our dreams bare this out. And I wonder if my visitors appear to me from out of space/time.

I am never dreaming when the two men appear to me; I am always wide-awake. Lately, I am usually writing at the computer or thinking about something I want to include in the book when I see them. They appear slightly above and to the right of where I am sitting. I perceive the man on my right as giving off an aura of great authority. The slightly shorter man, on my left, once pointed me out to the first man implying pride because I had been praying so fervently for the hungry children during a famine in Africa. When he smiled at me, I thought God had beamed a golden light down to me, and perhaps he had. I don't know who the two men are. I have seen them again and again, often, like I said, while I am writing. Do they mean to encourage my writing? One time they appeared to me when I was in dire need of encouragement. My paper, an art essay for the college class I was taking, had just been rejected; I needed to write a new, twenty-page paper in only a few weeks. I believe the reason that the paper was rejected was because I wrote about my visit with God, tying the visit in with my art and the art of other romantic artists. When the two men appeared, the tall man sent his love down to me with a smile saying, "I am pleased." I understood his words to mean that he was pleased that I dared to write about God. His words and smile satisfied me more than I can ever convey. I wished that I could do more to please him, to see him smile at me again. Now I struggle to write this book and fervently hope that it too will please him.

I can't tell you what mechanism is at work when I see the two men. I only see them for a short moment and then they are gone. I can't tell you what they look like either except to say they both wear long garments, seem manly and strong, and they "sort of glow." I feel their presence as much as I visually see them. When they are nearby, I always get the feeling that I am in the presence of great love and wisdom.

What is seeing anyway? Layers of illusion envelop our total existence. If we strip away one illusion after another, what will be left? In a sense, we see what we choose see. We select out of our total environment what we decide to see and remember. We must accept some illusion or layers of 'Maya' in our existence. When I go into a new room, I imbue it with what I expect to see. I give it my own ideas of what it should look like, and if I stay longer, I will keep refocusing and readmitting new images into my conscious awareness. I think that a totally strange place would be almost un-seeable to us. But also, it is well to remember that matter is matter, a rock is a rock wherever in the universe we observe it. So, as I have done many times, we tend to use our own referents to understand what we see if we go into a strange place, a place like an unknown world. Sometimes Jesus will take my hand and lead me to a new world but when I first get there - I can't see. The odd fauna or strange people are out of focus and hard for me to define. After a short time, my vision improves, but it may be that I color the new fauna with my own ideas of what grass or trees should look like.

It is the mind that sees, just as it is the mind that travels. If we could go to a strange new place and out again quickly, it would be hard to give an accurate, detailed description. What can we remember in only a few seconds? When I went to Nexus again, also a short visit, but this time with Jesus leading the way. I noticed a few more details. The figures all wore long robes of varying hues but not every one wore a hood. The ground where I stood was not cluttered with stalls or other buildings; nevertheless, it had a bazaar atmosphere or the flavor of a vast gathering place. I had more time to look around so I naturally looked up to where people were rising and disappearing at the top of the roadway or escalator. I wanted to ride up along with them but Jesus said, "no" that we would "go too far." The last time we went there, he told me that I wasn't ready yet. He didn't elaborate on either statement so I have no further explanation as to where they were going or why. Was it a huge pivot point in space? A transportation device on a specific world? A joining of wormholes? Or just one more puzzle to ponder.

I am not the only person who can mind travel, I think anyone can and I am sure many people have because the universe is made up of thought - thoughts run it and keep it going, God's thought, our thoughts. "The universe needs an observer to exist," said Stephen Hawking, the well-known physicist.[2] Physicists are the first to admit that they have only scratched the surface of the true universe. I asked Jesus once if our modern scientists would be able to understand the universe if they knew what underlay its mechanism. He laughed answering me and said, "It is stranger than they could ever imagine."

---

[2] Stephen Hawking has repeated this phrase numerous times in magazine articles and in his book, *A Brief History of Time, (New York, NY, 1988).*

If the universe is made up of thoughts, why can't we change it? "We live on a ball of frozen energy," Einstein said once. I have always remembered this quote because I imagine us as little humans standing around shivering and freezing on a small ball of ice. If somehow our thoughts don't manipulate matter like they should, maybe its because we're cold. Perhaps our thoughts are bent out of shape or reduced in some way that renders them less effective. I've found the fault is not speed, our thoughts can travel faster than the speed of light. The problem may be our prior conditioning. Perhaps with the proper training we could move a mountain or tell a tree to wither and die. Jesus said we could do it, that all we need is faith.

When I say that I see and talk to Jesus Christ I mean that he is 'there' for me. I know he is there, I feel his presence almost as much as if one of my children were standing next to me only not as long in duration. What is odd is that I am sure if I were a Hindu and called him Krishna or a Hebrew and called him Yahweh or a Buddhist and called him The Enlightened One he would be just as present and he would answer to each name. Does this mean that I see Jesus, Mary, and angels as archetypes, as Carl Jung might have suggested? I don't believe so because archetypes are dream symbols and I do not dream when I talk to Jesus. Also, I don't think archetypes interact with the person seeing them, as happens in my own encounters. On the other hand, in some way I can't understand, Jesus can be with everyone at the same time, even though he is there with me. Could he be an attribute of himself? That doesn't make sense, does it? At the same time Jesus is everywhere, he is within us. He said to me, "I am inside you." This idea has caused me a lot of problems that I prefer not to go into. I have asked Jesus to explain this inside-outside dichotomy, but his only answer is that "You will understand some day."

Whether Jesus is out there or in here sometimes I see him with my eyes as well as my mind. I do not go into a trance in order to see him. I tactually feel his light pour into and through me at times. His smile has warmed me, his arms have caressed me, and his voice has nudged me into action. Other heavenly beings have hugged me also. I will forever remember when the angels floated above me and poured liquid light out of heaven down into my body as I sat there meditating. This memory is still so vivid I doubt that I will ever forget it. This happened during meditation so it is more easily understood than visits when I am awake and writing or doing housework, these I don't understand at all. I get so frustrated from my lack of knowledge, my only resource is to repeat Jesus' words to myself over and over again, "Someday you will understand."

When Jesus gives me information and says we need a new paradigm he doesn't mean that he is telling us the ultimate knowledge of the universe. He is, instead, giving us what we can absorb and understand according to our present culture and time. And just like an itch that needs to be scratched, he gives just enough to tantalize and tempt us because that gives us the incentive to continue learning. We keep reading the Bible, not because it is smooth and easily understood, but because it is ambivalent and hard to understand in its fullness. Every time we read the Bible we can come away with a new awareness of what it says and means. This causes us to keep reading, to keep trying to understand. Our curiosity is aroused by discord and the conflict of new ideas, not by light reading or sweet goodness. Plus, sometimes, we need to be jarred out of our compliance with a shockingly new idea, a new idea that gets our thoughts rolling.

This morning I reinvented the need for God. After deep thought, I realized that God's value lays in the fact that he knows. I was re-learning that I needed God not because he is mighty or has such great authority, which he does, but because he knows the Future/Past. What a relief to believe, to have faith that there is a Being in the Universe who knows what is going on, what will go on, and why it will continue.

Like when a small child comes running in with a cut on their finger or a complaint that "Jimmy hit me, he took my truck" We can understand. We can see the child's future. We know that the child will be OK, that his finger will heal and the pain go away, that Jimmy will give back the truck soon when he gets tired of it. We know everything will be OK and say so as we comfort the child. I derive this same kind of comfort from God's knowledge.

Jesus does the same when He looks at me and smiles; he knows. He sees further than I, further than the traumas of rejection or fear I suffer. He tells me that I'll be all right. He often tells me that he will, "be here soon." But, I have finally learned to laugh at this because we have such different ideas about the word, 'soon'. He has been saying that for the last ten years. He smiles at this. I want instant gratification while he is the embodiment of patience. Well, some things take more than a willing mind and vivid imagination.

But imagination is a necessary base. To conceive the possibility of mind travel makes it so. It complements the new theories that even science, our religion of the Twentieth Century, must now argue, that things aren't what they seem. Read any book on quantum physics and your solid world will disappear into a nether-nether land of mist - called indeterminacy. Time can run backwards, you can blink Schrodinger's cat dead or alive, or quiff new stars into space. Since the advent of quantum theory, reality hasn't behaved as our common sense says it should—past, present, and the future are gone—they depend on the subjective viewpoint of the observer—space, objects, worlds, people no longer exist unless an observer—God or, if you prefer, a human—tells them to. I exaggerate but not by much, science seems to have entered the realm of magic.

Yet, few scientists can allow room in their theory for God or angels. Science shies away from most exotic possibilities such as U F Os, out-of-body experiences, and Marion visitations like boats from dry land for a simple reason, they can't be measured and science is the study of measurements. It's odd that gurus, mystics, and others with eccentric spirits may be experiencing the very tenets that science is now studying, yet are not considered valid informants. Nothing science has found, so far, prohibits the possibility of mind-travel, other worlds, other universes, other dimensions or messages from God. Lately, I've read in the newspaper that in the last few years, not only do a larger number of people believe in and talk to

God but that God is answering them back. Certainly, I won't dispute this, I feel a bond with these people. I may meet them up there.

What am I doing when I travel? It is easier to say what I am not doing. I am not Astral-traveling. While writing this book, I decided to cover all bases by searching out anything that resembled my travels. I couldn't find much. A book I read described what they call astral travels as going to different planes or levels of subtle matter where spirits and angels live. Jesus tells me emphatically, "No, You are not astral traveling." that is enough for me. But what is the difference? The difference seems to be what is called Theta waves that involve the super conscious mind which induces a trance state. This is opposite to my own experience, I don't go into a trance state.

Another thing I am not doing is channeling. Years ago when I read a book about Channelers and reviewed their statements, I was amazed at their knowledge. Why didn't I get answers like they did? I laughed at my concern; I didn't want to be a channel anyway. Jesus agreed with me that I wasn't a channel. This book does not serve the same purpose as channeling; it is not funneling information from one person to another. I worried that, though some channels seemed sincere, some shouldn't be trusted because they say too much. I hardly ever get clear and specific answers to my questions. I question why they do. Jesus, when he answers me, which is not often, gives me a cryptic phrase and a smile then leaves me to decipher it for myself. It may be that our purposes differ, mine being to grow spiritually theirs to relay information.

What exactly am I doing if it is not astral traveling or channeling? Is it out of body experiences or OBEs? I am not sure. I read one book lately that describes the person as going into a trance just before an OBE. Some of his experiences are like mine in the since that he can go anywhere in time and do anything on earth or off but I don't go into a trance. He does not refer to the people he meets as angels or Gods. I did not read the whole book so I am not certain who or what this being he meets is. Another type of OBE is the kind experienced after a trauma to the body, where the person floats over their own operation in the hospital. Then there is the near death experience or NDE where the person almost dies and experiences events comparable to some that I describe in this book. I believe my experiences are similar and therefore point out the repeatability of this kind of experience without trauma or a near death. Thus, we finally get to the nugget or purpose for this book; sharing these experiences may nudge more people to begin traveling. Maybe it will get crowded up there.

You might ask why anyone should travel? I can only repeat what Jesus told me, that we need a "new paradigm," we need to look outward more. I thought of the frightening idea that souls never die but our sun will. Humanity will need to be off planet, by whatever means, when the sun goes nova. Would you want your soul swimming in a Ghenna sea?

Traveling does involve effort and a lot of trial and error learning. It also may serve up some deep frightening fears before you get the hang of it. We can go 'there' with our earth smarts but still be woefully ignorant, like a street-smart kid visiting a farm and being chased by the horse. If you go expecting names and explanations of who someone is or what their purpose is, forget it—leave names at home. I am still learning how to travel and will never stop. Jesus lately tells me that I need to learn how to distinguish a lie from the truth (I'll leave the specific details of what I fell for to your imagination). Believe me, it is not easy to know who is telling the truth. How would you detect a truth or lie if someone appears to you in flowing white and tells you that you will win the lotto, or you will pass go and win two hundred dollars, or —but you get the picture. Believe me, you never win money in this game, no lottos, no pots of gold. If someone says that something great is coming your way, disbelieve it. It won't happen. I know because I am learning it the hard way.

Of course, you don't want to mind-travel for money but only to talk to God. God is the reason I began to meditate and then mind-travel. I needed to get my life in order, God, angels, and Christ helped me do that. Your reason to travel may be to delve into the secrets of the universe. Hopefully you will get more decisive answers than I do. I've learned not to ask too much. Now, when I search for information 'there,' it isn't factual information that I am looking for, it's the plus side of the universe, it is life's self affirming nature. I want to see all of life's beauty as Jesus sees it, to see life as others live it. You will establish your own relationship with Jesus and the universe for whatever the reason that fits you best.

Is mind-travel real? There is no way that you can check my experiences out to see if they are real. I can't prove a thing. I only know about my own travels, my own relationship with Jesus and heaven. You must make your own. I advise you to be careful and vigilant because there is a jokester out there who mimics Jesus and mocks any effort to learn about heaven. This jokester's antics could fill a book but doesn't deserve the credit, so I won't write it.

You may disagree with my terms - my use of the word 'travel' for move-ment of the mind or thoughts through space and time but I insist that it is a form of traveling because I always have the sensation of leaving and going to another place. I always feel that my whole self 'went' into a dif-ferent place or time. I don't feel any separation between my body and mind when I travel. If, by some chance, my body traveled too, how would I know? I hope to control the duration of these travels eventually so I can stay longer and gather more information, but at present I need to be con-tent with short visits.

This book may imply an unusual method of travel or an alternative reality mixed into our own but it doesn't stand-alone. I realized this the other day while I was reading about an anthropologist who was in the field studying about the theory of birds evolving into dinosaurs. Reading about that on-going dispute and the long study of ideas that lead to the concept, I recognized all the background knowledge that had been required, a mountain of ideas built layer upon layer, year after year, to support or dis-pel that one theory. How could I write a book with few supporting facts and no long standing body of knowledge?

Then, I remembered the many books I had read over the years on the edge of science, books about out of body experiences, near death experi-ences, religions and prophets, eastern philosophies, unidentified flying objects, the list goes on and on. I realize now that this book also stands on a body of knowledge and information, not concrete facts like in a scientific study, but knowledge of a different kind. It is exploring mental states that have been circulating in humankind for as long as we can find written records. Religious belief is as old as man. So if a psychologist were to state that we couldn't see visions or mind-travel, I would point out the infancy of psychology as compared to any religion. Religious faith has always meant a faith in beings from out there or spiritual presences of some kind. Like Jacques Vallee would say, "Not only are we not alone, we have never been alone."[3]

[3] Jacques Vallee, *Passport to Magonia: on UFOs Folklore, and Parallel Worlds,* (Chicago, Ill., 1969).

Blind Gift

Countless people stood gathered on the shore across from the swiftly flowing river. I called and motioned for the people to join me, but many refused to step into the water. I waded through the deep river pointing and pulling people off the land into the water. People began to wade across holding hands. Children were too short to walk in the river so we carried them on our backs to Jesus who waited on the other shore. More people, when they saw Jesus, jumped into the water to go to him. Soon the river was full of people crossing except for one man who stood alone on the far shore. He refused to cross even when I held his hand. It was Jake (name is changed), a man I knew intimately. I felt it was important to get him into the water. I coaxed and pulled on him until he consented to timidly step into the water and to Jesus. The river had risen until mid-way he began to drown. My feet had left the ground too at the same time I was trying to lift his head above the water. He would sink under the high waves then rise his head and sputter water while we struggled across the mighty river. Jesus stood up opening his arms to us as we climbed the rocky shore, dripping river water and steaming in the sunlight. Jesus in a white glowing, sunlit robe leaning over to help pull me to him. To join all the people gathered on this new shore

Nothing but a pleasant reverie, a quiet relaxing daydream, played out in full color one late night when I couldn't sleep. Filled with my own symbolism, nevertheless, the scene was one I played out often in my mind as a message to Jesus Christ that I was willing to help lead people to him so they could share in love. A beautiful daydream.

I run into Jake the next day. During our conversation he looked at me strangely and told me about an odd dream he had the night before. A dream in which he kept drowning. "Water kept pulling me down," he said as he looked strangely at me, "It woke me up." But he said nothing about

Jesus on the other shore. I was surprised because Jake was the first person I'd ever known who admitted that he never had an ESP or a deja vu experience, nether was he religious or spiritual in any way. He was an accountant by profession as well as by nature. Somehow, my nonchalant imagery had gotten through to him on a basic level, I felt proud that he had felt my struggle to pull him to Jesus. Nice thought but soon forgotten. It wasn't a big deal, people made comments like that to me all the time. It wasn't anything to take it seriously.

I practiced similar mental exercises often, sending my mind out to people during late evening, not trying to contact anyone but only to give comfort. That the visits might actually be real didn't concern me much; this thought was only a hazy background noise; besides, intention was what mattered. Jesus accepted my visits as prayer; it was up to him to do the actual healing. Jesus or his angels went with me into prisons and we hugged inmates. Here was a man sitting on a low cot depressed and crying, I hugged and held him for a short while, another man pounded the walls with his fists in anger and we tried to comfort him as well. We never stayed long, only a moment in each place perhaps because I didn't have the strength to stay long. I always assumed that the person couldn't see me but hoped that the inmate or sick person would feel the presence of love and concern. Regardless, I never went alone; angels always accompanied me on these visits. I wonder if the angels need us to care because it helps them do their own work?

Sick and handicapped people were on my visiting list more than inmates. Since I worked with senior citizens and later with people in nursing homes, I had come to know a large number of people with various needs. I considered myself lucky to have access to this knowledge so that I could reach out to them during the day and at night. It went like this: Quietly I would send my mind out into a person's home. I would imagine them in their favorite chair, bed, or busy with a common activity. The time of day didn't matter, because my image was independent of real time, it was mine to choose. The angels and I would hug that person for a moment then leave. I would do this five or ten times each night to different people I had known.

One limit I put on myself was that I wouldn't go to people that I was close to in the present, people that I was taking care of now or people I knew as friends. There wasn't any specific reason for this. I just felt that I shouldn't impose myself on them. Across the world to Africa or China wasn't beyond my limit, but across the street was. I could pray for someone I knew well but not send myself over for a nightly visit.

I went across the street only in the company of a multitude of angels. We would join hands above the treetops and shower symbolic rose petals down onto Detroit streets. In fact sometimes we began in Detroit but reached out and across America, over oceans and around the world. At other times we glided into Detroit homes, hugging and holding children and their parents. If I or an angel found an adult crying, a child cowering in fright, or some other desperate person who needed a lot of help, we would all gather around that person and give them hugs. I considered each hug a prayer, and so it was.

All wasn't roses, I am ashamed to say. I had a few love affairs over the mental airwaves, too. But then, I never said I was a saint. It may have been wrong to use my gift sexually, to visit with someone I loved. We all know that love is blind; I was lustfully blind for many years until one man straightened me out by making me face the idea that it wasn't all a dream.

I knew, deep down that it wasn't all a dream. But it is like knowing the definition of a word but not the real meaning, the gut feeling. One bright day, after a night of great sex with this certain person, he hinted strongly that we were through, no sex, not ever again. He had his reasons. I went home feeling devastated. Why not? It wasn't real was it? How could a little sex hurt anyone? Then I felt ashamed.

It opened up my awareness, blew apart all my denials, my refusal to see. Do you mean that he was really there last night that we really touched, really kissed and loved together? But I had been home in my own bed alone. My God, was I raping people over the air. Did people think I was using them? Was I forcing love on different people? Even just hugging a lonely stranger could be construed as hurting him through love?

My visits to everyone stopped for quite a while. I asked Jesus, "Why didn't you tell me?" I cried while angels hugged me. I flew into a rage up in the sky and Jesus called my name and told me to stop. I did. I began to calm down. It wasn't as horrible as I was making out. I was just ashamed of myself. Had I sinned? I didn't know for sure, but who doesn't sin? Is it a sin if you are ignorant of the rules? The worst part was using God's gift of love and mental visits for my own pleasure. How could Jesus have loved and tolerated me through it all.

Love was the culprit. I had been trying to broaden Jesus' love, love everyone, love more, use the Yoga of love. I was whoring in space. I still hurts me to think about it. Jesus and I loved but his love is different, not physical. It is more of a joining of selves, a union, an ecstatic oneness. Yet, I would love Jesus wholly and completely; then, in the next moment, send my love out to someone else. Hopeless and dejected, I realized that it was time to change. I did change. Since then, I discovered a number of things about my gift, my ability to send out thoughts; I learned that a gift, like a coin, could have two sides.

When is a gift not a gift? When it hurts someone. Ignorant use of my gift came close to costing a few people their lives and a few others some sleepless nights. My only defense is that I was truly ignorant, selfishly young, and lacking in wisdom. These are only a few examples of my near-sightedness.

The car was filled with groceries; I had just turned onto the street behind my house when the other car coming at me from the opposite direction suddenly swerved and hit the side of a car traveling behind us. I immediately saw why. It was because the man driving had looked over at me with a startled look on his face and neglected to watch for cross traffic. I felt guilty but because I was alone in the car, I kept driving. What could I say, I hadn't done anything. Besides, even though I didn't know the car or person, maybe he thought he recognized me. Why else would he have looked so startled at me? Actually, I believe that I had inadvertently sent him a thought and it startled him out of his composure. Shopping does that to me, makes me tired and stressed out. Cans used to bend when I would go shopping for the group home. I would be so tired and thirsty driving back that I think my wish for a cup of coffee bent the big three-pound coffee can.

A mild infraction but imagine being in a car all by yourself, radio off, then hearing a voice speak inside your mind. It could be frightening. More so if you are up in the sky flying. Once or twice I have sent a thought up into the air towards small airplanes flying overhead when I was at the beach, just for the fun of it. Naughty I know. I had fun imagining how startled the pilot was. Did the pilot hear me? I'll never know, but the plane swooped down a few times.

One time I almost caused a severe accident. A trapeze artist was swinging high on the rope ladder at the circus. Focusing intently, which I didn't mean to do, I watched him as he slipped and caught himself. I think I had inadvertently called out "hello," "great" or some other word to him from where I sat with my children and foster children. Soon a number of businessmen came walking over to our section surrounding it and watching people as if searching for someone. I shrunk in my seat and almost left early but after thinking about it, I doubted if there was anything to be afraid of. Who would know it was me? In fact, who would believe it? I tried avoiding the trapeze artist for a while but gave up and finally did leave early because the baby was crying. I have never been to a circus since.

As a rule, there is little danger sending someone a stray thought because, usually, if they hear a voice in their mind, they will believe that they just had a bad moment or it was a mistake on their part. This has saved me from discovery many times. A strong feeling or deep worry can sometimes jab a thought through to someone close by. One time it happened to a relative, an in-law's mother'. I have no idea what word I thought at her but I saw her up-start as thought she had seen a ghost. A sudden fear had crossed my mind that I had forgot my antibiotics at home and I hoped I wasn't infectious in the swimming pool. A silly worry but she had picked up on it. She is a religious person and spiritual people can often pick up stray thoughts. Religion and spirituality seems to bind people together into a single oneness whether they are aware of it or not.

Could thinking or sending thoughts to someone be the same as traveling with your mind? Is mind travel a type of extra sensory perception, ESP? When I travel, am I essentially just talking to someone out there? I think I can answer these questions with a negative because I don't see the environment as if I were looking out from another person's eyes, I always see it as if I am there experiencing the event in person. Besides, I just don't see out, someone sees me too, our reaction is mutual. When I popped into Nexus the lady saw me, likewise the sailor when I popped onto the old sailing ship. At least, in the case of Nexus, she didn't recognize me as a ghost image but a real person. I don't know what I am when I travel or visit. I have learned that when I visit people with angels, I can choose to be invisible or visible, noticed or not.

I remember when the angels gave me this gift of sight. In fact, a group of angels said, "we will help you." I felt the middle spot in my mind open up. It felt like bones crunching and snapping open. Even now, I can feel that same spot if I think about it. This spot is the same area in the brain that is used in the East to induce mind communication. On reflection I remember that I could think at other people before the angels opened up my mind. Their purpose must to have been to enhance what I already had, to finally realize that now I could do it. This begs the question of why. Why does it matter if I can send thoughts or travel, what purpose would it serve. I can't answer that question. Jesus' only answer is that "One-day I will understand." I've already explained that I am not a saint. I am not great at anything; I have done nothing that I know of for the betterment of humanity, except as we all do by acting nice to neighbors and relatives. Although, I fervently hope my actions bare out the three small peoples prediction that I save them. Only time will tell.

Jesus' time is different than our own, as I've hinted before. His soon is as far from my idea of soon as anyone's can get. Sometimes he speaks as though he is from the future or, he knows that an event in the immediate future is certain to happen. I said to him the other day, "I am going to go to that church tonight, aren't I?" even though I never go to church on a weeknight. He laughed and said, "yes." This was unusual behavior for me but he knew while I just guessed that I might go to church.

I am sorry to report that the other end, the evil side, the jokester, also knows the immediate future. I wonder if there is any certainty past this immediate future. He can predict what will happen and does to throw you off your stride. In fact it was yesterday, after work, while I was thinking that in the evening I would write in this book, he said in a mocking voice, "Not tonight you won't." Now we aren't talking Voodoo here, I didn't sit down and think I couldn't write because he talked me into it. Just as I was going into my office to work on the book, a book the jokester hinders whenever he can, when neighbors, who never visit, came over to talk about a project for the neighborhood children, I could hardly refuse to join them. Also be careful and don't get taken in by a man who appears and then tells you to do something, it is false. Slam your mind away from him. Oh, but he will persist. Jesus has never demanded that I do anything in all the time I've known and loved him.

Speaking of time, why couldn't Jesus speak from the past, future or outside of any known time frame? We think of him as being from the past, and at the same time, we give him the status of God. Well God must be in all imaginable times; so, Jesus must be able to see both ways into time at will, past or future, from where ever he exist in time (if such a thing as time exists at all). We think of time as duration, and surly duration exists? Not necessarily, physicists can postulate the possibility of time running backwards, a ball lifting and returning to the bat or a bullet flying back into the gun. The subject is too much to go into in this small chapter but perhaps duration only exists on our frozen ball of matter, world, a place where energy is changed into slow motion.

Still, the question remains, where or when is it that I go when I travel, into what time or place or universe. Like Jim Carrey in the movie, *The Truman Show, I keep trying to punch a hole through the screen, to punch through into reality, into the real world. Great thinkers through out history have observed earth as being a stage prop: Shakespeare in his poem, "The Seven Ages of Man," said, "All the world's a* stage…"[4] Edward Fitzgerald's translation of **The Rubaiydt of Omar Khayydm depicted us as, "Magic Shadow- shapes…."**[5] Many philosophers, writers, thinkers, comedians, etc. have questioned the seeming absurdity of our stage and the roles we play on it. I can't rest content knowing that so many beings are out there without us, watching us, leaving us behind?

I remember many instances of meeting or talking to a group of people from out 'there.' It was a group of angels who opened the thought-transfer area in my mind. Often, a group of angels will meet and hold me if I request it or travel up to them; and sometimes it seems like I am talking and receiving answers from their leader. Once, years ago, before I had any understanding of the intricacies involved, I woke up in the middle of the night to see a group of beings, all wearing white garments, hovering over my bed, talking over me. Trying to wake me up from my life long sleep, most likely. The next day, I wondered if it was some kind of hidden memory of a group of doctors. Now I know they were not doctors.

---

[4] All the world's a stage, And all the men and women merely players; They have their exits and their entrances; and one man in his time plays many parts…" William Shakespeare.

Oscar Williams, Ed., *Immortal Poems of the English Language*, (New York, NY, 1952) , p. 73.

[5] …We are no other than a moving row, of Magic Shadow-shapes that come and go, Round with this Sun-illumined Lantern held, In Midnight by the Master of the Show. *Immortal Poems*, p. 359.

Who are they? The same people who have always been there, angels, saints, lords, enlightened ones, people able to send themselves out there, as if that is any kind of answer. Where are they from in space? Where are they from in time? The answer seems to be anywhere and everywhere. Someplace, two people were talking against a white background when I popped in on their conversation, someplace I call Nexus people were riding up and down moving highways, someplace God sits in audience to answer questions from upstarts like me. Yet, aren't we also someplace? Aren't we also a part of this grand scheme of visitors and travelers? Or are we only a curiosity, a hidden by-way in the vast universe? Shouldn't we investigate the possibility? We may learn someday that it's the only way to travel.

When you look at a whale lifting itself up toward the sky, what do you think about? I think about the whale's communion with God and its futile effort to overcome gravity, its gallant attempt to rise above its surroundings and look up. We are certainly at least as varied and curious as a whale. Can't we also lift ourselves up out of our environment, out of our common surroundings toward our God? Mankind has always looked up, now we can learn to travel there as well. If my words are true, then not only do we have the ability to reach beyond our world, beyond our wildest dream, but God, himself, waits for our arrival with open arms.[6]

---

[6] I thought that I was finished with the book, that this was the end. I didn't know Jesus had other plans.

THE SOURCE

Last night I witnessed the most astonishing and unfathomable place in the universe. I was accompanied by both Jesus and Mary; this was the first time I traveled with both Jesus and Mary, as we watched what must be the first wonder of the universe, a Verde opera of immensity, a vast outpouring of life in un-measurable proportions.

We stood on the edge of a dark cloud, as if on a cliff, looking far into deepest space. Translucent streamers of soft glistening, pearl light flowed past us.

"Turn around," Jesus said to me, pointing. "Look."

A cinematic proliferation of life swirled at us from a single vortex far on the horizon. I saw eddies of tangled life curling away in all directions, as if birthed from a single source of energy, out of this point of energy poured a virtual potpourri of life: Gold people, black people, faces smiling, faces crying, faces screaming, groups of people huddling near fire, people dancing, humongous hoards moving, people clothed in reds and blues, pinks and green stripes, people running shouting, screaming; animal forms, indescribable contortions of heads, arms and legs, bodies with stiff spiked fur, glistening diamond scales, wet eyes, staring eyes, weeping eyes, webbed feet, needle toes, needle teeth, blunt crunching teeth with open jaws, an elephant standing in fire grass, birds filling the air with red wings. A panorama of worlds fanned out as if from a streaming cinema screen, whole cities, sky rises, glass houses, mountains, countryside's with green trees and yellow grass, oceans rubbing rocky land, pink suns, orange suns, suns dancing with moons shinning color wheel variations, plants, flowers, leaves, upside-down trees.

As I stood watching this cornucopia of world zoos filled with moving, living, breathing life, twisting out from its point source, I could only stare, mind-boggled with wonder, eyes flickering between chaos and normalcy. Normalcy because a real star

spangled universe surrounded this vast outpouring. Tiny pin points of stars blazed in a million dots of light against a dark velvet background, as if to frame an oil painting the size of a solar system. Then once again, my eyes would flicker back to the vortex of energy streaming towards me.

"But, what am I seeing?" I asked myself. "What is it?" Instantaneous birth? Riotous thoughts? Plato's perfect forms? DNA run amok? Egg yolk? The vortex created, multiplied, grew, became, stretched as we watched. A point source—of everything?

"Yes," Jesus suddenly said to me, "This is The Source."

I understood him to mean an out flowing from the All, the One, the Everlasting, the Eternal, the universal God: Brahma, Yahweh, Allah, El, Zeus, Vishnu…

As we turned away and left this spectral theater of life, I felt relieved because even though I yearned to absorb it all, to suck it all in, I felt overwhelmed with culture shock. Suddenly, I felt wrung dry of emotion; they were right, it was time to leave. After all, I am just a little person, not up to universal sightseeing.

"How would I ever describe what I just seen," I asked Jesus later, "I don't know if I could put it in my book."

"Write it in your book," Jesus instructed.

"But I don't know how. How can I picture it all? How would I describe what I saw? It was too much," I complained to him, but he was gone. My objection fell on the empty space around my chair. Sometimes, that is his way.

I have tried to describe to you what poured out of the vortex, The Source, to the best of my ability, and I think I did a fair job of it, but I cannot, by any means imaginable, understand or defend its logic. You and I are both perplexed, how could we not be? To me it remains an enigma of universal proportions.

Nevertheless, I derive great solace from the memory. When my mind seethes with doubts, when I question my own sanity, I need only recall my abrupt visit to The Source. The memory of its vivid outpouring, its actuality, and its perplexity always sets me back on a straight path, as does the memory of my visit to Nexus and audience with God. The Source also serves me as a kind of measuring stick; after this, the other places I visit are tame.

Tree World

How can you absorb the essence of a world in a single moment? That's what I tried to do this evening. I intended to smell it, suck it in, know it, and feel it. As it turned out, I could barely focus on any significant details. "Tonight," Jesus promised, "We will visit a new world." I had been hesitant and slightly uncertain of going to new worlds but now I was determined, ready to go; then, after all my mental preparation, we spent only a few fast minutes on the world.

We arrived on a road that ran up and down low hills. Suddenly, a square low-sided vehicle came racing over the hill right towards us. Zip, we'd have been squashed if we were made out of sterner stuff. The vehicle flew up and down the hills and away, a speeding roller coaster. I am sure it had wheels but I wonder if they ever touched ground.

And to think earth has crazy drivers.

If I remember right it was an open vehicle with low sides with six people sitting inside, three in front and back. They were moving around, nodding heads, waving arms and calling out, not I think in warning to us, but in enjoyment. It's a wonder no one fell out when the car drove up and down those steep hills. Considering the danger of the open car and their fast speed, all six people seemed extraordinarily unafraid for their situation. It made me compare them to earth kids out for a joy ride.

I had no way of knowing if they were young kids or not, but they acted in character, actually like cartoon characters on a Saturday morn kids show. Their faces, long and narrow, had large black areas where eyes and mouths should be. I remembered one person had a tuff of hair jutting up from his/her forehead. With no obvious windshield, I don't know how their hair or clothing stayed put, if it did.

The landscape looked normal: a picturesque blue sky stuffed with fluffy white clouds floating overhead, it looked no different than a sunny day in the country. The grass and trees looked a yellowish green, but this could have been their autumn season. Trees of various shapes and sizes grew on the hills in the distance; yet, only low grass and tiny flowers grew near the smooth road which wound up and down the hills like a narrow ribbon. Bright sunlight shinning through the trees made crisscross patterns across the hills and road. With the yellow/green scenery and speeding car, I felt right at home, the only thing missing was a blaring radio.

This was when Jesus pointed out to me that every world had its own social problems, implying that those speeders were one of this world's problems. Social complexity and the problems created because of them are a necessary condition for growth. "Each world is at a different stage of development," Jesus told me. He also explained that earth was unique in a number of select areas, but not in the social arena, conflict and strife run rampant on many worlds, struggle and change a basic way of life.[7] I think if the universe has any meaning, that meaning must be life—life in constant flux, moving to the dance of the universe.

Our next visit to Tree World [8]two months later, was more instructive; nevertheless, puzzling. We entered a city square, a wide flat area surrounded by tall buildings, jam-packed with tall, fast-walking, people. Their gait was odd, the bottom half seemed to move before the top half. Jerking would be a more accurate description than walking. The city was a bustle of high energy everywhere I looked.

I watched as a tall person came to a long row of tall chairs high off the ground. He/she sat down on one chair and the row of chairs began to move, rolling away sideways forcing people to step out of its way. All

---

[7] Jesus has offered to take me to worlds destroyed by its inhabitants. I don't want to go, but he tells me that we will visit one such world in the near future. I have always believed God would stop people from destroying their own world. It disappoints me greatly that God has allowed this to happen/

[8] I name the worlds that we travel to. Sometimes I give a world a name that I need to change after I've visited it a few times. This happened with Tree World.

through the city square crowds of people moved, almost running, in every direction. I looked a over low railing and saw lines of people, four abreast, hurrying below street level into a tunnel entrance, while, across the opening, another group stood tall, quiet, and silent, their rigid stance forcing other energetic people to stop, then go around. I watched as one person stopped, quickly in front of the group then detoured hurriedly around as if the group's obstruction were only a slight annoyance. The group that stood as still as stone was accomplishing or acting out what Jesus told me was a "Resistance Prayer."

I mentioned to Jesus that, Resistance Prayer, was a perfect description of events. This one group was resisting a whole crowd. People toggled into a new gear change at each step around the resistance group. Everyone, except the group holding the "Resistance Prayer" acted highly energetic. I saw it as twitching. I wondered suddenly what they would think of my walk if they could see me because I didn't think they could see us as we walked through their city observing them or I would have seen a reaction; although, I don't believe we were infringing on their privacy because we were in a public area.

As we walked amid a large group of hurrying people, suddenly, unexpectedly, popped a large ten (?) foot tall machine forcing people to scatter away in new directions. It had claws or brushes lined up on each side whirling and whizzing around; obviously, it was a street cleaning, monster machine. It didn't give any warning to people to move away, unless it used a silent whistle. Amazingly, I was the only one bothered by the machine's intrusion, the vast crowd took it all in stride; although, I noticed, they did move quickly away from its mandibles. Could it go berserk and run over someone? Certainly, this impolite machine must have some kind of life avoidance system; people were too unconcerned.

Further on, I saw another strange sight; a person was crawling, against a low railing, down the walkway on its belly. All the people, a large crowd of them, avoided the belly crawler as if the person were contagious; an empty space crawled along with the person. The belly crawler's skin (or clothing) looked like it was moving back and forth on his body as the person crawled. It gave me the shivers. Not only that but the person's movements were very slow and deliberate, as if acting in slow motion; opposite and contrary to the fast paced hurrying movements I had seen so far. Later Jesus told me that the person's slow crawl was an act of atonement t, that a necessary part of the atonement ritual included the avoidance of other people. The person crawling was assumed to be invisible to the other people walking by. I don't know how far the person needed to crawl to atone for sins or for how long.

These people look like giant, tall, walking sloths. They wear clothing, but I didn't notice if it was a special design except that only the mid-half of their bodies were covered. The dark hollow facial features, extraordinary long arms and legs, and gait made these people look strange to me and out of proportion; nevertheless, their humanity was instantly recognizable. Jesus told me this would be true of all the places we will visit; the people's humanity, intelligence and technology will be self-evident. I imagine this is necessary for my benefit. Tree World is so similar to our own it could be a paternal twin; still, I find it hard to visually comprehend most of what is in front of me. For this reason, Jesus said that we would go back a number of times to Tree World. I think he means for me to get accustomed to looking at strange behaviors and peculiar landscapes.

Our next visit was Jesus' idea. He said he wanted to show me something and that we would only be there a short while. We arrived surrounded by tall trees intermixed with large leafy bushes, a jungle. We pushed through an opening in the leaves and came upon one of the people, tall with white hair all over his body, sliding or rubbing himself on a pole or tree. The person was making humming sounds at the same time as vibrating the body at the tree. The pole and the person resembled each other both were skinny and tall. The person was sending a song by scent and vibration up towards the top of the tree or pole. As I followed the vibration to the top, I saw that above our heads, the trees joined together in ropes and walkways that snaked all over the sky between green leaves.

Jesus then caused us to become visible to the person at the tree. The person startled and bleeped away, I mean that the person turned, looked at us, and then disappeared. It looked like the person's head stayed a moment longer than the rest of the body. Later I was to learn that the person didn't really disappear but had slid sideways into the leaves; the movement had been so quick it looked like a disappearance.

Soon, heads popped in front of us seemingly out of nowhere. The heads looked at us and popped out again. Because of the abundant green foliage it was hard to see where they were coming from or going to. I think they came to see the show, to see us standing there amid all the green trees and leaves. And why were we there, what had we come to the jungle to see.

Sex? Was that what the person had been about on the tree. I don't know why I got the impression that it was sexual. If it was, was the person embarrassed by our sudden appearance, I asked Jesus. He told me no, that the person wasn't embarrassed at all; their sexual mores were more open than ours. They have much less shame and guilt. He added that it was not sex as we think of sex but a pre-play to mating. It was the person saying by actions, smell, and sound "I like you," or "Please be my friend."

"Like a cat rubbing against a leg?" I asked.

Laughing, he agreed my analogy was right and told me that I needed to get used to actions that might embarrass me. Also that I should be careful how I interpreted unknown actions by people on different worlds. If I formed my own interpretation of an action too quickly, I could come to the wrong conclusions. I should remain tolerant and open minded regarding other people's actions, especially odd, strange behaviors when we travel. I supposed that this lesson was why we went to Tree world that night, to reaffirm my tolerance of different cultures.

But, also, it is important to note that I can never gather more than small, minute bits of information about any world we visit. The little I learn can't possibly cover even a fraction of the social, psychological, or spiritual cultural of any world; all these worlds I visit will always remain clouded in unknown discoveries. After all, unknown discoveries and unique cultures still lay hidden and scattered on our own world, even after millions of years of search by mankind. This inability of mine to understand a complete, whole world is probably the reason our visits center on religious rituals and worship, the field is narrowed down so that I can absorb and understand what I am seeing.

In November, we went back to Tree World again. This time we visited two different kinds of buildings, public and private. The public building resembled an enclosed round amphitheater. It was huge and sunny with long sloping ramps rising and falling on the outer parameters next to the large, glass walls. I could see far across to the other side past numerous, giant, tall, white columns that were scattered throughout. The columns were concentrated in the center and reminded me of tall trees in a forest; they actually branched off near the top of the high building.

Large numbers of people were coming and going but the building wasn't crowded. As we rode up the ramp, a person in front of us walked into the wall, the new door grew wide to receive the person, then closed itself behind. I could not see where an opening had ever been and assumed that we rode the ramp past many such doors. We stopped at a platform high above the pole-trees; a blue sky filled the ceiling above our heads, then we walked over to another ramp and rode it down. It was not unlike riding on a tall, fast escalator.

The total aura of the amphitheater was hard to grasp because there was so much glass and light intermixed with tall people riding up and down the ramps and walking to and fro in their jerky, fast, gait. All the walls and ramps were glaring white, but perhaps it was the bright daylight that gave me that impression. The only vivid color I noticed was the people's clothing. Clothing was colorful but scanty, hardly what we would wear to work, if work place is the right term; yet, in here, I got the impression that people were attending to business, not play.

The first thing I noticed in the private residence was a narrow ramp inside the dwelling. The ramp rose gradually in a curved arc to an upper story. What I found most interesting, were the tall tree-like poles standing behind and under the ramp. I understood that this area was the nursery, that the tall tree-poles were for training and raising their youngest children.

The group of people, in this private residence, seemed to except our presence with aplomb. I had the opportunity to look closely at them. Each person had a very white, hairless face with black holes for facial features, a set of eyes, nose, and mouth, details of which I just couldn't see against the deep dark areas. The extensive arms and legs were covered with long, sparse white hair that resembled finger length strands of white silk. The skin color was not a shade of pink, olive, or chestnut like our own would be but an actual whitish white. In all, the person looked like a giant sloth except for its quick jerky movements, which belies my use of sloth as a comparison. But after my first visit to this world that was what I called it, Sloth world. I've noticed as my travels progress that my ability to see specific details improves with each visit. This is why we have visited this world so many times, so that I can train my visual acuity; then, just as I got used Tree World, Jesus told me that our next visit would be our last.

Our last visit to Tree World was enlightening. We went into a hollow sphere or covered saucer-like depression in the earth, which was dark with mystery and silence. A hidden, low light source glowed softly around the parameter. The floor wasn't dirt; I think it was made of a hard stone like substance. The underground cavern is thought of as "The Root," a place of worship and prayer.

We followed as one person entered to perform a worship ritual. The person knew we were there but because it is a private ritual, we stayed out of sight. The person groped in the dim darkness with long white arms reaching out as if searching for a way through a complex maze. Eventually, after a long trial and error session, the person found the route to a tall, narrow, dark stack opening in the roof and began to climb. We followed.

The person mumbled and twittered during this long climb up through the dark, tree-stack. Progress was extremely slow until sunlight began to shine in a narrow opening at the top, then his movement quickened. Finally, after much ritual struggle and a long climb up, the person reached the sun lit top. Imagine the wonder of golden sunlight after a dark dungeon, the sound of birds chirping and leaves rustling after a long solemn silence, the warmth of sunlight on your face after the cool, dampness of the underground cavern; imagine the goal, the end, the delight. This I imagined as I watched the person reach the final pinnacle then watched an outburst of joy as the person jumped out. Born again from the womb. Wondrous delightful green trees surrounded us on every side, sunlight spattered and waving in the soft breeze, branches hanging and vines crawling in many directions. I was elated. I felt as if I had suffered the same anticipation as I climbed behind, the same joy as I reached the opening, the light at the top of the world. I watched as the person swung down a long rope and across to a green rope bridge. Worship was over.

I suspect the worship involved the person's whole body, mind, and soul, that it centered the person within rather than outside the self. There seemed to be a deliberate slowdown climbing the stack as if to say time was measured different in this place of worship. Perhaps a 'transformation of being' took place during the worship; or, just as likely, I suppose, it could have been merely a repeated ritual played out repeatedly. My feeling was that it had been a solemn occasion for the person. It certainly was for me.

I have no idea what the people call their planet, I called it Tree World for the obvious reason that trees were all over the place - inside and outside; although, I visited only a few small areas. I am sure that it is vast and varied like our own planet. Jesus has told me that it ranges from tropical to arctic conditions, but it is not as varied as earth. I wonder if it had fewer continental divisions. I do know that the people of Tree World are past the self-destruct stage of development, the same stage we are still moving through. Jesus said they are past the danger point, that they made accommodations to preserve themselves and their environment worldwide. He mentioned that they still have serious problems to solve but they are working at solutions and making good progress.

RIBBON LIGHTS

Jesus promised me a unique and amazing experience for my next visit. We popped in to a new world for just a moment one night. Suddenly I was surrounded by wide streamers of intense color floating in a cobalt blue haze that filled the air. As the streamers glided past me I realized they were of various thickness, and transparencies. Each ribbon of light twisted and waved as if swimming in the ocean depths.

The view changed color for an instant as the edge of a bright yellow-orange streamer floated near my face. Mouth open in wonder, I turned around and the deep blue sea filled with streamers went on as far as I could see. The floor at my feet was rippled in waves as if we were at the bottom of an ocean. But, it didn't feel like water, "This isn't water, is it?" I asked Jesus.

"No, this is air," he said and smiled.

It looked like we were standing in a deep ocean, although; there was no sensation of wave movement, Even the vegetation was sparse and fleshy as you might expect beneath an ocean. Most of the light came from the various ribbons floating all around us; at no time did I feel like I was in the dark, I felt rather, like I was standing in multiple shades of blue sunshine.

We only stayed for a few moments, yet I already new that it would be the most beautiful and awe-inspiring environment I would ever see. Later I told Jesus, "I want to go back, I want to linger and stay a while next time." He promised we would.

Tonight, we did go back, after Jesus told me a few facts about Ribbon World. He told me that Ribbon World, as I called it, didn't cover the whole of that world, that it was a small unique area of land surrounded by mountains. It is believed to be sacred, a gift from God. Those who visit must go through introductory rituals before being allowed to enter. The entire population of the world, and even a few people from other worlds, know about the sacred area but only a select few are allowed entrance at any one time. We will not go through an introductory course but no one will notice. "You will be OK" Jesus told me. He mentioned that, if I choose, he would stand back while I involved myself in the sacred ritual.

Where to begin? I saw many people, very human in physical appearance, softly shadowed in blue and different ribbon colors, walking single file in long curved lines that seemed to curl into tight spiral patterns then curl out again. Some of the people were nude but decorated with painted stripes on their bodies, some wore clothing with wide bands of vivid colors, while others wore simple, long white gowns, like what I wear when traveling. I stepped over and joined the nearest procession then watched, as figures in front of me would reach a certain point in the spiral, then turn outward. I felt a momentary pang of fear, "How would I know when to turn?" I asked myself. But when I reached the turn I knew. I hummed along with others as we slowly walked step by step into and out of a long spiral that curled on and on and on. We twisted and turned as if entering the center of a deep flower, step after step after step around and under rose petals, fragrant with dew, down, down into the pink depths then step by step out over the rim, on and on. We forever knew when and where to turn; I had become one with the procession, one flow, one group, one soul.

As each spiral path led higher and higher and then down again spiraling into the pattern, I became so entranced, so one with the flow, I was not aware of any intricate turn of the procession, or of any final design. The flow, the movement, the involvement was all. I felt a great love for the person in front of me, a gentle, all compassionate intense love. I loved the orange thick glowing ribbon, I loved the emerald ribbon, gold, ochre, crimson, violet ribbons joining in the flow. All, ribbons and humans, together in a soft melodic singsong stroll, hands clasped in prayer, raised in wonder, feet stepping, sliding, floating on little valleys and troughs of soft sapphire sands. We, the procession, the flow became the wave, the movement of brilliant flowing ribbons.

Entranced, I became one with the sacred substance, I breathed it into my lungs, swallowed the hazy, cobalt, bright air into my soul with every breath, I became the sacred; the sacred became me. A living glow of gold light floated onto my chest and around my right arm, penetrating my body with its gold being, it lingered for a tingling moment inside me, then flowed on, exiting my back. For an instant, we had exchanged souls. Some part of myself flowed out, bonded with the gold ribbon, some part of its golden aura stayed as a living part of myself, soul-to-soul, life to life, its substance, my substance, our substance.

I fell in love with this evocative, holy ground. I left a part of myself there on Ribbon World when I came away, yet; I left with more than I can ever express.

Even now, I believe that I hold inside myself a part that holiness. I feel that each glowing ribbon was a spiritual power close to God, a kind of angel.

I hope to go back to Ribbon World often, when I need a refuge, a solemn place to meditate. I even hope that someday in this vast universe of time and space, I will live and dwell as a native on this blue world were the Ribbon Gods flow.

Since the visit I just described, I have gone back, but I still cannot relate to you in words the complete oneness and all-ness I feel there. I can add little more knowledge than I have already told you. I don't want to know any more about this land, just feel it. Besides, Jesus explained to me that it is considered taboo to study any part of this sacred, holy ground. No instruments or other technological gadgets are allowed inside the mountain range. He said that even when people from other worlds are allowed an infrequent visit, they come away awe-struck and always decide to leave well enough alone, to leave the sacred, sacred.

COTTON SEED

We stood in a white on white environment except for a few large gray forms that broke up the whiteness far in front of us. Huge white flakes of the stuff was swirling and blowing all around us. "Is it snow?" I asked. In answer he reached out and gathered a handful to show me. All I could see was a bunch of strings and fluff stuck together perhaps like cotton; although, I don't think I've ever seen real cotton. This cotton like substance filled the air so thickly it looked like a snow blizzard in deep winter.

Jesus took my hand and led me through the whiteness to one of the huge gray forms; it was a tree, wide and squat with deeply grooved bark. The few leaves I could see were clustered in upside-down bowl shapes hanging low from the tree. It looked unearthly, but its girth and bark design was so exaggerated it looked perfect for a Disney movie.

To my surprise, Jesus knocked on the tree and a door opened to a medium size room. Standing in the open door to welcome us was a plump man with as big a grin as could be possible on a human face. The room had a low ceiling and a few walls were tree textured in deep grooves, wood knots, and growth lines. We were led to a small, thick pedestal table by the grinning man who invited each of us to sit on a stool he pulled out for us.

Sitting, I watched as four or five adults, who were all short, square, and plump, came to greet us and nod their acceptance at our presence. Children with knobby knees and elbows scampered into the room with the adults and right away began laughing and playing across from us. All the adults were plump, acting merry and busy; they continued working and talking while we watched, except for our host, who kept grinning at us.

I was greatly fascinated to watch a young child with short white hair, that looked as if it were cut with a bowl, climb up an open stair-wall to my right. The stairs were carved into the wall but didn't look like stairs we would choose to climb; these were far too steep, more like a ladder. Oddly, the child climbed with his knees and elbow as well as his hands and feet. He looked funny but very quick and agile. I would have needed a rope. The child disappeared into a round hole in the ceiling. I think he purposely tried to catch my attention to show off how quick he could climb.

As I watched the goings on in the room, the feeling of warmth and homeyness, and welcome grew until I became very comfortable with my surroundings. Although, there was one item in the center of the room that I couldn't help noticing, it puzzled me. It was a huge rounded wood hill, about half my height, polished smooth. Exquisite patterns of wood grain swirled and twisted in odd contusions all over and around the wooden hump; it looked polished to a smooth glass finish. A round black hole on the floor next to it led to a lower level. I felt a little guilty that this hump kept pulling my eyes away from the other events in the room because the grinning man would nod and watch for my acceptance.

Jesus whispered to me that the man was grinning so happily because our presence meant a good omen for his family. At this time, a few of his people were walking outside in the cotton, on a spiritual journey; our presence would guarantee their safe return. Also, he explained that my presence wasn't a shock to them because they already knew about earth and were familiar with much of our culture.

I had noticed that they acted towards Jesus as if he were a close friend, but I don't know what name they called him by or whether they thought him a God, angel, or man.

Later, I asked Jesus about the wood hump. He explained that the hump was a family platform for each speaker, who would sit straddled on its pinnacle. Every home had one. Each family group attributed great spiritual significance and special meaning their own house platform. This wood rise, or hump had been deliberately nurtured into an overgrown knot of wood, selectively nourished and then polished to a fine gleam. It was the central pride of every family group. Jesus also explained that their unique life style was caused by their periodic need to escape the cotton fall, which filled the air and covered the countryside three and four times a year.

Much of their everyday business of living and working was carried on inside their trees and the root system that had tunnel connections below ground that reached around the world.

He added that their technology; although, at the same developmental level as earth, was very different from ours because so much was carried out and based on their trees. Chemistry was almost their sole industry. For instance, they could induce tree parts to grow in specific required shapes through special feeding or irritation of the wood. "They are extremely skilled at growing and creating everything they need."

From this, I assumed that they worshipped trees and asked Jesus if this was so.

Laughing, he answered, "No, they don't worship trees, they worship cotton. Cotton is everything. It is their main source of clothing as well as food. But don't think of them as primitive, far from it."

We went back to Cotton World about a week later. This time, when Jesus knocked on the tree, he explained that knocking was an important tradition on this world. Because so much of their root system is open to casual strangers, knocking at their home was a necessary courtesy. Even passing a work station in the root was an occasion for a quick knock on a hard surface to signal their near presence.

On our last visit, we were invited to visit their cotton industry, and that's where we went as soon as we arrived. We walked to the middle of the room, to the smooth wooden hill and then down steep stairs that was more like a ladder than stairway but we touched bottom quickly.

At the bottom of the ladder, the area where we stood was a large, vast room with openings that branched away into the distance. The ceiling looked like tree material, but it was actually the top of the root system. Many people were walking past us, coming from every direction. Everyone looked at us as they walked past, not staring, but very aware of our presence, as if we were the top news of the day. A few people paused, sending wide smiles our way, but no one intruded themselves uninvited into our group that I thought said a lot for their polite culture.

Our presence was a great honor to our host and he wanted everyone to know about his guests, so; I don't know if the walking traffic was more numerous than usual. I could see other ladder openings and assumed they led to other homes. Jesus told me that these people were like us in that they divided their time between inside and outside. Right now, because the cotton was flowing, they spent more time inside. As soon as it stopped flowing, they would go outside to cultivate their crop.

At present, we stood in one of the huge, joined root systems of a select group of trees, this was where they processed their cotton (cotton-like substance) into the many items they needed. They do to their cotton what George Washington Carver did with the peanut; they make it serve numerous uses. We walked over to the side were a number of low stands were lined up in rows. Workers walked us down the rows, pointing and smiling at odd forms that were growing in the square boxes; the forms reminded me of mushrooms and molds. The lighting was very soft and diffuse plus everything seemed to have a slight glow to it, fungus?

We stayed in the root system only a short time. As a guest, I climbed up the stair-ladder first and slowed everyone up. Upstairs, as we took our leave, each person nodded good-by to us. I was hesitant to leave such a warm hearth friendly place. Imagine every Christmas myth, a homey comfort next to a warm fire. That's is what it felt like I was leaving. Though, I had seen no fire places any where in their home. I was tired from the strain of long observation, but still felt a slight disappointment that we had to leave these fine, friendly people.

Later that night, sitting and reflecting on my visit, I wondered why we hadn't visited a place of worship like usual. Then suddenly, I realized that perhaps we had. Perhaps worship to them was working on the cotton; they may combine work and prayer. I didn't know but hoped to learn more on my next visit.

Which was very soon because we went back the next night. Jesus wanted to show me Cotton World without the cotton flowing in the air. It was beautiful. A deep cerulean sky with fluffy white clouds much like

Earth on a sunny December day with snow drifting and covering the ground. Except it wasn't snow and the trees were fat, and squat with green leaves hanging down in bunches from their round tops. In the distance, as far as I could see, people were outside scattered amid their short stumpy trees raking and piling up the cotton.

The family I had met was outside gathering up cotton. Children were scampering in the cotton. I watched as a few children put cotton in their mouths and ate it. This didn't concern any of the adults watching. Gathering cotton was a game to the children. The adults seemed to make a game of it too.

The sun was very bright and I wondered if the cotton would rot before they could rake it all in. "Oh, no," I was assured with a shake of the head, after Jesus asked the grinning man for me. He explained that the cotton substance needed to ripen beneath the sun for a short time to swell the pods. The man showed me two samples, one had very small seeds tangled in long strings and the other had larger pods, less tangled and stringy, more like fuzz. When the "Gathering" was complete, they would open trap doors all over the land and drop it down the shoots into large airtight containers.

Jesus told me that after the "Gathering:" they would party all night beneath the starlit sky. The dancing and drinking and games would go on all night and into the next day. They begged us to join their "Gathering" but Jesus told them that we couldn't stay this time, but promised we would visit one of their future Gatherings.

After we left, Jesus told me that the people on Cotton World have less problems and disputes than most. Their land is very integrated and made more so by they're large root system. They are a playful and happy people. Their struggle for survival hasn't been severe because the cotton supplies most of their basic needs. Jesus promised me that we would go back for another visit one day.

GOD'S WORLD

I am becoming a pro at traveling. Earlier in the day when Jesus said that we would go to a new world and stay longer than usual, I took it in stride, continuing with what I was doing at the time; until he told me where we would go. God's World! He said we would be going to God's Kingdom? But, but, but… I can't, I stammered. How will we get there? What if I can't understand? What if I can't see, what if I…? All the rest of the day I worried and made myself anxious about going to God's World.

"You are invited," the angels said to me with many hugs, "It is a gift."

Later that evening, I downplayed my anxiety as Jesus led me to God's World.

We entered a golden forest amid a riot of gold foliage: gold tarnish, gold orange, soft gold, brown gold silver gold, blue gold, red gold, yellow gold; the variety and selection of so many golden hues astounded me. Everywhere I looked were tall golden trees, golden bushes, golden leaves, golden flowers with golden stamens; textures of bright glittering gold and soft, diffuse gold, gold in shadow and gold in bright sunlight beneath a golden/yellow sky.

I stood gaping in awe and wonder at the scene before my eyes—a golden banquet fit for a King - or God.

"Can I touch it?" I asked breathlessly, afraid to breathe it away? He nodded.

The single gold flower petal I touched was pliable and soft. The flower had four petals with an orange stamen covered with gold pollen. It resembled a tiger lily. Its leaves were covered in soft silver fuzz. Curious, I bent down and brushed with my fingers at the undergrowth of fallen burnished bronze leaves. My fingers touched and sank into rich damp, black soil - it was real dirt. The complete golden tropical forest

73

was a real, living, breathing, diversity of biomes. This was no Midas world; it was too alive, too vivid, too actual.

Laughing, Jesus reminded me that I was only seeing a small section of a whole world, but it was all just as spectacular.

"What if it rained?" I laughed as it began to rain.

Rain fell in tiny diamond drops. Gold rain plunked down on flower petals, rivulets ran down our faces; then the rain stopped as quickly as it began. I laughed in wonder as we walked through the golden forest, sometimes brushing against dripping gold leaves. Drops fell from overhead trees creating a low golden mist that swirled around our feet, filling the air with sweet aromas and soft chirping bird sounds.

Soon we walked out of the dense foliage and arrived at a high outcropping of light blue/gray rock. The rock was not gold but the waters falling over it in tiny, braid rivulets was. Gold water dripped into a small pool of golden water rings, before it poured down little inclines turning it into a miniature rapids. Just beyond, many rivulets of gold water met gathering into a small stream that ran out into countryside of tall gold grass, waving high in the soft breeze.

"Is it real water?" I asked as I bent down and filled my cupped hand from the shimmering gold pool. I sipped the water out of my hand. It looked and tasted like real water, fresh and pure.

"It is real water," Jesus said, "It looks like gold because the sky is yellow."

I looked up into the yellow sky; white clouds flocked overhead like tuffs of dandelion seed floating in the breeze. A deep yellow orange lined the horizon over the top of the trees. There was no visible sun, just a steady golden glow that felt warm and pleasing.

We walked near the small curling stream; on one side was the gold forest that we had just came out of and on the other side a vast landscape of tall fluffy trees and waving grass—all dusted in golden hues. Rocks were scattered here and there and I think I saw faint orange hills or mountains far off in the distance. I didn't notice many birds or animals; although, I am sure they were numerous because this lush world of golden flowers and trees was a perfect milieu for life. Curious, I asked Jesus if people lived here.

He answered in the negative, he said that people didn't live on this world, but there was always people coming and going, even staying for long periods of time. I think he meant God's world was considered a parkland or nature preserve.

Later, I realized that my visit to God's World had been a great and wonderful experience, but I worried that something more was expected of me, that it had been too great a gift. I was afraid that I wouldn't be able to describe it adequately in the book I was writing.

"Don't worry," angels said later, "The purpose of the visit wasn't to give you material for your book. This visit is a gift to you, given freely by God."

"But what right do I have to visit God's World. I am not good enough. I am nothing special; I don't understand." I still felt concerned about being given a privilege such as this. I was unable to accept such a great gift graciously.

To quiet worry, Jesus said, "Other people will visit God's World too."

Then he made me a promise, a personal promise I will never forget, and this is the reason I have included a visit to God's world in this book. I wanted to tell you of Jesus' lovely promise to me. Like a lover offering the moon to a lover, Jesus said, "One day I will pick a golden flower from God's Kingdom for you. You will wear it always."

Heaven Alive

I've just realized that I should clarify a few major points about the names I throw out so casually, names often considered sacred and holy, nevertheless, real and valid names that I seem to take for granted because I have been using them for so long. It is time that I explained who I mean when I refer to God, Jesus, Mary, or angels. I mentioned angels in an earlier chapter but I don't think I've tried to illustrate my personal views of God. I keep writing about God but I haven't clarified my ideas of who and what I believe God to be. I am not sure that I can clarify these ideas unless I try to share by illustration my visits and my visions; doing so, I may learn enough to enhance my own knowledge as well as yours. I'll start by detailing my feelings during a vision of God one night.

One night in early evening, Jesus said to me, "I will help you with your second book; I will show you many worlds." At this time, his words shocked and amazed me; not only the many worlds part but also because I thought my book was complete, all sixty pages of it. My first inclination was to think it wasn't Jesus speaking at all; that someone was imitating him. Then I saw God smiling down at Jesus and me as if to confirm the seriousness of Jesus words. God's smile set a solemn aura of authenticity to Jesus' strange words.

God was right there in front of me; even so, it is almost impossible to describe God because he showed himself as transparent and barely detectable, only a whisper of air with a smile. In just this way, God has joined us in conversation many times, a phantom smile hanging in the air above me. If it's only a smile, how do I know the smile belongs to God? I don't. At these moments I rely on God's essence of being and my instinct, my own strong feelings of recognition, my knowing. Admittedly, this is not proof. There is no proof, only God's overriding presence. I find God's smile enough, or would you in my place dare ask for more?

This ghost smile aspect of God is different from my audience with God when I was placed at God's feet by two angels. Then I felt God's overwhelming, awesome power and might pour out as if from a golden tornado. I've seen God in many different aspects. Another time God showed himself in church as an intense golden luminescence, as though the sun were stepping inside the church to pray. And a few times God appeared as a vague human figure, smoky and transparent, nameless but sending an aura only God's presence could fulfill. Many other people have seen God, in the present and throughout history. We humans have seen God in a thousand altered aspects, given God a thousand distinct names for a thousand special reasons, do you think by now God cares which name we use to call him?

The recent visits are different, so different that I ask myself if I am seeing the same God? Which God am I talking to? Or, should I ask myself which form God is presenting himself as at the moment. Jesus told me once that God has thousands of names on our world, and that I could take my pick which name I wanted to use; still, I remain in a quandary—"But, isn't God *God?*"

Now I realize that instead of puzzling over God's many names, we should think of God as having many different aspects: Aspects such as power, might, love, character, forgiveness, universal being, all-ness, oneness. In other words, how dare we limit God or decide what God can be or should be at any given time. Who are we to ask if God is male or female, or personal, or universal, or one, or many? Why can't God be all these things at once, why not—everything and anything. Why can't God be a personal God for me at the same moment he is a universal God; or why can't God, who is everything, take on any form, large or small. I learned in an anthropology class that we Americans tend to see things as opposites, wrong-right, either-or, black-white; we shun gray and middle areas in daily life. We must shun gray ideas in religion as well, or why else wouldn't we let God be God. In the book, *Conversation with God: Book Two*, by

Neale Walsch[9], God keeps repeating that he *is* us, that he is inside of each and every one of us. God says repeatedly in the book, "I am you and you are me." This idea is hard for us little people to understand, the idea that we are God. We may agree that we are a part of God or that we can grow more godlike, but to be God? It is beyond my ability to fathom too. I read an interesting theory once that speculated the universe began with one particle that kept bouncing around and multiplying itself until it produced every atomic particle formed in this vast universe, including us. Talk about being star dust- we're not star dust, we're all one star. Though, it is a good explanation for how we all became *one*. So, perhaps we can't separate ourselves out of God but God can separate himself from us. After all, we Christians believe God stepped down and lived among us once.

I've explained my relationship with Jesus in past chapters, you could say it is probably the real subject of this book, but do you know that even now, after all the talks I've had, after all the visits, sometimes I still doubt.

Jesus said to me last night, "You still don't believe me, do you?"

I had to admit that I still had doubts. This made me feel humiliated and shamed. How could I still doubt Jesus? I think the reason is that he is so much there, his presence is so penetrating and vivid that it causes me misgivings and doubts. Even when I can't see him, which is most often, I can feel him next to me. I become so aware of his presence when he speaks that there is no doubt in my mind that a real man is standing there. It doesn't matter whether he speaks inside my head or outside; his voice feels just as substantial. This substantiality is what bothers me; it feels too real to be true, to human to be Jesus. I worry, sometimes, that it is an evil man or joker sending thoughts to me. So I asked Jesus.

"What if it's someone pretending to be you?

"I told you once, 'you always know'.

---

9 Neale Donald Walsch, *Conversations with God: Book Two*, Charlottesville, VA, 1997.

"Yes, but sometimes I don't know that I know.

I laughed at my own words then. I reminded Jesus that all of us have preconceived ideas about him. "How can we help it, you've been a God for two thousand years. Of course, I tend to forget that just because Jesus is a God or Lord, he isn't non-human.

Later I thought about my continuing uncertainties. We do tend to put Jesus up at the top of a heavenly hierarchy but he never asked to be put above anyone while he was on earth, why would he want to be put on a pedestal now. His message was not about who was had status in heaven or earth. It was about love. Its just happens that his ability to love so far exceeds our own that it boggles our mind. How can we help putting Jesus on a pedestal? It's almost impossible to think of Jesus as just an ordinary guy.

Still, maybe he is, if not an ordinary guy, a real person. Once, an angel whispered, "He is a very busy man." I understood this to mean that Jesus took time out of a busy schedule to talk to me, although I admit I don't know how this can be unless he is a multiple person who is many places at the same time. Or, is it that in a single moment he can send his mind to various places? Speculating, I have decided that Jesus has such a powerful mind that he can spread it out to diverse places and talk to many people at the same time. Factually, I cannot explain any of it; I just know it to be true. I have spent many hours in circular question and answer sessions with myself trying to understand Jesus. I finally decided not to question who or what Jesus is but to just accept him the person he portrays himself to be – Jesus Christ.

In the final analysis, whether Jesus is a God or Lord, I need to see him as a human companion and friend so we can travel and talk together with a similar base of understanding. Still, I am left with a very odd question that needs to be answered, a question that has been popping in and out of the pages of this book since its beginning; namely, "Is Jesus also a spaceman." The word spaceman conjures up little green men from Mars, but we know Jesus is far greater than any of our Mars cliques, if for no other reason then his immense love for all of us. We hear reports of entities from UFOs using force and cohesion on people; this could never be a method used by Jesus or any of his followers. Love equals respect. So, the answer is "No," Jesus is not a spaceman as we usually think of the term, nevertheless, we could think of him as the Lord of Space or a Citizen of the Universe.

Perhaps this is a new understanding of the Jesus who is alive today, the Jesus I've learned to know and love, the Jesus who talks to me. One day when I was alone at work, Jesus spoke of his return. Without warning, in a very determined voice, I was instructed to remind you that he is on his way to earth. I am to assure you that his arrival will not spell doom. Jesus will bring joy. He stated, "Yes, not doom! Write about my coming in the clouds."

Jesus spoke these words to me almost as he must have spoken them to his disciples two thousand years ago:

"...And 'you will see the Son of Man[10]

Seated at the right hand of the Power

And coming with the clouds of Heaven.' "

This statement of Jesus arriving in the clouds when he revisits earth is repeated six times in the New Testament.[11] Although if you're like me and never satisfied with a simple answer, you might ask why will Jesus will revisit earth if he never left? Read John 14th chapter, verse 16 to 20. "I will not leave you comfortless: I will come to you."[12] These verses seem to imply that although Jesus is leaving, he will stay on as a comforter. He does repeat that, ...but you will see me because I live, and you will live."[13] Isn't he here with me, with all of us? Or is it only his spirit that is here with us? Isn't it Jesus who speaks to me, the same Jesus I have known and loved these many years?

---

[10] The American Bible, The Revised New Testament, World Catholic Press, 1970, Matt 24:30, 26:64, Mark 13:26, 14:62, 1 Thessalonians 4:17, Rev. 1:7.

[11] Theophilos for Windows 95/98/NT, Version 2.6.0, 1997-98, Ivan Jurik. This bible was used for some references.

[12] Theophilos, John 14:18

[13] *The New American* Bible, John 14:19.

One night, tired, weary and sick of living, I told Jesus I wanted to give up because it all seemed so useless. "Can't you just end it for me, now?".

"What if I quit?" He asked me.

My heart suddenly thumped in panic. "But you can't quit. You're Jesus."

I had such a feeling of fear it was unbearable. Imagine if Jesus wasn't here – Gone the friend to lean on, gone the direct link for prayer, gone the person who always listens, gone the shoulder to cry on. I couldn't fathom such a loss. The very idea leaves my mind with a big hole in it, a sinkhole to nothingness. Jesus can never quit. He is here. He is with us forever.

Unfortunately, forever also holds for his death. He will always have died—horribly. We celebrate his death every Sunday in church during Catholic mass or other Christian services, we wear crosses on our ears and around our necks, we paint and portray his death image on cards and art. The manner of his death is forever with us and has tormented me for many years; it remains unbearable to me. I hate how Jesus died.

Once driving past a small museum I had always meant to visit, I parked the car on a whim and rang the bell. The museum, a small storefront next to a flower shop on East Grand Boulevard in Detroit was called The Cloister Museum. An aged and kindly priest who was the caretaker of the museum said I could look around. Various styles of religious paintings were scattered about, hanging on walls, leaning against stairs and walls, and standing on easels, all crammed and cramping the small room even smaller. We talked about art as I looked at the paintings and I told him I used to paint but never this good. He seemed to enjoy my delight as I studied the paintings in their huge ornate frames. He smiled and told me and said, "There are a lot more paintings upstairs."

I climbed the narrow stairs and entered a chamber of horrors. Every single painting, and there must have been hundreds in this huge, upstairs loft, was a depiction of Jesus Christ dying on the cross. The red blare of pain splattered and pulled my senses in every direction, blue eyes, black eyes, tortured eyes hanging in the air, dead agony leaching out of every face, white rigor death on every body, nailed, stabbed, scorned and hanging. Anguish poured into my bones as I walked, weak kneed, around in a circle and cried. I sobbed. Jesus Christ was dying over and over again, all around me. I had to leave, I couldn't stand it and I tried to wipe my eyes on my way down stairs but the old priest knew I'd been crying. He patted me and held my hands for a moment as I walked out the door and asked me to, "Please come again." I never did. Then one day when I drove past, I noticed the museum was boarded up and closed, dirt and decay the only occupant worming itself onto the building. I still feel sad at its passing.

Sadness and tears threaten to overwhelm me as I write this, I still feel like crying. I love Jesus. I can't bear to see him die. I avoid church events leading up to Easter for this reason. I hate that he had to die and one night, many years ago, I told him so.

He showed me how the earth would look if he hadn't died:

Looking down from above, the earth was a black, burnt, dead, cinder revolving slowly against a background of star dots. A testament to mankind run riot without inhibitions; worse than any animal because animals kill from need, mankind kills for pleasure. Without Jesus' life and death as an example we didn't sacrifice or share with each other enough to hold our world together. Without Jesus example, we forgot to love. We had reverted to a dog eat dog existence. Mankind had fouled and killed his own spaceship; the nest God gave us for nourishment and growth.

If death is all we primitive humans can understand, if death is the only fact that can penetrate our psyche, the only horror that can paint two thousand years red, then, "Yes," Jesus had to die.

He died but is not dead.

Dead is not death. It came to me in a flash of intuition one night that I will never die. I will go on forever visiting different worlds in the universe until I've absorbed all the knowledge I want or need. I know this for a certainty. My body will die, many times perhaps, because I may choose to live again in a different form on a different world. Something else that I suddenly realized was the tremendous value of living in a futile, impotent body, forgetting where we came from and remaining ignorant of where we go. How dull it would be if we already knew everything. Life is the thing. It's in the living of life that we experience life and each moment truly is precious. Though, living on the edge all the time like I do can hinder the enjoyment of life. Fear of the unknown, loosing a job, loved one, shelter, or some other treasure keeps us from experiencing the joy of life. Reading my own words makes me want to take stock and pull myself together, to remember the adventure of each moment. "Don't wait for death and life in the universe," I need to tell myself, "Relish life now." I wonder if our great saints, gurus, and holy ones were really space travelers who stopped on earth just long enough to live a life before moving on?

Most people would disagree and say we can't know where we came from or where we will go, but if you believe in evolution then the continuing idea of learning and growth after death would follow naturally. I believe that a soul can never die, that life is the purpose of the universe. Perhaps we are all transient visitors to Earth, putting in our time on the stage until our part is over, then moving on to points unknown. Jesus smiles as I write these words. Death is not death but life.

Neither is God dead. I remember when Jesus first told me, smiling and laughing, that God was coming to earth. It was about fifteen years ago and I envisioned a vast, huge 'something' turning around and coming towards us in space. Just recently, I asked Jesus if God was really on his way to earth. His answer was "Yes."

I asked what it would look like. If I understood Jesus correctly, God's Kingdom is as large as a solar system, and it is traveling through space, or some other medium, and coming towards us. I believe, and hope, God will arrive in my lifetime.

I want to mention something Jesus said to me one night in December while I was watching a PBS program called *From Jesus to Christ.* The program talked about the apostles, that they expected God's Kingdom to arrive soon, and how their writings were affected when God didn't show-up. Out of the blue, Jesus said to me, "He did come."

I felt shocked, "What, God was here?" Do you mean that God's Kingdom came to earth and people didn't know it? Couldn't they see it? Why not? Did God pick you up? Did God pick up the saints? Will that happen again? We have powerful telescopes now, will that help us see God?

Jesus didn't answer my grocery list of questions, perhaps because they were unanswerable. But thinking about it later, I wondered if we'd need a special insight to see God's Kingdom. Is it that only certain people could see God's Kingdom, in the first years of the current era and two thousand years later when it returns?[14] Must we find an extra element in our psyche, one that has gone missing for much of our evolution, a psyche ability that has been asleep; perhaps a psyche we are just now learning to stir up. Don't laugh when you hear of people talking to animals, healing the sick, or sending their thoughts around the world. Their minds are in the forefront, minds gathering new dendrites that speak. Our psyche is trying to wake up from its long sleep. How else could we call God to us? How else can we finally meet the real, breathing, live God?

Jesus said it himself, many times, "He is not God of the dead, but of the Living." Mark 12:27[15]. How many times did Jesus tell us this? How many times do we read the phrase, *living God?* Almost thirty times in the Bible, twenty times in the New Testament alone.[16] It follows that, if we can think of Jesus as a Citizen or Lord of the Universe, can we also think of God as the universe's Master Controller?

---

[14] I wrote this before I visited God's World. Also I hesitate to call God's World, God's Kingdom.

[15] *The New American Bible, The Revised New Testament*, World Catholic Press, 1970

[16] *Revised New Testament* list of Living God, Mat 16:16, 26:63, John 6:69, Acts 14:15, Romans 9:26, 2 Corinthians 3:3, 6:16, 1 Timothy 3:15, 6:17, Hebrews 3:12, 9:14, 10:31 I , 12:22, Rev. 7:2.

I wonder what God would look like as the Master Controller. God suddenly spoke to me the other night with a promise. He said, "I will show you something soon." I believe God intends to show me something to share with you, information to include in this book. Although speculation is useless, I speculate nevertheless about what he will show me. Will it be a vision of God as the Master Controller? Will I see the whole universe spread out before me? Will I be shown the future, the past. I don't know but I promise to describe what God wants to show us in a later chapter.

Names are unnecessary when I travel, but names and labels are necessary to write intelligibly, even most of our thinking revolves around names and symbols, it is the bases for our learning and knowledge. This is why I have always called the beautiful lady, Mary. I didn't know what else to call her, so I gave her the most respectful name I knew at the time. It fits royally because she is elegant, queenly, and Godlike. She has spoken to me off and on through the years verbally and mentally. I call Mary when I am in great distress. Because roses are her symbol, and I love roses, she hands me an arm full of red, white, or yellow roses when we visit and talk. It was Mary who told me how to distinguish Jesus from his nemesis, his imitator. She told me, "Only Jesus can wear a cross." It is a symbol, like a badge of honor or a crown of kingship that only he can wear.

At another time, about fifteen years ago, the beautiful lady spoke to me for a long time, telling me about heaven and its relation to our world. I was in a trance state; with the result that, when I woke up, I couldn't remember most of what she told me except the final statement, "You now have everything you need to know."

"But I can't remember anything you told me," I complained.

"One day you will understand," she replied.

This has been her message through out the many years I've known her, that one day I will understand. Now I constantly learn more and more but I still don't feel as if I know anything. I keep asking when will I comprehend all the information I've been told, when will I understand what Jesus tells me, when will I know who the beautiful lady is, when will I finally understand?

INSIDE TIME

I've learned a few things since I began writing this book in early 1998, consequently, by its near end, some of my original ideas are wrong and some terms overused or obsolete. My frequent references to time is one of these misused terms because time has limited relevance when mind traveling between worlds. Duration, development, evolution, generations, hours, days, and years, are all valid references

When living and traveling on a frozen ball of energy, Einstein's term for earth, but invalid when mind traveling. Then again, it may be important to arrive on a world at a certain time, for instance, during the appropriate developmental stage of its civilization, but it also may not. I don't know. I am new at this. My only clue is that Jesus often compares a current civilization's technological development with our own.

It may be that when traveling between worlds, you are stuck with whatever time you get there in, that you can't just snap your fingers and zip into a new time frame on other worlds. When Jesus took me to Cotton World, I remember that for us to see the sun shinning we needed to revisit the world at another time. It is all very confusing. I've determined that while traveling in space can be very complex and hard to understand, traveling in time can be unfathomable. It seems that although a specific time of arrival to match our present technology may be important when traveling to other worlds, on our own world, no rules are evident. I have mind traveled back through time by my own efforts and with Jesus. Once Jesus took me to his favorite place on earth—old Palestine. Traveling into the future may produce its own kind of problems; I have never tried to travel on my own into the future, though Jesus has taken me into earth's future many times. As you read this chapter you may find both past and future are archaic terms.

Although, time is half my title, I use little of it when traveling, in fact no time at all seems to be involved. My visits are shorter than the time it takes me to express them. Actually, the non-time aspect of traveling may have a profound effect on its happening at all. If it wasn't for time being what it is, or what it is not, traveling could prove to be impossible.

Time is such a perplexing subject I can't dig deeply into its mysteries in this small chapter. More so because we tend to throw time terms around like confetti, terms like in time, out of time, timeless, timely, nick of time, times, old times, etc. As far as our sense of time goes, As Larry Dossey, M. D. Explains in his book, *Space, Time, and Medicine*[17], we experience four different kinds of time. The first is the present, this is our feelings of now; the second is duration, as our sense of time flow; the third is temporal perspective; our self-experience of time; and the last is succession; our counting of time. This seems to be all common sense stuff, but what I find most interesting is the point he makes about time as experienced in past civilizations. He said that past civilizations lived in clyinical time while we modern people live in linear time. Past civilizations took it for granted that everything in time would turn back on itself and repeat the cycle, the heavens turned, seasons returned and crops reseeded themselves, and death was replaced by birth.

We on the other hand, live by clocks. The clock ticks off the moments of our lives, we go from year to year, day-to-day, workweek to work week. We don't think of it as repeating so much as flowing from yesterday into tomorrow, from birth into death. Our lineal view of time is important because it plays on our expectations, early in life we learn to expect time to flow like a

---

[17] Larry Dossey, MD, *Space Time & Medicine*, Boulder Col., 1982, p 23 - 24.

river, so it does. But, according to present day science time not only does not flow like a river, time may not even exist. Time is an anomaly.

There may be no such thing as time. What we call real time may be only a presumed quantity or quality that we acquire by measuring and counting. We count the earth's progress around the sun and call this duration of time a year. It takes time for the earth to go around the sun, we can count the months as the earth moves from January into December; but by counting months, have we described what time really is, what time is made of, at what place it exits the universe? Can we touch time? Oddly, touch may be the only thing we can do with time, touching the time inside ourselves may be time's only real definition. I feel time therefore time is.

If you ask what time is, the answer depends on which kind of time you are asking about: there is sidereal time, solar time, standard time, ephemeris time, perceptional time, and fourth dimensional time. Our own perception of time could be split into longer or shorter moments, according to how time passes for us. Who hasn't experienced the clock at work ticking ever so slowly or the opposite experience of becoming so involved in an activity that we look up and exclaim, "Where has the time went." This psychologically based sense of the elasticity of time seems related to our inner happiness. This kind of time flow is considered an illusion, but then, what kind of time flow is not an illusion?

And, in fact, we can't get out of it. We can't leave time, whatever it is, behind. Time is intertwined into the fabric of our whole life, our psyche, but perhaps not in our souls? Trying to decipher the meaning of time is like trying to study the self even though we can't stand outside our self to take the measurement. Time is so wrapped up in our perception of it that every kind of time may be nothing but inside time.

Wait a minute, you ask, what about decay? What about growth and change? Doesn't a flower change through time, doesn't a tree grow, or a baby? Yes, but these events boil down to cause and effect, and cause and effect has been proven to be non-existent in sub-atomic particles. "At the molecular level there is no distinction between past and future," explains

Nick Herbert.[18] And according to quantum theory, at that level, if you break a cup it doesn't matter if it suddenly falls into pieces because eventually the pieces could conceivably flow back together again. Time can flow backwards on the sub-atomic level as well as forward. There are time arrow directional problems in science but they are too involved for me to go into here.[19] As Paul Davies said of most scientists' view of time, "Time does not pass, and the past, present, and future are merely linguistic connections with no physical content… Dates have relations but they do not *occur*."[20]

He sites the words of Herman Weyl who said, "'The world does not happen, it simply *is*.'" In this picture things do not change: the future does not come into being and the past is not lost, for all of past and future exist with equal status."[21]

That may apply to sub-atomic particles but not to me, you could answer. But what exactly are you? You are made up of sub-atomic particles made up of atoms made up as chemicals made up of tissue and organs made up into gross matter. You and everything around you are made of electrons in a standing wave position around an atomic nucleus. Atoms that are made up of more space and air than anything else, air made out of the same sub-atomic stuff as you are only spread out so thin you can't perceive it. If you were made of not only neutrons and electrons but some photons too, and some of your parts surly are, you would not travel in any time at all because a photon doesn't perceive time. A photon travels at the speed of light, the highest speed attainable in the universe. A photon arrives

---

[18] Nick Herbert, Faster Than Light: Supraliminal Loopholes In Physics, (N.Y. 1988), p. 82.

[19] Asymmetry problems – Psychology arrow, thermodynamically arrow, cosmological arrow, quantum mechanical arrow, and weak interaction arrow. *Faster*, p. 81

[20] Paul Davies, *Other Worlds*, (N. Y., 1980), p. 189.

[21] Davies, p. 189.

as soon as it leaves. The electrons of which you are made, may exist as a quantum wave that fills the whole universe until they are observed or measured; there-fore, until you perceive each or any or all the atoms within your system, you are spread all over the universe. Luckily, you perceive yourself as there. You could also take this to mean that if you choose to perceive yourself at any other far away point in the universe, volla! You are there.

Fred Hoyle, an eminent physicists, and one of the few not afraid to philosophize suggests that time can be described as God shinning a light into a group of pigeonholes. In one of these holes, you exist. When the light enters the hole, you perceive yourself as living in a present time with memories of a past and hope for a future. When the light moves to another pigeonhole, you cease to know your own existence until it shines into your world again.[22] This idea is so beyond most of our common sense that we need to dismiss it as our reality, but it does give us some food for thought. Does this mean that God is shinning his light on me now?

If you've read this far into the book you know I am not exaggerating by much. If we are grateful for this potential gift, a universe united into one, imagine how God could experience time. I wrote a poem about it that I put in the back of the book.

Sense God is all knowing and aware throughout the universe, I wonder if God's time always means the present. Is God's present somewhat like the Hopi Indians whose philosophy only acknowledges time as being in the present by neglecting the past and future? God's past, present, and future must be one continuous present. This must mean that God can reach out into any single present moment of time throughout the cosmos from its beginning to its end. God who pervades the universe with his total substance, observes the universe, and allows us in on his observation. I believe this is the reason for our creation, to share the universe with God, also God allows us to actively interact in the universe, our beings joined to his being.

---

[22] Hoyle, Fred. *October the First Is Too Late*. New York: Harper and Row, 1966.

If all these ideas and speculations are too exotic or iffy for your taste, what about the theory of time that has been around for almost a hundred years — Einstein's theory of Relativity and Special Relativity. According to Einstein time is elastic, time stretches and bends around gravity and time and matter squeeze together if you travel close to the speed of light. These theories have all been experimentally proven true. Also proven true is the fact that time is relative to the observer. If you are on one world and some-one else is on a space ship, you will both perceive and measure time differ-ently, you will both age at different rates relative to each other and, more to the point, you will both be right.

Relativity determines not only the speed of light but also the speed of everything in the universe. If we measure and send a beam of light from Mars, it will take five minutes to reach the earth. Einstein determined light to be a constant in the universe, traveling at 186,000 miles per sec-ond. It takes light 100,000 light years; the time light travels in one year, to travel the diameter of our Milky Way galaxy and only 18.5 miles per sec-ond for earth to orbit the sun. All this time, but it only takes the mind a split second to travel to the other side of the universe or beyond.

If we agree that time is the fourth dimension then the past must still exist, back there. In fact, past and future have always existed but humans only perceive this "block universe" one moment at a time giving a view of a continually changing present.[23]

If even this is too much to take in, stop and take note of your next moment on earth. Think about the present moment you call now. Where did it just go? The next moment has already taken its place, now has moved into the past while the future moment has moved into the present, and the present has just moved into the past, ad infinitum.

Never ending moments of now brings us back, full swing, to the ques-tionable use of time in my title, what kind of time do I travel in? No time

---

[23] Herbert, *Faster Than Light*, p. 191.

at all. It may be the non-existence quality of time that allows me to travel in the first place. Time does not put any roadblocks in my path. So, even if my body remains anchored to earth, my mind or soul remains free to roam. With this in mind, it seems that the only obstacle to movement in time is our own limited perceptions. If the first half of my title is non-existing, what about the other half, space? You guessed it, space doesn't exist either.

EVERYWHERE SPACE

Since the introduction of quantum mechanics early in this century, we have been living in a world full of quantum weirdness. Quantum weirdness is matter at the atomic level. As the famous physicists, John Wheeler, stated "Nothing is more important about quantum physics than this: it has destroyed the concept of the world as "sitting out there." The universe will never afterwards be the same."[24]

What isn't the same? Bowling balls still hit pins, billiard balls move to the pockets, we sit on chairs that don't let us fall to the floor. These everyday experiences are logical results of Newton's laws of motion. Cause and effect, action and reaction that still work according to our common sense. But with the advent of quantum physics, sub atomic particles, the matter that underlies everything in the universe as well as ourselves, is not only no longer the same, it is no longer there. Matter has disappeared until or unless we choose to notice it.

Sense Quantum physics is so vast a subject; I will only repeat for you a few of its main ideas or theorems.[25] One of the more unusual facts is that electrons, and photons, in other words, all the matter we see, feel and hear, can act as both a wave and a particle. What does that mean?

We all know what a wave looks like on a still pond when we throw a rock in to the water. If we throw two rocks in we get waves that interfere with each other, little mixed up ripples. It is probably no surprise that when a beam of light is shined through two slits in a screen, the beam will show an interference pattern on the wall. But when scientists narrowed the beam down to one atomic particle or photon of light at a time, the

---

[24] Fred Allen Wolf, *Taking the Quantum Leap*, (N. Y. , 1981), p. 152.

[25] Please refer to the extensive Bibliography in back of the book for further reading.

series of particles still flowed through the two slits making an interference pattern. The question was, "How could a series of single particles know where to go to collect into the same interference pattern?" The answer was that the atomic particle or photon of light was a wave until we observed it, then, because of our observation, the wave collapsed. The same wave has now become a particle.

Another mainstay of the quantum theory is what Hiensberg called the Uncertainty Principal. This means that a scientist can never measure the whereabouts of a particle with total accuracy. The exact place of a particle can be measured or its motion but never both. Any one of us can predict which pocket a billiard ball will, or should, roll towards if we hit it just right, even though I haven't played pool for thirty years, I found out last summer that I can still predict which pocket the ball will fall into. Not so with an atomic particle, it can go any which way after you pinpoint its position. Or if you know the direction of a particle, you can't know exactly its position, only how fast it is going.

What this means is, as stated in the book, *The Ghost in the Atom*, [26] If we put a single quantum particle in a closed box, its wave would be spread all through the box. Now if we lower a screen in the middle of the box we would expect the particle to be in one half or the other. That is not the case. The particle is in both half at the same time, it only reverts to one half after we choose which side to look for it in.

So what, you might ask, this weirdness only applies on the atomic level, doesn't it? But then, in walks Shrodinger's cat, as the tongue-in-cheek theory is called. Shrodinger's theory pulls quantum effects up to our level of observation by asking what would happen if we put a cat in a box with a Geiger counter and a very small pile of uranium that will last about an hour. The counter has a relay button that will release an acid to kill the cat when it goes off, if it goes off within the hour the cat will die if not the cat

---

[26] Davies, P.C. W., and Brown, *The Ghost in the Atom*, (N. Y. , 1998), p. 21.

lives. At the end of the hour we realize the cat must be ether dead or alive. But in the rules of quantum physics, the cat is in a superposition of two states. The cat is alive and dead. It is our choice as we open the box whether the cat has lived through the hour or died. (All this supposes you have a very quiet cat). The theory states that we the observers, make the choice for the cat's life or death because we choose whether the particle has or has not burst into a ray of energy releasing the poison and killing or not-killing the cat.

Another proven aspect of quantum theory is non-locality. Since Bell's theorem and Aspect's experiment (I won't go into either here) physicists know that a particle has non-locality. This means that once two particles are correlated, and mere observation can correlate the particles, there is an instant copying of one particle by another without time for a message or signal to travel between the two particles. This holds true no matter how far away one particle is from the other. It would be like having cards picked from a random deck in New York being identical to cards picked from a random deck in Tokyo."[27]

David Bohm has a different interpretation; he compares it like, "a fish being seen as two distinct pictures in two individual television sets. Whatever one fish does, the other does as well. If the fish images are assumed to be the primary reality, this seems strange, but in terms of the 'real' fish, it is all very simple."[28] According to Bohm, "This means that the universe is interconnected in some deep and dimly perceived way, on a level where time and space don't count."[29]

The official view of quantum mechanics called the Copenhagen interpretation after Nels Bohr is the one most physicists agree with. It is the one that states nothing is there until we observe it. There is also the many

---

[27] Amit Goswami, Ph. D., *The Self-Aware Universe: how consciousness creates the material world*, (N. Y., 1995), p. 120.

[28] Timothy Ferris, *The Whole Shebang*, (N.Y., 1981), p. 285.

[29] Ferris, *The Whole Shebang*, p. 285.

universes theory of Hugh Everett where every time you make a decision you jump into a new universe. Another view is that of David Bohm and Basil Hailey with followers like Wheeler that could be called the Quantum Potential Theory. Bohm's theory says that the universe is really there but it is part of a holistic system that covers the whole universe.[30]

The focus of this book is the unity of the universe and mind travel within it, consequently, I agree with Bohm's theory more than the others because it describes the universe as one, unified, undivided whole. The same description mystics have given the universe throughout history. Jesus agrees with Bohm's theory, as well. Note – in an earlier chapter I stated that Jesus said the universe is not a hologram, it was my mistake to think David Bohm ever said that it was, Bohm said that the universe was *like* a hologram.

Bohm's theory of reality is that "the simple patterns we see come from a deeper enfolded order. Reality unfolds to produce the visible order and folds back in. Reality is constantly unfolding and enfolding at such a fast rate it appears to be steady.[31] I picture Bohm's reality like a spinning fan, when the blades are still, it is enfolded, when the blades are spinning, it is unfolded. Bohm further states that, "thoughts, feelings, and mind work in a similar way." He uses the word implicit to mean a thought can be enfolded into another thought. "Both mind and matter fold and unfold so they are similar in basic structure. This helps us understand they are related. "

He comes to this conclusion by the wave/particle duality of quantum physics. Similar to the mathematics of a hologram. He says a hologram is the *best example* [underline mine] of where we see a pattern enfolded and unfolded into a visual image. "The whole is unfolded from each part" He uses a seed as another example of enfolded order. The seed has information to make a tree. A tree uses air, soil, and nutrients to grow into the tree. The tree can make more trees. Now you can't say definitely the tree

---

[30] *Ghost in the Atom,* p. 123 -134
[31] *Ghost in the Atom,* p. 123 -134

was in the seed. The tree needed the whole environment. The forest grows from this seed, the forest evolves and changes, enfolding and unfolding. He adds, "I want to say that life, mind, and inanimate matter all have a similar structure."[32] He explains that matter in general is like "active information." "If you yell, 'fire,' every one moves. Interestingly, he also says that this quantum potential doesn't lessen with distance. This is similar to what I have experienced.

Bohm states that his implicate and implicate order are only the tip of the iceberg. And that we stand where Galileo once stood, at the brink of a new order. "In his view, quantum weirdness is a keyhole through which we have caught a first glimpse of another side of nature, one in which the universe is neither deployed across vast reaches of space and time nor harbors many things. Rather it is one, interwoven thing, which incorporates space and time but in some sense subordinates them..."[33]

Bohm's view is not the favorite among scientists but many keep going to his corner but some scientists think of Bohm's view of non-locality as made up of cold hidden variables which tends to make consciousness non-creative. But Jesus commented to me that Bohm's view of the beyond is just the opposite - he implied that it is full of life. This beyond is the universe where I travel so I understand first hand what Jesus means by agreeing with any view that fills the universe with life.

But does the universe still need an observer to exist if it is enfolded. Perhaps, because both mind and matter are enfolded, the observer can still collapse the quantum wave. I just had the sudden realization that our minds are *non-local*. This means that our minds can send instantaneous signals or travel the universe in no time at all, which agrees with the last chapter on time and, not surprisingly, what this book is all about. Non-locality also explains bi-location, this is where a person is reported to be in

---

32 *Ghost in the Atom*, p. 123 -134.
33 *The Whole Shebang*, p. 283.

two places at once - some great Sufis and saints have displayed this ability. Teleportation could also be explained by non-location, perhaps our mind is the driver, the body just a follower. Non-locality's greatest importance is that it clarifies for us how Jesus can be with me and you and everyone else at the same time. His mind is non-local as is ours, but he knows how to use his.

Soul Talk

Kneeling during mass one Sunday not paying attention to the priest, who could on a day like this when suddenly long sunbeams enter through the window, transforming the near-empty church into a cathedral, the colored stained glass into a prism, the dark wooden pews into gold, and the clear chilly air into a honey yellow mist; so, instead, I knelt telling Jesus how beautiful the sunshine was. Jesus agreed smiling but then looked at me sadly and stated his often recurring request, yet again:

"Show them the way."

There in the heaven filled cathedral, I felt as if a cloud had suddenly darkened the sunshine. Perplexed and dismayed I said to Jesus, "But I don't know what you mean. Do you mean that you want everyone to talk to you?"

"Yes," he said.

"You want more people to become mystics, everyone"

"Yes," Jesus said with strong emotion, "Yes, yes, yes."

His 'Yes' still reverberates inside me because I am not sure how to erase the urgency, the swirling pit of in-completion I feel; what key will open the door and let this unfulfilled emptiness out. What can I do? All that I know to do is write this book, this request, this call to arms – talk to Jesus. Those who already do, talk more, those who do not, start talking today. All of you—become mystics.

What is a mystic? A mystic is someone who talks to God or Jesus. A mystic, you, does not need to be in an ecstatic state, or in total union with the one, or to have an out-of-body experience, or even to be meditating; no, the only requirement to being a mystic is that you talk as sincerely as you know how with heaven. Communicate with Jesus, the rest will follow.

Jesus[34] will lead you step by step up the ladder of mystic wisdom and learning. All you need to do is talk, not in prayer, but honestly and with emotion about what you think about our world, what your worries are regarding your children, what your neighbor's need, what your country needs, what beauty and love you see around you. What you hope and dream and think about. Please understand that I am not against prayer, I am just saying that you need to take the time to share yourself with God, in your own words and with your whole mind and soul. Talk to Jesus as if he were your best friend, he will become one. Question your best friend, he will answer.

Probably, answers won't enter your consciousness immediately, only hints, then your psyche may stretch into a broad smile as you both laugh at your own silly questions, and finally you may see Jesus standing next to you, 'his continence shining.' Leave it to Jesus to lift you, step by step, up the ladder to heaven. All you need to do is begin. Listen to what Donald Spoto says in his book *The Hidden Jesus,* "Jesus comes not to offer a new code of conduct, but to announce the accessibility of God for humanity. Utterly free in his own response to God, he came to set the world free from a slavery to its own limitations. We are still sitting on our limitations."[35]

This book is only a record of my experiences traveling and talking to Jesus, therefore, it leaves out the negative aspects of being a visionary or mystic. For one thing, mysticism is almost a dirty word in most social circles. If you talk of mysticism, or even of being spiritual, you are automatically assigned to the loony-bin side of society. Most segments of our society think this way; even modern religious painting isn't considered serious art. Supposedly, education relieves a person of the need to be spiritual or 'weak thinking.' This is nothing more than a rebound reaction to

---

[34] Or Buddha, Mary, Saints, Allah, God, in short, anyone from heaven, if you prefer.

[35] Donald Spoto, *The Hidden Jesus,* (St. Martin's Press, New York, 1998).

the national, dogmatic church of the past—five hundred years in the past—the debate between superstition verses rational thinking. Early scientific thinkers had to believe in themselves rather than the church, they had to push their theories outward, they were the underdog. No longer, now science is our church and our refuge from discovery, its ideas often ring dogmatic in the popular mind giving us experts in medicine, psychiatry, engineering, and other disciplines. We delegate only a specific, short time and place for God; whether in a Church, Synagogue, or Mosque; but God would have us close to him at all times.

Another negative image we have of mystics and mysticism is that they are always walking around with their head in the clouds. I consider myself a mystic but I can go days or weeks without mediating and don't feel mystical at all. Although it is important for me to touch base with Jesus every day, the knowledge that he is always present doesn't overwhelm my daily activities; it enhances them. I go about my daily life as if nothing unusual has happened, and it hasn't. I consider talking to Jesus, knowing Jesus, loving Jesus ordinary and normal. Jesus should not be an exception but the rule. Although, I admit that there are times I'm not in a hurry to talk to Jesus. Like last night when I just wanted to be within my own thoughts while thinking something out for myself. It was only later that I sat back and asked for Jesus' opinion. So please understand, even though Jesus is always with me, he isn't always in my awareness, though I hope I am in his.Being a mystic has been likened to climbing a high mountain. It doesn't mean you are always on the peak, you needed to climb some rough terrain to get there, but after the long struggle to arrive, you stand at the top and yell "Eureka!" what then? Then it is time to climb back down. In other words, if you find ecstasy, you can't revel in it all the time. If you find great wisdom, an outlet must be found in which to share it. If you find yourself standing alone at the epic of the world, and like it too much to come down, pull others up to the top with you. If or when you walk back down the mountain, you can't miss the road signs, the signs that point you further along your zigzag path. The gift you carried down may be invisible to most people, but give it away, anyway. Here is a small Sufi story that I can't remember where I read it but one that I've never forgot: the mullah was making his followers work all day in the hot sun for hungry and needy people. Except one fellow who just stayed in his tent and prayed. Finally one of his followers came up to the Mullah and said, How come we need to work every day while that man just gets to sit in his tent and pray. Why doesn't he help the needy? Why can't I sit and pray every day like he does? The Mullah answered, "Are your prayers effective?"

Now that I have a more mature, humane understanding of the world, I feel that I can serve it better, that my integrity and knowledge of who I am will stay with me no matter what I bump into. Now that I see beyond my own needs, I can see what must be, what must become, what must happen for the cycle to continue, for evolution to follow its course. One thing more - once a mystic always a mystic. As a mystic, you will forever see the world as changed, interrelated, and undivided. Once you have climbed the mountain, you can never un-climb it, you will be forever changed.

Do you read the news and identify with the person in their tragic moment. I do more and more. I fit the other person's tragedy or joy onto myself, wrap it around and compare it on for size. An odd photograph of an aged old person's face can send me sliding into other times and places with them, back into the German horror camps or 30's dust bowl or the Great Depression. One Nubian or Arab or Scottish or Ethiopian face in a photo can grab and hold me in rapture for long moments while I mind-walk into their lives. The soul-some eyes, deep riveting lines of angles and wrinkles, sculpting the nose and mouth into a testament of life. So perfect, so telling, and so timely, though perhaps that is only my artistic sense of beauty. Growing more empathetic towards all humanity seems to be one of the steps we climb towards oneness. It is part of our constant push forward towards God. Who knows where it will end, what we can become when even the sky is not a limit. The whole universe is there for us to explore, all life ours to become, all sorrows and all joys.

Enough, I get carried away sometimes.

Back to mysticism. I think I became a mystic because I didn't know how to pray. Since I didn't know any prayers, I told Jesus of my dreams instead, I speculated and bombarded him with questions about earth, heaven, and God. Eventually, I began to realize that Jesus did help the people I told him about but not in ways I expected. Usually, the person would tell me they felt better, their depression was over, or they had turned their worries over to Jesus. Now I've learned to always pray for what God thinks is best for the person, not what I think is best. For myself, I felt prayer would be shameful if used selfishly; when I did pray for something I wanted, Jesus replied that God knew what I needed. So I had to learn to leave my needs to God, a hard lesson, still unreachable and still unlearned.

Just recently, Jesus told me "All will be restored." I think he means that everything that I lost or that was taken away during my period of learning or testing, twenty or thirty years worth (?), will be restored. I joke that I never had much anyway but I am pleased at Jesus' words. And I wonder if that makes me the modern equivalent of Job? Jesus has also promised me that, "nothing will breakdown until you don't need it any longer." I joke with Jesus about this too because it means I'll either be dead, rich or married; and, "Do I get to choose?"

One odd problem relating to mysticism that bothers me greatly is that I need to come down from the clouds to write. It's as if I am too close to the light to see and consequently for a short time afterwards I stay blinded by the sun. As I get further into the book, the problem isn't as limiting as it used to be. Perhaps because it has become habitual, after a visit with Jesus to sit down and write a few notes to help jog my memory later; though, I still find it hard to find the right words to express what I've seen. Plus, the need to put into words what I just experienced takes something away from the vividness of it. Just try to write about the rose you just smelled or the flavor of butterscotch ice cream and you'll know what I mean. Needing to write in words about my travels with Jesus separates me from the emotional impact, the intensity, the vital scenery, and visual stimulation. Often, after leaving a new place, my senses are saturated with color and feeling that I can't adequately describe.

This inadequacy also affects my ability to describe my relationship with Jesus in correct terms, Jesus does not treat me like a child, though this may be hard to detect from my writings. Perhaps because I am attempting to share feelings and sights that are unexplainable and un-reportable. How can I write in clearly understandable words my feelings for Jesus that are almost sexual in their intensity? Most often, though, our relationship is friend to friend, even if one friend has a much greater wisdom to impart to the other. As a friend, I've often played and joked with Jesus. Once I suggested that he was made out of neutrinos. And he joked back that perhaps it was really anti-neutrinos. We both smiled at this. Yes, let me restate this concept – Jesus can laugh as well as cry.

I have always supposed the instruction of Jesus, "Be as little children," should be taken literally. To me it has always been a mandate to become more childlike, to use my imagination and to try and love as simply as a child. Mother love comes close to this ideal. The idea that as Christ's mother she also loves us unconditionally has always pulled many of us towards Mary. As a catholic, it may be natural that I join in attributing to Mary the same deep respect and reverence that most popular Catholics do. Their love has held for so long and is felt so deeply that the official Church has been unable to sweep her many appearances, called Marion Visitations, under a rug. The official church doesn't like things they can't explain. Mary can't be easily explained but I believe her visitations are an attempt, to warn us of coming danger, to gather us under her wing, to reach out to us. Mary is one of the overseers of earth; she stands guard for us. Her love pours down to us in the form of her visitations. Would we dare not listen?

Mary showed me something that I was told not to write about in this book. Of course I won't write what I saw but I could try to send it to you in a vision. I think she meant that the knowledge of what she showed me wasn't for everyone. Don't worry; it isn't a message for now, but a vision far into the future. Mary showed me with deep love and concern; I may try to show a few of you as well.

The universe is driven by love, but because we can't always feel it, we think heaven's affection doesn't reach down to out little ball of earth. It does but we just can't see it. I suspect that it works like this: you make a choice, perhaps to go to college. God loves you so dearly that he makes your choice valid. It is God who collapses the quantum wave; it is God who makes your choices real. His love would also work if you chose to pick up a gun and kill someone. God knows you choose this action for the good of your soul. Perhaps your soul needs to learn and feel what hell is like behind bars or what death means to the other family and yours or some other learning event. This in no way means that suffering should be encouraged, quite the opposite. To suffer should only apply to what we need, asked for, or want. We need to learn to share love, not revenge, hope, not despair, but some people are still slow to understand, slow in growing towards God, so slow that they may need horrible experiences in order to begin that long reach upwards. There are probably people, though they never speak of God, who are nevertheless spiritual in the way they live their life, they revere God's principals if not his name. And some people may not learn in this life, but need to wait until the next one, if they are so lucky

Moral maturity is probably the first necessary quality of character to becoming a mystic. At times, it becomes vitally important to know what principals you hold as right or wrong; otherwise, how could you hope to distinguish a truth from a lie. Both will pour into your psyche, pulling at your soul. The devil and an angel standing on your shoulder whispering into one ear then another is not just cartoon characters. Temptation is a real phenomenon. I've always been afraid of being led down the primrose path with a joke at the end, and I have started down this path a number of times. Mystics tread the edge of sanity as well as good and evil, and I've wavered back and forth across this edge a few times, but Jesus always pulled me back. Years ago, I figured out my most helpful moral; though I can't always live up to it: There is only one sin, and that is to deliberately hurt another life. Of course, this is the same thing Jesus told us two thousand years ago, "Love one another as I have loved you." We can't always practice this love; so, I reasoned that if you can't love everyone, at least, don't hurt anyone. It sounds easy but even this simple moral can be hard to follow.

Though the idea of 'love your neighbor' is not easy, it is up to us to keep trying. Many of our social ills could be solved by asking, "Where is the love? Who needs love? In which direction lays the empathy? How are you hurting? What will fix the heart pain?" This, of course, assumes a more mature social population then we have at present. But our ability to love will change as we continue to grow because we're going to grow up faster than we know, the people of the near future will be more spiritual by necessity. This I was told and believe but I don't want to study the information any further, I don't want to know too much because some things are better left unknown, some visions are better not visualized.

Part of being a mystic is visualization. Visions can come at odd times and may seem weird or just your imagination. It may be hard to tell which is which, but if the vision persists, it is probably true no matter how unfounded in reality it seems. This is hard for most of us to accept because we have been taught since infancy not to believe in visions, in far away vistas or scenes we see with our mind's eye. Once you begin looking inside for information, you will be amazed at your newfound perceptions of truth and knowledge. For example, I keep seeing a short and plump man and women calling me. They are the two hosts I met on Cotton World. They want to tell me something but I was too busy cleaning house to sit down and meditate or pay attention. Suddenly it didn't matter if I had time to sit down or not. Their message came through regardless, they said, "We have agreed." I don't know what they meant but I know Jesus is involved in their decision. Perhaps they will give us another gift. They gave earth a gift three thousand years ago. The Manna that the Israelites ate in the desert was what I called cotton. I didn't include this when I was writing about their world, although Jesus suggested it. I thought it was too unbelievable. I thought people might get upset. Now I realize that everything I write in this book is going to upset someone. So I might as well tell all. I do hope their new gift, if gift it is, will last in our memory as long and enduring as their last one. Jesus has not yet explained what it is all about.

Jesus knows and wisely says little. Sometimes the results of his knowing can be funny. For instance, often Jesus knows what I am going to write before I write it. The other night, he told me that I wasn't done writing yet although I knew that I was. It was later that night when the new memories popped into my mind and I had to go back downstairs, find my notebook, and then jot the new memories down, two pages worth. Jesus also knows that this book will be printed but he doesn't tell me when or how or even if it will be printed post-humorously.

When Jesus speaks, I don't question his words. I recognize that his knowledge is far superior to my own, so much so, that my questions to him are probably childish. Nevertheless, I wonder, how does he know so much? Is it because he has lived so long, for two thousand years or has he been alive since the beginning of the universe? If so, has he kept up with our growth in knowledge and science or is he always complete in total knowledge? Jesus has stated to me, "I am not invincible." Does this mean that he doesn't know everything or he can't do some things, (makes sense or evil would be eradicated?) Imagine Jesus having our modern equivalent of knowledge two thousand years ago and then agreeing to die for us. The thought tares at my soul. What if one of us agreed to step down to become a chimpanzee for a span of life. Imagine us as trans-chimp being told by a human, through sign language, who and where we came from and that we would revert back into being a human after death. (This would make a nice science fiction story and probably already has) My imagination runs wild and all I can think of is that chimps are dirty. I've strayed from the subject again; this idea is hardly mystical or is it?

If we could contemplate all the knowledge there ever was, would this knowledge equal God or the totality of all spirituality? Is quantum physics the first step towards a scientific understanding of religion, God, spirituality? Perhaps all knowledge is nothing but a mental construct in our mind and the mind of God. The whole point of my book is that imagination is a valid means of traveling the universe. Imagination touches and enwraps God. It leads us to a mystical union with God. We are all active participants in the idea stuff of the universe; do we also help create the universe? Do we share in God's creativity? Does the universe form itself to our imagery of it? Is the universe a growing, alive, aware, matrix of all that is, was, and will be? Yes to all. I have learned through my talks with Jesus and our travels that the universe is not the cold, dark, unthinking place that our instruments measure and that it also has many layers (dimensions?) that we are not aware of.

I call this multi-universe God. God who is personal as well as universal. God who can be a substantial, separate entity apart from us who, at the same time, can be an ethereal substance within our minds, all this while holding and keeping the quality of the whole cosmos together. It is more than I can imagine. Besides, I dare not get into a philosophical discussion of God because I would loose every time. I only have my own best reasoning and what I have learned from my visits. Visits that I hope I've encouraged other people to try. That is the purpose of this book.

When you get a thorn in your shoe, stop and take it out. When you get a thorn in your heart or mind, it is time to move to action and remove it. After I graduated from college, a few years ago, I began feeling lonely and set apart from people. In the past, although I was alone a great deal of the time, I didn't feel lonely. That changed and keeps getting worse as I finish my book. Jesus has not relieved me of these fits of loneliness; he has allowed these aches and pains, this thorn, to fester until I do something about them. Pull the thorn out. Now that the book is almost finished, it is time that I get out and practice what I preach. It is time to get more deeply involved in something. Am I waiting for the right moment? It is no longer enough for me to stay home and befriend children in the neighborhood. I think its time to broaden my horizons, to reach out more. I don't know.

The reason I write this is so that you can see my reasoning and how Jesus encourages us to change. He gets his message across with subtle hints or, if need be, a hammer blow to the psyche.

It is your soul that needs these hard, life changes as events to learn from; it is your soul that delights with you and keeps you going even into disaster. Your soul has lived many lives and will live many more - so enjoy. This life is just a platform from which to grow like a flower nourished by soil. The Eastern religions are right, our soul gropes towards bliss, towards the Nirvana. But then what, what does a soul do after it attains bliss? Why, it goes back down the other side of the mountain and re-enters life. We in our topsy-turvy life styles can hardly imagine everlasting bliss and perhaps wouldn't want it. How dull. There may be a few Buddha's who think bliss boring too, so they step back into life again and again, as prophets.

But for us who have not achieved bliss states, we climb down from the mountain and walk back into life, back into a sea of struggling souls crying out for empathy. Empathy we may now give more fully. I no longer feel tormented and abused by the evil one. I am now sheltered from harm by a mental shell of knowing. Jesus has repeated this to me over and over lately, I cannot be harmed any more, though I still worry, I still feel pain, I still cry out for help. He has also told me that my children will be protected from severe evil. He means all my children, my birth children, grandchildren and my neighbor children, the many different children who have been visiting me for the last fifteen or twenty years even my former foster children. This doesn't mean that they won't get into trouble at times, but, on the whole, they will grow up all right, that my influence on them will bare fruit, and that because I loved them, Jesus' love will shine from them too.

Those of you who seek union, who want to be mystics, remember this, Jesus is always present even in suffering, especially in suffering. I remember that each time I was threatened, sneered at, mocked, or ignored, Jesus watched out of my eyes as the person behaved badly towards me. Jesus felt my anguish, my pain, my naiveté, my horror. Fate will give to each person what they have given. Is this what God meant when he said, "There will be justice?" I believe so. I too have sowed what I reaped. We all do, if not in this life, then in the next. For now my conscious is clear, my many sins and faults have been burnt away through time and suffering; consequently, in my next life I will be exploring the universe with Jesus who promised to put a golden flower in my hair.

DISASTER WORLDS

These next worlds are places I didn't want to visit, worlds I was afraid to see because of the conceivable horror involved. Reluctantly, I became Jesus' companion as, night after night, we visited these disastrous worlds. You needn't be afraid to read further, none of these worlds were as vividly horrible as my imagination could make them, no fire and brimstone, torture, or death and dying, just world wide problems that we can hope never occur on earth.

Gray World

We stood suddenly, on a high ledge overlooking a large, built-up city with towering high-rise buildings as tall as the sky. Everything was gray, not a dull gray, but a polished, gleaming gray, giant steel gray cylinders, some square squat blocks of burnished silver/gray, intersected with broad gray avenues and cross streets. The sky overcast the cityscape in slivers of gray and silver, not unlike a sunless, drizzly day on earth. I noticed a few tall white buildings that stood out like clouds amid the gray but overall everything was washed in silver light under a steel gray sky, clean gray, nothing was dark or dirty. The scratchy clean roadway between buildings was interspersed by small square courtyards planted in light green trees. I noticed only a few specks of color scattered throughout the city, small signs or flags.

As we stood watching, I asked if we would visit their countryside too, like we did on Tree World. Jesus' answer startled me. He told me that there was no countryside left on this world, that most of the land was developed. He explained that the only undeveloped country left was areas of extreme hot and cold, high mountains, and deep oceans.

I found this hard to imagine as I watched the few scattered figures below scamper to and from, out one building into another. Then what was few in number grew into a large crowd moving in long narrow lines that defined the geometry of the city, like a colony of soldier ants marching to a pheromone call. All the people walked, I didn't see any cars or carts or buses only people, people moving down streamlined avenues from one end of the city to another.

"Do their faces look human?" I asked Jesus.

"We can go down if you want to see them close, " He answered.

"But won't our presence bother them?"

"No," he explained, "We can stand in front of them to block their path but they will not see us. They refuse to see.

This happened just as Jesus said it would. We went down and stood in the middle of the swarm of walking, running bodies, but as our unmoving bodies blocked their progress, they turned and moved around us defining a new path down the avenue. Something there had to be avoided at all cost, something invisible, something unmentionable, a taboo of some sort. We stepped on to the next avenue, no confusion, just a turning away from our bodies as if we were a hole in space. Not one person stopped or looked at whatever was blocking their shortest route from point a to point b. No one bumped into us or their neighbor. We were nothing but a chuckhole in the road.

"They really can't see us!" I yelled above the humming buzz of the city.

"No, Jesus said, " And that defines their disaster. They are blind they refuse to see.

These people refuse to recognize or acknowledge any form of spiritual belief, any idea not reducible to fact, he told me. Any unproven philosophical idea is regarded as belonging to the outer fringes of society; they abhor speculation that doesn't lead to concrete results.

"It has been like this for a long time," he added explaining that they stubbornly refuse to acknowledge anything contrary to their usual belief system. They are unwilling to change or bend, he explained; also saying that the problem was not a local one but worldwide.

I was beginning to understand. Their problem wasn't that they lived on an over-crowded and mechanical world so much as it was their blindness, their refusal to see. They would hold to their blindness even up against some of our earth's most cherished spiritual concepts.

"Is heaven trying to help? I asked

"We set up anomalies in a few odd places around their world." Even though he had implied earlier that it was too late for this world to change or reinvent itself, it was hoped that some people would stop and puzzle about the anomalies set in their path. The whole point would be to cause enough perplexity to jar them awake and out of their self-made compliance, their blindness.

I still understand. "But why are they doomed? Where is their disaster?

"Their disaster," Jesus answered, "is after death, no one is leaving the world after death. They keep coming back to relive what they refused to learn the last time. He told me it was like an infection feeding on itself, the more they kept intensifying their non-beliefs, the more they kept living, dying, and multiplying within the same precepts of factual beliefs. Beliefs that kept proscribing religion or any form of spiritual revival. Because of this stubbornness, a person had no other resource but true death – like a caterpillar that could never become a butterfly. A caterpillar rotted inside its cocoon.

"We are done with this world. Jesus said to me. And we left.

I suspect that each world will have a specific message for us. We on earth seem more able to see new ideas and spiritual possibilities; at least, we are not as blind as these people.

Jesus said it was too late for most people on that world. These people are not represented in the universe even though they are an old race. When the real disaster strikes, they will be unprepared for it, they won't be ready.

Cracked World

Through a gloomy, cloud filled sky; I saw a deep dark crevasse of a jagged land, dirty with rocks. The deep gorge cut off one huge, bare area from another, bare except for sparse tuffs of grass and low bent trees growing around the scattered rocks. Bare rocks and sparse vegetation was the norm on this world Jesus explained to me. Beyond the crevasse, where we stood, I could see small round hovels; no other word defines this scattered group of homes, hovels centered on destitution and sacristy. A fine, misty drizzle of rain continued to fall while we were there, giving everything a bleak and blurry look.

"It always rains and storms here, " Jesus told me and explained that the people celebrated with joy any time the clouds let the sun shine through for whole day.

I wondered why didn't we visit a city first, like when we visited the most other worlds. Jesus told me that there were no longer any cities on this world, only substance living conditions and unremitting hunger. They gather together in small groups to share scavenged food and bedding. There is not much left of either. "This has been their way of life for a long time,' he added, "a life without hope.

These people are the last remnants of what was once a large and thriving civilized world, a world that can no longer support more than a few scattered groups. All of the remaining people must inhabit a narrow band in the temperate regions of the planet. There is no longer a livable tropical region.

"Will they see us if we go over for a visit?" I asked.

"They are a very spiritual people. Their circumstances have driven them toward deep spiritual beliefs. So to answer your question, yes, they would see us if we made a visit but it would have a negative impact on them. A visit from us tourists could only remind them of all they had and lost."

"Can you help them?"

"The people, yes, their world, no,"

He told me that their only exit is death that they know this and they also know how deeply they are loved and welcomed when they leave this world.

"Their world is so horribly gloomily and sad." I said.

"Once their world was like Earth, with green grass, blue skies and fluffy clouds. It was very populated, a fountain of life. Now there is very little fauna left or animals."

"What happened?"

In answer, I received a flash of insight that showed me the sudden disruption of energy balance between their star and world. They kept building on; heedless of the choking black smoke they released every day in combustion. Industry run riot. They didn't listen to warnings from the scientists or heaven. All the evidence pointed to disaster but they turned away from making a collective decision to correct the problem until after it was too late. Once the balance begins to drastically change on a world, it is hard to bring it back into equilibrium. Finally stress from the lessening of resources flipped the scale over into the dead zone. Now their world is dark and gloomy forever. They are not much alive, only going through the motions of life because life is tenacious and holds on to whatever it can cling to. Guilt wears them down as much as need.

If it weren't for spiritual release, their lives would be completely hopeless. But we are there among them, trying to keep their spirits directed towards heaven. "We have not abandoned them," Jesus told me.

I felt sad for these people as we left yet somewhat relieved that there's wasn't a hellfire world.

Black World

One place kept popping into my mind just before we left for any disaster world. It was a place I wanted to avoid, one fleeting glance was enough. I was instinctively frightened of the brief scene that flashed in and out of my consciousness. I don't know how I knew it before I ever got there but finally Jesus said we had to go there for a visit. No, I didn't want to go but I did, or write about it, but I will. I shudder still when I remember it for a moment. But I must describe it for you or how will you see?

The picture that kept flashing to me was a crusty and cracked ground swelled with red flowing cinder intermixed with shinny black rocks. The scene in front of me where Jesus and I stood was the same only worse. The air was clear and cold except when the wind gusted, blowing black dust particles around in small rivulets and dust devils then the air became dirty and the ground seared bare. Large black flakes of burnt, charred something swept up and twirl a little dust eddies at my feet—I couldn't stand it.

In some places the black, shinny, ground lay bare, stark, and naked, in others coal black and soft, intermixed with ebony rocks. Far off in the distance, twists of metal and thrown beams like black sticks in the ground. I think the layers of crispy flakes would have been as hard as rock beneath my fingers if I had touched it, but I didn't. I couldn't wait to get away. It was a dead burnt world; a world that I assumed had once been filled with life.

"What happened," I asked Jesus.

"A solar flare," he answered.

I shuddered and cringed within myself.

"Don't worry," he added, "Everyone left in time."

"They got off"! They didn't… I couldn't say the word burn just then.

"No," Jesus smiled "All the people got off."

I felt wondrously relieved that they had escaped.

"They had to leave because they were aware that their sun was unstable. They had to learn how to get off as soon as possible."

"They all left!" "Every single one of them!" "But how did they get off?" I asked him. "Did they leave in a space ship, or some other way? Then I realized that they probably didn't have time to invent and build enough spaceships for a complete populated world. They needed a quicker solution; they must have used their minds.

"Yes," Jesus told me, "They sat down and sent their mind out into space. They left by the same method we use to visit other worlds – their souls took flight.

There are other ways to travel, aren't there? To travel like we do requires the ability to direct your mind, to concentrate, to believe, to know. What about the children? Suddenly I realized how inept children were at concentration. I felt a growing horror at what Jesus' answer might be.

"They stopped having children a few generations before they needed to leave."

I thought the togetherness of their society was almost unbelievable. They really had it together didn't they? Imagine a whole society collectively making a decision of that magnitude, and then carrying it out. They were an old, mature race of people weren't they?

Jesus nodded in agreement.

I felt relieved that they had gotten off this round hell of a world but then I had the sudden realization that none of the animal life could go with them. "They couldn't take anything, Could they? I said. "They had to leave it all," I whispered, as my mind conjured up Fluffy and Lassie and Benje and Smokey and trees and roses and lilacs and daises and Dune, and Moby Dick, and The Bible and the Mona Lisa and …butterflies …and oh, so horrible to think about. There have been times when I couldn't pick a leaf off a plant because I'd hear it cry. The cry from this world must have vibrated through all of heaven, the psychic shock must have been unendurable.

All they could take with them were their memories of their history and culture.

Suddenly, I felt anger. "But aren't you supposed to be showing me worlds that are destroyed by their own people. God caused this destruction," I cried. "Those people didn't make their own sun blow-up." Oh I felt like crying for the lives left behind.

Jesus asked me gently, "When someone on your world dies, who causes it? Does God? Or is it what you call nature?"

"Usually nature," I answered, "Unless it's a tornado or something." Then we call it an 'Act of God,' but that's when it is really nature and not God. No, we don't say God kills people when they die.

But nature also runs its course throughout the universe, he explained to me. Worlds are born, they die, some sooner, some later. Whole civilizations grow and die just as civilizations do. This is a lesson for all civilizations. You learn to understand this when you study your histories. Change is the way of the universe. Life is process, life is change.

"There are some worlds where people don't get off in time," Jesus added.

"But how can God let whole worlds die?" I asked. "God is the universe, does he let himself die?"

Jesus didn't answer. Perhaps there is no answer. Or perhaps I wouldn't understand the answer if he told to me. I don't know. I don't know.

On another day Jesus told me something strange. He said that often I pick where we are going. How can that be? How can I pick a place that I don't know is there? In the black world, I kept thinking about not going there, did I see it before I went? It reminded me of the picture Jesus showed me of the earth if he hadn't died. I feel weak-kneed thinking about it.

Divided World

This world looked unusually strange. The first thing I saw was a low oblong building set deep into the ground. The rooftop and about two feet of the beige sides stuck up above ground while the rest of the large enclosure was sunk beneath, somewhat like a berm house. Jesus and I watched as a single person caring a large item in their arms walked down a long sunken alleyway leading to a door deep-set into the building face. Jesus told me that the person was carrying a tray of food to the inhabitants of the building, food that was grown by these same people living outside and above ground. The people living inside the building never go out unless they ride in huge steel armored vehicles.

"What's wrong? Are they afraid of the people outside?"

"No, air," Jesus said.

At one time the air became poison to a large group of people, as I understood Jesus explanation. Those who could go outside helped those who could not, until their culture grew and solidified into the division of inside and outside people. Physically, the people are similar, only their clothing style defines them as different from one another. The people on the outside do all the work, they tend to the people on the inside. The outside people grow the crops. They live outside in the elements. It is a mild world but a past disaster long ago sent the leader and people inside for cover from fallout. Each group grew and repopulated itself.

Now it is hard to say who is the slave and who the keeper. The people on the outside are free to roam over their whole beautiful world beneath sunny skies and green trees. While the people on the inside are able to travel on machines in vast corridors of underground tunnels along with other technology but insiders can't ever leave their shelter (or prison?). This behavior is now so deeply ingrained in their culture that the past reason for the division has become clouded in superfluous myth and logic.

The sad state of this worlds division means that the two people can never interact except as slave and master, owner and servant. This prodigious keeps them blind to each other's value. Their narrow view of humanity keeps them from heaven because their kind of heaven is unworkable.

I knew why, it was because heaven equals oneness, and unity.

"Yes, intolerance is not a part of God's Ultimate Kingdom." Jesus agreed.

Each group competes against the other in their blindness. The powerful went inside long ago but kept their hold on the people outside. But in turn, the insiders can't enjoy the sun, breeze or oceans of their world.

Jesus says there is no help for these people because they refuse to reach out to one another. A new disaster, not of their making, will soon hit their world. It will be gigantic in proportion and sudden. It will crush the buildings and turn over the land—few will survive. Those few who do survive will be forced by circumstances to join together. If their inbreeding and class division proves too great an obstacle to reunion, the people will parish forever.

"Can't heaven teach them to adjust to each other after the disaster?"

They are also lacking in deep spirituality; worship to most of them has been reduced to ritual, religion has decayed into meaninglessness, Jesus explained, that their stubbornness has outweighed all the help heaven has sent to them.

I told Jesus I didn't want to write about this world, that I think of myself as tolerant and broadminded so, it is hard for me to understand how people can be so divided and close.

"There are uncountable worlds in the universe," Jesus told me. And then explained further that some societies act more atrocious towards each other than these people, our own earth has seen worse. At times we earthlings have treated each other with horrendous hatred but usually for shorter periods of time then these people. He also said that when any world meets its final catastrophe, it is nerve racking horrible but that God gives all beings autonomy—the purpose of the universe is life in all its variability's—beings must grow to finally become a part of heaven or parish. No one can be born into adulthood, all must be nourished to grow in wisdom."

"You can think of these disaster worlds as modern parables," Jesus added.

The next morning, I woke up disturbed by some of the worlds we had recently visited and specifically the stubbornness of these last people. Reflecting on what Jesus has showed me; it seemed to me that once the pot is stirred, it follows its own momentum. Why wouldn't they change, why couldn't they see the obvious, or did they? Perhaps they didn't want to see. I am sure the answer would be love if we knew how to practice it precepts. But perhaps only a deep, mature love could reverse a disastrous situation on any world. Perhaps once found and nourished, a mature devotion cannot die in a person, system, or world. A soul cannot die, but it can go on repeating itself indefinitely until it learns to love.

Love must be extremely important—it seems to underlay the universe to its core. This would hold true if God is universal love. We could argue that creation is an act of love. On a mature earth, love would prevail. Most social dilemmas could be solved by asking, "Where is the love?" But this learning to care and empathize must be learned, experienced, and evolved. We could say birth is a prescription and duty to learn to love. But there is one argument that has always bothered me and can unhinge all our talk of love. That is the death and pain of children, children who we consider inexperienced and innocent. We can hardly ascribe their pain to this life. I believe the answer must be that their soul knows and has found love. Evidence of after death experiences from children seem to bare this out. Our soul knows when to depart for new horizons, even the souls of children. "But, I ask myself, "aren't we all children?'

Jesus suddenly answers my speculation, "Yes."

I feel better now. My fear for those people was caused by their own folly, their own stubbornness. Jesus said that heaven tried repeatedly to help them through writings and prophets but no prophet prevailed.

Disaster World

Jesus told me that it was important that we include our visit to this disaster world in the book. For some reason he must consider its message important for earth. On my first visit to this new disaster world, I was unsure of where I was because I kept flipping back and forth between two places. One moment I would be standing, clouds beneath my feet, surrounded by a beautiful azure blue sky, the next, I would be enveloped by a thick, gray/white fog peeking with mysterious dirty, gray forms. What was happening was that Jesus was showing me both the upper and bottom layers of a world and I found the difference so difficult to adjust to that I was flipping back and forth.

When I recovered my equilibrium, Jesus showed me that I was standing in the glass tip of an extremely tall building. He said the building was so tall that I could hardly imagine its height so he showed me what it would look like if I could see its total length. It looked like a needle, a needle with its full length and tip stuck up out of the ground, half its eye and end looked sunk and buried. Jesus was right; it was an unbelievable feat of engineering. But the building wasn't build for pleasure, its towering length was necessary to suck in pure air and energy from the sun. There are literally millions of these needle towers all around this world.

At street level again, I took another look. The atmosphere was still white, not a pure, innocent white but an oppressive grayish white, one I thought I could choke in. Huge building corners and edges stuck through the murky fog like phantom sentry posts, I needed to reach out and touch one shimmering, dark surface before I realized it was an actual solid form.

If fog covered most of their world, how did these people survive without sunlight penetrating to ground level, I asked Jesus? He said that was the purpose of the needle buildings, to gather sunlight and its energy. Energy was so treasured on this world that it was used as a monetary system. They place so great a value on this energy that their sun has become their God as well as savior. Only the very privileged can go up to the top of a glass tower to view the blue sky and sunlight except on holy days. It is considered a holy rite and on certain days, people climb the long twisting stairs up to the top and receive a minute of sunshine and blue sky before they climb back down again in a long descending line. Almost everyone who climbs to the top on holy days, cries. The tears have become a part of the ritual of worship, a gift to the sun. On these holy days, they walk past their God shinning in the sky and are ashamedly aware of all that they have lost. Yet, even after seeing the holy sky, no large enough number of the population will step down from their privileged life. No one will agree to consume less then their neighbor, no one will have fewer births even though over population is killing their world.

In general, these people look and act much like we do. Their air problem is caused by a constant over build-up and growth. They have more land and fewer seas then earth which increases the problem because even their seas are over built. Actually, their crowded, underground, condition isn't their worst problem; their most entrenched problem is their attitude towards change. They stubbornly refuse to change their customs to benefit their own civilization.

They value their population too much, so much that they refuse to put a halt to its expansion. Over population caused many past wars, which increased, the population because the people killed had to be replaced increasing the stress and pollution, which added more problems leading to more wars. They keep growing, people upon people, and all these people need to have food, shelter, transportation, and entertainment. Since no one will give up any privilege, it becomes impossible to cut down on technological growth, as well. After the sun, their most valuable possessions are new births. The long-standing custom of their whole world demands a high birth rate.

Balance is the message from this world, Jesus told me. Balance is very important. In a closed system, the definition of any world, everything is in balance. If you take away from one part, it builds on to another. No matter if it is water, air, land, sea, population, energy, food, housing, etc. It is all in balance. When this balance is disturbed, it causes great distress that builds upon itself like a volcano, which eventually blows its top. This also holds for mental balance. One area builds and spits out hate and anger, corrupting its surrounding area and spreading until half the minds of a world are weighted towards hate. The result is an imbalance in the equilibrium of the system.[36]

---

[36] Please remember that here and throughout this book, most of the words are mine, not Jesus'. I elaborate on Jesus words as I try to understand them. As an example, in this last section, all Jesus said, with strong intonation, was that imbalance was a serious problem, I supplied the rest of the comments.

Currents of unbalance are natural to any world, like small breezes that blow hither and there, but tornadoes and whirlwinds of unbalance are not. A world that is over stressed and over crowded is heading for danger; it is on a downward spiral towards collapse. The people on this world are now gathered so close together with no room up or out of each other's way that they are like rats in a small cage. They have no place to go.

They have the technology to invent ships that travel to other worlds but all their energy is used for survival. They don't travel with their minds either, all their knowledge and resources go into keeping the population fed and alive. They are on a treadmill of produce, consume, and grow.

"Are saying that they need to control their birth rate?" I asked Jesus. Don't ask me to write this, the Catholic Church is totally against controlling births. "How else can any world prevent such a large population?"

"The problem needs to be prevented before it escalates," Jesus said, "There are other ways." [37]

I think Jesus meant that pills to prevent birth would be ok and that people who don't believe in using pills can use other means. People can change their habits and customs regarding honor and privilege. We could honor women with out children as well as those with children, we could encourage small families, and we could insure higher education because educated people contribute to a lower birth rate. We could demand that the population in third world countries receive an education. If we think about it, there are many ways to control the population, but it takes effort and understanding.

"A deep respect for life includes the understanding that a new birth is preplanned and treasured." Jesus also said that in a mature society, no birth is ever unwanted, unloved, or unnecessary. As Spock would say - the needs of the many outweigh the needs of the one. These sentiments are really too

---

[37] Notice here that Jesus has not condoned any form of abortion or infanticide, he only speaks of prevention.

unworkable for our world at this time. We cannot imagine loving so greatly or wisely. This thought brings up sentiments we can easily imagine—war and hate.

"Is earth moving towards its own disaster?" I ask

Jesus says that NATO bombing Yugoslavia is the beginning of a long siege of atrocities. (At first I didn't know if I should use the word 'atrocities' but Jesus said to use it) Even as it dies out more will flare up. I think this means that a definite evil force is directing some people to agitate and work against others. Jesus says that great problems are coming to America and, I assume other nations. He has warned me. His words bare repeating, "Great disasters are coming."

Events are fast out pacing my book.

My granddaughter is typical of this generation. She is very naiveté in thinking that "its all over there, all the bombs and stuff." But it is this generation who will pay our price, it will be their job to learn the spirituality we did not, their job to gather together in affection we couldn't feel, their job to travel in ways we refused to see? We spoil them with material goods while giving them a world of fear and violence. Theirs will be a hard lesson but a lasting one.

I don't know the details of what will happen and don't want to know but it will happen. Atrocities will multiply and create more and more anger. I believe that the coming events will change our world forever. It will be more spiritual by necessity. I may have written earlier about prophecy serving as a warning for change, but it is now too late for prophecy, too late for change. This is no warning because it can't be prevented. Events are even now overtaking what Jesus has hinted at. The ball rolls down hill.

Our near future may be horrible, but it isn't doomsday. Jesus assures me that we will persevere; we will ride out this storm wave just as we have always ridden them out. Imagine someone from the fifties or sixties generation suddenly entering our society; they would look at our current movies and television shows with disgust and horror. But we take this same society in stride, we roll with the punches. This is how we will persevere through the coming hardships, with guts, hope, and faith. Nevertheless, our children will be forever changed. It is them, their trauma and eventual spirituality that will carry the day. They will embrace the earth and give it rebirth.

This is why I consider it so important to love and give validity to the children. We aren't leaving them much of a world. I dedicated this book to the people of the future; I just now realized what I meant by that dedication. The people of the future are these children living now, the children riding their bikes outside on the sidewalk, the children in Mesoamerica sleeping under viaducts, the children laboring in Chinese factories making shoes for us, the children living in sewers in Romania. (My own writing frightens me so bad I don't know how I can write it). Many of us already know this in our hearts. We know we need to take care of the children because they are so precious, so important—earth will be their world.

Interesting that Jesus tells me I am not done writing tonight, that I have something more to add. But I don't know what? Sometimes I'm forced to realize that Jesus knows what I am going to write before I write it, as if he is reading this book in the future and making suggestions on how it will be.

Armanda

It was very late in the evening. Jesus asked me to go with him. He took me up above earth and pointed. Space moved towards me on fast forward. I saw a—the first word that popped into my mind and the only one that fits—Armanda. An Armanda of vast proportion made up of worlds and planets and ships and streamers of light and golden clouds and stars—all aiming for earth at tremendous speed, or so it seemed to me as I watched. The Armanda is on its way to earth but it is from someplace else, another universe. Jesus agreed that universe is too strong a term but we don't have the words to define where they are really coming from. I wonder if they are coming from another place and time. Future time? Then Jesus spoke hard words.

"We will be too late," He said, "Hold together until I arrive."

"Too late?" "Too late for what?" "Yes, of course I'll hold together, all of us will" But I had a sick feeling in my stomach.

"Don't worry," he said.

Then felt such an overwhelming love inside my soul, a hunger for nearness, absorption, entwinement, and a yearning for heaven that can't be completely satisfied. But one day I will be filled.

With Jesus close and at my side, I thought again of the Armanda coming our way and asked him why the Armanda was turned towards earth. His answer shocked me.

"You called me, remember"

"No, I don't remember," I started to say but then I did remember. "Yes, I do remember. I remember calling out to you during catholic mass once that we needed you now, here in the twentieth century, that everything was collapsing, rotting, falling apart and that we were in too much pain, I was in pain." Selfish pain that is why I called you. Then I caught myself up short, I realized that a grand Armanda of worlds would hardly turn in space and head our way because of one voice calling out in pain. Thousands have screamed their pain throughout history.

"You are growing up," he answered.

He meant earth was finally growing up, that because our minds could send thoughts out to the stars, we were coming into a new age, that my scream was only the tip of an iceberg, a siren call. Our psyches are waking up, growing new tendrils of thought and intuition.

"You called me while I was on earth too, don't you remember?" Jesus asked me.

Suddenly I did remember, I remembered screaming my pain down through the centuries. In answer, to my shame, I saw Jesus Christ on the cross. Jesus as painted by the greatest master of all, life. There before me was the real dying Jesus, mouth agape, nose running, dark bluish gray skin, dried caked brown blood and fresh red blood, deep set eyes, wounded eyes, agonized eyes, eyes looking into my soul, his soul into my soul. I couldn't stand it. I left. I popped out of there as fast as I could.

Guilt and horror drove me away but I had to go back, I had to tell Jesus how much I loved him, how much we all loved him. But I couldn't go back to the cross; instead, I went to the garden, the garden where Jesus was in agony. [I feel chilled remembering it]

I was still crying and sobbing when I found Jesus. He comforted me. His smile wrapped my soul in warm cotton bedding on a cold night. His sun dried my tears while I gasped and pulled myself together enough to explain who I was. I told him that I was from the future, two thousand years into the future, that people from my time revered him, called him God, prayed to him, loved him deeply, studied and wrote books about him, and wept for him.

"We will never forget what you do for us. We will never stop loving you. But you know this already, don't you?" I said all this as I hugged and enfolded him with my spirit arms. But even as a man in agony in his last moments, he gave comforting words to me, and said, "I will come when you call."

When Jesus told me in church, "You called me, I am on my way," I didn't know if I could believe his words at that time because I was still floundering in my understanding, belief, and fear. Some fears I have overcome but I still fear; I fear for our nation, "These things must be," Jesus had told me.

I often wonder if Jesus coming closer makes it easier for him to communicate with us. This idea is probably not true, because Jesus has been communicating with various people down through history, people such as St Catherine of Sienna, St Francis of Assisi, St John of the Cross, and Saint Teresa of Avila. Perhaps Jesus is taking more notice now because the times are right and he knows that he is needed, or perhaps it's true that I called him from the depths of space and his concern for us has called him to the forefront. I don't know. Most of this book is about questions I don't know how to answer. I can only keep repeating, "I don't know" Although, here is something that I do know. Jesus told me that you would receive proof that he has been talking to me. He didn't tell me what this proof was or when it will be noticed. He just said that it "will happen." I said at the beginning of this book that I had no proof for what I was about to write; I never expected any. Our tendency towards scientific rational thinking would tare and dissolve any kind of proof into shreds of confetti anyway. So why bother and I told Jesus as much, but he insists. You will see the truth.

Mars Again

I am only speculating but perhaps this proof is on Mars. We went to Mars again last night. This time it was in bright daylight, the sun was so fierce it hurt my eyes. Mars, where we stood, was littered with layers of broken, washed down rock. It was a valley of rock. The air was so clear it made the whitish rocks look sharp and empty, almost empty because Jesus showed me a plant growing between crevasses on the side of the Martian rock. It was a sponge-like plant, brown and dry looking with wrinkles. Straight, straw like branches or tubes were growing from a single horizontal middle stalk or backbone, I say this because the plant disappeared as we watched, I think it crawled away. Though, of course, it could not, or could it? Well, it was gone. All that was left was light yellow-orange ground layered with yellow to white stone ridges. The moment was over so we left. Please don't ask me why I included Mars in the chapter of disaster worlds; somehow I believe it belongs here.

Empty world

Tonight Jesus took me to a strangely beautiful world. Vividly stark and barren, its vast horizon imbued me with quietude and solemnity. This even though a fierce wind was blowing our cloaks with whiplash frenzy.

Wind whistling its mournful cry and the billowing clap of our cloaks was the only sound.

"But, it's beautiful," I said to him.

Jesus agreed with me and just as I thought he was about to include this world as one of the disaster worlds but I shook my head, "please no." So we stood there together, looking out to sea. I didn't want to know; I preferred to think of this world we stood on as an empty moonscape, a moon without life.

Although, I could see a moon above me in the sky, a sky that was pink with a green, washed-out yellow band floating across its width. The sand at my feet, squeezing between my toes, was a deep maroon, almost black. The sea by which we stood reflected the pink-green sky but a lighter shade standing frozen and still. I wondered if it was a huge flowing sheet of water ice or some other chemical because colossal black rocks floated on the surface. I know this because I watched a rock move relative to where we were standing. Except for the wind, all was soundless; no bird song or chipmunk twitters or other animal calls could be heard. The silence was awesome.

Jesus said to me "give me your hand." I put my hand in his and we stood leaning against a porous odd shaped rock or perhaps it was a block of rusted metal. As we looked out over the sea, in spite of the wind, it was so restful and peaceful standing there with Jesus. I felt in Jesus, a sense of wistfulness, of longing, or deep attachment for the place where we stood. It made me feel the more entwined with him, more loving, if that were possible.

I liked the odd movement of the rocks, so buoyant and drifting on the water. I watched as they moved across my vision. I couldn't see Jesus face but I felt my hand enclosed by his and heard his white cloak snapping in the wind with mine. I felt such great love and comfort standing near him even on this expansive, barren world.

Jesus spoke to me of liking the place where we stood. I agreed it was beautiful.

"You will paint it one day, " he told me.

"I'll try I promised.

God's Show

When Jesus told me in September that he would help me write the rest of my book, I was astounded, and overjoyed by his offer. He said he would take me to many new and different worlds, but, of course, I had to do the writing. Delighted, I couldn't wait to begin, or so I thought, but then weeks went by and I kept putting it off. "It isn't time," I kept saying. For some reason I wasn't ready to go to these new worlds. Jesus agreed with me. "You are not ready yet."

Usually when we hesitate too long we're afraid of something, so I began asking myself just what was I afraid of. I've dreamed of humans going to other worlds all my life, and here Jesus was giving me a chance to follow my dream and I hesitate. Why?

The truth, when I discovered it, was simple - I was afraid of my own imagination.

How will I be able to tell the difference between my imagination and what you show me? I asked him, "How can I differentiate between truth and fiction?" I've read so much Science Fiction, how will I know when I am influenced by what I have read?"

He answered telling me "If you hadn't read the Science Fiction, you wouldn't be able to travel."

In other words, I needed an extensive background in all the permutations possible in order to believe and understand what I was seeing; or, to dare imagine a mind could travel to different worlds. My hope is that this book will give you the background and knowledge to travel too. Speculation by a few scientists has played with the possibility that some authors unwittingly zero in on actual, ongoing realities they believe to be their own invention. Although the author creates the plot of the story, the setting or people may be a real place in time or space. This idea has been brought up by the idea that all things are potentialities waiting to be realized; that somewhere in the universe everything exists. This speculation, if true, would hardly detract from an author's skill; it's the writing that tells the tale. In a universe where we are all one, ideas should and probably do flow interchangeably around the world and throughout the universe for anyone who dares to grabs for them. Jesus has told me, almost in these same terms that all things exist, all possibilities are, and that all space is potentialities waiting to happen. The science of quantum mechanics agrees with this view.[38] Still, this leaves a huge open question that begs for an answer, if everything is potential and possible, what is real? I find myself back to my original question, "What is truth and what is fiction?"

Of course, the answer is that *it is all truth and it is all fiction.* So, what is real? What is this stuff we think of as solid, anyway? All objects are mostly space between atoms, we can touch and feel solid objects because the vibration of our space between atoms agrees with the vibration of the object's space between atoms. We are just space filled with some particles made of energy. Not only that, but the whereabouts of these energy particles can't be exactly pin pointed in space. At the same time, Jesus assures me it is "all real," that all possibilities are realized, that the universe is filled with a potential that is geared towards life, that the purpose of the universe is *life.* It also follows that the variety of life in the universe, in all its permutations, must be staggering

We're like fish in a pond who know there must be more to our world than water but, we just can't define or detect it, we fish can't imagine the sun-shinny air up above us. Actually, I think the 'dark matter' that scientists can't find is a good candidate for where heaven resides. Dark matter is an unfortunate name, it would be better to have labeled it missing matter, but first names stick. Dark matter, though it makes up 90% of the uni-

---

[38] There is not space here to explain quantum mechanics beyond my small chapter called "Non-Local Space." There are a number of good books listed in the Bibliography.

verse, is undeniable, un-measurable, and un-findable; even so, it exists enough to have gravitation because scientists can measure its pull on stars and galaxies. It is this dark matter, and its eventual detection, that it is supposed, can, "predict the fate of the universe, whether it will keep expanding, stabilize, or collapse of its own mass.[39] Dark matter in the universe is an exotic subject but suppose the space between our atoms is made up of dark matter, suppose this dark matter is filled with thought, suppose that God walks between the quantum quirks of an atom.

What throws me for a loop is what God told me once, "Heaven isn't what you think." Implying, perhaps, that Heaven is "out there" which would make heaven a concrete, solid, reality in space kind of place. This bothers me. If heaven is concrete where does that leave spirituality? The answer must be that heaven is tangible and, at the same time, intangible, definite and numinous, there and not there. It is there all around us, we are just missing it. Perhaps we can't detect heaven because we don't have the right radar—our radar is either missing, underdeveloped or neglected. Our psyche is probably that detection system. It may be that when I go to other worlds, I travel through what the scientists have labeled as 'dark matter'.

The other night I went with Jesus to just float among the stars and be alone with him. He showed me many wonders I won't write about here, except for one that I want to tell you about because I think it will help you see the universe in a new light. Jesus showed me an approximation of the universe from where we were that looked like this: For that instant, universe was a gold filled light instead of a dark background with tiny stars. It had no depth, no twinkles; it looked touchable and solid with stars and planets indented as if they had been hammered out of gold leaf. Strangely, its total essence seemed within view.

Jesus told me later that, "Worlds need darkness."

---

[39] The Detroit News

I imagine he meant that worlds made of matter need darkness to use as a cloak, a rest, as a blind from the light, and to count the seasons. I also got the impression that any one point was just as accessible as any other, that movement through this universe was easy. Why not? In a single, connected, universe, it may be commonplace to mind travel, to share ideas and realities. This ease of spiritual existence is not for us yet, we are too mired in matter, still evolving, still growing, still groping towards heaven.

Even after swimming the byways of heaven, I am still groping towards it. The more I learn the less I know. This uncertainty often causes anxiety instead of peace, the struggle to understand, is often taxing, the effort to live out what I think Jesus wants, over-whelming. These are worry-mountains I have grown and built all by myself, silly I know, but; still, my relationship with Jesus isn't all sit back and watch the pictures. He keeps asking me to, "Show them the way." I was in my neighborhood church one Sunday when he said this to me. He stood beside me and said in a gentle voice, "Show them the way." Jesus has repeated these words to me many times; they keep running through my mind along with my question, "How?"

Jesus does not explain exactly what he means by these words, I can only infer that he means for me to teach people something, but what? What have I learned through the years that could possibly show another person 'the way'? If you knew me, you would wonder too. I know many of you have found 'the way' through your own unique trials and suffering. Perhaps my trials and sufferings can show some other people the way, though, I doubt it. As far as I know, I have only one, solid, worthwhile trait, and that is tenacity, the guts to stay the course with enough stubbornness to keep to the straight path. I only know that through all the suffering, temptations, trials, loneliness, heartbreak, hatefulness, and broken dreams my love for Jesus has remained in tact. This could be the most valid message, the only message that works. Hold firm in your belief and believe he loves you unconditionally. One night I raged at him, "Why don't you love me, you give to everyone but me!" Jesus tolerated even this rage and when I calmed down, said to me, "You are deeply loved. You are never alone."

Holding to our belief in God and Jesus seems to be all the advice I have to give except this book I am writing. If this is what Jesus means by, "Show them the way," then I'll do the best I can by writing it. It may not be what he meant, but I'll write it anyway, just in case. One message that I feel is growing and forming as I write this book is the notion – show them the way *home*. Home, back into the universe that birthed us, back into heaven.

Remember I am nothing special; I am not a saint or prophet, even if I do consider myself to be a mystic. I have done so little for the world and still owe so much. My small effort in this book is nothing compared to what many other people are doing: Will Glennon, for example, who started the Random Acts of Kindness movement, Mother Theresa's sacrifice throughout her life for the poor of India, Nelson Mandela's political imprisonment, and the innumerable other people who work and give every day. One of my greatest messages may be that if I can grow so close to Jesus, close enough to ask questions and receive a few answers, anyone can.

Paradoxically-by relating to you my travels with Jesus, off world, I may have brought him back down to earth-re-humanized, our God, Jesus, once again a humble, loving, teacher. By showing you my own closeness to Jesus, you will see how easy it is to become close to him too, if you aren't already. All he asks is that you join his classroom, join him as his close friend. If you don't believe me, ask for yourself.

"No one will believe my travels with you," I said to Jesus.

"They will someday," he answered.

I am afraid that someday may be sooner than I thought. You may be forced, sooner than I expected by circumstances to believe me. During church today, Jan 24, 1999, Jesus told me that America would be devastated, would be brought down to its knees, (those weren't his exact words). He didn't tell me what would happen, whether this would be a series of natural disasters, war, or an economic collapse. I don't to know. Don't want to know. I felt dreadful after he told me. "But this won't happen for a while, will it?" I asked, "Maybe five or ten years from now?" He seemed to nod in agreement.

"Why did you tell me?" I cried. But I know why he told me, I know why he told me today; it is because I am almost finished writing my book and this information needs to go into the last chapter. He was very specific that I should include this in my book even though I don't want to write it. I felt shaken and grasped out for hope.

"But, it is also true that God is coming to earth, isn't it?

"Yes, but much will happen before that time."

The writing's been on the wall for quite a while - weather disasters, failed economies overseas, bombings in diverse places, global warming, wars and famines—our usual daily news stories. We could bet this grand prosperity in the west won't last forever, a shame because it's the first time I've ever seen prosperity 'trickle down' until almost everyone in America has a job.

I admit one of my first thoughts, when Jesus told me, was for myself and family, only my second thought was for the poor of the nation, myself included. It is these people, the people of few means who get hit hardest when disaster strikes, the family that can't put something aside for a rainy day, single mothers who don't have a cushion to pad the harsh reality of job-lessness, street people who don't have cloths or other material goods to see them through severe times. It is the children in the third world countries that I worry most about. What if more disaster strikes them? How much worse can it get for them? Yes, I am doubly fearful for the people on the bottom, they always get hit fast, hard and first, and I said as much to Jesus.

"Not this time," He said.

Not this time? Silence for my answer.

Now, that I have reached the near end of the book, I wondered, finally, what it had been about? What was its theme? What did I intend? Cart before the horse, I know, still, it wasn't until this moment that I realized that my whole book could be summarized with one word - real, real in the sense of true, actual, existing. God is a true, actual, existence, a real being;

God's Kingdom is real, Jesus is real, angels are real, other worlds are real, other people are real, Heaven is real, evil power is real. In other words, it is all really, really out there, yet it is inside too. We really are growing towards God's Kingdom. Are we also creating a mind set, a psyche that will accept God inside as he arrives outside? I don't know. I do know that Jesus lives; he is a Citizen of the Universe.

I mentioned in an earlier chapter that God spoke to me saying he wanted to show me something. Just now, September 99, I still do not know what God wants to show me or when he will do so; I decided to share with you as much of the book that I have written so far and when I learn more, I will share that with you too.

Now that I have seen, the whole world is new. I struggled for hours because I didn't know how to explain to you what God has shown me. I was stuck. Then God said to me, "Tell them like it is." So here goes…

My enemies are gone, vanquished. Those people who were spiteful, hateful, mocking, snobbish, or mean to me are gone. Those people who lied, tapped my phone, spied, or abused me through these many years are gone. Those people who spread rumors, shunned, or avoided me are gone. Not gone as in disappeared, of course, but their sinful barrage against me is stilled, or soon will be. Though a few enemies will always lurk in dark corners waiting to pounce, suddenly the day blue sky shines clear. God had used me as his anvil to reveal what is inside your heart. Your heart is open to God who can read your heart as easily as you read this book. I was so flabbergasted and startled when I realized this that I stood up out of my chair awestruck at God's way of 'showing me something'. What an understatement. I expected to be shown something spectacular, wondrous, and strangely out of this world. Events sometimes take amazing turns, don't they, especially when orchestrated by God. . Don't feel as if I have escaped scot-free. I have also reaped what I sowed, gathered my just deserts, received my portion, and felt the wrath of God's power. Justice has descended on me as well as you. When I said in the introduction that we would learn together, I wasn't kidding or being facetious; "No," I was being very truthful. I still had much to learn Jesus told me a few weeks ago, "Heaven is going to speed up humanity's spiritual growth." This may be a part of that speed-up.

All this has implications far beyond my trite tribulations, it speaks of God's overwhelming power within ourselves and our world, it speaks of God's all-ness and omnipotence. It speaks for God, period. God fills my life and surrounds me with himself.

I learned another little dust-bunny lesson hiding beneath this grand carpet— money isn't the greatest gift to have acquired in life—God's favor is. God's smile is worth more than any bank vault filled with gold, jewelry, and money. God owns the bank, the vault, the gold, the jewelry, the money and its keepers.

During my audience with God, I was promised, "There will be justice." Lately I see justice beginning to spread open like flowers to the morning dew. I say, "Thank you God," because I finally realize that our world and its inhabitants truly are all God's Show.

Part II

MESSAGE IN A CRACKED BOTTLE

I have a few comments and even an apology concerning Book I but first I want to share with you a surprise Jesus gave me just as I was to begin these book notes.

Jesus said he was going to take me someplace special. He seemed to smile in secret delight while we moved though the deep black of space and diamond stars. We left the darkness suddenly as though shedding a cloak and entered a lighted area of faint color that brightened as we moved forward.

"I am going to take you inside your painting" Jesus said to me with a smile.

"My painting? Which one?"

"Your universe painting."

"Oh, the one I keep trying to fix. But won't that be sort of fake? I just made the painting up on the computer."

"You'll see."

We continued to advance through a vivid rainbow region of stars toward a mass of bright white stars surrounded by vivid reds and blues and suddenly I recognized my painting in front of me. Billows of red and blue and green flared out from in front of a brilliant central swarm of light. I was delighted and said so as we kept moving forward. My interest was in the details within the bright mass of light, this was where I was having the most trouble with the painting but as we moved further into the area, I became completely blinded by the dazzling reflective, quality of the light.

"Close your eyes and open them again," Jesus instructed me, "You'll be able to see better."

I did as he instructed. The blare now seemed toned down but my confusion didn't lesson. I closed and opened my eyes again but confusion still reined. Everywhere I looked lighted space moved and jumped and twirled. Nothing stayed still. I couldn't seem to grasp or catch anything to hold or steady my vision. Luminous green-yellow-orange lights swam everywhere around, it was as if I was floating on an underwater, bio-luminous stage advertising with neon lights. There were millions of glowing shapes all around, above, beneath me, but it wasn't as if they were swimming or flying but rather growing and stretching in, up, and out in odd contorted billowing movements into giant cages, stripes, twirls, and spirals then suddenly flowing, stretching, and snapping back together again. The neon forms constantly grew and moved against a pale yellow luminous background. One form, in front of where I hovered, was shaped like a giant narrow leaf that had different colors constantly running up to its top. Surly not writing? With all the contorted wiggles and sliding and stretching I didn't know where to feast my eyes next. Petals of light swelled and contracted, rivers of chartreuse goblets streamed around and past, motes twirled and danced. At one point, I thought I saw a checkerboard pattern actually flash into different colors before disappearing. It was too much.

"Can we leave?" I asked Jesus.

Then I was suddenly back sitting in my chair and reeling from the bright afterglow and sense of wonder. I didn't know if I had been on a world or inside a sun.

When I asked Jesus, he told me that it didn't matter because I wouldn't understand anyway. "The answer is both," he said, then added, "This life is unique."

"It pleases you to show off special places in the universe like this, doesn't it?

"Yes." He smiled. "I love you."

His love seemed to wrap around me and it felt so good. I was still perplexed though by the idea of a visit into my painting so I asked him how we could we go inside my painting and at the same time be outside of it.

Jesus laughed. "I looked for an area that resembled the painting you have been working on for your computer program.

"But it was almost identical, I still can't believe it."

"Remember, all things exist."

"I still feel a little amazed, that's all."

"I promised you a surprise tonight."

"Yes you did."

Pleasure swelled within me as I realized his gift to me. Now I could try to complete my computer painting; although, I knew I could never portray what I had actually seen in so small an area with pixels on a computer screen, but the visit also gave me ideas and new avenues of approach for other paintings. This first surprise from Jesus proved to be only one of many gifts he gave me as I struggled to write this second book. One gift, a most beautiful and important one, I will not describe until the end so you can share in it's promise and hope.

In place of an introduction, an apology is due you that I wasn't aware of until Jesus told me that I had overstated his warning to America. I am sorry for my tendency to over dramatize disaster. What happened was that the drama of possible events, even catastrophic, became such fun that I over-wrote about the potential danger instead of what Jesus actually meant, Jesus didn't state specifically what was to happen, but only implied danger of some sort. I will try to forewarn you next time my tendencies run to exaggerating the danger or drama of events. Don't misunderstand, there is still a huge problem or crisis brewing in America, a crisis that I don't know anything about except that it *will* occur, but you probably won't need to run to the mountains to escape it. By using the word, 'devastated' I may have given a false impression. I admit I don't know what specific crises is coming our way but whatever it is, I hope and believe we will have the courage to overcome it; more than that I don't know.

I do know that I've grown in maturity and knowledge since I first began to write these books. Although it may seem to you as if I've leaped suddenly into new avenues because both books are now put together, but remember they are months apart in conception and writing. I mention my maturity because I want to explain that it reaches a high point or zenith during meditations with Jesus. My personal knowledge, comprehension, and ability reaches deeper than at other times. It's almost as if I am living two different lives, on two different levels of understanding; when I am with Jesus I know on a more intense level concepts that I ordinarily would find hard to grasp, new concepts seem to flow effortlessly through my mind during our visits. I think this may be one reason I forget to ask him pertinent questions because I forget that I need to know the answers. I remember actually making a list of questions to ask him during a visit but as soon as the visit is over, I noticed that I didn't ask even one question. If this seems strange to you, believe me, its no stranger than trying to put into writing what is essentially wordless; those mystical concepts that can't be written because there is no analogy in our language. Thankfully, my ignorance can also be a useful tool; if it weren't for my level of ignorance I wouldn't be able to write even this small account. Imagine if I were some genius trying to speak about the true meaning of music or mathematics, everyone would be bewildered by numbers and formulas that only I could understand. So be thankful for my ignorance but also applaud my honest attempt to overcome this deficiency while I write.

Another interesting fact you may want to be aware of as part of this introduction is that I never talk about my travel experiences with Jesus to anyone, the greatest reason is that no one has asked. At first, I found this extremely odd, I expected a lot of questions about these travel experiences and their validity or, at least, curiosity. Of course, the largest question should be, "Are you really talking to Jesus?" But so far nothing. I have concluded it may be like the subject of sex, too embarrassing for most of us to talk about. Also, my talks with Jesus have an intimate quality that I hold close to my heart. I don't choose to speak about them nonchalantly to just any one. Even now when people talk about trips they have taken on vacation, I don't volunteer the information that I am also taking trips, very far away ones. How would it sound to people if I went around spewing about travels into the universe without also giving a more complete understanding of why and how these travel events occurred. Perhaps the spoken word falls short because we don't have time to sit down and listen well, also, I am not a good orator; so I remain silent but speak loudly on the written page or computer screen. Regardless, as I write about the universe and our place in it I hope you will learn along with me because, believe me, we are both in line to ride on a roller coaster of ideas undreamt before in our reality. Our journey awaits.

I didn't know I was going to write another book. Jesus decided otherwise. I was sitting in the back yard last summer, leaning back in a lounge chair watching the tree leaves sway in the breeze because it was still cool this early in June. I felt as if my first book was a job well done and over with and breathed a contented sigh. In truth I wondered what I would do next with my life and had just started to meditate and expand my thoughts outward when suddenly Jesus spoke and told me that I would write another book. I must have acted dumbfounded because Jesus' next words were, "It is necessary."

My immediate thought was, "But what would I write about?" I speculated that the only reason people read the first book, which I published on the web, was to catch the sparse and cryptic statements of wisdom from Jesus; not for my own views or adventures; so I felt astounded and worried at Jesus request. Perhaps I'd left out something vital but it seemed to me that boredom would grab and quickly dispose of any reader if they had to read another whole book filled with nothing but my popping into and out from one world after another, like a tourist jaunting from country to country. Perhaps such monotony that even Jesus' words couldn't give excitement to.

But Jesus answered my thoughts by saying, "Yes, we will continue to explore the universe together," then added, "I will help you."

I still didn't understand why or what I should put in a whole, new, big book. I remembered the reason Jesus gave me for our original travels, "So you, (humanity), will recognize the worlds when you see them." But humanity is so far from building a vehicle that will carry people to even Mars let alone other worlds that my mind just couldn't fathom how another book would fit in importance. Without doubt, I would write it because that was Jesus wish that I do so. I would write ten books if Jesus asked me to and may. There was something else to consider, during my first writing I realized what a great pleasure it was to write down concepts and ideas. I learned that I liked to write. Now I had a few children's stories and magazine articles swimming around in my head. Without Jesus request and my effort, I might have never found this kind of satisfaction. So, although, Jesus didn't explain to me why another book was necessary, the challenge of writing it was beginning to grab me. His enigmatic smile told me, as if repeating once more the words he has spoken many times, "You will understand one day."

A silly thought flittered through my mind suddenly and I laughed as I said, "You've protected me from danger so many times, are you still going to protect me when the books are done?" I had been joking but Jesus wasn't when he replied, "Your work will not be done."

This quieted me. My thoughts ran to imagining all sorts of scenarios and daydreams of what Jesus meant about my work not being done. What did he mean? Would I finally take that walk around the world I had imagined once so long ago, would I need to give speeches about my travels, I shuddered at that thought. Will I become well known and famous and, after playing with this for a short while, shuddered again and honestly hoped this almost nightmare did not become true. I like the simple life. So I played with ideas and have yet to realize what Jesus will mean.

I worry that my first book, by consolidating twenty years of spiritual experience into less than a hundred pages, may have given a lopsided impression of my travels or a significance that I don't deserve. You'd get the same effect from describing all the big fish you'd caught over a twenty-year period or the many baseballs you'd hit during a lifetime, which might give a false impression of batting ability. Please keep in mind that I am not great or saintly or holy. The opposite would be more true; the whole point of relating these travels and talks with Jesus are that if I can do it, lowly, nothing, me—so can you.[40]

---

[40] At the time I wrote the first pages of the second book, I thought that was the only point, to teach you how to travel, but learned later that it was only part of the truth.

In fact, it might surprise you to know that I am not sweet or soft or sentimental. I have had some hard knocks to overcome in life, most of them of my own doing, with the result that I have grown a thick, tough, outer skin that serves me well. My manner isn't always pleasant, my words are sometimes loud, my thoughts sometimes run to jealously or anger, though when I notice thoughts of this nature, I try to cut them off. One day I felt so ashamed of my angry, hateful thoughts that I needed to ask Jesus to forgive me. I told him as a solution that I always try to say a Hail Mary when ugly thoughts enter my mind.

He laughed and said, "That is the only thing that works."[41]

His implication was that other people use the same method to drive away bad thoughts or words and taunts from the evil one. A sudden memory of nuns wearing dark blue habits and stiff white collars beneath blue headdresses mumbling to themselves and fingering brown, wooden beads as they walked past rows of pretty flowers on the school grounds came to mind. I felt a sudden unity with them, though they must be long gone by now. I also felt joined to the millions of people around the world who are sloughing through ruts of evil and cracks of temptation, sometimes enduring torture and mockery, living unseen, nondescript lives, saying whatever prayers will hold off the evil for just a moment, to keep their mind on a steady keel, to hold to the good side, to cling to their ideal, no matter what. We are a stubborn group.

Many stubborn people have been serving God their whole life, gurus, priests, nuns, teachers, missionaries, preachers, parents, writers, maybe even a few politicians work for heaven now and then. Each of these people in God's army working through their own agenda and purpose, their own agreement about their specific job, their pact with heaven, using their special talent. The complexity of it all amazes me when I try to imagine the

---

[41] Jesus didn't mean that latterly only the Hail Mary prayer would work, he mean it was one of many solutions.

vast dissimilarity of people who sow devout seeds around the earth each day. Then add to this each person's life work that is not only necessary, but right, right for whatever religion or belief or system the person holds to be true. Amazing that we all have our own ideas on how to serve God and, yet, each of our actions fit so snugly into serving. I think it can be unfortunate that many of us don't learn until very late in life what our real job is, this job we were born to do.

Fifty years. It took me more than fifty years to finally realize what job I seemed destined to accomplish. I have finally learned that my job is to simply see, to see beyond the ordinary, and then, of course, relate it to you. It is for me to see new worlds in the universe but more commonly to see a spiritual layer that surrounds our earth too, a layer that perhaps surrounds all earths, and of course the presence of Jesus and Mary and angels and…because sometimes I see other strange beings, beings of different sizes and luminosities, just barely detectable in the lamp-lit air. For this I believe I was born, to see, hear, and report. It is a great pleasure but an awesome responsibility and hardship as well, to finally find and accomplish the job you was born into. No matter how difficult the job may be, it still satisfies the soul in a way that no other work can. Probably we all look crazy and weird, those of us who have found our true calling. I sit here, unpaid and un-kept, struggling with a part time job writing while other people are out working and living a full life. I know my family wonders about me; nevertheless, I have to do it. I feel compelled to write what I write for Jesus. And like Jesus said, "It is necessary." Yes, my job is to travel, to see, talk to Jesus, and to bring some outmoded ideas of Jesus up to date. Or does Jesus mean to bring me up to date?

I am well aware that I am not the only person to speak with Jesus during the last two thousand years but I was surprised to learn that I am not the first person to have traveled to other places with him. My research had zero to slim results, at first, but eventually I found or was led to the right book. I was beginning to consider it a hopeless cause to find other strange travelers, especially travelers with Jesus until one day while browsing in a small branch library in Detroit I felt the urge to pull out this specific book, *Mysteries of the West*. I almost put it back on the shelf because the chapters didn't look interesting; then thought better of it and stacked it on top of the other books to take home. Restless and bored one evening, I had already read the fiction books, I picked up the *Mysteries of the West book and flipped through the chapters until suddenly the words 'traveling* with Jesus' caught my eye and then the word 'bi-location." I sat down and sunk into the chapter, amazed to find that a nun named, Maria de Agreda, had traveled with Jesus to the New World, America in 1620 (Many people may have heard of her but I am not familiar with most religious writings which makes my research doubly hard).

Maria was a nun in the Franciscan Order, in Aragon, France. Her travels with Jesus occurred between 1620 and 1623. She said she had been taken by God to the New World, but when the inquisition came to visit, she reversed her story to say that the travels had been only visions. Her Franciscan confessor and friend believed that they were travels out-of-body. (I didn't know anyone used the term 'out-of-body' experiences before modern times). He referred to her travels as, "corporal bi-locations." "This was the first time I realized that some of my travels with Jesus were actually a form of bi-location. Jesus agrees that this is an accurate description of many of our travels, although, as I've stated before, I am not a saint like Maria who also had miracles attributed to her.

When the missionaries first arrived in the American West, many of the Indians begged to be baptized right away before they were taught about the religion or instructed in baptisms. They reported having seen a women just like the one whose image the missionaries carried, a nun wearing a Franciscan habit. The friars wrote that they saw miraculous savings and mass healings that they attributed to this mysterious Franciscan nun. Eventually it was learned that that nun was Maria de Agreda. But when people representing the Inquisition came to visit her, although they left declaring her visions truly from Jesus, they must have frightened her because she begged Jesus to stop the spiritual gifts. Jesus did stop taking her on the travels, so they ended three years after they begun, in 1623. Maria was also reported to have levitated and, at times, her face glowed in ecstasy. She is now considered a saint by the Catholic Church.

The article I read about her referred to a book she wrote which interests me greatly. She said that she received a divine command to write a book about Mary's life and named it, "Mystical city of God." I see in Mary's request a similarity to Jesus' request that I write this book I hope to find a copy of the book and read it one day that is if I can find an English version.[42]

The only other reference I found with the concept of travel and Jesus in the same article just happened to be in the same small library. It is a modern book based on a specific method of mind travel, although this method of travel is independent of Jesus, the author does eventually talk to him. The book's title is *Cosmic Voyages* by Courtney Brown, Ph.D. The writer belongs to a group that practices remote viewing in a strict scientific sense as they search for information. Their method is exact, precise and careful; so careful, that they use a double and single blind method and use comparisons of reports by many viewers. Often the viewers do not know where they are going before hand and all visual sights and impressions, without emotions or judgments, are recorded during the travels, which are guided by a monitor.

According to the author, for a short while, the CIA developed and investigated this method in an attempt to see beyond enemy lines. The writer's group "The Monroe Institute" has no military involvement but was an out growth of the knowledge that the CIA had gathered. This group wanted to push further into knowledge the military would only skim over or dismiss, such as unidentified flying objects. In his book Courtney concentrates on visiting a civilization he calls the Grays and a

---

[42] "Miracles or Mystery, Maria de Agredas's Ministry to the Jamano Indians of the Southwest in the 1620's," John L. Kessell., *Great Mysteries of the West*, edited by Ferenc Morton Szasz, Fulcrum Publishing, Golden Colorado, 1993, pp 121-144.

dead Martian civilization, as well as, visiting great thinkers from earth's past. One of these great thinkers is Jesus. I will give further information from Courtney's book in other chapters. For now, I want to quote a direct statement that Courtney wrote in *Cosmic Voyage* because it applies to my own dilemma when I arrive on a new world with Jesus.

> Remote viewing is a lot like being blindfolded and dropped into a foreign city. You take off the blindfold and look around. You have no idea of where you are; yet you notice buildings, people, strange languages and many physical sensations. You may be able to perceive everything but you may not understand anything. While the unconscious mind tries to make the information understandable to the conscious mind, the job is easer if the conscious mind already understands basic concepts related to the viewed data.[43]

When I began reading *Cosmic Voyage* it looked familiar then Jesus told me while I was reading it that I had read it once years before but forgotten. He added that it was he who caused my forgetfulness because it was the ideas I found in this book that spurred me on to begin writing my own. His implication was that if I had remembered reading about Courtney's remote viewing, I would not have written my first book because I would have been too afraid that it would copy his.[44] As it turned out, the only thing similar about our two books is that we both travel or see beyond the ordinary. The subject matter, theme, and means differ greatly, so I needn't have worried. Regardless, I am thankful that he

---

[43] *Cosmic Voyage*, Courtney Brown, Ph. D., Penguin Books USA Inc., New York, N. Y., 1996, pp 129-137.

[44] It was for this same reason that I put off reading the Conversations with God series until my first book was finished, though I later put in quotes from the book.

uses such stringent scientific methods for his own remote viewing; his scientific method gives a validation to mind travel and revote viewing as a true method, and can be used by people who are not spiritual. Our modern society admires and in some respects even worships the scientific method so greatly that many people would refuse to believe anything that science hasn't proven as factual first. If you feel you could relate easer to remote viewing rather than to speaking with Jesus, then by all means, *Cosmic Voyage* would be a good place to begin.

As you have guessed, Courtney doesn't depend on Jesus for his remote viewing but, surprisingly, his group does meet and talk with Jesus. His comment after talking and speaking to Jesus was, "It took us a while to get over the surprise that Jesus was a friendly personality who did not mind that we approach him for advise in a highly controlled type 4 setting."[45] The statement Jesus gave to Courtney is extremely important to all of us; so important, I will quote it twice in a later chapter.

Of course any statement by Jesus is important but our well being in the near future is of great concern to him. Jesus told me, "Spirituality must be rekindled on earth soon."

These words of Jesus are hard for us to grasp because many people don't yet realize they have a soul, let alone that it should be rekindled. Then, also Jesus' task seems doubly impossible because we humans have a hard time taking a long-term view. We find it hard if not impossible to sacrifice for a future generation who will not be alive until—some day. Imagine how the new Christians two thousand years ago must have felt as they were thrown into the lion's den, totally ignorant of the importance their death would have on future generations. They had no understanding of how their sacrifice and Jesus' words would endure through the long centuries. Just as it is hard for us to visualize the why or how of Jesus' words that heaven will "Rekindle spirituality on all of earth."

---

[45] Cosmic Voyage, Courtney Brown, Ph. D., Penguin Books USA Inc., New York, N Y., 1996, pp 129-137.

I had toyed with the idea of writing a mystery novel before starting this book but that will need to wait now, the importance of this book over-weighs any mystery novel I could write. Although, and I laugh at this, Jesus said that my murder mystery novel is, "a part of it." I don't know what he means; although, he may be referring to the idea that whatever I write, I am true to myself and my love for him, so in that sense even a murder mystery may serve as a stand in for his message.

I have worried that this book will cause trouble for many people who read it because of its unorthodox subject matter but then I remember what Jesus said about the people of heaven.[46] He told me heaven is going to "Step up our spiritual growth." Perhaps this means we will face turmoil regarding our long held belief systems. If we stop to think about it, our treasured belief systems more or less show how our cultures have incorpo-rated the words from our great religious thinkers and applied them into our cultural practices throughout the centuries rather than being true to an actual representation of the original leader's ideas. This certainly applies to Jesus. Any religion that can last two thousand years has grown negative connotations as well as positive. During one of our conversations, Jesus made a statement to me to me that I will never forget, He said, "Spiritual growth is always painful." So, all of us had better plan for a few upsets in our belief systems, our cultures, our governments, and our world. Heaven will be busy.

And I must be busy at my own job—writing. If you think that I am not a good representative of Jesus life, you are right. That many other people are more holy or better, you are right again. If you believe this clay is not of good enough quality for Jesus to mold, you are again right, but Jesus needs each one of us to do our part, and this is mine.

---

[46] Usually when I refer to heaven I mean the people of heaven, ie, Jesus, Mary, Great ones, Angels, etc.

When Jesus told me I would write this second book he also told me that we would be going to one specific world most of time, a sister world to earth. I wasn't happy to hear this information, it is difficult enough to visit many different places, but I thought it would be more troublesome to keep visiting the same world, repeatedly, and digging deeper and deeper into its culture, so I asked Jesus why.

"Why take me to another world just to show us their problems? Why not just take me around the earth and point?"

"You can't see yourselves," was his answer.

He's right, of course. In order to see ourselves, we need to step back from our own polluted jungle and let a slice Alice's looking glass reflect, however bizarrely, what runs amiss within our own souls. So let the distortions begin. Almost every chapter in this book will end with a visit to a world I aptly named, Silver World.

Jesus took me to a world tonight that he said we will visit numerous times. He explained that it was a very earth like planet and civilization, so much so, that it could be considered a sister world to earth. The thought of visiting a world so earth-like, comforted me and I felt relaxed as Jesus lead me to the new, misty, green, Shangri-La.

My first impression was silver, silver everywhere; a soft silver light that shimmered like a misty fog with just a faint hint of rainbow beyond the insubstantial curtain. As my eyes quieted and adjusted to the area, I realized that everything looked silvery and wet because it was covered with a thin film of dew. A silver mist covered the whole forest area where we stood. It was obvious that it was a forest even though it wasn't dark and shadowy or sharply defined, as you'd expect in an earth woodland, it smelled damp and earthy but also included a faint tang or odor I couldn't place. My immediate impression was a silvery softness of unreality, of clouds painted on a fuzzy, soft terry cloth towel. Browns and greens predominated but other colors showed up here and there, softened as if by pastel crayons and tinted with a silver fog.

The silver green leaves hung low from light brown branches and Jesus reached over and picked a leaf off one of the trees to show me. It was slightly darker up close, and it was shaped like a fat star, a round center with five protruding tips. He put it into my hand so I could feel its velvety texture. The stem was damp and dribbled a watery sap on my finger when I touched it. Suddenly, I ridiculously wondered about harming the life force of the tree, perhaps because I was on a strange world and who knows what will do harm. But Jesus assured me that it was only a tree and the leaf dropped off in the fall season just as it would on earth.

This started me to thinking about any world we visit and how fragile it could be if you didn't know about the fauna and life ecology. How would you know what could be moved, or picked up or displaced or eaten? The idea opened up new possibilities that I hadn't thought of before and I made a promise to myself to be careful; although, with Jesus as my guide, what harm could I do? What if I were here on my own? Would I be paralyzed by fright, afraid to touch anything? Then I realized that without Jesus next to me I wouldn't be able to interact on a physical level with anything on this or any other world because I wouldn't be solid enough. Does it take his magic to make me real? Does it take his presence for me to be here at all? Perhaps but there are exceptions: places where I have been invited back like Ribbon World. Oh, we'll, questions to hold for later, right now, I was just overjoyed to experience this world's soft, quiet colors.

I knew immediately to call this place Silver World because of its silver mist but also because it shimmered as though through a rainbow hid just around the corner. As I looked around to my right I saw a deeper, chocolate shadow lying on the ground next to mint green bushes and trees. A decaying log. We walked over to get a closer look. The log was lying on top of the ground, its edges decayed and rotting with light green moss and with one tiny red flower rising up from its center like a standing soldier, its tiny golden center protruding from an umbrella of red petals. I wondered at the odds it braved to stand there on its slender silvery stem. It was tiny and looked like a doubled up poppy flower, not much different then the ones sold on every street corner on Veteran's day. The fallen log was covered with a fine coating of silver dew that seemed to make it glow. The little red flower was bright against its silver tinted background. I decided that it must be dry but decided not to touch it to find out. The ground nearby was covered with various shades and shapes of murky growths, some spots were covered with yellow moss and some spots were red but not as red as the flower, most colors blended softly into the green ground cover along the edges. These odd placed colors looked like soft islands amid the green. A few taller and bushier growths were scattered around between the trees and its total impression was of an un-kept and natural fairy garden.

We walked up close to one tree and I put my hand out to feel its bark. It looked just as any tree would and was a dark shade of raw umber up close. The rough bark felt wet to my finger touch and the grooved ridges, running up and down the bark, had moisture between them that was running down in rivulets. I surmised that because objects got darker as we got closer, the silver quality must be caused by the reflection of the silver sky and the damp mist in the air. The mist had a sweet and sour tang to it, a pleasant smell of—perhaps lemon rind. The odor was very faint and I may have picked up on it because lemon scent is a favorite of mine.

The whole area of forest looked like a Romantic painting of the nineteenth century. The clearing had an early spring aura to it, and a feeling of magic wonderment. Jesus told me that this whole world had a misty silvery atmosphere. That the sunlight was seldom intense and a thick cloud cover was normal for most of the world. The dew and dampness that I saw was an integral part of the whole ecology. I looked up at the sky and it was brighter than an overcast day on earth but still silver. I assumed the silver rainbow coloring reflected the quality of sunlight as well.

Then Jesus quickly reached down into the ground cover and pulled up a tiny, long shouted, gray animal with big eyes and a curly tail. It sort of puffed a screech at us, twisted, somersaulted in air, flew to the ground and scampered to the other side of the clearing. Its face and size had been mouse like but its tail was like a squirrel monkey's. I think it was more monkey than mouse but the long nose and large eyes made it look like a miniature Lemur. Its skin had sheen on it as if it had just taken a bath. I laughed at its antics as it somersaulted to get away but amazingly, it had been curious enough to stay near by as we walked around the forest clearing and I thought its two black eyes followed us from underneath the moss even now as we trampled upon its world. This reminded me that we must be visible, that the tiny creature wasn't afraid of two unusual looking strangers said a lot for the little creature's mentality.

I asked Jesus if we would be visible during all our numerous visits to Silver World and he told me that it would be counter-productive to be visible most of the time but agreed that we might become visible if circumstances warranted it.

We stood a little longer basking in the gentle breeze and eerily lit copse of woods. I loved it. I stood in wonder, holding my breath while waiting for a leprechaun to step out of the bushes. A few small birds did fly high among the trees although I didn't notice any bird songs, perhaps our presence disturbed them or I wasn't listening hard enough. Perhaps the soft contours and quiet, gentle atmosphere dampened their songs. I wondered if perhaps we stood in a barely detectable fog and was curious to see if fog lay all over this world. A small opening beneath the hanging branches seemed alight with a brighter sunshine than where we stood, the color in the distance promised a creamy rainbowed atmosphere.

I very much wanted to go through that opening but Jesus said to wait until one of our next visits. Then he added, "Wait until you see the people of this world. You'll love them."

"Do they look like fairies," I asked, because the forest seemed to invite fairies and butterflies.

"No, " he smiled, "but there are worlds with real fairies living on them."

There wasn't anything to say after that as my imagination played with the image of fairies and other possible delights in a universe so vast that only God could devise it.

Later, that night, I told Jesus that I felt uneasy about the difference between imagination and actual seeing, "What if I see it wrong?"

"You can't see wrong." He told me. He explained that I can't see anything that doesn't exist somewhere in some form or configuration of forms. It all exists but only God can know or see it all at once. God is the universe and only the universe can see its total self.

EARTH SOUL

I went back to Ribbon World tonight. It is so serene and solemn. Jesus said that I didn't need him to go with me when I visit this world. I can understand why, I feel completely at ease for the few minutes I am there. I don't think the other people notice me or if they do, they don't care because it is common that people enter and leave the solemn ritual at all times.

As I got into the rhythm of the spiral and moved in and out, stop by step, I watched a ribbon flow through the arm of the person in front of me. I felt or sensed the person' delight. After a few minutes a blue ribbon flowed through my right cheek, then soon after three more ribbons flowed through me all at the same time. It was a sensation of buzzing lights or as if a prayer clouds had kissed my soul. I felt amazed and honored.

A short time later, I left the line and went to the side where the ground rose up towards the mountains and the green vegetation was thicker. I looked at the whole area once more before leaving. From above, it looked like a clear fish bowl set in the mountain with fat streaming lights floating everywhere in the blue tinged air.

Later Jesus told me that this was one of the most unique and rare places on a world where people lived. He also told me that the ribbon lights sensed that I was from another world and so gathered my whole past as well as information on earth's past and future when they moved through me. This is their joy, these Gods. Everything I knew was now incorporated into them. They would have shared their knowledge and gatherings with me if my ability has been large enough hold the concepts, but it wasn't. The ribbon lights are a part of a larger whole whose nature is unfathomable to us humans and most other people in the universe, but we should remember that earth is unique too.

At home it was late evening and winter white snow lay beneath the street lamps, but where Jesus and I rode a canoe down a narrow southern river the air was menthol green and daybreak was sneaking past the tree tops. Swirls of mist and fog hugged the giant rooted trees that rose above the water while moss hung down from emerald trees meeting together like fingers clasped in prayer. Jesus was talking to me about the countless variety of worlds and cultures in the universe because earlier, I had been reading a fiction novel about a New York Indian tribe in early America, and asked him if there could be Indians living now somewhere on another world. He answered in the affirmative and was telling me about these various life forms and cultures.

I was startled at first, but finally realized that it shouldn't be surprising that an Indian culture could exist someplace in space at the present time. After all, it was only a specific level of culture. A level of tribal culture that most of earth's civilizations lived through at some time or other though with different forms of art and pottery. From what I knew about tribal cultures, they were egalitarian which means they shared their resources with each other on a more equal bases then our modern culture does. An ideal, by the way, that all the great religious thinkers strived for but only a few cultures ever acquired.

Jesus was explaining to me that life is so varied in the universe that I can't begin to fathom its diversity. He has said, "All possible variations exist in God's universe." I supposed that would be true of cultures too. Sure, why not, tribal cultures with many levels and different forms on other worlds, although, so far, we haven't visited any. This may be because Jesus usually takes me to worlds with a similar level of technology and set of problems, which though earth-like are hard enough to grasp; so, I am content to keep it that way. Jesus had just asked me if there was a specific place I wanted to go and I shook my head. I just wanted to stay here floating down this quiet river on earth with him listening to the waves slap against the canoe. We had been traveling to Silver World almost every night lately; if I get too busy traveling and writing notes, I begin drifting away from the central core of love that holds me to his presence. I have a real fear that I might get so sunk into details, that I'll stop perceiving the mystery. This night I just wanted to reconfirm his presence.

We still had many places to visit he informed me but that there was no hurry, so we continued floating on the emerald river, here and there dappled by the brightening sun through the treetops as if it were beginning to rain gold. I was thinking that this green, earthy wonderland could hold its own against any river on any world I'd seen so far and Jesus agreed with me.

"Earth is a strikingly beautiful world," he said, "Even to people from other planets. People come from other worlds in the universe to observe earth's splendor and beauty." I can easily believe it; although, I speculated there may also be an element of desperation to their visits; they may want a last look and feel before the splendor is gone.

I wonder if my closeness to Jesus has given me a more intimate awareness of earth's beauty. On an outing with my son and his family to Harson's Island last summer, I remember the deep blue reflections of sky on the open water riding on waves topped by silver sparkles. The magnificence of sky and water combination struck me so deeply that it felt like I was undergoing an epiphany. Riding back in the boat in the early evening, as I watched the sun, a big, orange orb floating over the dark land sitting on the horizon like a majestic king surveying his domain, my throat caught on fire with renewed admiration and wonder at earth's beauty. It took my breath away.

Oh yes, Jesus takes me to visit many interesting, lovely, amazing worlds but none more beautiful than earth. Earth, the blue green marble riding against black velvet space. I fervently pray that we learn how to rescue it because earth is in serious danger. I often wander if the whales and other marine animals already know this.

When I see whales jump out of the water as if to lift themselves up into the sky, I understand their purpose to be a kind of prayer, a communion with the universe, an attempt to thrust themselves up closer to God's realm. Fanciful perhaps, but one night as I watched a PBS program about whales,

I replayed these thoughts and wanted to know more about them. I wondered what it would feel like to be near a real whale. I saw Jesus' smile beside me and I was suddenly transported into the deep blue water of the Pacific Ocean, floating near the largest head I could have ever imagined, that of a huge whale. It kept moving so I swam to keep up because I wanted to touch it. For one second, I wanted to be a real, solid, wet, drowning person so I could feel the whale's skin against my fingertips but I had to settle for the near presence of the big king of the deep as it swam past. My arms wouldn't go around even a portion of its girth. Its eye was half as big as I was and seemed to stare at me unblinkingly. I thought and believed at the time that the whale accepted my presence as benign and harmless. This pleased me because I remember one time, more than twenty years ago, when the whales refused to let me share their ocean world.

The day it happened I was feeling so depressed that I wanted to die. My feeling of woe and despair was running so deep that I wanted to bury myself beneath the muddy ooze of the ocean bottom and never come out. I imagined myself diving down into the deep hidden depths, deeper and deeper, down so far it was inky black. I lay there on the bottom in the mud and slit wishing I could dissolve and become morsels for fish to munch. This wasn't to a whale's liking because it lunged at me where I lay. The swirl of water lifted me from my muddy grave and then other whales and porpoises joined the game of joggling me back up to the surface where I belonged. I wasn't welcome. I was startled and shocked by the whale's behavior at the time, probably shocked out of my depression too, though, right now, I can't remember why I was so depressed. My thinking was that since this was all a made-up scenario of wish fulfillment anyway, why and how did it get so far out of my control. Why couldn't I stay on the bottom if I wanted to? Regardless, I learned a lesson about whale etiquette and never tried to visit again. I felt rejected for a long while afterward.

Now that I am able to look back through new glasses and a sense of wonder, I ask myself if that event could be based on reality, a reality that I am only now beginning to re-find. Now that I am traveling the universe with Jesus I can ask if I also traveled beneath the sea that long ago day. Maybe I didn't make it up after all. But what pleases me the most is that the whales no longer reject my presence. I didn't carry melancholy thoughts into their deep realm this time around, just a sense of fun and adventure. I felt pleased and welcome.

Later thinking about the size of the whale's head and brain I realized, like others before me, that a whale might be vastly more psychic then us humans. We humans tend to think of ourselves as supreme because of our technology but; instead, it could be our technology that holds us back from knowing our own psyches or souls. The whales could have beaten us to it. In our arrogance, we believe that our intelligence is enhanced by technology but what if our technology is children's toys to the huge mind of a whale, signaling a low stage in development they may have long ago surpassed or skipped? To the huge whales we may look silly with our busyness while they spend their own time thinking thoughts beyond our ken. They could be conversing with each other mind to mind or talking to the universe, or...

While were on the subject, why not elephants too, with their large brains, they could also be psychic. I wonder. We know some dogs and cats are psychic. Could we be missing a whole range of animal behavior because of our own haughtiness? I have listened to mice scamper in the kitchen then when I hold still waiting, they suddenly stop their movement and become quiet too, as if listening to me listening to them. Try it sometime for yourself, see if they don't become quiet while you listen.

I'll never forget when I took my young children to the Detroit Zoo, and saw the huge, old great ape sitting on the cement floor in its small cage. As our eyes met, our psyches joined for a single moment. I shuddered in horror at its circumstance and couldn't look away. I felt a sudden intense pity for the deprived state of this intelligent gorilla. It seemed so pained with sorrow and boredom that I felt mesmerized by its horrible fate. Finally, I could turn away, but I could never forget. Years later, I read in the newspaper that this same gorilla was moved to a new humane, environment away from the zoo. Evidently I hadn't been the only person to recognize its deep pain and anguish.

Many animals are more intelligent than we give them credit for. I had the weirdest thought while watching "Thinking Animals: Part I" on television. I had the peculiar notion that the dolphins who were jumping through our hoops and playing hop-scotch while being studied and photographed were actually acting out, on a rudimentary level, a ritual sacrifice—that they were sacrificing themselves for a cause—the cause of teaching us humans that they are worthy of respect. Ironic if we humans are the ones in school.

Yes and we have much more to learn in that school for it is not only the biologically living earth with its whales and trees and monkeys and humans that is extraordinary but its surrounding outer planets and moons as well. They are just as exquisitely unique as earth.

Early this year I read an article about Jupiter's moon, Europa and told Jesus I would love to go there, "But not as a visit to write notes about, just to go."

He agreed and suddenly we were both standing on a flat, bumpy, black and steel gray surface next to a deep crevasse. Thin silver lines and small upheavals radiated around us. The sky was black but I didn't really notice because I was more interested in the mountains outlined and framed by light in the distance. We stood there a minute taking in the eerie coldness and beauty of the scene.

"But where's Jupiter?

"Turn around," Jesus told me.

I turned.

"Oh my God." What a sight. Jupiter wasn't a ball in the sky. It was the sky. It was hanging on top of us, a swirling, speckled, awesome majestic God of a world. It was enormous. Its colors were not as sharp as I would have expected this close up, whatever the features were showing through the thousand of deep layers looked hazy as they moved and turned. Looking into this firmament was like looking into God's eye, an endless ocean of mirrors. I was enthralled. It must be incubating a virtual fount of life.

"Yes, a diversity of life. Life too strange for you to grasp," He added that he may be able to take me there some day but not at present. And I suddenly, for an instant, thought I saw an image of a smoky, giant worm haloed against a swirling current of darker smoke and I shuddered and agreed with Jesus. Really it was all too much for me to take in, even on this simple, cold, hard surface.

Later I asked Jesus about the mountains I had seen, I thought it was strange to see such large mountains on a moon. He explained to me that those hadn't been mountains but asteroids and other moons. I felt stunned by my own stupidly, at not recognizing the obvious. It was beginning to sink in that even though I am finally getting used to traveling to far places in the universe, the grandeur in our own back yard is enough for many lifetimes of wonder. I am sure that life beneath the ocean crust of Europa would be too strange for me to grasp as well. I hope our scientists never send a probe to stick its claws down below the crust. We do not have the right to contaminate or destroy life on any other world. The probe we sent to Mars was going to execute and annihilate life at the same time that it tested for life's presence just so scientists could study its composition. That is not allowed. We can look but not kill. I couldn't believe this when I read it in the newspapers, the fact that we would destroy life on another planet. Precious, precious life. I felt very strongly against the Mars probe when I learned of its attempt to analyze by destructive heat any microbes it might find. Even microorganisms have the right to life. On our own world, it is part of our ecosystem, a part of the balance of life that we kill microorganisms every day as protection or by washing our hands. How could we not? But other worlds have their own balance and we do not have the right to disturb that balance, do we?

Maturity is the first step to the stars and an understanding of the value of all life.

Jesus said, "You can put this visit to Europa in your book if you like."

I wasn't sure if I wanted to at first, but on reflection, I realized that Jesus wanted me to include it so I could explain that killing life on other worlds is prohibited. An idea we should take to heart on earth as well.

Jesus took me back to Silver World tonight, to the same wooded clearing we left on the last visit. After standing for a moment, as I gathered my mental bearings, we began walking through the woods. I was anxious to see what the people looked like, I couldn't get it out of my head that they would be fairies. Jesus said we were on our way to see them now.

The woods were not unlike earth woods but were swirled by mist and silver drops that trickled down the trunks and fell off low hanging branches. The dew covered everything turning the soft greens and browns into softer and lighter tints. The skylight seeping though the scattering of treetops still gave a silver tone to everything below. The trees tunneled us as we walked because they were sparse and far apart enough that the branches hung low enough above our heads to touch. Only a few branches stood in my way, though Jesus bowed his head a number of times.

I noticed that the ground was spongy with dead growth and bumpy in places. I began to notice more color, red birds and blue flew through the treetops and some tiny animals kept jumping from branch to branch above us as we walked. Soft tweets and twittering followed us as. The soft day shadows kept changing in the light from gray silver to brown or greenish silver. Flowers grew here and there, not a profusion of flowers, but their sharper colors stood out against the varied silvery forest tones. It was still a fairy forest of delights and I couldn't get used to its loveliness.

We entered another clearing, this one three times as large. About twenty people were in this clearing, stooped down and gathered around in a large circle. As they squatted, they held to each other with their arms so entwined I could hardly tell where one left off and another person began. Their legs and arms seemed integral to this type of pose, the entwined legs and arms made a zigzag pattern around the circle.

One person from the circle's middle, right across from us, was standing up. Oh how this person gleamed and rippled, its body a reflection of the soft light and silver shadows that beamed down from the sky. The person's body was outlined in silver with small clear veined butterfly or dragonfly wings that undulated in changing rainbows. The whole person was a rainbow and truly awesome in its beauty.

Like the forest, none of the colors on the person was sharp, only soft and shimmery, almost as translucent as silvered glass and just as hard to see in detail. As the person stood and spoke in a singing voice, its milk-glass body changed colors. When the person moved arms up and down, both wings moved too, the whole body and wings reflected the green trees, the browns of the bark, and the silver of the sky. I was glad that I was invisible because I would have looked bad, standing there with my mouth open, staring. I couldn't take my eyes off this silver bird-like being gilding, throwing its mane too and fro, as if to jump across the moon like a mythic unicorn. Jesus was right, these people weren't fairies, but exquisite orchids floating against a forest sky.

The leader swayed and moved his gossamer wings (or membranes as I later learned) in different poses and gestures, like we would use our hands to add meaning to our spoken words. His long, silver hair disappeared into the foliage green and sky as its head swayed in singsong talk, its style oddly gathered up on top of his head and then left to free flow in conjunction with the whispering trees. His rainbow body reflected and basked in the life of the forest; birds seemed to glide across its face while flowers grew and waved through its arms. The person's chest was covered in a soft woven green cloth, the only part of its body that wasn't a reflection of some other life amid the wooded green, the only part that I could actually see. Though narrow in structure and tall, he looked to be shaped like any earth normal human. The other people stood now, and I noticed that they also wore short tunics made of soft forest colors. My eyes were getting weary of trying to make sense of the soft flashing images that kept floating and gliding off the people and speaker who seemed to be getting agitated and louder.

It was too much, too beautiful, too moving, it was time to leave.

Later Jesus told me that even though the people have wings, they no longer use them to fly but glide. Gliding is their favorite pastime. He reminded me that earth people don't climb trees anymore for the same reason people on Silver World don't fly. I couldn't imagine evolution turning people away from a propensity for flight. It seems like one trait that evolution should have left well enough alone.

MYTHIC PORTIONS

Jesus told me earlier today, "The chance of saving earth is very slight." He didn't tell me what it is we on earth are doing wrong because he also told me, "It wouldn't do any good." He probably means that the message would fall on deaf ears, that we would still hit the freeway for long hours of commuting for work and play, still shop to exhaustion, still buy more and more cars, clothing, and other what-knots. In other words whatever we are doing wrong, we would keep on doing-regardless.

Remember the movies, *Terminator I and II*, where Arnold Schwarzenegger goes into the past to prevent the earth from being nuked. Under the circumstances, any and all means to stop the bomb was legitimate because everyone was going to die anyway, very soon and very horribly. Earth was about to be burnt to a crisp unless the hero could prevent it. Of course, that was only a movie, a fiction dreamed up by a Science Fiction writer. But maybe Jesus and the people of heaven are trying to prevent a similar disaster in our future. I don't know exactly what it is they are trying to prevent at this point, but I do know it is not a fiction or movie. It may not be nuclear, it may be some other form of calamity; one that we can't see yet. I mentioned the Terminator movies to re-state the obvious that if Schwarzenegger had traveled back in time just to talk to people and tell them what was about to happen to the world, do you think anyone would have listened? Neither will we listen. No, the only way heaven can prevent earth's coming disaster is change the venue, change the culture that will set it loose, change the society that would stop enlightenment, change the group who's power prevents change, change the status-quo, change us—somehow.

A statement Jesus has repeated again and again to me is, "We are going to speed up your spiritual growth." He isn't referring to my personal spiritual growth, although I am included, or only America's; no, Jesus was referring to the spiritual growth of all humanity. People in the east and west, people in Afghanistan, Africa India, Europe, Alaska, Mexico, Russia. People all over the world are going to be given the chance to modify their behavior, to grow towards enlightenment, to recognize that we need to step forward and make serious changes.

Jesus didn't elaborate to me on how heaven is going to accomplish this goal. But if you were a highly evolved group of beings looking down on our world, how would you go about changing it? I am not highly evolved but my guess is that one tool is to introduce strange events or anomalies that will wake people up in some way. Perhaps anomalies such as strange physical or social events that we can't decipher immediately, events that puzzle us into new areas of thinking, pushing us into new pathways that stir up preconceived convictions and beliefs, like a sudden stone falling into a still pond. At the very least, a series of odd happenings that trigger us to stand up, rise to the surface, and shout. This all brings to mind the little Cuban boy, Elian, I wonder if he is one of these anomalies whipped-up by heaven.

Only heaven could have planned the many symbolisms that surround Elian: One small six year old child, suddenly motherless, drifting alone on an inner tube in shark infested waters, riding toward a country that boasts about its great freedom, saved and rescued on Thanksgiving day, 1999, the ultimate day of freedom at the turning of a new era. Neither storms nor sharks could be allowed to finish what his drowned mother began-the push towards freedom for her son. He is called "The miracle child" or "A little angel," by the exiled Cubans living in Little Havana, Florida because their intuition tells them that Elian is a gift from God. "Elian reportedly told the two fisherman who rescued him that dolphins saved him from sharks."[47] Elian named his new puppy, Dolphin

---

[47] Detroit Free Press, 1/31/00.

Unfortunately, roots of hate still run deep in Little Havana, the Florida enclave of earlier survivors from Castro's Communist Cuba. They blame Castro for separating their families and denying them freedom. They believe that Cuba is so horrible that Élan's life would be a disaster if he returned there. The exiled Cubans believe that the grandmothers and father are merely puppets for Castro's communist regime. Across the ocean, many Cubans must also think this way of their leader Castro. To many of them, freedom, jobs, free speech, food, and pleasure is only 100 miles away in Florida. Since 1959, more than 75,000 Cubans have drowned trying to get to the United States. Elian's mother was one.

Throughout these many months Elian's legal status has been seesawing between his staying in America or returning to Cuba to his father. And while I write this, Little Havana people are locked, arm to arm, if necessary, to prevent his return. Finally the President of the United States seems to have solved the problem by having Elian forcibly removed from the home he'd been staying in. But the final scene may not have been played out; the final court decree not handed down, the final lesson not yet learned. Jesus tells me that, even now, the dilemma is not resolved, though Elian is back in his native Cuba and just beginning a new school class. I don't know what we Americans and Cubans have learned or will learn from this young boy's terrible experience or what other problems, mix-ups, or anomalies may still be in store for us, but God must be smiling.

Elian's story has turned into an icon, a modern day myth and serves as a first-rate example what a real myth is not, a myth is not a made up story. The real definition of myth as found in the Oxford Dictionary of World Religions:

> But while myths may be both intended and understood as factual, it is clear that more often they are stories which point to truths of a kind that cannot be told in other ways, and which are not disturbed if the apparent 'facts' of the supposed case are shown to be otherwise...Myth endures because it engages

human attention at the extremes of terror and delight; and also because it illuminates, and is illuminated by, *ritual.[48]

Myth is universal and common to all peoples everywhere. Also myth is not a falsehood but may seem to be so because myth goes beyond the explainable. On a personal level, I am beginning to learn that myths can be more 'true' than our usual supply of information and I am coming to the conclusion that it is myths that keep society moving, not realities and established truths. Myths are more potent than fact, and in this regard, Jesus can be considered a myth. But some people use myth in a derogatory sense. They would have us suppose, that the Epistles are different from the man Jesus, that Jesus' life is exaggerated, that the facts from the New Testament don't add up, therefore, we are wrong to believe in them because they are only myth.

Why should they add up and what difference would it make if they didn't, although, I believe they do? Some writers have a very small opinion of mankind, they tend to reduce our humanness to only body and brain and then weigh everything against this absurdity. This attitude adhered to by countless people is wrong. We are much more than brains walking around on a stick. All great thinkers admit that our humanness includes an ethereal essence that goes beyond mere matter. Even eminent scientists and physicists will agree to this though they may not be able to define what this essence is. But ask any mystic, monk, guru, sage, holy-man, or deeply religious person what this essence is and they may be able to tell you. If Mother Theresa of Calcutta was still alive, she could tell you, or Ghandi. Perhaps we could accept their lives as examples of this essence made manifest.

---

[48] *Oxford Dictionary of World Religions*: Myth is a human universal. Edited by John Bowker, Oxford University Press, Oxford, NY, 1997. pp 671-673

It is our job, our mission in this perplexing and modern time to search out this essence and learn its nature for ourselves. We have the obligation to learn of this essence, to become a part of it, to grow into it, to transcend our bodies and experience its universality. To do this, we need to use more than our bodies and brains, we need to use our minds, our intuition, our feelings, our psyches, and our souls.

Jesus continues to live on as myth precisely because he was born as a mere man, who with only this indefinable essence at his disposal, grew into a superman who could defy life and death. Or if you prefer, he became one of the most highly evolved beings the world has ever known. Jesus essence will continue as one of our greatest myths, and it would be a mistake to mix up the man between the pages of reality because we find it hard to distinguish the one from the other. His value to us as a man is-unbounded. That he sweated, slept, ate, cried, laughed, loved and angered is important but not as essential as the fact of his holy spirit's availability to us through time. This Holy Spirit has been teaching us throughout the years. This myth is real.

Heaven uses the strength of myth to teach us because they know what drives and pushes us through life, and it turns out to be our beliefs, not facts. The image of hope that flows around inside our minds is more valuable than what we call reality. Memories of green grass during childhood is more vivid than the green grass we see today. We all know that religions are based on myths, the myth of prophets, and saints, and gurus, and heroes, and gods, and golden isles. Myths, and yet we follow and treasure and fight for these religious beliefs because we instinctively know them to be true, even if on a level we don't understand. On the level of logic alone, it might be impossible to join and gather all the religions into one; on the level of myth, spirit, and the holy, there is only one possible religion and we are all joined into its oneness.

Myths have great value to us humans. Creation myths are universal around the globe. In the west the Adam and Eve myth is still so prevalent that it can be used in cartoons. Historical myths like King Author and the

Knights of the Round Table can still draws crowds to view armor and swards. Robin Hood is a never dying myth loved by young and old and was the base for countless movies. Noah's flood went around the world, although the names of the participants were changed. It was useful for the leaders in the Middle Ages to keep the myth of purgatory and hell going in the mind of sinners. Yes, myths and their usefulness abound in all our cultures. On a more modern level, the Kennedy myth of Camelot is one that we can all relate to.

Then there is the myth of the flying saucer, a myth that has lived with humans as long as we can remember as leprechauns, fairies, elves and other visitors to earth. It's usefulness as myth may be one reason why we haven't seen a real, solid, extra-terrestrial land on the White House lawn and say, "Take me to your leader." Alien as myth is much more potent and long lasting than alien as fact. If an extra-terrestrial became a fact on front page news one day, it would be usurped the by short skirts or a football game the next because many people's short term interest only wants to include what is happening now; what is bigger, what is best, or new or most exciting and of course, its monetary worth. Our urge towards Hollywood glitz would turn even a real extra-terrestrial into the newest sensation or biggest freak on the block. I can't see any person from a different planet landing on earth just to become a trite fad. Better to keep it a myth. The myth of flying saucers has been an ongoing phenomenon throughout human history and its continuing presence is probably due to that fact it hasn't dropped down to our level of physical reality, as myth it plays a more valuable and instructive role. Throughout history, the flying saucer myth has been played out as leprechauns, flying machines, funny lights in the sky, witches flying on brooms, fairies and fairy rings.

While watching a program that speculated about, "Life Beyond Earth." [49] I was thinking about these various aspects of the subject and felt proud to be

---

[49] PBS show, Life Beyond Earth, Wed 11/10/99.

an ambassador to the stars even if I am the only person to perceive myself as such, when suddenly Jesus smiled and one of the people I had met on Tree World stepped into my living room. He wasn't a solid person; more like a 3-diminsional movie persona or hologram until he reached out and touched my hand with his. His hand was sheet white with tissue thin skin wrinkles in odd places. He looked at me full in the face as I sat dumbfounded before he disappeared again. If it hadn't been for Jesus' smile beforehand, I might not have believed what I was seeing.

I felt so proud to see a being from another planet walk into my living room, and had no prior conception that people I had once visited could turn the tables by turning around and visiting earth. Was my visit to Tree World instrumental to this person's visit, or do highly evolved people visit earth all the time?

I think it helps when we attempt to travel to first know that the civilization exists, that people are home, so to speak. Now that the person from Tree World knows we exist, he may visit us more often. He will want to look at our culture, how we raise our young, support ourselves, travel, worship, work and play just as I have looked at their culture. What will he find? Perhaps it will be as hard for him to grasp the many intricacies and variations as it was for me, but hopefully our best values will stand out, not our worst. Regardless, let's get ready for these mythic visitors. They may enter your living room some day too.

They may or may not arrive in flying saucers, but they are coming and we are continually learning of their possible existence. The general population has been learning to look up and search the sky since the first UFO's in the early fifties and this helps us see ourselves as being only a small part of the vast universe. By recognizing that our earth is a spaceship that encloses and protects us, we can consolidate and homogenize all earth humans into a single group living and breathing beneath the same shell of sky. Instead of separate nations of Russians, Chinese, or Americans, we will begin believing ourselves to be humans. Earthlings in common, earthlings who share a single myth—earth. This will move us one more step forward to an awareness of our oneness in the universe.

It is vital that we do so. Everyone may need to get off earth within the next 300 or 3000 years, I can't be more definite because Jesus refuses to state any specific time frame. I don't wish to throw out idealistic, unworkable ideas and I never thought I'd need to write a doomsday book, especially one without a clear cut solution because I abhor books of that nature but here I am writing one. I believe in its importance because the ordained events are birthing now, in our lifetime. The cusp exists at this time, the beginning of the twenty-first century, and the fate of the earth has fallen onto our laps. Earth is at a pivot-point and our actions for the next ten to hundred years will swim or sink it. This is hard to grasp, I know, and it is just a small indication of what will be in later chapters about the coming problem. At this point I am only guessing at the possible scenarios but Jesus knows and sees the whole picture. He has stated to me, "I will help." For my own part, as I write of these problems, I'll try not to get too dramatic. When I think about earth's future, I get frightened. Jesus looked at me with a bittersweet smile and nodded as if to agree that I should be frightened.

We had a conversation about Silver World before I went back for a visit. Jesus wanted to give me more background information about the people and their world. He also explained that we must remain invisible because these people's mindset wasn't much further evolved from our own. If they saw us they would be frightened or in denial. One difference between us is their greater technological ability to travel to their moon. I thought this odd because their sky is so overcast that the sky must have always been strange to them but perhaps this spurred them on towards greater adventure in space flight or the impetuous may have been their gliding ability. I don't know.

As far as their civilization goes, he told me that their suburbs are laid out differently than ours, in clusters or groups with small copses of forest as dividing areas between regions. The people have just recently added brighter colors to their clothing and this was a big change in development for them. He said their complex, modern era has ushered in much sharper colors and brighter designs that at any time in their past. Their commerce is much the same as ours and he will take me to see some of their industry later. He told me that in some areas these people have as much to learn as earth people do, if not more. He asked me to remember also, that they are not as diverse as earth's nations or as complex, that their evolution, like on most of the worlds we visit, has been less fragmentized than earth's.

"Is this because we had more separate continents?"

"No, there have been other issues that added to earth's complexity."

"I am not sure I will be able to take in so much information about a single world."

"Yes, you will. You'll see." Then he added, "I have specific reasons for taking you to Silver World. Reasons that will come to light as we visit different areas and events."

I hope you, the reader, understand now what I meant when I said you would learn right along with me. I have no idea what Jesus intends or why.

Tonight, at my request, we went back again to the original forest clearing on Silver World because I still wanted to walk towards the cream colored rainbow that I saw shimmering in the distance on my first visit. We had to bend beneath overhanging tree limbs and leaves before we stepped out of the clearing. The light was slightly brighter but other than that, it held few surprises. The forest gave way to rolling yellow and green hills that held sway to the same aura of silver mist and silver sky inside the forest but it all seemed brighter because of the larger view.

It was like an overcast day on any farm or countryside on earth with early morning dew still on the ground, the atmosphere felt slightly dryer then within the enclosed forest canopy but still misty and damp. We walked down a meandering dirt path lined with the forest on one side and open fields on the other. Possibly some of these were planted gardens. Light green grass with tiny flowers grew in tuffs and clusters on the side of the path amid larger bushes further in towards the woods. I wondered if the grass was kept short by some means or if it grew that way. We turned to our right along the forest line and with the forest behind us, we entered what Jesus told me was a typical suburb. A ribbon of dark pavement began as the dirt path we had been walking on ended.

The houses were small and set in short rows, maybe five or six to a row. They looked to be made of wood and single story. To my eye, they looked like playschool houses because all the windows and doors had large trim around them. The trim was about one or two feet wide and curved into soft edges. The house I looked at close had light green trim and cream plaster color on its sides. The roof was flat in front but bent down in the back.

Jesus repeated what he had told me a few times before, "This is a sister world to earth."

I had to agree. Except for a few stylish decorations and the silver mist that softened all the contours, it could look like earth. The only harsh edge was the roofline in front of the house. The edges on the dark road were softened by short green grass that grew up to the pavement. One or two people walked around near the homes. One person left the front of a house and got into a vehicle and rolled away. The vehicle didn't seem to be made of metal but some lighter material and it had a large leaf roof that folded down like glide wings.

The two or three people I saw looked the same as the people in the forest except they wore longer clothing that also covered their arms and legs. Their skin and hair was different shades of silver or white transparency, a milk glass kind of silver. These people were so beautiful I didn't think I could ever get used to them. It almost seemed an affront to cover up and hide their bodies beneath so much clothing especially since the weather was temperate and mild.

When I spoke these thoughts to Jesus he said, "Some people that visit earth feel the same way about your clothing."

Interesting but dumb. We'd all look so funny with our fat bellies and butts hanging out without support. Oh horrors what photos for an ET. Let's all keep our cloths on.

As we walked I began to notice little items that stood out as different then what I had seen in the forest. The colors of clothing the people wore were still soft and forest-like but the dewish, watery look had disappeared. The houses didn't look wet and neither did the grass and road. I wondered why not. But I could see wood grain in the trim and assumed that they built with lumber just as we do.

Jesus explained to me that much of their culture was still very dependent on their forests for industry but were also used for religious ritual. Their forests are more important to them than our parks to us because they served a different purpose. He then added the statement that the forests were dying all over their world. He didn't explain why just yet but I assumed that they had the same type of problems we do with over population and technology. He did say that our next visit would be to one of their many cities.

PLAYMATES FROM HEAVEN

This night, August 7, 1999, we went on a short visit to a rock in space. We arrived in deep space on a jagged, rocky surface. It was lit in a brilliant orange red light with deep shadows outlined everywhere. We walked to a small hole in the rock and climbed down a ladder.

The first room I saw was filled with bawdy, loud men, yelling and laughing and playing. It must have been a party. We only stayed in this first room a few seconds, the next room we entered, we didn't walk but just arrived, was a profuse jungle filled with strands of green stuff and other colored leaves flowing all around. A riot of greens and reds and blues all growing in every direction as tall as the rock ceiling. Some plants were attached to the ceiling and crawling or growing out of it.

Jesus showed me strange plants that looked to be producing gemstones. Many of the plants were twisted and growing into various designs, twirling and curled and wrapped around each other. Jesus said they are turned and positioned into the different designs. Some plants were hanging sideways and upside down floating free, there wasn't an up or down. The room was in free fall.

Jesus told me it was predominantly a mining colony near a red star as we floated back to the main room. I didn't see any children about, and agreed it probably wasn't a place for families. The men I seen looked to be normal humans but small which could be a requirement for employment? As the undersized men shouted and drank, they floated in different positions, which gave the room a circus atmosphere. Jesus said that these men partied when they weren't working because they were stuck here in space for long periods and mining was hard work.

But then, Jesus reaffirmed the value and pleasure of all life by declaring that the life these men lived as beautiful even though it was full of hardships. He wanted me to see that even though these men were rowdy, unlearned, unreligious, and at a bottom class level, they celebrated each day as if it were their last, and in fact, it could be. They worked hard and fast, they played even harder and faster but Jesus loved and treasured them just the same.

He said to me, "We shouldn't be critical of other people."

I didn't know if I had been criticizing people and looking down at them or if it was an important message for everyone. Regardless, I will try and listen to his advise. But what of people who hurt other people? What if these men enslaved women or raped them? Then how should you think of them?

He agreed that some people cause pain to others. "Only an ignorant person would destroy or hurt another life form. Only a child would look on another person as less than treasured and valuable. Every and all life is valuable." He told me to write these words down in the hopes that you and I would keep them in our hearts.

"But what about pain." I asked him. "What about my pain?" I have cried and dreamed and begged for a lover/companion for years. What about my pain and loss and hurt? How can life be great when you're in extreme pain? Is it that our soul needs the pain, the experience? The soul can suck in pain? I can't stand it, I am so lonely. Doesn't my soul care? Don't you?

It seems to me that evil rolls over my life in waves, as if some malevolent mind takes notice of my direction once in a while then turns my dreams into pudding and my desperate emotions to charcoal until the malevolent mind happens to turn in another direction.

Jesus has not answered my cry except to tell me that evil really is desperate and hungry for souls at this time. I thought evil almost got hold of mine today but I gulped down my fears and persevered one more time.

Jesus said that heaven intends to speed up our spiritual growth and transformation into higher spiritual beings but some people pose the question, "Why be spiritual at all?" I know I have asked that question and the thousands of Chinese people who choose to belong to the Falon Gong might be desperately asking themselves that same question as their government throws them into prison. Currently they are being persecuted because they made this choice of spiritual faith, they are now deprived of freedom and subject to mental abuse or even physical torture because they choose to follow their consciousness and their right to meditate. China's dictator government is afraid of this growing, silent movement. The giant is afraid of this little mouse, and it should be. Jesus has told me that the current regime will be changed to a new one before too long. Ironically, the group probably didn't intend to over throw the government, just practice the religion of their choice. It is their government's overreaction that may have blown the religious movement out of proportion and given it the resolve to keep moving forward. Jesus assures me that the Falon Gong's sacrifice will not be in vain. But what about mine and yours?

I have always thought of spirituality as a feeling or attitude of faith but I have finally learned that it is much more. Jesus smiles as I write this. Spirituality is the ability to know yourself as spirit and move within it and say, "I am spirit." Spirituality means being in touch with your own soul. I have learned to touch my soul by traveling with Jesus. Unfortunately this new spiritual outlook has given me poverty, loneliness, plus more enemies then I can count, and since I have never did anything or said anything to justify anyone's hate, I can't help wondering how and why I acquired all these enemies. I have often asked myself if evolving into a higher spiritual person is worth it? I've had second thoughts, believe me, but for some reason, I usually conclude that the other extreme would be even more horrifying because it would be stagnation or mind death. This would be worse to me than a room full of cornered rats, so I push on against the tide, twisting in freedoms path, gulping in new corners of mind, commanding my spirit to speak, propping the door open on my unrelenting need to know more of my spiritual relationship with God.

Jesus said, "Once you have it, you won't loose it."

"But I've paid such a steep price for mine."

"Everyone does," he explained, "It must be." He added that spirituality is how we expand ourselves and, "It is always painful."

Painful or not, I see a furtive spiritual growth everywhere I look. Many diverse groups are groping towards the same goal I am. Even newspapers, which are very secular, are reporting more spiritual events and mystical beliefs then they once did. Newspapers tend to be less sensational convey-ers of news than television; therefore, beliefs and mystical events that make it into the newspapers can reflect what is happening on a larger scale elsewhere. Recently I read about groups of Pentecostal believers who were finding gold in their teeth. Naturally this was also debunked by the same news media reporting it, especially because it seems a silly way for God to show his face, but a few gold flecks are real. God told me that some instances are actually true if only because the Pentecostal people believe in it so deeply and strongly. Perhaps God's words are a message to us all to just believe, never mind worrying about it making sense. That may be our problem that we need to be sensible and rational. I have already men-tioned Elian who some people in Little Havana Miami call Moses. Also there are the Child Twins, only twelve years old, who lead the Karen Minority Army "Gods Army" it is called. They battle against the Myannor military. I have never heard of either of these places before I read the news article. What caught my eye is the mystery. It seems that the fighting sol-ders see ghosts when they try to shoot and aim at the Twins army. Most of us would quickly file this as another silly superstition and forget it because it doesn't make sense. When did we become so afraid of things out of the ordinary? Why be afraid to look around corners? Is it because we have been taken in by charlatans before and don't want to be embarrassed again? I think this is true in my own personal thinking. It can be easer to see facts, safer. There was a photo in the paper showing the little boys smoking and standing barefoot, looking for all the world like ghetto kings. I expect we are going to hear more of the child twins who lead this army because my intuition told me to hold on to the newspaper clipping, I may need to refer to it again one day.

Heaven is taking a more active roll in the world and needs to. People are crying out for spiritual help not only on a personal level, the realization that something more is needed is evidencing itself in larger groups as well. This trend towards greater spirituality may not show up for a long while except where counting is easy but I have heard that all the religions are increasing their numbers, and that the Catholic Church is definitely growing around the world. We are all beginning to feel a desperate need for change, we feel that something is lacking that needs to be put back. We all wonder and fear at the extant of the Taliban's cruelty, China's dictatorship, Cuba's communism, India's class structure, Africa's upheavals, and least we forget the beam in our own eye, America's greed and squander of resources. Somehow we know these are just symptoms of an ever expanding rot. My view of the world is narrow and limited, I can only see a few of the major problems, none of us can see them all. Many are becoming afraid and are turning back towards religion because we feel a desperate need to fill up this hole we dug ourselves into. The angels are pushing and cajoling us in this direction and we can look for heaven to increase the pace, "Heaven is speeding up your spiritual growth."

There are thousands, perhaps millions of people out there working for God. Not only preaching, and living by example but teaching in other ways, books magazine articles, churches, institutions and other organizations. All a vast hoard of people pushing for the good of humanity, pushing for change. And I think heaven is now asking all these people to push harder, move faster, and scream louder.

We are not alone in this struggle to reach spiritual perfection. Heaven, the angels with Jesus and Mary are constantly trying to help us grow and always have. As I read into our past searching for information I see heaven's influence all through our literature. Sometimes it seems no more than heaven smiling down with favor on works that get our juices rolling but at other times heaven seems to kick us in the rear as we move up a whole step. Plays in the early centuries about the war between angels and the devil, Paradise Lost by Milton, Dante's Inferno, Faust, the list goes on and on, ever upward.

I am convinced that in these modern times heaven guides us by influencing shows like Star Trek. Shows that tease us to look outward yet hold to ideals of togetherness. Perhaps you never thought of it that way but the Star Trek Federation can help us prepare for visible angels and real aliens. Heaven may have encouraged its long playing run on television. There are many entertainment shows that show a trend towards our acceptance of space, aliens, ghosts, sub-space, other worlds, psyche phenomena, special gifts, mental telepathy. You could argue that the time was just ripe for these ideas but I think heaven helps create the right time, that it is heaven's influence that is constantly pushing against the force of self-interest and spiritual apathy that evil would have us wallow in. Our souls cannot be lost; therefore, heaven must win, and will. But how to know which thoughts to follow, which path in which to cling?

One of my favorite poets, William Blake, said, "All deities reside in the human breast, and no element of the psyche is wholly good or evil. True evil arises from lack of integration of the psyche elements, true good from the balance, union, and integration of the opposites." He was referring to opposites like love/hatred, passive/active, reason/energy, yin/yang, peace/war. It would seem nothing human is pure; the psyche always has its dark side as well as light. We are fated to be forever on edge, choosing one side or the other.

I have noticed this myself, that if Jesus is inside me, evil resides there as well. The evil inside my psyche can speak with a voice just as vividly as Christ's, but, thankfully, I have learned its character is noticeably flawed. This overriding flaw is detectable most of the time but not always. I have been taken in by evil more times than I can ever count, just as most of us have. It is usually when I have been busy and away from Jesus' nearness, when I feel hurt and neglected, or needy that evil has the louder voice. Being on the side of love and spirituality isn't so easy as just wanting to be right, it takes a conscious effort to keep yourself on this side of the street.

When I need to, I shrink this evil inside me by imagining it reduced to nothing more than a squealing little mouse chattering at my feet. The battle is constant and seems quite intense at times, and I have often wondered if this is because I am closer to my journey's end, closer to Christ's grip on my soul. Weariness overcomes me at times; this constant battle for territory within my own psyche can feel draining and demeaning. I told Jesus one night that I needed a rest.

Jesus said. "Rest in me now."

I put up my hands and Jesus stood in front of me and became a golden cross that kept expanding until it covered me and went beyond where I was. I kept saying, "Oh, its so beautiful, so grand." I was looking at a golden swirling universe expanding and filling my living room. Resting in Jesus I felt the full realization of Jesus as God and I too was one with God. "We are all Gods," I blurted out with joy when I dared let out a breath. "We all have three parts like you, Father, Child, and Spirit?"

"Write it," Jesus told me.

So here it is. We all have three essences within us, God, personhood, and spirit. As we evolve more and learn more about ourselves, we will understand this. Many people in the universe already know about their different aspects of being, their own godliness. I keep trying.

The spirit within may be the answer to my question of how Jesus can be so close and real at one time and at another time so elusive and hard to see. Also, how can he be with me and you at the same time? How can Jesus be within us? I searched for an analogy and Jesus agreed that it fit reasonably well for my purpose: It is like we are water molecules floating in an ocean of God and the currents are Jesus personified and the rest of the ocean is Jesus as spirit everywhere. Can we think of this as potential? It not only takes the current to flow around us, but also our perceptions of that current to realize the potential. Or it is like playing a good poker hand out of all the possibilities and making your hand the potential winner. Or it is like inventing a different idea from the usual mix of possible ideas and running with it. I kept worrying these questions to myself then I realized that mind is the real answer. If my little mind can reach out into your home, the block, the sky, or the universe, imagine where Jesus' mind can reach. Jesus can reach out as a specific being to any point in the universe, to any point on any world, into any heart, into every psyche in existence—at the same time. Jesus can use his extra-sensory perception, it is a cheap word to use for Jesus but perhaps it gets my meaning across. Jesus' mind can form his being by your side, Jesus' mind can speak within you, and Jesus' mind can send love around the globe, the universe, the cosmos.

I wonder if that is that how the little people, the grays travel to us? With their minds or do they use some other means. The same people that Whitney Strieber told us about in *Communion*, the little people who came to my bedside one night and said, "You saved us." The little people…ah but I have learned more about these little people since the first book.

I have seen them, as I sit in my chair in the early evening. My dinning room light is on and they walk right past me. One, not so little but perhaps because I was sitting down, stopped and looked directly at me while I watched. I see them only as outlines, ghosts or whispers of beings, insubstantial, almost not there. Are they traveling in the time stream? Or are they just imaginary life forms, like a child would see an imaginary playmate.

Jesus explained about imaginary playmates to me one evening.

"It is so beautiful, the idea, the reality," I thought, "I must write it down but I don't know if it should be revealed in my book or not."

Jesus said, "Put it into your book."

So here it is:

I was remembering an article in the newspaper I'd read that weekend about imaginary friends. I laughed and said, "Jesus, maybe you are my imaginary friend."

With Jesus smile, a burst of sudden knowledge filled my mind. Now I understood that a child's imaginary playmate isn't anything to laugh about. They are not imaginary, but real. They are the little people, the Gray's children; they are our ancestors visiting from the future.

"They send a child back through time to play with your child," Jesus explained by adding that that if they didn't, their child would never understand what a normal childhood could be like. It is part of their schooling.

I suddenly realized with horror that we use up so much of the earth, that we don't leave any for them. Nothing is normal where they live. We used up their air, soil, metals, and water, and maybe we turn the earth into some kind of hell and maybe the evil one is right to attack us, maybe the evil one is also from the future and hates us for our arrogance? I began crying and couldn't stop. This settled into my heart and stayed. I couldn't bare the thought of children never playing or running or skipping rope or laughing.

Real tears streamed down my cheeks because I understood more than I ever wanted to know. This night I prayed for us in our sins of pride. This was the night before Christmas, the most opulent spending spree of the year. This night Jesus also told me to describe the vortex that Mary had shown me to anyone who asks.[50]

From now on I will look at everything I consume and waste and use up with new eyes. We must learn, we must teach different habits, we must stop polluting earth. We are all one on a single earth; we must increase the effort towards change. Remember what Jesus told me, "There is only a slight chance of saving earth."

Suddenly, we stood in the middle of a strange city. The first thing I noticed was a sail shaped object in the central open space. It was white with small writing on it. I also noticed small sail shaped or triangular signs with what looked like writing on them on the front of many buildings. Up

---

[50] Before Jesus had told me to only mention it in private instead of putting it in my book. That's why I didn't put it into the first book. Perhaps Jesus doesn't want it to be a one day sensation so it must be kept hidden. He has now changed his mind and allowed me to write it in this book.

close, the writing looked to be made up of triangles and diamond shapes. Another large square sail covered the front of one very tall building. I don't know what its purpose was I thought at the time it was for information as well as decoration.

The streets were filled with people bustling to and fro in front of the buildings. They looked like the people I had seen in the forest and suburb but oh they were so colorfully silver. Their styles of clothing was so varied I couldn't focus on any one style except that most of the clothing was short and didn't cover the arms and legs. A few people wore bright, neon colors and one person wore an orange and white striped body shift and she or he had bright red (dyed?) hair.

That is when Jesus told me that she was the equivalent of one of our teenagers.

"How can you tell the sexes apart? If they have sexes, that is." Everyone's hair was shoulder length or shorter but always hung down straight.

"The males are larger, and yes," he added, "they have males and females."

I don't know why this surprised me, Jesus keeps telling me that this is a sister world to earth plus it is probably the most advantageous type of mating for intelligent evolution. Soon, I became familiar enough to notice differences, each person's skin and hair shone in different shades of silver, from white to gray to glass, though everyone was transparent to a degree, which made it hard for me to see them well. I found it easier to focus on their clothing because the translucent quality of their bodies made them blend into the surrounding cityscape. If the buildings had been brightly painted too, instead of the dull earth tones, it would have been impossible for me to focus on the people. I wondered what strange beasts in their past had caused them to develop such great camouflage ability.

Then I looked around at the strange three or four story buildings once more. They seemed out of alignment because they were clustered in odd arrangements. It isn't that the streets weren't straight it was that the buildings didn't seem straight up and down or have sharp contours at their edges. Even the city looked scenic and countrified and then I realized why, the large windows had wide trim around them just like I'd seen in the suburbs. The whole effect was picturesque and out of this world, of course.

Jesus suggested we go behind the tall buildings. We did. When we arrived, I was surprised to see litter and dirt and a mixture of crowded objects all jumbled together around a central opening. It didn't smell bad, though. The inner street or alley was narrow with canvas awnings leaning out into the street. A single narrow lane lead into and out of the back cluster of the buildings.

I forgot the dirt and grime as soon as I saw the children. A small group of children were playing behind the buildings. They were sliding down off one high triangle shaped awning on to a lower white sheet that other children were holding up. I watched as one child climbed out the window and jumped on the highest awning and glided down to the lower one. The child's rainbow wings were extended as he or she glided down.

Jesus said that the children weren't supposed to use their wings because they were delicate and could be damaged easily. The people used their wings only for certain rituals and for adult gliding. I learned from Jesus that the wings weren't really wings but membranes with many veins running through them like a dragonflies. The people had more control over the movement of the membranes than if they had been merely wings. Now they were considered archaic and of little use except for gliding pleasure but that took training and practice. The membranes folded up against their backs and were usually hidden by clothing. When Jesus told me this I realized how true this was because I hadn't seen any wings on the people walking in the streets of the city. These children, like children everywhere, were yelling and laughing as they neglected the rules against gliding.

Like their parents, the children looked made out of silver glass, but they were chubbier and shorter and resembled cupie dolls. They had large eyes and fat arms and legs. Silver hair flew around a child's head as he glided down the awning. The other children laughed in singsong trills and yelled among each other. I liked hearing the children's voices; even their loud yelling had a pleasant sound. They seemed to be happy children as most children are whatever their circumstances. Some were running, some scooting down on other awnings, and one climbed back up to the highest window and jumped out again. I caught my breath as I watched. They looked too delicate to be moving with such speed and agility. I didn't see any adults supervising their play. I fervently hoped that they wouldn't get hurt and Jesus assured me they were fine.

The thought of danger reminded me that they must have blood running in their veins. But what color is their blood? It must be silver, or white, or gray? Oh these children are so beautiful, I can't believe anything on this world could be really ugly or dirty. If behind these building was their equivalent of slums, they were beautiful slums. I wanted to hug one of these children they were so plump, playful and beautiful.

"Many think earth people are beautiful too" Jesus added, "Visitors love the different skin colors, from ivory to ebony. The variation of people on earth amazes many."

"But I think we are so ordinary, not nearly as stunning as these children. I want to hug and talk to them.

Jesus smiled and promised me that I could talk to a few children before our last visit. He said the children will be able to see us and perhaps understand that we were visitors from another place. They won't be as frightened of the idea as their adult parents would be. "We'll see."

ETHOS AND PATHOS

I know you don't want to hear my views or too much about my life, you want to hear the words of Jesus and rightly so, but I need to put myself in somewhere because my experiences directly relate to Jesus' visits and statements. Besides Jesus doesn't speak many words, I can turn his simple nod of agreement into five pages of writing. I am warning you ahead of time so you can skip this chapter. You may find it boring rather than instructive.

If I suddenly feel like Jesus is far away, I panic and worry. If I can't immediately tune in with him or feel his closeness, I become afraid that I am not good enough, or that my mind might be loosing its ability to reach out, or that I will never find him again. Silly but there it is. At times, heaven seems to fly away from me because I forget to love or pray, for days on end. The angels assure me I am ok, that they are still here, heaven is here. Jesus is here. My panic subsides. Jesus is where he was all along—beside me, inside me, all around me.

He tells me, "You will never loose me."

I believe him with all my heart because he is within and without except for the days when I let panic and doubts seep in. I am just a novice after all; I can't grasp all the ramifications of his being or how he is close to me. It is only at odd, infrequent moments that my fear and worry jump into the forefront.

One time I asked Jesus if there was anything he wanted from me. He asked me to stop worrying. He would prefer that I just go through life with a childlike trust in events. I am working on this problem and think I am succeeding. I watch the other people's problems swirl all around me and I am able to smile within myself because I have learned to ignore some of the tornado of emotions that still sweep other people up into a turmoil of fear and silliness. Am I wizening up?

Jesus made another request of me. He asked me to keep trying to visualize him during a specific session; he must have felt it was important at the time for a reason I can't fathom. Focusing until I really see him is hard to do because if I strain too much, I loose his image. It is only when I relax and *know* he is there that he is vividly near-by. I need to look at him loosely with my heart. Once when I looked at him in front of me, he looked like a silver outline and I wondered if he was there. He said follow my hand. Where is it? And I nodded to my left, then right, then up. Jesus said, "Do you still doubt?"

"No," at that time, I no longer doubted his presence, but I laugh that am God's little monkey because my attention span is so short that my doubts begin to fester again almost as soon as they ended. I hunger for the infrequent times when Jesus presence is concise and clear, when he is so vivid that all doubt flies away in his presence. I don't know why this is not always the case because at times he seems to be only an image, an outline of himself or a voice without substance. I don't know the answer. I do know my heart fills with love as my space fills with Jesus and Mary and angels and roses and clouds and seas and trees and Jesus twinkling eyes.

I hope you could know Jesus as I do but of course many of you already know him in your own way. Father Thomas said something I found very worthy of note in a Sunday sermon once, he said, "Jesus absorbs into us when we receive communion." He was quoting St. Augustine who said that instead of us absorbing communion like we would absorb food throughout our bodies, in communion, Jesus absorbs us so it is just the opposite from eating. As Jesus absorbs us, we become more Christ like, we become more of Jesus. I loved this statement about communion when I heard it because it reconfirmed how Jesus is continually working within us. Jesus has told me he wants everyone to know him, to see him, to believe in him, even to travel with him.

I suddenly wondered; if everyone on earth decided to travel at once with Jesus, how could he possibly accommodate all of us.

He laughed, "Don't worry, there is enough of me to go around."

He wants a one on one relationship with everyone, but of course, we need this relationship, he does not. We need to initiate an opening, a willingness to see ourselves in his presence and keep working at it.

Jesus told me earlier that we would go someplace tonight, he didn't specify where so I asked if we could go somewhere, 'off the books.' I didn't feel like going to Silver World tonight. Since each visit was a learning experience it could also be tiring. Jesus told me that we didn't need to go to Silver World every time we traveled and that tonight would be special.

He said, "Hold out your hands to the front."

I put my hands out front and lifted my arms up and closed my eyes.

He then said, "Don't close your eyes."

So I opened my eyes.

Then Jesus seemed to materialize slowly in front of me. At first I couldn't see much but a slight outline then I felt his hands laid inside my own. I could almost see them. I began to see white glowing in front of me and then a soft light so bright it seemed to fill the room. His face and figure became less transparent, and as I watched, the features of his face began changing and reforming. His face became a multitude of different people as it flashed in and out, converting into one face then another. The facial features changed from the darkest ebony to reds and browns and shades of every ivory, his eyes blued then turned black, then brown again while his changing hair style grew or shortened or blew against the wind. Every face was different in shape, color, tribe, or nation and style of headdress. These bright colored costumes moved around most of all, their patterns a kaleidoscope of stripes, folds, leathers or shimmering silks jumping before my eyes. Only the twinkle in Jesus eyes and his smile stayed in place. Jesus hands, still within my own, changed colors and shapes just as the faces had.

As the multiple Jesus' began to fade away he said to me, "My preference is to wear the clothing of holy men."

I smiled at this obvious humor and was delighted in Jesus gift tonight; instead of traveling to an other world, I had traveled around our own through a vast array of people living on earth. If I missed something, like womanhood or an age difference or a strange mode of dress the fault was probably mine. The symbol was the message. I will let you ponder it as I did.

There are times that I ponder who I am too. What my value is, besides seeing Jesus and writing his words. I finally concluded that I am the questions that I ask myself. That each question is really a search for self-meaning, and the trail each of us blaze through life may be nothing more than questions we have chosen to ask and solve. I spent twenty years searching the question, "Who and what is God?" with the result that I came to travel the universe beside Jesus. I find it interesting to speculate and wonder, "Who am I now? What question am I asking now?" As I type this note Jesus smiles at me within my mind as if to imply, you'll find out. If I could clarify my most recent question, it would define me. I laugh at this because while writing I can sound so sure and intense, but believe me I am as weak and unknowing as many of you, if not more so. I think it is important that you realize the sudden difficulties and doubts I sometimes go through, that they are normal and that you might go through similar doubts one day.

One night, I almost lost it, my sanity or self or heaven, whatever. I kept thinking how heaven has never helped me in the long twenty years that I have been struggling to become, to evolve. It seemed to me that the more I reached out to heaven and Jesus the more troubles came my way. Heaven has not stopped the rumors or helped me find a lover. A lover who would work and help pay bills, help me socialize, or just be there as a companion. It seemed such a simple and small thing to want, but evil put an invisible wall around me years ago and this night I knew, I believed that heaven was helpless to crack thru that glass wall. There was no help going to fall to me from above. My fear became intense as I screamed into the empty room, "Why can't heaven help me? What good are you, what good is spirituality if it can't help me? What good is love? What good is heaven or angels? It is all just mist and fog; there is nothing real to hold on to. What do I need spirit for anyway? I need help! I cried but to no avail.

These thoughts wormed screaming into my soul and twisted around inside my head. Their strength and staying power was overbearing and weighed me down. I felt like I had found hell and reveled in its darkest pit. Doubts about Jesus, our travels, and the rationale for my last two years all went up in smoke. My mind was bound and splitting with agony. I remembered in *Conversation with God* that God said that all people choose where they go when they die, so why struggle, why suffer, why love, why change and worry and try since you can choose to go where you want to go anyway. What difference did any of it make, I kept crying to myself. *Why* am I here? Just to suffer? Does heaven like my suffering? That night I think I was close to a psychic breakdown.

When I began to cool down, because nobody could keep existing inside the hell I had created for myself and stay sane very long, I forced myself to think about heaven, to call on the angels to hug me, cover me with their bodies and wings and love. I forced myself to think about what the world would look like without love or the other intangible qualities that I knew within my heart to be important just hard to grasp this night. I imagined a world gone to hate, the whole world a Nazi death camp or slave pit and I shuddered. I told myself that spirituality must have great quality, even though its quality eluded me at the moment. People have died and suffered for this spirituality, that same intangible grace that I had just cringed away from in my dark pit. People have been tortured because they dared hold to their spirituality, their love for Jesus Christ or Yahweh or Allah or some other principal long held dear by the wisest among us. Though seeming weak, porous, insubstantial, the opposite must be true, the principals of love, belief, ethics, and integrity are the bedrock of life. They are all qualities that evil would like to destroy in us. That alone makes them worthy of acquiring and holding on to. Is that why I was suffering? I dared hold on.

As all these thoughts raged inside, ironically, thoughts of the evil one was what brought me around that night. I remembered attack after attack by the evil one and realized that I must be doing something right if the evil one keeps hating me so strongly. If hate and destruction keeps pecking at me from every direction, then I must be a thorn in its side. This made me smile because heaven must hold me dear if the evil one does not. I finally understood that even my doubts this night were really an attempt by evil to hurt me, evil in disguise trying to destroy my sanity, trying to turn me against heaven, against Jesus. "I will not listen, I will not listen." I couldn't even bring myself to believe the words I was repeating but I started praying anyway, over and over until I went to sleep. My distress must have followed me through out my dreams that night because when I woke up the next morning, I still felt sorrowful and hurt, betrayed by heaven. I dragged to work.

I arrived at work feeling as if I had been rung and hung out to dry, my spirit sickly and torn asunder. Since I was the only person there, I sat down and began writing my feelings down which began to shape into a poem. I called the poem Soul Torn. I stopped and read what I had written.

Delight suddenly thrilled though my mind like a tingle of lightning. This poem is good. I laughed out loud. My doubts and hate and worry and hurt and despair evaporated like mist. I was back to normal and all it took was a simple expression of my feelings. Jesus smiled at me as I sat alone in the dull brown office. "Yes, I am back, thank you Jesus." I clapped and danced around the central cabinets laughing. When I sobered up I began to wonder, "Was all the destruction and distress I felt last night really good? Or had I just turned the tables on the evil one who tried so hard to kill my spirit? What other traumas in life could be turned around with a simple poem, or walk through the flowers, a song or smile. Easily said once the feeling of hell was finally over but hard to grasp while the trauma was in process. Perhaps it is only the artist in me that sends me on these disastrous slides into dark mind space, perhaps they are my psyche cleaning house, and perhaps Jesus tolerates my storms because he knows all this. But somehow this seems too simple an explanation for the depth of depravation I had felt. I realized I still had much to learn.

Oh I suddenly felt so ashamed of myself. I begged Jesus to forgive me. I was about to promise that I'd never doubt him again but then I caught myself and stopped because it probably would happen again, although, I hoped, never again to this depth of agony. I am only human after all; with all the emotions we are all subject too rolling around inside me. Jesus is very tolerant but I worry that if I was to throw too many fits he might stop loving me. I don't intend to take that chance so I pulled myself together. I refuse to live through another, Dark night of the soul.

More relevant for our discussion is the fact that the answer to my question, "What good are intangibles, truth and spirit?" has been staring me in the face the last few days. The news has been full of what happened in a small town when these truth breaks down. Five people dead (21 later as a final count) and a thousand gravely ill from e-coli in the small town of Walkerton, Canada because the people supposed to be making the correct decisions—didn't. They knew something was wrong with the chlorine dispenser, they knew they had a break down in their purification system, yet they made the decision to keep trying to use it. I don't know at this writing whether it was from lack of money or some other excuse but whatever, when they did finally realize their mistake, they still were unable to make the courageous decision to notify the public about the contaminated water. With the result that people who got sick with the e-coli bacteria were told by their doctors to keep pushing fluids, in other words, keep drinking the contaminated water. It wasn't until three days later that an announcement was made to boil the water used for drinking and bathing.

The point that pulls at me, besides the retching sickness these people are going through, is that each step of the way could have been prevented if those people making the decision had more integrity, courage, morals, or wisdom. This happened in Canada, usually considered our nice, quiet, crimeless neighbor to the north. So what must be happening in boardrooms, labs, offices, and factories all across America among the people who make decisions? How many of their decisions are based on the spiritual, ethical, intangible of life qualities that are just as important as profit motive, even though, like the soft red scent of a rose's splendor, we can't define it? Not nearly enough.

Just to get elected, our politicians actually depend on the opposite qualities—greed, disparagement, grabs for the top place, false promises, and untruths. We all hope in our hearts that once elected they will convert back to the person of integrity they said they were before we put them in office. But more and more we see money and power make the decisions. Development intensifies, it keeps pushing, keeps bulldozing over the little houses and people or fauna that were there first. All in the name of progress and prosperity.

I am not sure how to get back or keep hold of these long held truths, I am not sure if we can. Heaven and those of us who think we see through the façade have a long road ahead of us if we think we can jump start a change. We can each look at our own life and change it, and perhaps that's all the success allowed in this war of wills.

I intend to keep my eyes open to the dark but at the same time outwit it by learning to pity my enemies not hate them, by rolling with the punches not punching my own holes. I have found the dividing line between the extremes, the demarcation line. It is the ability to recognize the different forces at work around me and to not let the wave overtake me. It is an attempt to walk in the shoes of your enemy and yet have the ability to *draw your own line.* It has taken me more than fifty years to learn this little witticism. I stand and watch the loves, smears, triteness and other human fragilities swirl around me but at the same time I can see strengths in some people, the strength to not believe the rumors, the strength to stand up for honesty, the strength to make the right decision, the strength to stand your ground even through a job loss, the strength to keep pushing ahead against overwhelming odds, the strength to look past the traps evil sets against us.

Probably any one of us could look at co-workers and see these emotions: slurs, weak and deliberate snares, cheating, or fear of loosing a job, flowing in and around the work place. I have every place I have worked and it seems to be getting worse. It is a constant battle of wits these days to remain clear headed, to disbelieve what people may be doing against me and then try not to react when I see that they are having the same problem as I am by believing that I have acted against them. Sure, some of the attacks may be true, some people may be out to get you but be weary of lies. I personally must disregard most subtle attacks like the plague because if I let myself get caught up in them I would be wallowing in the twists and turns that the evil one weaves. I refuse. I also refuse to sue any one for damage to my psyche or person. The very act of suing would put me at evil's advantage, a patsy to his whims. This applies to my life because of certain constraints of my own ethics. Your life may have different battle lines. Remember it is the evil one who causes dissention and anger between people; so, be ever vigilant especially in these times because, as Jesus tells me, evil is desperate, the battle is intensifying, the grab for your soul has never been so far reaching or effective.

Anyone with psychic ability, and it is growing among us, is ripe for evil's rapt attention. Be especially careful when you start to travel in the mind's psyche, you have hit dangerous ground. I wouldn't advise it without Jesus to call upon for help because of the potential danger besides psychic effects can last a lifetime.

When I build an emotional bond with someone that bond stretches like a rubber band, taunt or relaxed, which ever is the case, but it never snaps apart unless I make a deliberate attempt to cut it. When I was young, I hardly noticed this kind of bonding; I think it has grown as my psyche and spirituality grown. Sexual bonds are the most gripping and fragile yet long lasting. When I first noticed psychic bonding, I thought it was only sexual because our sex drive is so strong it can overwhelm our preconditioned thinking and therefore create a powerful psychic bond. But I was wrong. I now realize that strong psychic bonding is possible between mother and child, grandparents, friends and even between casual acquaintances.

I remember when my youngest son went to California with his father, long after our divorce. My son liked to read which assured a close bond between us, but I never knew we were bonded mentally until he left for

California. At night I would lay down to sleep and even before I closed my eyes my mind would be traveling with my son and his father down the desert highway. All I could see was the never-ending road coming at me. It actually made me dizzy. This sudden togetherness never lasted more than a few minutes but it was very real, so real that I worried that his father might be drinking and driving crazily. But my son never complained on the phone so I didn't say anything either.

When my young granddaughter got in a car accident, I knew something was wrong but not what. I was working at the time but I kept getting the sensation that I needed to call her. When I got home I did call her but my other granddaughter answered the phone and told me everything was fine. I was puzzled but relieved. Later I found out no one knew about the accident at that time except her mother.

Even now I can mind-touch a former lover but I usually don't bother. I have learned constraint and thoughtfulness. Consideration is important when using our psyche. While reading a Sufi saying that one should always enter a room through the door, it suddenly hit me that I could be invading a person's privacy by visiting them with my mind. I try not to visit people un-invited, but I don't mind if other people visit me.

At times I am mocked and taunted in my own mind by the evil one, an evil who pretends to be Jesus. As an imitation Jesus he makes outrageous promises of money and wealth to me but Jesus says heaven doesn't make promises. At the other extreme, the evil one threatens me that I will loose my job; this seems to be his favorite pastime, that I will never have a lover, that I will loose my home. Evil knows our deepest desires and has deprived me of mine. His attack has been so effective that, to me, it is comparable to Sampson loosing his hair, my strength was taken away. I have always needed a significant other, male companion by my side. I believe if would have had a companion during the last twenty years, I could have re-made the world of gave it a good try. As it is, my strength has been reduced to almost nothing, all I can do now is write and hope enough people will read it. Jesus and angels keep pulling me out of this morass, somewhat reducing my handicap, but its sting holds on.

I wonder if I will ever have a friend to talk to, a lover, a companion. I hold to Jesus and try to hold back the doubts and worries. I keep remembering what Jesus told me a few years ago, "All will be restored." And since heaven doesn't make promises, this must be a different sort of statement; this must be a guarantee and will be honored when I least expect it. Like last New Years Eve.

Jesus had said we'd do something special on New Years Eve because I was complaining that I would be all alone so Jesus smiled as if we would make it a special night. But my surprise came early, the evening before because as it turned out, I did have someplace to go that Friday. Thursday evening as soon as I finished watching a movie and sat in my armchair, I was suddenly back at Nexus, the way station for many people in our part of the universe? I was standing slightly apart from Jesus and the beautiful lady with golden hair was once again in front of me as if I had never left.

I looked over at Jesus startled and he nodded "Yes," that I was back at the same time and place I had left months ago. This time the lady took my hand and led me to one of the escalators. It was made of clear material except for the railing that was trimmed in silver. Everything high up was trimmed in silver - like silver lines crisscrossing and running together. Many other people were also riding on escalators. One hooded man, his purple hood was pulled to the back of his head, nodded at me as I rode past in the opposite direction. I wondered what made me so obvious. I now believe it was because my image or presence flickered in and out because I wasn't able to hold myself together well. I looked down at Jesus to follow but he shook his head in the negative.

The lady and I rode all the way to the top; we stopped at a curtain of light and stepped off the escalator into a jungle of trees and huge leaves. Nearby was the oddest animal I had ever seen - it was moving towards us and had a rider on its neck? Its walk or climb resembled gorilla but it was slim with long hairy arms. It had a small head and its legs were long and resembled its arms but I didn't see this until we were out of the jungle.

We got on one of the animals, which I suddenly understood was actually an intelligent species and rode for a short while before we began to descend. The gorillas climbed down very fast into mountainous country with big boulders sitting between mountain crevasses and ridges. Here the vegetation became sparse and irregular but we moved very fast. The gorilla's arms and legs ran over the ground and then climbed down mountainsides by jumping and reaching for hand holds. It was enlivening and exciting and frightening but I seemed to be the only one scared or concerned.

One of the gorillas was carrying a small, slim girl with long black hair; She was the one who greeted the lady and me when we arrived so I assumed she was some kind of leader. Finely the gorillas climbed over a giant bounder and down into a bare rock crevasse where huge doors opened into the side of the mountain. We went into the gigantic cavern with its modern lighting and appliances and machines all blinking at once. It was like a modern city, which surprised me although I knew they had some form of communication over long distances because at one point in our journey the black hair girl opened something on her wrist and talked into it. It was radio or some other type of connection. The gorillas, after we got off, stood up and walked away to their own pursuits. I was told that the arrangement for both species was a type of symbiosis and both the people and gorillas had their own type of jobs to do.

I asked the young girl who seemed to be my guide why the heavy doors. Was it because of war, like a fortress? She answered that it used to be but now it was a part of their culture to live beneath the mountain. The cavern we were in was so huge that it felt open and above ground, they could have flown a plane in there if they wanted to.

It was all too much stress for me I wanted to stay and see more but I was tired. I was ready to leave but I didn't know how.

An older person with gray hair walked up to me and said that was fine. He said, "There are many ways to visit our world." He meant that I was there as a mental construct and no one minded it although most of the others were physical.

Suddenly Jesus was at my side. I asked if it was ok to leave. I was worried about just disappearing with all these people walking around and all the machinery. Jesus smiled and nodded. The lady with the gold hair stayed behind when I left. She may have lived there.

Rested and relaxed now, let me describe what I remember of their world: It looked just like earth and so did the people except it was very mountainous. Where we had been there was no flat surfaces at all until we arrived at the cavern. The crevasses were like V forms tortured into the mountains that at some point must have went through great upheavals. It was no wonder they needed the gorillas to get around, it must be the only way to travel though they probably had airplanes too.

Everything looked earth normal until I looked up into the sky because there were two suns in the sky, a sky that resembled earth except for a slight pink tinge as though the sun was about to set but the suns were high in the sky. One sun looked odd, like a ring around another moon, how an eclipse might look in a day sky but it wasn't an eclipse. The trees looked normal and green, the rocks and mountains tops were white and gray but mostly a light gray. The green vegetation grew in shadows on the sides of the sharply tilted sides of the hills and valleys. It smelled earthy in the jungle and breezy out on the mountains. I didn't notice if the trees were conifers like on earth. I didn't look too closely at the vegetation but I did at the fascinating gorillas, which were not, of course, gorillas but a symbiotic species of some sort. They were light haired-brown to blond to almost white in differing shades and colors. When I seen them walk, they walked upright like a human would with their arms swinging. The idea of their evolution and symbiosis with humans is interesting and I hope to learn more about the subject another day. For now, this visit soothed my soul because it completed a journey once begun at Nexus and apparently moved my apprenticeship up a notch.

Jesus suggested that we visit an area deep in poverty tonight, but I rebelled. I didn't want to see these beautiful people suffering so I begged Jesus to wait until another time, and he agreed. We'll I do have some say about the places we visit. You'll have noticed that on the worlds we visited so far, we never visit a sports arena or political event. I dislike sports and politics and Jesus knows this; besides, my disinterest for this type of environment would detract from whatever lesson was in store for me, I would leave as ignorant as when I entered. On the other hand, I realize that Jesus has a rationale for the places we visit, that every visit has a lesson to be learned or a moral to teach which may be why the theme is usually a religious ritual or a small-scale cultural event. I also think Jesus prefers to visit the lower layers of civilization rather than the higher but seems delighted to walk among all the people and their diverse cultures.

Regardless, this night I didn't want to see young children hungry or neglected. I don't think I am a Pollyanna but I have my moods too. Besides, I won't win, we will eventually go to a slum on Silver World because it is necessary, but I hoped to hold the ugliness off for a while. On our last visit I saw those dazzling, silver bodied children playing and romping, gliding and shimmering beneath the soft sunlight and I didn't want to spoil that view yet. When we visit the slums, I will drag you there along with us, but for now, instead of visiting the lowest place, we went to the highest, the heights of Silver World, literally.

We stood aside and watched as a few of these silver people ran off a cliff and glided over the countryside. I noticed one person, his silver skin glowing beneath the silver sky, who looked naked because he wore a silver tunic, run up the foot worn path to the edge of the cliff, grab the edge with his long toe, and push off with a spring up into the air with his arms spread out. He caught the breeze just right because he lifted up on his glide wings and soared. Soon he became a shadow outline barely discernable against the silver sky.

We stood and watched as more people ran up the slope to the cliff edge and jumped off gliding. This cliff was natural but I understood that many cliffs were built for this purpose and most cities had their own gliding cliffs. Gliding was the most prevalent leisure activity on this world.

Colors were brighter this high up in the air too. This cliff was brown with orange streaks running in horizontal layers and deep brown in shadows. All the people were tall, small boned and usually thin and seemed to be expert gliders but Jesus told me that there were a lot of gliding accidents. That even though they were expert at maneuvering and taking advantage of the wind currents, some people crashed because they were intoxicated, not unlike our drunk drivers.

"It's too gorgeous for accidents," I said. We were standing on the side of the cliff, which was in deep brown shadow with gray rocks scattered around amid short stubby grass clumps and weeds growing from cracks. It seemed wild and in a natural state except for the foot slop where the people ran off the cliff. The sky was still silver but the air was clearer and didn't reflect the sky as much.

We could see over the countryside for a long distance but the horizon turned milky sooner than it would have on earth. I could see farms down below with crops growing in different arrangements of straight rows as well as triangle and diamond shaped areas and some odd clusters. The texture was varied and colorful though still softly subdued by the silver sky. The birds I saw were too far away to see and I thought of possible predators and how the gliders were protected by their invisibility, this might have been why a few people wore silver clothing while gliding.

It was also interesting seeing the straight rows because it reminded me that any modern civilization would eventually come to the same conclusion, space is valuable; therefore, use it as efficiently as possible. Jesus told me to hold on to this thought because I would need it during our next visit. He told me that our next visit to Silver World would be at the water's edge, we would visit one of their many shipyards. I thought this would be interesting because I've never been to a shipyard. I was suddenly reminded by Jesus smile how much he enjoys our visits.

At the shipyard, we were like small ants amid huge metal giants sitting on the dock or floating. The ships were dark mountains against the silver sky as we walked past them to the other end of the marina. Here there were thousands of boats, much smaller than the giant ships, but still roomy enough for a large family as I found out.

We stood among a family that was sharing the cooking chores on a central burner and pot. They were gathered in standing positions and I didn't see any chairs at this time but later noticed a few benches. We couldn't be seen, of course, so we just watched as they ate their food and talked. There was a roof over us with a number of rooms leading away in many directions, not just in one direction, as you'd find on one of our small boats. The gathering seemed lively and, after eating, many people left to go ashore. Jesus told me they come and go to their jobs and other business but sleep and live on the boats.

We rode on the boat when it left to go on a fishing trip. There were a lot of people on the boat at this time doing work with ropes and other ship equipment that I was totally ignorant about. This boat was one of about a hundred that were going out to the deeper water to fish.

As soon as we arrived at the deep ocean, the people began throwing fish lines over the side of the boat. They pulled fish into the boat one right after another. The fish seemed to jump into the boat, then into the hole in its center. This kept up until the day was done.

Jesus motioned me over to a fish laying on the deck so I could see one up close. The fish was actually more transparent and glass like than the people but it also had silver in various spots. Shape wise, it was normal, six to ten inches long, with fins, tails, and, I think, scales just as you would find on any earth fish. Its glassyness was dull in spots and it was not as beautiful as the people that caught it.

Jesus wanted to point out to me that these fish shapes followed certain lines of evolution, and fluid and quick motion in the water was an evolutionary staple. I think this lesson also included most natural formations along with intelligent decisions about the arrangement of planted rows, writing, and other activities by a people on any world. Most of all, it probably included the people we had met on every world, they were all different but followed obvious lines of evolution, they all walked upright, with limbs on both sides of their bodies, and numerous digits for dexterity. Jesus had mentioned before that evolution was "directed" by heaven and suddenly taking another look around, the fact became obvious to me as well. The people were good and swift at fishing, their bodies moved gracefully and, shockingly beautifully, with hidden strength when they needed to pull in a larger fish. They were aptly suited for any job they would put their minds to. The usefulness of their equipment, though I had never seen it before, was easy to identify, their cooking pot had been so ordinarily round as it sat over the heat source as to be laughable, cooking was cooking on any world, as was fishing line.

I didn't see these specific people use nets but presume nets would be used at other times or placesThe people pulled in other kinds of fish too, without the glassy look, these were more colorful. A few fish were shaped in wild contortions but seemed rare and were thrown back.

The people partied, eating and drinking all the way back to the shore and this seemed very human and normal to me too. Darkness dropped down on us so suddenly that I couldn't remember what the sunset looked like. As soon as the boat got back to the dock, a large number of people piled in and began eating and drinking and I presume sleeping, but Jesus and I left at this point.

CONNECTED SOULS

We went to a strange place tonight. We walked down a tunnel that was so strange I felt afraid to keep going deeper. With each step, it seemed to me that the tunnel was more alive with pulsations and whispered breaths. Even the color was fleshy, not like inside a red mouth, but whitish pink and gray with light and dark streaks running in concave circles all around, like throated veins. I stayed close to Jesus.

We then entered a larger area filled with struts that crisscrossed from floor to ceiling in long diagonals until finally we arrived at a large shimmering gray curtain wall. The wall or curtain looked like a hundred shear curtains hanging in multi-layered folds crossing and joining each other and billowing in a soft breeze. The wall seemed to send my eyes away each time I stared at it; I couldn't really take it in so I glanced at it sideways with peripheral vision. The cave or tunnel we had been following was completely empty as it branched off to the left. When I tried to look at the curtains again my glance still kept sliding away. The curtain was slippery but this time I noticed it had a great defuse of color depth in the center.

Jesus told me to wait and not try to force my vision. "Close your eyes and then open them again," he said. He meant that I needed to see with my emotions, not just my eyes. I did as he suggested and closed my eyes and opened them again. I watched as some strange person, I don't know where they come from, stepped inside the curtain, turned and walk away disappearing behind the curtain folds.

With Jesus' encouragement and half push, I followed the person's example. I stepped into the curtains which turned out not to be there at all but only an optical illusion. The illusion persisted as I stood inside the curtain, which now surrounded me and Jesus in twisting folds of purple rain. Now a million rainbows surrounded me as I suddenly realized that there was no floor, that I was suspended in air.

It seemed that our next move could be on any direction, forward, back-ward, up or down and Jesus let me take the lead when I fell in the direction we should go. Our random direction pulled us out into a large garden area.

I called it a garden because it looked to be a well kept and tended. The flowers were arraigned in beds and rows and various arraigned designs. For some reason my view could travel for an extremely long distance although I wasn't standing on high ground though, thankfully, it was solid. I think this world or place was small because it looked like the horizon was curved upwards towards the sky instead of cutting off in the distance. The crisp air was so clear and sharp it turned far off flowers into vivid dots of lolly-pops and canes. The sky was light blue with tiny oval clouds in the far dis-tance. A great profusion of brightly colored birds, butterflies, and other flying life filled the air near us. The air smelled wispy clean and summer breezy, fragrant but not overpowering,

Then Jesus reminded me that this was supposed to be a short visit but I was gazing around in wonder at the vibrancy of the colors and sniffling in the sharp tang of clean air, made fresher after the closed in space of the tunnel. The whole looked like a jumbled up Van Gogh painting with brush spatters here and there. My artistic sense was awake and enthralled by the vivid painting I seemed to be standing in. Reluctantly I returned with Jesus, stepping back into the purple curtain where I, instead of land-ing in the tunnel, suddenly arrived home again, sitting in a chair.

I asked Jesus about my feeling that the tunnel had been alive and he told me that my feelings were correct, that the tunnel had been alive in the same sense that a tree is alive. That we were the worms or bugs traveling inside its passageways. It served as a vehicle of transportation for little beings like us. He added that the garden we went to was really a ship but one as large as a small world; it looked smaller because the air was so clear air, with only the flying life hindering the view. He also confirmed my notion that it was a hollow sphere. He explained that the curtain I had walked through was a transport node, a system that took you to any part of the ship you choose to go as well as places beyond the ship.

Jesus told me to write all this down as correctly as I could remember because, he explained, "The readers will have strong opinions about this small trip one day," but he didn't explain further what the opinions would be about.

What if a big, intelligent, pink blob of flesh were to set down at the intersection of Woodward and Adams in Birmingham to meditate? How long, after the excitement, and t-shirts and dolls, until the fad turned cold, how long do you think it would be before we shoveled the pink blob mess into the trash pile perhaps disturbing its century long sabbatical or new path to meditation. Or what if a flying saucer landed in Central Park in New York City and the aliens decided to go shopping. How long before they were mobbed and trampled or worse. Jokes? Fiction?

Well ok, joke. But it points up an important message—we can't tolerate an alien walking, living, visiting, or landing on earth yet. Oh many of us could, but what about the fringe, the bad mouths, the drunks, the crack heads, the down right bigots, the narrow-minded, the strictly whites, the black is power, etc. the list goes on… the fact is that if even one person felt hateful toward a visitor to earth, hateful enough to take a swing with a baseball bat, we all took the swing, if one person shoots an alien, we all picked up the gun and killed it. We are all responsible for each other's actions because we would no longer be singular earth persons, we would be earth people. We, each and every one of us would now define the collective—earth. Earth whose intelligent species are called humans or earthlings.

In the same light, any extraterrestrial visitor would be a representative for their whole world. That pink, blob that sat down in Birmingham would represent a world, a whole species of pink blobs. Our actions would not be against a single organism but a world of organisms. So it isn't enough that some people are tolerant, or that some people are loving human beings. In order to allow any visitor from another planet to visit earth, we need to know that all the people on earth will treat that extraterrestrial with respect. We are earth people and we need to begin teaching and living this fact.

Although neither Jesus nor heaven expects us to loose our individuality anytime soon, they may expect us to be capable of joining morally, psychologically, and emotionally into a more homogenous social matrix. Our minds have collectivity and bonding powers that we have hardly touched on as an immature society. You may not believe it but our thoughts are not held strictly inside our little round heads but continuously broadcast outwards beyond our bodies. As I suggested in the chapter on space, non-locality defines us and is never so demonstrably true as when tragedy befalls us and we are hit with a blast of extra sensory perception. The mental broadcast didn't suddenly birth itself in a blast of knowledge from afar, No, the blast was you're sudden perception of what was there all along. Mind is anywhere and everywhere at once.

Even in a physical sense this is true but the idea is unfathomable to us as yet. We have a lot to learn about the diversity of the universe and the possibilities it enfolds. It is not impossible to be a single entity yet be composed of many diverse moving parts, our own bodies could be an example of this idea with its blood cells and mixture of microscopic organisms flowing around within us

I think I visited a body like that once that existed as a whole forest: This place was strange but at first I didn't recognize how strange because we stood on fallen leaves in a forest that could be anywhere on earth. But the hues of browns and reds and oranges had an odd note to them, less intense. On closer inspection, I noticed that the leaves were square shaped and had a whitish-gray coating with the corners curled up from dryness. The veins were all small and looked like tiny ladders running from one end of the leaf to the other. I couldn't put my finger on it, but this place felt strange too.

As we trampled through the leaves it sounded just like it would if we were walking through an earth forest in the fall season. The colors were wrong though because some leaves were blue and some yellow with dryness but no real bright red or oranges. As I walked to a slight rise in the ground trying to look beyond the immediate area, the land began moving in undulating waves, in a slow rhythmic rise and fall. The trees shook and swayed while dark green bushes with pointy leaves rose and lowered in rhythm. Soft sounds, complex and hard to place, rose in pitch and fell with the wave movement. The ground was undulating in spasms of earthquake?

Not an earthquake as Jesus explained it, but because the ground we stood on was alive and moving in phase to its own bodily needs. This large parcel of land crawled or slid at a snails pace across its world. It carried a whole natural biosphere on its back; it was its own ecology. After Jesus told me this I looked closer. The variation was so true that it even had bugs of different sizes and worms and other life forms scampering about.

I asked if there were people living here too and Jesus told me "No, not here." I didn't know if he meant that no people lived on the whole world or if they just avoided this false landscape, and didn't think to ask right then, or even if this moving forest was the whole world.

Later I felt like the forest had been a fun trip but fun with a kind of message; though, I am not sure what the message was if there was any. Often we go places with out a detectable purpose because the message doesn't show up until later. Jesus will often see what is lacking in my writing and take steps to fill it in. This may have been a message about togetherness? Oneness? Evolution? Singleness of purpose? Or have no message at all? Some messages I grasp at once and some I need to flush out or investigate, not this next statement by Jesus. It is clear, precise, and unambiguous. He means what he says:

"No one person can go forward unless he or she helps the others who temporarily remain. It is a law of evolution, the opposite is selfishness and greed."

Jesus didn't say these words to me, he said them to Courtney Brown as quoted in his book, *Cosmic Voyage*,[51] the book I mentioned earlier. Courtney is a social scientist and remains true to the scientific method as he remote views distant places, a method that has been ongoing since the1980s. By this method he gathers some astounding information to report in his book. He has even remote viewed Mars and the Pleiades. I am grateful for his rigorously controlled scientific study and especially his courage to write about his results in areas of knowledge that most scientists won't touch; nevertheless, it doesn't go far enough. Science can be limiting as well as instructive.[52] I admit I don't use any method; I place my trust in Jesus and let him lead me. Only Jesus knows how he wants these books to be written, which is why I often remain as much in the dark as you.

Courtney calls chapter sixteen of his book, "The Collapse of the Gray Civilization." It is so important that I want to quote a large paragraph from it:

> "Following the signal, I am moving in on the concept of environmental collapse. There is total pollution here. Literally, these beings are swimming in their own feces. Their entire consciousness is orientated toward self-gratification.
>
> I am probing the concept of sex now. It seems that these folks are extremely sexually motivated.
>
> Moving on to food. Their food is mass-produced. There are many individuals to feed, literally billions. Over time, the food became highly processed and very far from a natural design. The source of food was the oceans originally. I get the idea that these folks eat fish.

---

[51] *Cosmic Voyage*, Courtney Brown, Ph. D.

[52] For those of you who prefer science to mysticism, please read his book and perhaps begin a program of your own remote viewing.

Again, following the signal, I sense that these beings were corrupted by some type of subspace war. It's as if they were collectively seduced by an arrogant, rebellious, and very powerful leader. They later felt betrayed, but the damage was too far-gone. They had to recover from scratch."[53]

Courtney's report is certainly vivid, it is also accurate, but there is one information track that he has failed to pick up on. The people he calls Grays, you know those small, white beings with the big wrap-around black eyes that you've seen on book covers. The same beings the Whitney Strieber wrote about in his book *Communion*, are not extra-terrestrials, they are a part of us—they are our own children, our grandchildren, our great grandchildren, our descendents. Jesus explained this to me when I re-read the Cosmic Voyage book, and has repeated it over and over. When Courtney describes the destruction of what he calls the Grey civilization and world, he is unknowingly describing the destruction of our own, his description reveals what *we* will do to our own earth. He says the Grays damaged the atmosphere with pollution, and radioactivity bombardment caused by an evolutionary mistake. "The focus on the self for self-gratification led to a behavioral dysfunction on the part of the vast majority of Grays."

As Pogo would say, "We have found the enemy, it is us."

Jesus said he will help me complete the knowledge we need to prevent the destruction of earth. He said, "What was hidden will come out." All the secrets held by many groups, the hidden watchers on earth and much more. This information is needed so that people will finally believe the danger earth is in. "We must save earth," Jesus said to me many times just as he told me again tonight, "We must save earth."

I told him I was beginning to feel afraid, "I am getting fearful."

His only answer, "You should be."

---

[53] *Cosmic Voyage*, p 132.

When Mary showed me what would happen in the future, I assumed it was a long way off, perhaps 300 years, perhaps even 3000. I couldn't be sure because it was just an impression, but at the time Jesus said to me, "A lot can happen in three hundred years."[54] If we think back to three hundred years ago we were in the late sixteen hundreds, we were wearing breeches and wigs, Catholics, Quakers, Puritans and mis-fits were trickling in to the New World and the fur trade grew along the Great Lakes. In Europe, Halley predicted the return of the comet, Bach and Handel had just begun to write music and Newton's laws turned the universe into a believable and easily understood machine. Peter the Great founded St. Petersburg and William III began to share power with parliament. The events of 300 years ago seem far in the past, a long way off in history; just as three hundred years into the future seem so far ahead as to be beyond our imagination. True, all true, but the cusp or pivot point is now. The drastic change for earth and mankind's possible down fall is beginning now, in our time. Our modern, fast paced, speeded up civilization is threatening to overflow the cup.

I assume what Mary showed me was a symbolic representation of danger to earth. Watching it I understood our world to be in great danger of some sort but I couldn't grasp exactly what or how. The impression was that earth was being sucked into a black hole, which of course couldn't be true, but at the same time, I wondered at Jesus words in the New Testament, "I go to make you a place for you."[55] I wondered if he meant a new world, that maybe he would terra-form a new world for us because we were going to need it after the old one died? My vision was right but my interpretation was probably wrong. In fact, because I stayed in such a quandary about

---

[54] I just realized that Jesus might have said three and I took it to mean 300 or 3000 because only three years was unbelievable to me. It has been three years since the time I wrote this to the bombing of the World Trade Centers.

[55] *The New American Bible.*

what Mary showed me, Mary came to me again one evening and asked me if I wanted to see the vision again. I told her that I did.

I followed Mary up into the dark, star-lit night sky. We stopped in front of a swirling vortex of streaming matter turning in a tornado like wind, it resembled a small, dirty, gray galaxy against the black heavens. I stepped closer to see better and suddenly fell towards the center, turning and dropping fast as it sucked me down into its maw. Then once again I stood outside with Mary staring down at its ugly center. This had been a reenactment or image of a future event, somewhat like a movie and now I was able to stand back and reflect on what I had seen. Obviously Mary didn't mean that I was in danger of falling into a hole, No, I must have represented earth at the moment of my fall and the swirling vortex represented death. Earth is in grave danger. Mary nodded at my thoughts as if to solidify them.

I still wasn't sure if I understood, the message was certainly real, but the actual event, of course, couldn't be. Most of us know that the earth's environment is in danger. The weather has changed drastically in recent years, our measurements have broken all sorts of records, winter through fall. We've all noticed and wondered if we should worry. We should. The warming of earth is more serious and real than we at first thought, the drastic effects of tornados, draught, floods, and hurricanes will increase dramatically in coming years.

Our scientists are aware of this problem but disagree on its cause or solution. The disputes have been on going for many years with one study confirming or another contradicting the first. Only lately have geologists confirmed earth's warming as factual. By digging down deep into the rocks to the 500 year old depths around the world they have discovered that in the last 500 years the earth has warmed up by 1.8 degrees. 1.8 degrees may not seem like much but as an overall system change it's effect is far-reaching. The most dramatic effect may be the most damaging—we can't turn down the thermostat. We now know that the decade of the 90's has been the hottest decade sense we have begun recording earth's temperature. In fact, first 1998 and then1999 have been the hottest years ever recorded on earth.

Some scientists say this can have a good effect for a few nations, they are wrong, drastic change is nothing to play with, above all because we don't know the rules of the game. Ask the people living in Mongolia, sheep carcasses are laying frozen all over the desert in their coldest winter in thirty years, while the rest of the earth is heating up like an oven. Ask the people living in Mozambique, they had flooding and re-flooding and then more rain and re-flooding continuing for more than two weeks. The list could go on and it's only the tip of the iceberg.

Earth's problems didn't start and won't end with only global warming, everything on earth is being affected by frightening changes. When we learned about the possibility of a few major animals and birds becoming extinct, we fought hard to change their fate, and won. But how will we win the fight for frogs and toads? How could we stop the extinction of the amphibians when the cause of their demise is the loss of wetlands to development, fertilizers and pesticide run off, ultraviolet beaming down through the thinning ozone layer, and the over growth of roads, apartments, swimming pools, and bigger houses. In order to reverse their end, we would need to stop our own growth. No one is ready to change their life style that much, yet.

Not only the amphibians but all extinctions are more dangerous than once thought; we now know that it takes 10,000,000 years to recover from a minor or mass extinction. Many biologists say that by destroying tropical forests and other habitats, humans are driving species extinct at an accelerating rate that, if unchecked, will result in one of the major extinctions in earth's history.[56]

Will we be one of those extinctions? As I watched the program, "What's up with the weather" I was appalled to witness the common views

---

[56] Free Press 3/9/00

of average people. When it was suggested that one way to help would be to increase the cost of energy to limit its use, one lady said she couldn't afford fifty cents more per gallon of gas because money was tight. She had just killed her great, great grandchild for fifty cents a gallon. Surly there is something that she and her family can use less of in order to save the ecology of earth, the planet she needs to sustain life. This is the crux of the problem—selfishness.

Do you realize that it is the good Ol' U. S. of A. that is destroying earth. We're not the only cause but our sizzling consumer based society is destroying it more quickly and thoroughly than the other western nations. And, God help us all, the third world debtor nations can't wait to get into the fray with their own brand of consumerism.

Guess who is pushing the Dow Jones up and up and up, spiraling the economy to mountain highs? It is our old friend, that newly, self-defined, prosperous, modern, evil one. An evil one who will be grabbing souls right and left as soon as they *must* have more and more and more. But this more and more and more is destroying the earth by using and heating it up into faster and faster growth. The evil one is laughing all the way to the bank, his kind of bank.

Greed is becoming the normal state of affairs in America. Don't feel bad, I am as subject to much of this greed as you are. I can't count the times I have been caught up in wanting more money with the excuse, "It's so I can help other people." I had an old copy of the United States Constitution that I starting thinking might be valuable. I started dreaming of the millions I could spend, of course, I would give half away. It was all a lie but I fell for it hook-line-and-sinker. Later, I felt somehow poorer than I had been.

I am afraid that our push to succeed, the energy that made America great, has now distorted itself to such a degree that it has become the push to 'succeed at all costs.' Our modern mantra is also our road to destruction. Our push towards success, money, fame, grows but never do we ask, success on top of who? Money accumulated for what? Fame for what? Power over who? Let me restate the modern quote from Jesus here:

> …No one person can go forward unless he or she helps the others who temporarily remain. It is a law of evolution, the opposite is selfishness and greed.[57]

Well we all need to live, you might argue. And you would be right. We all need the basic substances for life plus entertainment and education and other pursuits. I suppose the problem rises in degree—how much of these normal pursuits beyond the basic do you need? The answer is different for everyone. I know many people who crave 'things.' They need to know they are surrounded by their things. Whether beautiful things, or collected things, or useful things or stylish things; it doesn't matter, but in a future world gone mad 'things' will no longer have much meaning. It would be nice if a few people would see this fact sooner than later. It might help save our planet.

I was feeling upset and lonely tonight, sorry for myself and angry at heaven for not pulling miracles out of its hat for me. For Jesus sake, I tried to pull myself together because he had told me we would go someplace tonight. I suggested that we wait another night.

"No." Jesus said.

This surprised me and shook me out of my fatigue. "What?" Jesus has never told me "No" before, this must really be a super event but my questions were left unanswered except for the warning that the visit would not be what I expected.

So we stood on a world, where or when I didn't know, but I trusted Jesus decision to bring me here to this beautiful place. The soil was black but the sky was blacker. A million scattered rock edges shined a silvery

---

57 *Cosmic Voyage*

green reflecting the light of a hidden moon, I thought, until Jesus told me the moon wasn't causing the rocks to glow. He said that it was internal poisoning - radioactive poisoning to be exact.

I now saw that we stood on radioactive black, loam, soil radiating its poison upwards into a beautiful patterned light show. In the distance the green white glow became more obviously unnatural. This whole, large flat area, I now noticed, was absent of people or any other moving animal life.

Jesus bent down next to a plant and touched a very dark leaf with glowing green edges. The plant was growing in a round hump, its leaves falling over and around that somewhat resembled a hosta plant. The leaf crumbled to dust as Jesus' hand touched it. Its green-black beauty had been dissolved in an instant, to me it looked like the whole plant shriveled up in a death throb. Looking closer at the soil I noticed what looked like veins growing through out and beneath our feet. I imagined them as death fingers reaching out further and further to kill and grab. .

This must have been a catastrophe of great proportions. I imagined much death and destruction of life and shuddered that such disaster could happen on any world.

"It's such a large, dead area."

"Yes, a whole continent."

"Did these people have a war?"

"No, an accident caused this blight."

I thought the results were just as bad as any war could be. As we moved across the dead landscape, I noticed one or two people far off in the distance. They were wearing protective clothing that covered their whole bodies. The edges of the clothing glowed with a greenish phosphorous light so I assumed they must have been collecting soil samples.

"It wasn't always this huge," Jesus said. "It is growing."

"Growing?" How can radioactive soil grow? I thought about it for a minute. I had heard of chain reactions possibly growing and reaching down into the earth but this slow growth seemed too tame for a chain reaction, which I thought, would sort of explode. But, then, I am ignorant about this whole body of knowledge.

"Could it be some type of water osmosis making it grow.

"No."

"Is it living as it grows?"

"Yes. Jesus told me.

He explained that it is alive in the tiny soil organisms that evolved after the radioactive accident. The survivors incorporated the contaminants into their system of reproduction. At present, they are thriving, growing, and spreading, slowly but inevitably killing out all the normal fauna. The organism's growth can't be stopped. It is eating the world.

The people have learned to travel to their moon so they could someday escape the disaster that is spreading on their world and consuming it. On the moon they dig out cells to live in for themselves and their future decedents. They don't have a Mars (I couldn't help my sigh of relief at hearing they have no Mars) or other close planet, they only have a dry, cold, dead moon. No one is sure if they will succeed past the next few generations. Many of these people believe that moving to their moon is the only solution.

"There is some other solution?"

"Yes and we will talk about that at another time."

"But what world is this? It isn't earth?"

"No,"

Jesus has implied that earth could have its own form of radioactive disaster someday, but not this day. "It's not earth," I heaved another sigh. "I have never been here before."

"Yes, you have, many times. This is Silver World."

"What? Silver World? The world filled with beautiful glass people who worship God in soft green forests beneath a silver sky. Silver people with silver wings?"

Jesus remained silent because he knew my questions were a rhetorical reaction to beauty being rubbed and smeared against reality. The truth hurt. I felt like crying.

"There is more," he sighed, "But it will wait for another time."

THE SILENT WAR

We are already at war; many of us just don't know it because it is a silent, subtle, sneaky war, taking place between friends and enemies, mind-to-mind and heart to heart. Betrayals and schemes are common, friends are turned inside out and revealed to be something else. Most of this is caused by fear. Fear of not belonging, fear of loosing what we have, fear of being exposed, fear of change. This silent war being fought today is only a symptom of the next battle, the real one, Armageddon. A war that will not be fought on any battle field as many suppose, but mind to mind, within our hearts and souls. Jesus nods as I write these words. You might ask how this will be accomplished, even how it could get worse, but my guess is that evil's taunts will become stronger and harder to turn away from, harder to notice the malevolence inside them, the untruths that they sow. Will evil ever cease?

A number of days ago, after I had a horrible dream of hiding from a political system that was threatening to take over the world, Jesus told me that I had been in Nazi Germany during World War ll. He added that I had "suffered greatly." I didn't want to know any more than that, especially after that bad dream except that Jesus also told me he was instrumental in saving me. I wouldn't mention any of this here but I learned something of vital importance along with the other information. Jesus said, "It will never get as bad again." His implication was that in Nazi Germany evil had reached its final apex, an apex that rose to the surface, choking nations, destroying whole nationalities, and enslaving races. If Hitler had won the war, the whole world would have looked like the Southern United States during the slave debacle. Perhaps all people with dark hair or skin or some other obvious trait would have been dehumanized beneath Hitler. The holocaust consolidated and mirrored in modern times how slavery affected the souls of perpetuators and victims alike a hundred fifty years earlier.

Now, in the present, evil hasn't gone away, it just moves insidiously through our society only erupting to the surface now and then in bloodshed. We hardly notice the depth of its virulence except when we read about another shooting in the newspaper after the damage has seeped into a person's mind as insanity or injury, which the person then twisted into dislike, hate, and finally, attack.

One thing about evil that is very frightening is that we need to be right all the time. We humans cannot face wrong opinions of our beliefs or actions done in the name of wrong ideas. I think about the women in Nazi Germany who must have kept telling themselves, convincing themselves, that everything was ok and normal, that during war these things happened and then proceeded to put evidence in place to insure their own opinion. The same thing happened a hundred years ago as happened fifty. People assured themselves how right they were to believe and use slaves. They wrote laws to prove themselves good citizens while they labeled other people sub-human. Does evil over-reach itself every fifty years? I don't know, we'd need to check back through history. Regardless, we tend to put a candy coating on our sins, or point our fingers at every one else, so we don't need to face what we wrought.

What is evil or malevolence? How do we recognize it? If it cloaks itself in fake clothing all the time, how do we know it for what it is? Some people ask, "Is it really there?" Humans have always associated evil with darkness because all its symptoms lay on the dark side: it demeans the spirit, spreads hate and dislike, amplifies jealously, and intensifies selfishness. Light does just the opposite, it feels good to share with other people, our spirit feels raised up, and we find comfort in being loved, in sharing, in giving. Evil can't exist in the light, which is why a prayer or even a kind word or hug can send evil scurrying back down into its dark sewer. So simple a solution yet often so hard to put into actual practice.

I was stupefied to read in the religious encyclopedia one definition of evil as "banal." That evil could be, as banal as following orders or not thinking about the consequences of actions. Many people on trial after the Holocaust used the argument that under a dictatorship they had no choice but to follow orders. This is how we can get so caught up and entangled before we feel its sting, because we always feel its sting when it comes back on us.

Modern life tends to hide the steps down the sewer until we have already fallen between the cracks. It's often hard for us to recognize when we're on the right side, the side of good. At what point do we have too much power or riches or anger, at what point does malevolence overgrow our hearts. When did we step over the line to the other side. Wouldn't we all like to have a definite line drawn across our path that tells us we must stop now, go no further or you will be on the wrong side, the side of evil, that your new marching orders will spiral you downward towards damnation. If only it was easy but its not.

The warning signs are there though. You can look in any direction and see spitefulness at work. Overt and subtle happenings that impinge on all our lives. You can also recognize those people who are most easily influenced by evil's pull. People who have a deep-seated need to feel powerful, who crave riches, who need high status, or hunger after anyone or anything too intensely. It is easy to see that people who drink a great deal have let down their guard and the same could be said for any type of addictive substance, people on crack haven't just let their guard down, they have stepped into evil's embrace. But aren't we only talking about ignorance and incompetence at life, stupid acts that finally turn into disaster for that person and those around them. Maybe, but this slacking off on morals and creeping in of ignorance applies to the destruction of our society too. It is up to us to halt its progress because if we continue this downward spiral into chaos our grandchildren's children will never forgive us.

My granddaughter told me something while visiting during the thanksgiving holiday. She has a pimple on her scalp that she didn't have two weeks ago. She showed me where. I have a pimple in the same spot-left side of temple. We aren't talking genetics here, I remember many years ago when I found it and knew it didn't belong there although I finally accepted its presence. When I learned that she had one too, I was freaked out with worry. It upset me that my grandchild, and perhaps everyone, has this beacon in their head. I guess that's what it is, I don't really know. It is such a small item but with such mind boggling, potential for misuse that I was livid with anger. I knew where it came from, I knew who put it there. I knew that Jesus also knows the children of the future so I asked him about it.

He told me, "Heaven doesn't need it. It is evil's attempt to copy heaven." He also told me that heaven doesn't work that way that the war is intensifying. It is very important that we grow in spirituality soon, "Evil is getting desperate at my coming."

My anger evaporated finally because there wasn't anything I could do about it. I am not even sure if I am on the right track about its purpose or composition. It may even be made out of real flesh to camouflage its existence. Check your own head, your left forehead, diagonally from your eye. Probably half the people in the United States have a similar mark someplace on their body.

I was fascinated to read in Courtney's book, Cosmic Voyage, what he says about the evil being he sees in one of his remote viewings. It is an amorphously shaped dark-light being and Courtney actually enters its mind. He goes to a subspace area of chaos searching for external agents to the problem of the Grays and finds a layer of subspace with tremendous connotations and chaos that is almost over whelming. He explains that they are the Grays before birth who must take orders from an evil leader. I don't know if this is evil one or just some being who is evil but his next statements are as interesting as they are applicable.

> Strangely, they had been ordered to self-indulge and destroy (both in subspace and after physical birth). Indeed, I entered its mind only to find that it has an extremely dark mind.

Something was wrong here. It was as if the being was psychologically ill. To begin with, it had a pathological fear of dying. It
seemed to think that military fighting and conquest was
needed in order to survive. It knew that mistakes had been
made, and it was afraid of punishment. The leader seemed
unable to devise a plan for reconciliation—fear prevented it.
Then it became clear to me: this leader was a terrorist…the
Grey souls were being held as hostages during the crisis. He was
using them against the others in the realm. The dark mind
wanted a negotiated settlement that would establish its right of
personality survival, but with changes. It wanted control over
its own dominion. It wanted to establish itself as a sovereign —
a dictator. Indeed, the leader desired worship (of itself). [58]

Courtney then states that the being descended into his office as a dark
shape and then dismissed him as if he was just a small fry.[59]

Jesus and I have talked about these Grays, our ancestors, before, and I
asked why some are treating people so harshly, sneaking up on them at
night and taking them away like zombies then bringing them back. Why
didn't they just ask for what they need before abducting people? Why were
they doing it? Jesus answer was that the situation resembled our present
day morality, some people disagree and side with evil. He promised that
only a few worked for the evil one, which was comforting and satisfied me
at that time. But some people perceive them as acting out a necessary, evil
like forcing a child to get a shot at the doctors? I can't help feeling that a
rotten core hangs around any setup of this nature, even if good is the ultimate aim. I don't wish to be a part of un-cooperative selection. Ask me

---

[58] Cosmic Voyage, p 135.
[59] Cosmic Voyage, pp 136-137

and I may well agree to give what ever is needed but don't treat me like an unthinking head of cattle in the cow pasture.

Jesus laughed when he informed me that the other night I told these Grays how angry I was at their antics. I don't remember any of this, meeting them or what I said but I hope it was ripe with feeling. Though perhaps, like Courtney says they are just following orders from the evil one, they are themselves zombies.

The subject of the last page probably disgusted a lot of people who 'don't believe in that kind of stuff.' Half of me don't believe in it either. But I know how maliciousness works. I have seen it worm itself into a mind and twist it against me or someone else.

I have noticed certain steps that we seem to go through before we fail in our efforts to surpass malevolence. One scheme could go like this:

- We feel a lack or depravity,
- We begin craving something that we believe will satisfy this need,
- We often hide the craving or act out of pride,
- Then meet a group of like peers,
- The act or satisfying the craving is acceptable by the group,
- The group feels togetherness and feeds itself and emotions of comrade,
- Other people are against group because they are against this specific behavior,
- Someone in the group makes a request that you do something towards helping your group.
- You act out in some form in order to brag to group,
- But the next request becomes a necessity,
- You must do it if you are to stay in good standing in group,
- Usually this request is a small act against someone outside group,

- You rationalize that it is ok if you can, eventually, your rationalize each action's value
- You are now bought and bound by evil.

From a small step to the last you have now fallen in the thrall of evil, so far that your next act may be to physically harm another person for the groups sake. Or to save yourself from discovery of what you have already did. Only God's forgiveness can save you now.

But ignorance is easy to fall into. Unless we can perceive and put a halt or limit our own wants and needs, even a spiritual person can fall into evil's grip. I need to be ever vigilant and keep in mind that Jesus visual presence is not something to crave or I too can fall off the edge.

Lately someone has spoken and showed himself for an instant who looks like Jesus but who I think is fake-why? Don't know exactly. This happened in church. He seemed hard and unyielding and said." I don't like that prayer." The church had been saying the Our Father the most common and well-known prayer. I realized it wasn't Jesus but not because of his statement of dislike for the Lord's Prayer. I know myself, and am aware of my own strictures and so does Jesus. Would he speak in such a manner? Jesus has said many odd, strange things to me that turns our culture upside-down, enough to shake anyone's narrow mindedness or stand their faith up side down, but this seemed out of character. The personality didn't seem to fit. I think if it would have been Jesus he would have made a statement about how we said the prayer, not that he didn't like it. Jesus would have said that we need to say it more with our hearts. Then again, this prayer above all others joins people together into one group as we hold hands, and sing. I don't think Jesus would have made a statement against this prayer. So don't worry, just try to think of the words more. Jesus is very tolerant; I believe he would slowly break our hold on an idea we loved not abruptly shatter it.

Even an angry Jesus still feels like Jesus. His personality stays intact. Jesus is not usually against something that doesn't hurt anyone. Jesus is for togetherness, love, unity. So the statement in church wasn't from Jesus. I am showing you this self-argument so you can see my dilemma of making a quick decision whether it is Jesus talking or some one imitating him. Besides Jesus might leave me hanging with questions, but always with kindness so I will struggle with the quandary and find the answer myself. Let me tell you something Jesus told me about the evil one. I asked if he could act good in order to deceive us.

Jesus laughed and said, "He can't."

So Jesus agrees with what Courtney found in this beings mind, that he is defective. Nevertheless, we must stay diligent, and never underestimate its cunning nature, the imitator is an expert at what he does. The reason I am telling you about this is so you can be warned not to believe everything you see and hear or even feel. Look within yourself and your own needs to find the truth, then take care.

I am certainly not immune to evil's whiles. I have watched as other people throw their dislike or anger at me and sometimes I at them. Even so, I know through long experience with corruption, that I need to try to overlook their actions. I have learned the lesson Jesus taught us long ago, to turn the other cheek. I have had to because not to do so, opens my mind to hate. Hate is the evil one entombed inside the mind.

We all see evil every day in the news. We can see the scenario. Someone builds up dislike and anger for whatever reason. He gets confronted by this person who has hurt him, he has a lot of guns he has been collecting, suddenly his anger flares up, the guns are available, he hurries to the place and begins shooting. Later, during the trial, he wakes up and wonders what made him so angry and mad. He now can't find any reason for his anger. Sometimes we make it easy for evil to get inside and do its dirty work of twisting our minds to do his bidding.

One night many years ago, evil stepped into my mind and threatened me with a promise. He said "You will never have a lover or husband again.

You will die first." At that time I was young and still pretty and thin, so I didn't believe the voice. But so far it has proved to be the case.

Recently when I asked Jesus why evil has won so far in my life he answers, "Evil has not and will not win." He told me that I would get married again some day. For most of my life, I was in love with love. A real love for Jesus has overcome this defect and satisfied my hunger as well as broadened my abilities to love other people. My love for Jesus is spiritual which leaves room for social love, although Jesus will always be the most important person in my life, and any mate will need to accept this. I keep remembering what Jesus said to me once that "All will be restored."

I don't think evil will win either. My book proves that. I have come to the conclusion that evil has intensified its efforts against me specifically because of this book. For a long time, I felt confused because I didn't know why I kept getting attacked by evil while other people seemed to thrive until I began writing this book. Of course, the evil one knew that I would write these words some day and began its efforts against me long before the fact. Take heart from this lesson, if you seem singled out by fate, perhaps it is because you will do something good one day. I think this book will have a positive impact and influence on changing the world for the better, so much so, that the evil one has tried to destroy my credibility. He has used rumors, personal attacks, and my own lack of self-esteem and tried to keep me from gainful employment. He has tried to destroy my character by any means possible; yet, I have persevered.

If you feel evil's wrath, you are not alone. I have felt evil's sting over and over and I often wondered what it's rational is, what purpose could it possible have for destroying lives.

Jesus tells me that, "I already know." He also said, " You will come face to face with evil."

"Oh no. I can't even imagine what Jesus means by that statement. But "No, not that, I can't face evil," I cry out, "I don't want to meet evil." But silence greets my call. At some other time I intend to discuss this question with Jesus I promise myself, but I keep forgetting to ask.

But whether you believe in an evil being and his workers or not, you should believe in radical evil. It exists and must be dealt with. We must minimize its grip on our world somehow.[60] Jeffery Russell asks and answers many questions in his excellent book, The Prince of Darkness. Here is a quote from the book:

> If the Devil does exist, what is he? If the concept has any meaning at all, he is the traditional Prince of Darkness, a mighty person with intelligence and will whose energies are bent on the destruction of the cosmos and the misery of its creatures. He is the personification of radical evil, and he can never be irrelevant because humans have always sought to understand and to confront that evil. That search, that need, is a sign that meaning is there, however obscurely it seems to be hidden from the intellect.

He then goes on to say that "perhaps love can do what the intellect cannot." Most of us certainly agree.[61]

The big question, of course, is radical evil, is there such a thing and Jesus answers that question in the affirmative. Radical evil means evil as a cause in itself. This is the answer against evil, as we evolve and grow spiritually we become less and less weakened by evil. In the end because as growing beings we keep evolving, evil must loose out. I am myself aghast at my past capacity for evil. When I was younger, my personal feelings were very self-centered. This must be the case with most youth. Youth must be ignorant by necessity. But on the other hand, youngsters have the least ability to see anything wrong with the world. I love their innocence and exuberance and love of life. They have no inkling of what may be in

---

[60] Paraphrased *in The Prince of Darkness*
[61] *The Prince of Darkness*, page 176

store for them as they grow into adulthood and I certainly am not going to disillusion them. So we will leave evil to us thinkers and complainers.

Jesus has told me that evil is a force in the universe, a psyche force in space that centers on emotional nodes like earth because earth is so immature. How is this force conjoined with God? Is it like dark against light? Could it be called a natural force? Is it necessary? What I saw out in space a few years ago during meditation was, I believe, a being of gigantic, universal, radical evil. Even now I shudder to remember this dark force. Does it permeate earth space somewhat like a god? Does it direct certain beings on and off earth? Can it affect only people on earth? I don't believe so. From what I have seen of other peoples and worlds, with little exception, all intelligent beings seem to be more or less in the same boat regarding the temptation of evil. This is disturbing, to be sure, but you may derive some hope and comfort to learn as I have that evil cannot penetrate God's golden light, that Highly Evolved Beings are higher up than evil, and that there are some worlds where evil is almost non-existent. Evil cannot enter all doors. The Bubble Worlds Jesus and I visited were one example of a civilization where evil does not penetrate.

The other night we went to such a strange place in the universe that I got stressed out very quickly and we needed to leave. We saw red blobs surrounded by dark space, as we moved closer they became orange transparent bubbles floating around a central star. It was too much for me. Jesus said he would bring be back to this group of worlds because there was something specific he wanted to show me.

We went back later and I got a better look at the bubbles. They still looked like bubbles, bright red circles floating in dark space around a central star, then as we moved closer to one of the bubbles, the bright red color dissolved into a reddish orange transparent sphere. We moved up to the orange sphere and pushed through its skin like it was a membrane.

Inside was busy with floating forms of different sizes and some of the floating or flying forms looked like small people traveling up and down and sideways as lightly as any bird or butterfly. Everything I could see inside the bubble looked like it was in free fall, I mean nothing was anchored to any floor because there wasn't any floor to anchor to. Objects were moving seemingly in any direction or place they wanted to go and it was very confusing to my earth eyes. Plus, it was huge, it could no longer be described as a bubble but an inside-out world. Its size was so vast I couldn't see any sides or top or bottom.

Well everything floated by us or we floated by it, one object was a round floating abode or dwelling. Jesus told me that these dwelling places weren't owned by any of the people. They were used by anyone who desired to stop and rest for a time or who felt like taking a nap then sleeping or eating if they choose. Like a floating bed and breakfast only free, or at least, not paid for in a monetary sense. I presume there was some system setup where everyone cooperated to provide substance for all.

Nothing was crowded even with all the parts and parcels and abodes moving willy-nilly around. We moved to the front of two huge pillars with a shimmering multicolored soap-film wall between them, this, Jesus told me, was their mode of transportation through the universe.

If they choose, this soap film doorway or transportation node would even take them to Nexus. One of its links was to the tunnel transport system Jesus and I had visited on another evening, the one that seemed made of curtains filled with different colors. Many peoples on different worlds have these transportation systems they use to travel throughout the universe. Jesus then showed me a vision of transportation paths through the universe like the flower pattern in a multi-dimensional lace curtain. It went on forever over and under and around itself. This super-highway wasn't physical, but made out of veins of light or some kind of ethereal-like matter running and flowing throughout space. Jesus mentioned that some systems have been mapped by a few civilizations but no civilization has learned the whole of it yet, or ever can. Which brings up the question, "Are these paths natural or man-made?" I remembered to ask Jesus this question later and his answer was "Neither."

Just before our next visit, Jesus explained that we would always stay invisible in the Bubble Worlds. He didn't' explain why but I later understood that the reason was so as not to infringe on the people's psyche or minds who inhabited these worlds. They were very highly evolved and lived gentile lives. I wondered if even my thoughts, being lowly and not very highly evolved, would disturb their equanimity. So Jesus must have blocked our conversations from their awareness. I understood better how highly evolved these people were as I traveled their world. At one point I asked if we were going to visit a place of worship in the bubble and Jesus answered, "No, these people don't worship God or the universe through ritual." He explained that they live their reverence during each moment of their life, that every act, whether they are playing, eating, working, or learning is a form of devotion.

As Jesus lead me around inside the bubble world I saw so many strange and wonderful shapes and forms of life, too numerous to mention here except for the few that were so amazing they stay in my mind even today. We visited a lake that was round, I don't mean round and flat, I mean round like in circle, like a ball. It was incased it its own bubble skin. He pointed out large multicolored flowers that grew in round balls too that floated around. He said that the people living in this sphere choose to have a lot of flowers and color around them.

The bubble had a blue sky with clouds in a few areas and in other areas there was what seemed to be strings or twisted regions with different color of atmospheres and degree of light. I understood that the people could travel to areas of daylight or night or even a season of spring or summer whenever they chose. I saw fog or mist strings swirling gently around in some places and thought perhaps they gave the world variety as well as decoration.

What Jesus wanted to show me most were the people who inhabited this paradise. They flew around their world as easily as birds or butterflies would travel from one flower to another. At first, I only caught glimpses of them from a far off view and thought they were birds. But they were small people who looked earth normal in every way except that they were floating and flying. They were tiny with long hair, both men and women wore their hair extremely long, in stripes of different weird colors, colors I can't easily put a name to, colors like chartreuse, mauve, sea-green. Their hair flowed out around and behind them as they danced through the air. On a number of people, their pubic hair showed and was colored and decorated as wildly as their head hair. They all wore vary bright colored costumes. Their clothing was like the wind, flowing in strips of different colors so it was confusing looking at a person and wondering what part was person, what part hair, or just decoration. Jesus said the people in this bubble delighted in odd colors and flowers for decoration.

While in some of the other bubbles or worlds, each half the size of earth I learned later, people stayed nude. Some people had changed themselves genetically so that their wings or flaps become a permanent part of their body decoration. Here in this bubble the people chose to wear their wings as decorated attachments, which to me looked like they were made out of clear plastic with beautiful abstract designs painted on them. They looked like a fashion item, as a part their clothing that could be changed at will. The wings were different sizes and kinds too. Some were shaped like butterfly wings and some small ones that reached from wrist to waist. The purpose of the flaps or wings was maneuverability, not flight, because there was no gravity here.

The people were experts at odd turns and twists and soaring and stopping in mid air. They seemed to me to be a playful, happy, and free people. I never saw a person stand on a solid surface and walk, but perhaps there wasn't any straight flat surface.

I wondered how they grew their food and asked Jesus. He explained that they have a central sun (self made?) and that their food is grown in bundles of trees and earth. He added that they used to devote whole bubbles to agriculture but they learned it was better to scatter their farms throughout each bubble for variety and ease. I supposed it also would be safer to scatter the wealth of produce but then doubted if these people needed to worry about safety. It didn't look as if they had any bad vibes or enemies inside or out. Jesus agreed with this sentiment by telling me that no evil could penetrate here.

The colorful, little scattered forms I found most fascinating were their birds, they served as the cleaning system. These vacuum cleaner birds were of varied designs and sizes, some very small, and like everything on this world, wore bright colored feathers. I watched as one flew at a floating item and scooped it up in its mouth. I supposed it knew what to eat just like any earth bird would know what to eat and what to leave alone. And since everything floats here, I had the sensation that I was under water because of the constant movement of round abodes and rivers and flowers and bubbles that kept floating around us. There must always be food for the picking, and crumbs left floating to feed the birds. Perhaps they could scoop up non-food items too, don't know but it makes good sense. I couldn't' see if the birds had real feathers or not, it didn't look like they had wings like a normal bird would so I don't know what propelled their movement. They looked more like fish twirling and curling up and dashing around, certainly they were perfectly fit for the job they were doing.

With everything moving, turning and twisting and flying it soon became too much for my senses to take in. Especially at the round lake where I watched a person dive splashing into the water, turn and flip then dive back up into the sky. What a way to take a bath. I suggested it was time to go and Jesus agreed. I hoped to visit again, and thought I wouldn't get as lightheaded next time.

Today Jesus told me that we would visit a place that is worse [or just as bad] than the radioactive accident. He said he wants to speed up our visits and get to the real reason for our travels.

I just read how some Gray people used humans as ginny pigs, controlling our minds, creating robots, turning people into robots. There are many reports of this happening. The good ones always give people a choice, the other side does not give choices, and they treat people as if they had no merit or worth. I had a premonition that I would visit a similar horror with Jesus tonight.

It didn't seem so horrible. First. we revisited a number of places on Silver World. We went to the leader's office that was high in one of their cities and watched some people talking and arguing. Even I could see the anger and discord between the people in the room. After the visitors left, the leader walked over to the large window and stood looking out over the city. We went back to the original forest glen of our first visit. Jesus reminded me of the many scattered forest areas that these people use for worship, then mentioned the hammer blow, "Listening devices, for the purpose of spying, are intermixed between the trees and bushes of every forest glen."

He quickly added that the leaders didn't use strong-arm tactics against the people, they aren't put in jail, shot, or physically abused in any way. Instead a subtle propaganda has been used against them, propaganda created from information during worship gatherings. Worship gathering for these people is a valuable means of communication and joining of ideas. Gathering for ritual prayer and discussion has been increasing lately after stagnating for many years. Their gatherings in the forest is not only a means of worship of God but also has the connotation of togetherness on specific ideas. I couldn't think of an analogy like it on earth, but I understood that important decisions by ordinary citizens were made at these meetings, somewhat like our voting method.

The leaders want to relocate all the people to the moon. This would give them complete control over the people, their reproductive rate, their status into work groups, and their food rationing. The people's complete life style could then be manipulated, in their supposed best interests, by the leaders in power. This is the reason for the listening devices. The leaders who direct this world are pitting one group against another in an attempt to maneuver them to accepting the moon position. They have turned many of the people to their way of thinking.

But the leaders, themselves, are being used by an evil force, our old friend and antagonist? The evil one has taunted them with the dream of power and convinced them that there is no going back to the old natural way of life, that their future lays in technological solutions. They now believe that worship and gatherings will not save them, that even that beauty is old fashioned, that they have outgrown their world and the next choice for progress is a move to the moon. They believe strongly that they are right.

But many people want to hold fast to their world, to fight the blight and beat it back. All the people feel the shame as they watch the other world continent die, but not all want to fight. They hope, at the least, to preserve a few of their sacred green forests. Some people hope and believe that a concerted effort and concentration of mental energy will change the course of the blight that threatens their world.

"They are right," Jesus said. But then he added that it wouldn't be easy, that it would take everyone on the world working together with love and devotion and understanding to effectively turn the blight around. The battle is subtle with each side believing they are right. Practical people don't believe in mental power or energy, they then prove their correctness by subverting the mental power around them through skepticism and cynicism.

Young people are entering the debate and joining the gatherings. Worship by the young has increased tremendously since the blight disaster was admitted. Diverse groups are trying to increase their understanding of the mental energy that would be necessary for change. The groups who believe that the blight can be turned back, also believe that loss of mental togetherness caused the problem in the first place. Too great a dependence on modern technology, some have come to understand, may have caused the divisions and rifts between the people in the first place.

Their prophets are spreading the belief in mental energy and heaven is influencing the prophets in this knowledge and wisdom, and has been for quite some time. Heaven is everywhere active on worlds that are in need of help, especially during fragile, historical turning points of world evolution. This is obvious if we search back through our own religious history.

This might be a good place to mention what Jesus told me one night about Joan of Arc; I was watching a program about her life and refused to watch the ending when he said, "She didn't burn." I implied from his words that he saved her at the last minute by lifting her into heaven. I know your relief is as great as mine.

Cosmic Voyager

So many times I question what is going on. I should get a doubt trophy. But this morning before church Jesus presence was so strong that there wasn't an inch of doubt left in me. His authority and love poured out as if from a never-ending fountain. He repeated what he has said many times, "Everything I tell you is true. It is all true."

True; nevertheless, it can be tiring with worry and hope. I told Jesus I would be happy some day to be back with him. "I need a rest."

Jesus said, "Rest in me now."

I put up my hands and Jesus stood in front of me and became a golden cross that kept expanding until it covered me and went beyond me. I kept saying, "Oh, it is so beautiful, so grand" I was looking at a golden swirling universe inside my dinning room. It was then that I realized that Jesus was God. That at this second I, little nothingness me, was joined with God. We were one at that moment. I realized something else too, we are all swimming in a God-sea. We are God. The golden moment dissipated because it was too intense for me to stay longer.

I suddenly began wondering if we all had three parts like Jesus, father, son, and Holy Spirit so I asked Jesus. "Are we all god, people, and spirit together?"

"Yes, write it down," he told me. So I wrote it down before I left for church. Nothing more was said about it but it seems self-explanatory. We are all part of God's ground of being, we all have physical bodies, and we all have souls or psyches. It is up to us to touch base with our different aspects and learn to know them.

Another time when I was very tired, tired of trying and pushing and writing, God spoke to me. I had complained that I felt finished with the world, that I was always on the bottom, struggling, that I didn't have a friend or companion so I wanted off this earth for good, I really wanted God to end it for me.

Suddenly, God said to me, "After you finish writing the mystery book, you can leave if you still want to." I was surprised. Another time when I worried that a full time job wouldn't leave me enough time to write, God spoke by saying, "Write it."

I can't imagine what will be worth writing in a mystery novel that even God agrees that I should write it. Perhaps I mixed up the intent, God may have been referring to this book. I intend the theme of the mystery novel to be good verses evil and how evil sneaks its way into and through us, turning even good people against God, which is not an unusual theme in fiction novels. I do agree that these Travel books are important enough to require that I stick with it. The message needs to be said and Jesus wants me to say it. But I am running out of superlatives when I think of God wanting me to write a murder mystery. It is almost funny but I am afraid to laugh. Then I do laugh because sometimes I get Jesus and God mixed up. Jesus spoke and said, "That is ok."

Sometimes when Jesus speaks, I turn around and ask, "Where are you." As if I expect him to standing there every time he speaks. He is not. Most often he speaks from beside me or inside my mind. I think I have solved that puzzle though; I may understand how he can be with me and you at the same time. He sends his mind out to touch us, all of us. His spirit can dwell within all of us because he sends it there from where he is. I reason it like this, that if even my little mind can send a thought or emotion to someone else, ESP is becoming a well-known quality, then imagine how greatly more powerful Jesus' mind is and how more easily he would send his thoughts to us. That may be how his spirit can be present within each of us and, at the same time, be in numerous other places in the universe. I suspect that even we can do it or will be able to some day. He has tried to teach me to expand my mind outwards in all directions at once; though, I am still unable to do it well, but keep trying. Even so, I am not able or don't choose to go into other people's minds because I feel like I would be invading their privacy, not so Jesus because he knows everything as God. Also, don't worry about Jesus' ability to be everywhere, Jesus assures me that if everyone began traveling and talking to him; there would be enough of himself for everyone, enough to guide each and every person forward. Ah, what a wonderful quandary that would be.

As it is, I feel guilty because so many nights I talk to Jesus about myself that I forget to pray. I seem to go through long periods of selfishness. Though I believe talking with Jesus is a form of prayer; still, I should be thinking of other people not myself all the time. This night, I caught myself going in circles, stuck on my own problems, so I pulled out of my self-morass and began to pray for others. I wanted to pray for the people in Afghanistan and Mozambique tonight. I read a quote in the paper that hurt me badly. An Afghanistan man said, "They treat us like dogs." He was referring to the Taliban, which is fighting a war while leaving its own people to go hungry.. Mozambique had just flooded for the third time in two weeks and there is a growing draught in India, plus Africa still has multiple wars going on. War devastates a people to mere existence. There is no lack of people in need of prayers.

I don't know how valuable our prayers are at the moment; even with the help of angels we seem unable to gather enough concerted effort to push back the Taliban or the hundred little dictators in Africa. But we will some day. Jesus said, "We will need to." We will fight a war of good against evil. This must mean turning corrupt governments up side down and cleaning house within our own. Idealistic dreams, for now all we can do is pray. But how? I realize that I am still not sure how Jesus wants us to pray.

"How should we pray?" I asked Jesus. "How do you want us to pray? With spoken words, reading prayers, emotional love, sending feelings, mantras, or mind travel so we can hug people."

His answer was, "Any way you can, any way you want."

We can feel assured that Jesus will make our prayers as valid as possible. Our love and concern calls on Jesus to help. Our prayers call on Jesus to use his power. When Jesus was alive he could heal the sick, drive out evil, feed the hungry, absolve sin, raise the dead, correct deformities, and raise himself from the dead. So the prayers and thoughts that flow from our mind through Jesus' to help someone are certainly going to the right place. As I was thinking these many thoughts about Jesus and prayer, Jesus said, "I still have those powers."

I believe Jesus will show us he still has these powers, perhaps more now than in the past. I used to think it was because he was traveling closer but now I think it may be because we are growing closer to him. Does that make him stronger or his presence stronger and more able to affect our well-being? I remember what he told me once, "We must step-up your spirituality" Jesus and all of heaven is trying to increase our faith and spiritual growth to save our future.

I know I have mentioned before that when I refer to heaven I mean the highly evolved beings who work for God and Jesus and Mary, who I often think of as the female aspect of God. I hope I don't throw you off by talking to Jesus and talking to God and then getting answers as though from different places. I do this because I need to. In order to understand Jesus I need to think of him as a person, a man who I can relate to, though, as I grow further in wisdom I find God can be recognizable as a person as well. Jesus doesn't seem to mind. Perhaps Jesus is such a highly evolved person that he is God. He told me once that he was as much God as most of us could understand at this level of our evolution. So for most earthly purposes, Jesus is God, as much God as we can handle. I remember when Jesus told me to call him Lord. Now I think of Jesus as Lord of Space and Time. A Lord who knows and can take me to any place in the universe. That is God enough for me. A Cosmic God.

I was delightfully surprised to read God referred to as "A Cosmic Voyager," in the book *Divine Encounters* by Zacharia Sitchin. He is a professional linguist so when he talked about Olam as mentioned in the Bible as meaning *many worlds* I understood it as the place I visited, God's World. Sitchin has used many new ideas and linguistic interpretations to re-read and re-interpret the Bible. I have paraphrased a small part of his interpretations of the words Olam.[62] You would need to read the book to get the full idea.

According to Sitchin, Saddai as an epithet for Yahweh is uncertain etymology. New studies suggest the word is related to shaddia, which means "mountain" in Akkadian so El Shaddai means "God of mountains." Biblical referents to Yahweh's throne stated it was located in a place called Olam. Modern translators render Olam as everlasting and forever or eternity. The Hebrew bible, more strict in precision has Olam often appearing with its root ad to denote its everlasting nature was a noun derived from a root that means disappearing: mysteriously hidden. The numerous biblical verses in which Olam appears indicates it was a physical place, not an abstraction {as everlasting} "thou art from Olam", God is from a place which is hidden.[63]

> No less eleven times the bible refers to Yahweh's abode, domain and "kingdom" using the term Olamim, the plural of olam-a domain, an abode, a kingdom that encompasses many worlds. It is an expression of Yahweh's Lordship beyond the notion of a "national God" to that of a judge of all the nations beyond the earth and beyond Nibiru, to the "Heaven of Heaven. Deuteronomy (10:14, Kings 8:27, 11 Chronicles 2:5 & 6:18) that encompasses not only the Solar System but even the distant stars (Deuteronomy 4;19, Ecclesiastes 12;2) "THIS IS THE IMAGE OF A COSMIC VOYAGER"[64]

Actually it would be more accurate to say that God is the Cosmos or God's mind roams the cosmos but even this fails our understanding

---

[62] Notes as variously taken from *Devine Encounters*, Zecharia Sitchin, Avon Books, New York, N. Y. , 1996, pp356-357.

[63] Divine Encounters, p 372.

[64] *Divine Encounters*, p 379.

because our minds are not adequate to take it all in. We must finally just accept God as God and leave it at that.

Sitchin's book was an accumulation of ideas from his first five books, *The Earth Chronicles*[65]. Heaven has implied to me that what he wrote in his books is true. I hesitate to refer to these books because some of the factual information is quite detailed, much of the detail are from the Bible and other historic sources which some scholars tend to change at every translation. Heaven's whisper may have meant that these books were true in essence, but not in every detail? Of course, Sitchin, as a scholar knows manuscripts are subject to change and must take this into account. I have often wondered if the angels told him that he is on the right track, or if heaven encouraged his books. Because he is a scientist he would probably disavow this idea. If you're curiosity drives you to want another interpretation of heaven, besides Courtney's sub-space, and my heaven filled with helping hands, read Sitchin's books.

Of course, there may be many interpretations of what heaven is, and with many layers to choose from, all interpretations could be partially right. Remember Courtney refers to heaven as subspace, I have often thought of heaven as space-plus, but all our ideas fall far short because heaven is much more than what any of us can understand including what modern science calls space/time; and certainly God or Jesus is much more than some astronaut traveling through it. You know this already if you love Jesus.

Our culture tends to belittle anything the sounds like space and aliens in the same breath, which is unfortunate because we will need an improved connotation of these concepts in the near future. The mockery of space aliens as clichés has been partially induced by the evil one. If we learn to mock what may be real and helpful to us, then we stay in his corner, perhaps doomed forever. We must realize that the next step in evolution will

---

[65] *The Earth Chronicles*, Zecharia Sitchin, The 12th Planet, Avon Books, New York, N. Y., 1978.

be through space culture and mind expansion outwards through our souls. We must learn to touch our souls, even though many of us first need to learn we have one. Remember—Armageddon will be fought inside our minds. And who knows, evolution may be selecting for the ability to survive death of the birth world, the ability finally to leave it and go forth into the universe.

As a mere glimmer of this mental tendency, I see evolution working within us at the present time. I notice we try to gather and belong to esoteric clubs. People in each kind of group believe they know each other and recognize their own kind, this is an aspect of extra-sensory perception that is waking up inside us or waking us up, however you want to look at it. But a problem arises when a specific group believes themselves to be elite and set apart. This identity sorting can be dangerous because it can drive one group against another. In other words, we humans tend to join groups, but lately, my guess is that many groups have had a certain sense of belongingness and subtle knowing between its members. Many of these groups consider themselves elite, with special powers of knowing or understanding inclusive to their group. This is not true. ESP ability is not inclusive of any specific group. This is important to know because all these groups will need to join together in the future skirmish for souls. Not only that but many churches will loosen their differences, until finally, the lovers will join together against the haters. As Jesus says, "It is necessary."

Yes, The writing is on the wall for a horrible war or disaster.

I knew opulence could cause disaster but I never thought of prosperity as dangerous. Yet, it is dangerous and pointing us towards the unending or final disaster. The history books remember the disasters of the 30's, the Dust Bowl, The Stock Market Crash, the Depression. The effects were so devastating that many older citizens I've taken care of still hoard tissue paper, Kleenex, and other paper products that were so scarce during that time. The point is that America has had some bad times, belt tightening times, crying times, and no one wants to go back wards or re-experience such hard times. But now in the year 2000 it looks like forward *is* backwards. Our spiraling prosperity may invite the first blow from a nation or faction within the eighty percent who are left out of it..

There are other possible disasters on the horizon. The weather patterns are changing and disasters are increasing around the globe and will continue to increase. I am sure of it because when I read about Mozambique flooding Jesus said, "These things must be." He has said that phrase to me to me a lot lately and, "More will happen." So I am warning you we can expect more bad weather conditions, which cause more travail and woe among the various populations of the world. But, maybe bad can lead to good, perhaps the growing severe problems around the world will teach us Americans to give more.

I know we are a generous nation, we help other countries, but we are not generous enough, we only give a minor fraction of the wealth, yet use up 80 to 90% of the resources. Somehow we need to develop a more equitable world economy and government. We can afford it. We are so rich that we brag about it. Our total entertainment system takes glory in this richness of ours while it should be doing just the opposite—down-crying our immature wallowing in money. Our whole society is based on materialistic wealth, on consuming and buying and the power money can buy. But, at the same time, we feel shocked when we read of atrocities people used against each other long ago, people's cruel antics, their injustice, the inquisition, the torture and clash of swords, we wonder how any human could have acted so childish. But our own children, our decedents will ask these same questions about us, they will look at our antics with a vivid, living horror and ask how we could have acted so neglectfully; how could we have so stubbornly held on to our vaporous riches, even at the cost of breathable air and life giving water.

The World Watch Institute warns that our strong economy is actually blinding us to environmental catastrophes, leading to, "rising global temperature, increasing destructive storms, melting glaciers, falling water tables, shrinking forests, and disappearing species threaten the health of the earth and its people,..."

I was reading the Detroit Free Press about women's history month and how women have finally joined congress because we have been given rights unheard of a century ago and still unreachable in a few other countries. In the same edition of the paper, there were photos of women dressed in black in Turkey and Gaza Strip trying to improve their rights. I felt proud of America for its achievement in liberty and freedom (although it still has a long way to go) and suddenly Jesus said to me, "That is why I stay my hand."

I stopped reading and thought about his words and then remembered other words of his, "These things must be." Jesus has implied to me that America's greatness will not last. I believe we must change soon because he will not stay his hand forever. But I can see why he has stayed his hand. We have started so many great improvements and ideas for human liberty. We have, along with other western countries, raised the idea of the worth of every human out of serfdom and substituted the pursuit of happiness. But at the same time, we wallow in such riches as to be unheard of in the history of the world. Riches that depend on backbreaking labor from the have-not nations to keep the supply flowing. These riches are also squandering the wealth that was held inside the earth for eons. Yet, we act as if all the world's wealth is due us, and us alone.

Any change for the better will probably mean we must increase our global awareness. At present, we throw out crumbs to other nations and peoples in need, crumbs are not enough. This finite world is just that, finite. We truly are living on a spaceship built by God. Technology will not save us from all of our own follies. Worse, in our own opulent country, we deliberately isolate ourselves from those who have less, this way, we can say, "We'll, I gave to charity, didn't I?" I hate that word *charity*.

Collectively there seems to be a lot more we can do. Most especially the large conglomerates, the world institutes, the banks, the agriculture and manufacturing companies. Some large firms are doing that and some people are single handedly making great changes. Then I read about a Rancher out west who is buying up land to turn into a preserve. Another person in Michigan is letting a golf course go back to the natural state with wild flowers instead of letting builders move in with their high-rises and condos. The government along with various groups are trying to bring back a lot of the Florida Everglades that have been eroded over the years. It will be a monumental job and well worth it. Around the globe we see nature being brought back into form. But is it enough to undo the damage? Can the damage ever be undone? Not as long as our cities keep growing and spreading and spending and using up everything in their path. The real solution seems to be less business then usual, that we change our cultural structure to take pride in less, less gadgets, less land, less sizes, less cars, less of everything, even less money. If we could make pride our goal rather than money or power we will have met nature half way on its way back to saving earth.

I don't think people need to live in poverty to save the earth but we must learn to use less of everything and share what we have extra. Selfishness is the opposite of a healthy world. Unfortunately our society doesn't have a mechanism set up so that wealth could be shared if we wanted to. I know people who deplore that some people don't have the basic needs for life yet they don't know how to spread the excess they themselves have. The system of charity falls far short both for the giver and receiver because it is a statement of class, an "I am better than you" statement. Not good.

We need a more equitable means of distributing wealth. A mature and wise society would find a way to spread wealth and necessities around to all its citizens. But laws will not change our selfishness, it must be voluntary. One means would be a ceiling on wealth, definitely not created with laws, but created from pressure of pride, a pride that raises mature people above the triteness of wealth. A mature society would also limit its own growth. We all aspire towards living in a mature society some day, don't we? Then we should be working towards it now. And by growing mature faster we might save ourselves and our earth. Jesus has said to me a number of times, "Save earth," and when I asked, "How?" he promised to show me. As soon as I understand I will share it with you.

I keep thinking about his warning, "It isn't true is it? About the vortex? It's only a symbol, isn't it?" I asked. "If we don't create a vortex are we going to do something radioactive like they did on Silver World?"

"Both," was Jesus answer.

He did not elaborate or explain the extent of the radioactivity damage or about the scene Mary showed me because he wants me to figure it out myself. I remembered the view of earth Jesus showed to me once and how the earth would look if he had never been born. He showed me earth as a dead, black cinder turning in space. But he was born and he will help us save the earth.

Perhaps it isn't Jesus birth that will prevent the disaster, but his existence through time. He is still active on earth, and will not allow us to destroy it. I strongly suspect that if we don't eventually reverse our culture to a negative growth one, heaven will do it for us.

I am sort of shell-shocked. Earlier I wondered what I would put at the end of this chapter, Jesus replied, "You will know." As if to imply that I would find the information I needed to complete it. I certainly did.

I began reading the last chapters in Cosmic Voyage and found that Courtney also fell into a vortex. He was directed to go there by Jesus. But the rest of his experience is the opposite of my own.

When he arrives at the vortex, he gets a clear signal of where life began. Jesus informs him he needs to know the reason for life. Courtney asks what he should do and Jesus tells him to go into the vortex. Courtney does and focuses on God within the center and how God loves us because we ended his loneliness and that he will never allow the demise of his creatures. Then Courtney experiences an explosive shift and great joy in God's new existence. Then Jesus tells him that this is the end.[66]

---

[66] *Cosmic Voyage*, P 294

When I read this I asked Jesus, almost pleadingly, if I had misinterpreted my fall into the vortex and its meaning. Jesus said, "No." "You are right. We have been trying to show all who are willing to see the danger."

I remembered Mary telling me, "We all love you." And I didn't understand. Perhaps it is because I am finally picking up on the message they have been trying to send us for a long time. My mind swirled into its own vortex. Black holes, (my term not Jesus') are still only theories according to our science. It is supposed that one exists in the center of our Milky Way galaxy, millions of light years away and perhaps tiny ones are scattered throughout space. This puts the danger so far away as to be negligible, so I smiled.

"No," Jesus said again, "Earth space"

I haven't even had a first year astronomy class, so how can I understand if Jesus tells me where it is, I thought. But I'll certainly try.

I asked Jesus if he would give me more details.

"Yes," he told me, "At another time." But he added, "it won't make any difference because by the time earth's problem becomes observable to your science, it will be too late.

Then thinking of Courtney's words of God's great joy, I remembered The Source I had seen with Jesus and Mary. Was that the beginning, the joy I experienced as I watched life flow from the point source of God? Then was this dirty swirling ball of dust and light its opposite, the end point?

"No" Jesus said, implying that this only involves earth.

All this is really, really, unbelievable and I wouldn't believe it myself except that Jesus has presented it in such a way that its truth is finally sinking into my psyche. He is giving me the truth in stages and I am presenting it to you as I receive it in the hopes that you will believe it too. Really you could say that Jesus directed this second book so it would have its present impact. He is not finished either. He didn't instruct me to write a doomsday book without giving us some kind of solution. Remember he said he would show us how to save earth? I certainly hope he has a workable solution because I can't imagine one. For once my mind runs blank.

Jesus says the world will change for the better because it must. Thousand and thousands of people are writing, preaching, talking and acting towards this goal. It is safe to say that this is already an army, an army for good, a mighty force pushing and shoving our new found psyches together, outwards, and upwards, soul to soul, mind to mind, heart to heart. Here is a sample of what our new earth can grow to be.

We went back to the same future time as before where I met the acolyte trying to lift something off the table with his mind. At first we stood on the same low hill as before with wild flowers and white rocks scattered in the wild tall grass. In this way, I got my bearings before we walked through the Rainbow City of earth. We walked a path with grass and flowers between glass buildings and homes. The city in which we walked was made up of different colored glass buildings but these buildings were not square or oblong. they were made of various triangles and diff shapes. I understood that here the people are motivated by pride, not greed or status or money. Here there is no money. The mind provides protection from lions and other wild animals that are allowed to roam free. Wild is preferable when possible. People still go to work to make and build things, they still use and depend on some technology but they return to a home surrounded by nature and simple gardens.

We went into a home and met a family group. When we entered the home, as Jesus walked through an oblong door, he laughed, turned to me and said, "See, some things are the same." And, "Yes" people group into families in this time because Jesus also said, "Families are back again." The people I met in the home were small and thin, with large eyes and small facial features, short hairdos and smiling. They seemed composed and gentile. They were aware of our visit to their home and seemed pleased. We had entered a large, round room with a huge window covering its whole circumference and lined with couches. This home was so large it was probably a place for many families ?

"No, I guess not."

Much of the earth is allowed to grow uncultivated. The population is sparse and grouped in nuggets around the world. People teleport to other planets and that is why few people are on earth at any one time. I met an extremely tall, sleek person who bent far down at the waist to smile and look at me. This person was not human.

Remembering earth's risky future I asked if we were on the old earth or a new one.

"Does it feel like earth?

It felt like earth, a much less crowded one, a sweet spring blown earth. Then the earth must have been saved?

Jesus did not answer.

I wanted to learn more about the people's ideas on the blight they had caused. I learned that many people want to relocate to the moon even though it won't support life because they have been persuaded into acceptance but also because they will be able to use gliding as a normal means of transport. The engineers are building the moon tunnels and caves to allow for the people's natural gliding abilities in lower gravity. To me, the choice for freedom would be easy, on the other hand, the ability to glide through the tunnels and caves of the moon may be beyond my understanding. But they will need to make oxygen and water out of rock with hard labor, which would force new social rules and rulers. I see clearly how easily people could loose their freedom if this happened..

Some Silver people also realize this. They want to stay on their world, to deliberately take a backward step from technology, to reawaken their souls and their natural surroundings. They also realize that they could be stepping into a dictatorship. They are afraid of loosing their freedom along with their world.

Jesus says they have some prophets among them who are telling them that the runaway microorganisms can be defeated if they relearn to join forces with spiritual and mental energy. But because almost half their world is already eaten up by the blight, many people have chosen to follow the leaders advice, they have given up. Some say that nothing will help and that God is dishing out a just punishment while people at the opposite pole insist that only God can save them. Their confusion reminds me of earth.

Unfortunately, their divided ideas and split factions of differing opinions are killing them. Jesus said if they could all agree to gather together and fight the organisms they could save their world. As it stands now, they have only a slight chance against the blight.

"Will they do it?" I asked.

"I don't know. Jesus answered me. All intelligences can make their own choices. It is this choice that determines the future course of events. Some events cannot be known until they happen."

I am suddenly reminded of the similar statements Jesus made about our own world's survival. He has said many times to me that there is only a slight chance of saving earth.

I certainly hope the people on Silver World come together to save their world. I picture people standing in a ring at every position around the blight and sending their love and mental energy towards its edges to limit its growth. Life against life. This is only my own fantasy. It probably isn't what Jesus meant.

At least now, I am not afraid of going with Jesus into the slums on Silver World, it can't get much worse. Tonight we went back to the forest glen. It was awesomely beautiful, more so now that I know how fragile its future is. We watched as, one by one, the silver glass people entered the green cathedral of forest and arraigned themselves into a circle. This very old form of worship was all that might save them. Sadly, their every word was being heard by dominant leaders who intend to manipulate the people's ideas to fit their own grasp for power.

I don't know why we came back to this forest glen. Perhaps to realize anew its beauty and loss of hope. Jesus told me that our next visit will be to the survivors from the other continent. They are now refugees living in crowded conditions on the edge of the only viable continent left on this world.

The first thing I noticed was that the people still have their natural beauty even surrounded by the dull colors and general messiness of the slum area. The sky is still silver, in fact, now that I think it, I haven't seen a change in the weather on any visit then again, why visit during bad weather. The ground where we walked wasn't covered with dew like inside the forest, here even the earth looked dull and lifeless. The houses looked unstable, built of wood and metal but, amazingly, there was large trim around the doors and a few windows. Fat trim decoration around openings must be a very strong cultural trait within this whole civilization but I suspect that the trim has utility purposes too.

Many children ran and pushed through groups of standing adults, like children do everywhere. Interesting that they weren't immediately halted or disciplined. They looked somewhat tarnished to me but this may be because I expected it. One child's green outfit looked dirty and dull. I wanted to talk to a few children but we couldn't talk to any of these because they were surrounded by adults. So we walked through the crowds. There was too much going on for me to notice any details right away. I did see some people cooking in large pots on the ground and other people standing around talking, but our purpose was to find a group of children we could talk to.

At length, we found a group playing off by themselves near a tree. The trees in the refugee camp looked to be scarce and this one was growing by itself on the side of a small hill. We stood near the tree and watched the children run and play for a few minutes before one of the children noticed us. Curiosity overcame any fear the child could have had as she walked over to where we stood. Her eyes popped out like she was scared but she stood her ground and soon another child noticed us then another.

Now that we were visible to the children and had their attention, I couldn't think what to say. So I blurted out with the first words that came to my mind.

"You are very beautiful." I then reached out my hand to touch the child and she stood there and let me touch her cheek.

I had the sudden notion that I must look terrible to these children, like some old hag. I am almost sixty years old and my skin is an olive pink, definitely not silver. I must be the weirdest thing these children ever saw in their little lives.

Jesus suddenly said, "No," He told me that I am fine looking and young when I am with him, that I just look different to these children, not shockingly old or haggard.

The child didn't speak, but none of them ran away or moved, they all stood looking at us.

So I spoke again, "I have a message to give you before I leave, Try to save your world. It is very beautiful like you are." I smiled as we disappeared and don't know what they told their parents if anything.

When Jesus and I left, I asked him if heaven was trying hard to save these beautiful people and he assured me they were. He explained that there were prophets and speakers among the people right now, encouraging the people and trying to convince them to battle the growing blight on their world instead of giving in to the leaders demands.

He added the fact that this world was small compared to earth. That even before the accident that destroyed half of it, it's population was small, and the intermix of cultures much less complex. Their technology; though, is on a par with earth's. The land is also less varied with large tracts of flat areas, they had to resort to building their own cliffs in the sprawling cities.

Jesus said that my message to these children was good and because I was strange, it may hold a deeper outcome and import for them.

I hoped so, and also hoped there was enough time for one of these children to grow up and become a leader against the blight.

RIDING THE HURRICANE

What can we do. Heaven must have known for a long time- perhaps heaven has encouraged our learning and discovery about the universe for this reason. I remember back to some of the disaster worlds Jesus told me about, On one world all the people got off but not the animals. I suppose if we began teaching spiritually to every one, even our children, we might be able to escape earth by the time it falls into the vortex or the vortex falls into us or whatever the last major disaster will be? This doesn't seem an acceptable solution because it lacks a very important item-earth. Earth, with all its fauna and animals and beauty. I suddenly thought of the whales, and Jesus surprised me by saying," The whales could leave." Still, it would be better if they didn't need to leave, better if earth could be preserved. I wait for Jesus to show us how to save earth.

When I saw a picture of a hurricane in the newspaper it grabbed at me, it looked like what Mary showed me. Could this be what I saw? Could I have been looking down on the earth from space and witnessing a huge hurricane? But this hurricane had no water at its edges, there was space all around it, unless it was a planet wide hurricane, impossible, how could any hurricane be planet wide? As soon as I thought of this, the idea felt right, as though a puzzle piece had just slipped into place. Still, most spaces remain empty.

Jesus tells me I already know the answer that I was born with the memory of what was going to happen so I could help prevent it. If what I perceive Jesus to say is true, then we need to start changing now. But even if we were to accomplish this great change how could we stop a huge round world like earth from moving towards this hurricane or vortex or other phenomena that is putting it in danger? I asked this of Jesus, "How can we prevent earth from dying?'

Jesus replied, "I will help."

I felt such a thrill as he spoke these simple words. His love seemed to surround me with comfort. This comfort was so engrossing that I neglected to ask Jesus how he was going to help or what was turning earth into a whirlpool or if the vortex was real?

If I follow this new knowledge backwards 2000 years and even further what will everything look like? All the warnings about saving our souls may look much different and clearer. Oh God it is terrifying. Jesus held me in his loving way as I said, "You knew 2000 years ago, didn't you, this is why you are on your way to earth now, this is why you will lift people off who are ready? This is what you have always meant by saving our souls from eternal damnation? Oh, it is to frightening, I can't imagine any person going the other way. I don't want anyone to fall into a black hole for eternity, even the evil one., no not even him. I want everyone to escape.

After my outbursts I realized that I was becoming dramatic again, that in all likelihood there wasn't a black hole growing to receive us but just a huge, world wide hurricane, a hurricane sucking into the earth like a tornado and lifting up the oceans into space? Am I being dramatic again. I better learn the facts before I leap.

But this is awesome, we, our souls are in great danger and like Jesus has mentioned in the past, "Not everyone will be saved." I can assure you, those of you who don't even believe you have a soul, that you do have a soul, and not only a soul but also one that lives after your body doesn't, a soul that lives forever. Imagine if you will falling into a black hole forever, sliding into a never ending time-status, neither growing nor changing nor moving nor falling, just a soul thinking upon itself—forever.

Do we need to escape into space. Perhaps learn to travel with our souls or move to the outer moons or asteroid belt. Oddly enough I visited organisms can and do live in space because they were genetically fit for their special environment, we are not.

Earlier in the day I was feeling hurt and lonely, so Jesus told me he would take me to a place in the universe that would make me feel better.

After I watched Fraser and sat down thinking my million nightly thoughts and worries. I reminded Jesus that he promised to take me someplace special tonight. He smiled and I closed my eyes.

When I opened them, I had a hard time concentrating on what I was looking at. My mind seemed to keep drifting back to my own thoughts. First I would see a bright light then my mind would be thinking of my utility bills on the table then back to the bright light. Actually, it looked more like bright smoke when my mind finally was able to focus on where we stood.

We stood amid smoky colored swirls and twists of color all glowing like tiny streaks of lightning. It was as if we were inside an ocean of swirling dust motes. We were.

"These are minute organisms that can only be seen because they give off light and chemical energy. The tiny dots moved like schools of fish, schooling in one direction then another, swarming together in circles and crazy eights.

The strangest thing about this life was that we weren't standing on any world. We were standing in space. I could see clusters and single stars far in the distance. When the mist forked apart I could see layers of points of stars riding in their own clouds.

The life swirling around was thick but still transparent. Streamers of tiny organisms kept glowing as they moved near by. Each school glowed in its own color and then intermixed as one swarm flew behind another. The multiple colors were interesting and lively but I wondered how these organisms could live in the vacuum of space.

Jesus said that space is not a vacuum throughout the cosmos. These organisms were using energy from the far off suns to process their life force and the chemical interaction that keeps them alive.

I thought it so amazing that Jesus knew the whole of the universe so intimately.

Then he told me, "You could fill the universe too, all of you." He added, "you could go alone on many of these visits if you wanted."

"But I don't want to go alone. I prefer being with you."

Jesus smiled at my words as we left.

We are earth bound, we need land beneath out feet, preferably earth soil and could not live without it. We had better hold and treasure the soil we stand on now. Personally, I've always liked the Gaia hypnosis's, the idea that earth has the ability to compensate for changes in the various systems of biological life that is thriving and producing on its outer skin. Nevertheless, its compensating system can be overwhelmed just like out own bodies can succumb to fever and die. So even if the Gaia Theory is true, and there has been much debate about it, it isn't enough to save a very troubled earth.

We all have a beautiful life—all of us—even the very poor because we can breath air and walk on soil and look up at a deep blue sky. By this measurement, even the poorest of the poor lives an exquisitely, breathable, functional, fruitful life.

Tonight I was thinking of all the ramifications of the vortex, or hurricane and thought laughingly, "Well, at least now we have a common enemy" I remembered a science fiction story I read about once that pulled earth nations together to fight the common enemy of mankind and was thinking along those lines, that perhaps it is only a wish fulfillment of my own fantasies or maybe God put it there as a challenge.

Suddenly Jesus said, "It isn't a game, Diane."

He seldom uses my name when he speaks to me, this startled and sobered me. I get scattered and dizzy in my thinking sometimes. Jesus told me today, May 14, 2000, "We can detect it." Meaning that the vortex or whirlpool or black hole or whatever it is, is already churned into an eddy, a tiny spinning seed of itself?

Actually I was kind of hoping it was a game and could foresee kids at their new joy sticks already shooting down the enemy vortex and driving it out to space. I think I felt like becoming hysterical because I don't want to be the barer of bad tidings. A doomsayer. I don't want to be ridiculed for shouting, "The sky is falling." But Jesus said it isn't a game and I need to return to somber reality, or a sort of reality, I guess, back into the thick of it all.

What must Jesus think of me, I can't even take the most destructive future imaginable and not treat it as a joke. Perhaps this is hysteria? I don't know what's wrong with me. I keep playing with the idea as if it was only in my own head because I don't want to face up to the possibility of its reality? Perhaps it is because I am unhappy? So my unhappiness will cause all the earth to die. Will the vortex go away if I become happy? Dumb thoughts but hanging in there and needing to be thought like a wrinkled curtain needing to fall. But this is not a game, not a game, not a game.

Heaven can see it, whatever it is, it already exists near earth, or on it, or inside it—and all I can think if is myself, my own self image-Oh please Jesus have patience with me, your stupid, little, minded monkey. To Jesus it must be like trying to have a conversation with someone who can only listen every five minutes or so because the person is busy fiddling while Rome burns. This reminds me of the developmentally disabled adults I used to take care and how happy I was when one of them actually looked into my eyes for a moment with complete attention. I must look like that to Jesus—the whole earth hangs in the balance while I twiddle away my time with nonsense thoughts. Stop.

Jesus spoke and said as he smiled at me, "I can be patient."

"So it isn't a joke? No one set it there to pull us together with fear, there is a black hole punching into another universe threatening to suck us up?"

Jesus said, "Something like that but not quite."

Now I need to wait for Jesus to tell me again what it is because I felt so scrambled at the thought that I couldn't understand or didn't want to.

In the New Testament Jesus said "Let the children come to me, and do not prevent them; for the Kingdom of God belongs to such as these." Matt 19:14, Mark 10:14, Luke 18:16 who adds, 81:17 "Amen, I say to you, whoever does not accept the kingdom of God like a child will not enter it." It seems to me that 2000 years ago Jesus was possibly referring to these, small, large eyed, beings who are our gentile descendants; though, I am not sure that they have all proved to be gentile, but then, they are our descendents, after all. Blaspheme you yell. We'll it is time for what was hidden to be reveled. These little people are in children bodies, with gentile minds for the most part. They inhibit heaven or God's Kingdom, have often been mistaken for angels, and they travel on waves of time. Their way is the future, it is our way of life whose days are numbered. We are the dinosaurs inhabiting Jurassic Park, the beautiful, fearsome dinosaurs being lead or pulled into a more stable future by these little ones. Dare I call them the people of heaven? Alas it is our job to understand that as dinosaurs, we can't take our gadgets into that future with us; our cars, road runners, weed wackers, TV, Cell phones, etc., will all need to be left behind if we want any kind of future at all.

These small gentile children, who roam heaven's time waves, or at least a layer of heaven, have been trying to tame us, to teach us but they terrify us still. I am not sure why. I am afraid of the dark too, of seeing a slight white shape in the dark below the stairs or a small statue move into life or the dark beneath my bed or around corners where they still lurk from childhood. I am trying to decipher why our hearts pound in fright at their presence. Is it because they resemble us so much, they don't look enough like monsters? If we could see them in the light, would we still be afraid?

There is the answer I was searching for, they are not all of the light. Some work for the evil one, forced, I believe, to do his bidding like zombies. No wonder just the suggestion of their form strikes terror in our hearts. It may have been planned that way since we were children. As children we were more reachable, pliable, playable, and loving. But perhaps both sides have been calling and teaching to us, no wonder we are afraid and confused.

The subject matter is no less frightening. Led by these children through walls, what we thought was real becomes illusory, insubstantial, un-real. It is enough to scare us out of our wits? Our memories of them when we were children and the secretness that surrounded their presence, sometimes in the dark and being forced out of bed, can send chills up my spine thinking about it. Is it all true? Yes but remember what Jesus told me once, "Only a few work for the evil one." And those few are trying to imitate heaven. Most of these beings are like angels, angels in children's bodies, children trying to lead us down new life paths. They surly are more terrified of us, in our big lumbering, hairy, bodies full of muscle strength and anger, then we are of them.

I must have been visited by a group of them last night. I don't remember it at all but Jesus told me that I was angry and I let them know it. He didn't tell me so but it must have been the little Gray people who I vented my anger on. I hope I gave them an earful of my wrath. I don't know what I said but it probably related to their treating us as specimens. I believe my goal is to set up a meeting. If they need something from us to let us know and we may supply it voluntarily. I don't know if they can step into our sunlight but something could be arraigned. Also if we could see them on television or learn they are real and common to us, it would lighten our fear, which may also eliminate theirs. We could promise not to study or harm them in any way but we do need to satisfy our curiosity somewhat. Actually, Jesus said as much to Courtney in his book Cosmic Voyage. Jesus said that it was a law of evolution that we help others, that we must.

I can already hear some of you enterprising readers thinking that maybe we could trade, we could give them what they need but they could teach us how to travel in time. Forget it. Could you imagine dinosaurs traveling in time. But besides that, it takes a certain mind-set to travel in time, not mechanical gadgets, they would probably be a hindrance. I suspect that we left our descendents so little to survive and work with that they had no choice to learn time travel with only their minds.

They have tried to teach some children how to travel in time. Whitley Scriber's book, Secret School, describes some of these attempts to teach him time travel when he was a nine-year-old child. Whitley remembers as a young boy being directed in time travel during the nights by a very old Sister of Charity or teacher who was actually a Gray. His teacher helped him to visit or exist in three places at once, Rome, as a slave in a country villa near Rome and as a visitor to his own city, St Antoine, Texas. His teacher had put some kind of salve on him to help send him off on his time travels. He was with a group of other children and they lifted up over the city at one point singing. These children sang and prayed because "prayer is a key to escape from the illusion of life, and so a critical link to timeless reality." [67]

In the country estate and in Rome he has become a Greek and is aware of things from this point of view as well as his own. All thirteen boys in his group are Greek. Whitley describes himself as being an actual boy who is cold because he doesn't have a coat. He is also a slave in 50 BC Rome. Whitley speculates that there was danger each place he was sent and this may have been why his teacher from the Secret school sent him and other children to that specific time. To teach, to show and to grow up and change the world. Later as an adult he re-visits Rome and finds a temple he saw during his time visits. He suggests that he may have entered his own past lives during these trips through time. I believe this to be the case because Jesus has told me that many of our dreams are actually memories; although, he didn't explain to me how these memories sit in time, if they were past or present or ongoing.

Whitley says that when he walked the streets of Rome they were very real streets. "In this sense, there is no time. We create the present. It's an invention. But we can reinvent it, and if we do that on a large enough scale, we may gain on a learning contact with out past and future, and even become able to change them." [68]

They also sent him very far back into the past earth where another human civilization exists. A more technological civilization than ours. They know a great danger is approaching in the way of an asteroid? Or

---

[67] *Secret School*, Whitley Strieber, Harper Collins, New York, 1997, p128.
[68] *Secret School*, p 134.

something else from the heavens, which Whitley is shown, that looks like a hundred moons. He says this happened about 10,000 BC and that the whole civilization is destroyed by the impact, an impact predicted as Pisces moves into Aquarius as the Milky Way galaxy turns on its axes.

I quickly sit up and take note, was this what Mary was trying to show me? Something destructive is coming our way from the galaxy? An impact?

Suddenly I am irritated. I don't want to get into this aspect of a possible future or past disaster. A disaster only 10,000 years ago is too close, it was probably more like a 100,000. Jesus suddenly said, "At least that." But Jesus will not get more precise. He will never state dates or specific times perhaps because of the simple fact that he doesn't live in time as we think of it? All I can understand is that earth has had super civilizations in its long history that have been obliterated and completely destroyed except for the remnants of myths they left behind.

I began complaining that all mystic books finally end in doomsday ones, that no one will believe in any doomsday that might befall the earth. We have been too bombarded with this kind of scenarios and think of them as clichés, as jokes.

Jesus said, "They refused to believe in the times before Noah too."

"Yes, and people now-a-days don't even believe there was a Time of Noah." Because we can't find any scientific evidence for the flood; therefore, it follows that it must have never happened.

"They are looking in the wrong place." Jesus said.

Troubled, I mentioned to Jesus that we couldn't have an impact from the sky and a hurricane too because both events don't fit together.

"Yes you can," was his answer.

I didn't want to think about it any more, the idea needed time to worm around in my brain.

"It is necessary. We must discuss it soon."

"But I need time to think."

"Yes."

"If I am to write about a coming disaster then I'll need some facts and more information." I told Jesus.

Jesus said, "Facts put people to sleep."

No comment.

We went to the first clearing again because that made it easy for me to get my bearings then we walked to where the people were meeting. The circle was three and four people thick. Usually they were interlocked because that facilitated their concentration. (It may be the opposite on earth. It may be better for us to only touch with our minds when we are first learning because this will strengthen us). Each Silver World person or group imagines a section of edge of the blight to push against. It has been divided up into segments for this purpose. The prophet who whispered where the listening device was located had been explaining how to fight it. He learned from a dream that they needed to practice changing one particle at a time and keep practicing until they accomplished their goal, which seems impossible to them. They have exhausted all other solutions, all other hope, they have no choice but to try this new tactic or move off planet.

Most of the people decided to die rather than leave, that death was preferable. Still some held out, and don't sit in on the circles or join in the schedule of attack. Others keep at it day and night in valleys all over their remaining continent. When one group of people gets up, another takes their place. The children are even included and do quite well, better than expected.

Jesus has been explaining to me why their efforts against their government and blight may be successful. They group their cities and towns in small self-sufficient clusters. Although there is commerce between clusters, the commerce is not vital or necessary for survival. Their prayer centers are also arraigned in small areas that help them join in circles and join together as a strong unit with mental outpouring. A part of their culture reminiscent of evolution, their tendency to form into circles for prayer and discussion. By having their prayer groups normally in their suburbs and surrounding their towns and cities, as well as within them, they have an ideal mechanisms for creating a mental shield around their parameter. Jesus explained that heaven is trying to work with them and teach them what they need to know. And that because their plight has become so desperate, their life depends on winning, they will have a good chance of succeeding.

We wait for a few minutes because Jesus mentioned they are about to receive good news. They have the first evidence that their effort is pushing back the blight in some parts of the edge. (Up till now I have received much of this information in a burst or packet of information) As I watched, a person came running and jumping through the forest, almost gliding, up to the leader who was sitting at the edge of the circle and sang in a low pitched voice. The leader got up and trilled the news in a shout that sent the birds flying. Many people broke ranks. An older person from the middle nodded that they were to get back into formation, they probably would celebrate later.

Then Jesus took me to the refugee camp. We watched the people run around and glide off the roofs of houses and anything else they could find. The cities were lit up, it was night, and people were gliding everywhere. Silver streaks filling the sky. It didn't take long for the message to spread. It seemed like everyone was celebrating. After all, this was their first inkling that this method would work, and this was after long weeks of seemingly endless effort. All they had left to try had been visualization, they had sent tender thoughts of love and caring to the part that was still clean and without corrupted microorganisms. They had a right to be proud because they had learned to gather and concentrate mental energy to drive back and purify the ground. They did this by "knowing" that each tiny area of ground was clear. Eventually they could turn each small area into a clean spot until the whole blight was gone. They would drive it back through space/time as if it never happened and make each small segment clean again. With heaven's help, they learned to use time as part of their method, like going back to the Source of the Universe and re-weaving reality until this small segment never has been touched by the blight in the first place.

I am sure the people on Silver World will have a long struggle ahead of them, but now they have hope where before they had none. Oh I was so happy to see the lights and people streaking through the air and running and playing. But what does any of this have to do with earth? Our problem isn't the same as on Silver World, so how does all this apply to us?

CRACKS IN TIME

No one has ever doubted that the world will end someday and perhaps the universe. Even our scientists agree that the world won't last forever but no one knows how or in what manner it will end. We tend to believe that it will be a long time from now, maybe someday the sun will go nova or during the next million years a comet will impact earth and destroy us like it did the dinosaurs. There is some speculation, oddly low key lately, that mankind might destroy itself with hydrogen bombs, but, even so, the earth would endure. Humanity only spreads itself over a thin layer of earth's skin, after all, even our oilrigs and mohe-holes can't affect anything deep inside the earth. Can it? Earth is big. And we assume, tamper proof. Yet, polluted rivers, land, and lakes are beginning to have disastrous effect on the rest of earth's animal life as well as our own. What would earth be without its vast cornucopia of life that spills in every direction over its surface?

Jesus has shown us what earth emptied of all its biological life would look like when he took us to Empty World in Travel book I. The world with the green and red striped sky, a tomb of blistering wind, harsh sand and floating mountains of rusted matter. I didn't know. My surprise was total. How did it happen? How will it happen? How will it possibly not happen?

I have a hard time believing that the earth could be moving towards such an immense emptiness and then I have a harder time believing that the people of earth could ever prevent such a wide-ranging catastrophe. Regardless, however Jesus teaches us to prevent it, it will be directed at future generations, not our own. This current generation can't limit carbon dioxide emissions effectively or make any major decisions on a global scale. The World Kato Convention held in Japan last year was a nit-picking farce.

Now it was May 18, 2000 and Jesus tried to show me about this hurricane but my brain just couldn't take it in—What plugged up my mind was Jesus statement that we, humanity, are causing this problem, this vortex or crack or flaw whatever it is. Yet Jesus and those in heaven can detect it. It is already apparent to them but we can't see it. This is too much. And I couldn't take it in so I begged off our talk and went upstairs to bed.

The next day, feeling refreshed, I decided to get a grip on myself and pull the questions and perhaps some answers out of a hat. I made a list of what I knew and still needed to know, so far.

What is it that will try to destroy the world?

1. Statements made directly by Jesus:
   "Only earth space",
   "We humans are creating it.",
   "Heaven can detect it now."
   This may be a flaw of some kind that they detect not as I assumed at first, a growing vortex.

2. It looks like a galaxy, hurricane, whirlpool, or vortex.
   It may react with combined effects already on earth, Antarctica, Vibrations, or the Bermuda Triangle?

3. Radioactivity or nuclear war.
   He has already said we will have some radioactive elements to take into account, but he didn't say if it was the major problem or a part of it.

4. Something is coming? Does this mean asteroid near miss or impact? Or some other type of impact?
   While I was reading about the nuclear deterrence in the newspaper for United States and Europe verses the rogue countries like, N. Korea, Iran, Iraq, Pakistan Jesus hinted that we will need it. But it would unbalance the super powers. Besides it is unworkable at this time.

Some of these facts seem to correlate with what Courtney said destroyed Mars. But he saw this through remote viewing so there is no prior evidence that these events occurred; nevertheless, I print it here because something strange did happen to Mars once and I suspect humans were on it when it happened.

Cosmic Voyage chapter "The event that destroyed Mars":

Small object skims through thick atmosphere, creating high turbulence in area of intersection. Gradually, object caused a circular ripple to form in atmosphere, ripple grows into atmospheric tidal wave. Circular ripple meets itself on other side, bounces and passes through itself again and again. Eventually produces osculation's and vibrations and then resonance. Resonance becomes "primary driver of atmosphere conditions, swamping all other sources of influence, such as heat from the sun.

Apparently gravity was not sufficiently strong to dampen the osculation's quickly. Thus they continued for a long while." "The beings on the planet were affected gradually. all weather patterns changed. The conditions on the planet slowly began to deteriorate. Food became a problem, since crops could not grow. Rain became a problem. There were both floods and droughts eventually." Gradually the atmosphere was thrown off into space.[69]

Courtney admits earth's larger gravity would prevent this same series of events on earth. If this was actually what happened to Mars, it may also have caused Mars to move further away from the sun. Is that possible? Does this have any relevance for earth? Maybe. The vibrations are what I am interested in because they frighten me. I don't know why but they seem vital to earth's current problem. I have no understanding of planetary motions, wobbles, vibrations, or resonance's and I suspect as far as science goes, the subject is still greatly unknown.

---

[69] *Cosmic Voyage* by Courtney Brown, Ph. D.

I have read about possible pole shifts in earth's past, this may be what the Bible describes causing the flood in Noah's time. As Sitchin states in his book "The 12th Planet"[70] many writings from the Bible and Babylonian papyri hint that the Ross ice sheet in Antarctica slid into the ocean causing a flood around the world. But Isaiah even states at one point that, "Behold, the Lord maketh the earth empty, and maketh it waste, and turneth it upside down, and scatter abroad the inhabitants thereof..."24;18-20. And most of us have read Immanuel Velokovsky's book *Worlds in Collision*[71] where he sites evidence from the Bible that Mars kept swinging close to earth from outer space before it settled down as a new planet. He grabs our attention with Joshua's unbelievable tale of the sun standing still for a day and gives evidence that on the other side of the globe the sun didn't rise for a day. All this is speculation and much of it has been dismissed as untenable today, but perhaps it is time for some-one to re-examine all the Biblical and historical evidence with a more insightful view. This I am not qualified to do, so its back to our questions and speculations.

We already have an anomaly at the Bermuda Triangle, which makes me wonder if there is a connection. This site may have begun as a ripple that became a vibration of space/time gone wrong, or out of kilter? Somehow the Bermuda Triangle may be tied in with the hurricane or problem? Only a guess but they could go together, one end in space and one on earth?

All these questions and I feel wrung dry. I can't figure any of it out. Jesus tells me that, "I know," it is why I was born, to help stop it. Hay! I didn't come here alone? Where is everyone else? Out there fighting and marching and coming together for a cause?

---

[70] *The 12th Planet*, Zecharia Sitchin.
[71] *Worlds in Collision*, Immanuel Velikovsky, Doubleday & Company, Inc., Garden City, New York, 1950.

And why not just give me a simple answer instead of making me go through all these changes? I guess it's like Jesus said, "Facts put people to sleep," even me. Just this morning Jesus told me that events in my life will change soon. I waited for more but he then said, "You wouldn't believe me if I told you."

And while I am throwing questions to the wind, I'd like to ask just who are these heavenly beings who detected the flaw? Could they be a group Federation in subspace as Courtney says, but there must be more to it than that and don't laugh, they may be the reason Star Trek lasted so long on television. These heavenly beings must be highly evolved in their own right, perhaps from many worlds, which can include angels and even great earth minds from our own past. More than that I can't imagine.

I know they are capable of setting up elaborate stage effects for our benefit. They will use props and do the acting out to convince us of their truths. An example would be Courtney's view of a being pumping ethereal matter from a machine at a person while he slept to awaken his spirit. After reading this I thought of angels pumping on a machine and sending white, smokey ethereal matter stuff into a person's head and I suddenly started laughing out loud. This scene is so deliciously funny and fake. What Courtney saw was obviously a set up created especially for his understanding. I still laugh whenever I think of it.

All we humans can understand are machines, hence, a machine pumping ethereal smoke. Reminds me of the flying schooner in full sail someone once reported. Courtney needed to see the stuff, see the spirit at work, so these highly evolved beings obliged him. It is not unlike my evolving view of God. When I first began seeing God it was almost like a stage set up from the Old Testament filled with fire and brimstone. I was given only what I could perceive and understand at that time, as a spiritual infant, I wasn't even sure I believed in God or heaven. Now my understanding has grown and I see God in a more mature light. God's words have also changed to fit my ability to accept and give honor to them.

Even my vision of Jesus has changed over the years. He sometimes looks more like a man to me and less ethereal and luminous. This frightened me so much at first that I asked the angels, "It isn't the evil one is it, pretending to be Jesus?" They assured me it wasn't; although, Jesus and the evil one's facial features can be made to resemble each other, their aspects are as different as day and night. Their psyche and auras are different and they are both here on earth, at this time.

I have just read, in the Problem of Eschatology, that Francis of Assi's life was a "full blown imitation of Christ, who was ready to appear; Christ's coming was the news that Francis had to proclaim." I have a lot of faith and love for Francis of Assi, and if he believed Jesus was on his way, then I trust that he was. Jesus may have arrived and left without anyone noticing, God's kingdom may have passed by us in space. How many times has Christ come to earth expecting it to be ready, changed, and redeemed? Although I don't understand it, Jesus likes what I write here about his coming back again and again. Yet, he also tells me he is here now. He has said these words and similar ones to me a number of times. His holy spirit will always be with us but does Jesus come and go physically? As God's Kingdom approaches, does Jesus' strength and power become stronger; is he more able to pour his spirit into us? So I ask again, how many times has Jesus returned to earth without being greeted by us. Did He come and leave with no one wise enough, pious enough, spiritual enough, imaginative enough, loving enough, to meet him? How many times will he come back to pick up his faithful? Not too many.

Jesus tells me, "One more time after this return."

After that there will be no other. Is this because there may be no earth to return to? Jesus has also told me that soon piety will infuse the earth like it once did during the dark ages of the 12th and 13th centuries. Though, I suppose, in a much different form, but according to Jesus, coming events will drive it forward, like cowboys herding cattle. This may be why Jesus and his angels are here now. And why I can't tell which direction he speaks from, he speaks from all directions calling all people to him.

In their time, the apostles knew immediately when a group had received the Holy Spirit. Their thoughts or awareness of each other was self-evident. They felt an immediate awareness of other people whose psyche has woken up.[72] Their ability to speak in tongues was mental telepathy on such a strong scale, it has been unheard of since the time of the apostles but is being reborn today. "The churches throughout the area grew in numbers" Is it because they were all feeling the wisdom and closeness of the Holy Spirit.[73] Much more evidence could be cited that Jesus' physical closeness may make his spirit stronger but I will leave it for your own search. You can flip back through pages of time in your own Bible and don't forget the history books; the middle ages are ripe with evidence that Jesus may have been near by.

A book called *The Secret School* by Whitley Strieber,[74] the same author who wrote *Communion,* has a few reveling ideas about time and taking trips through it. I mentioned his book earlier when I stated he had traveled to the past as a Greek slave with the help of mystery visitors. Those visitors showed him an image of their concept of time:

> To them, the future is like a pool of water to their right, the past a block of ice to their left. The present is the force that fixes the potential that lies in the future, turning it into the ice of the past. They seek back into the past to melt, change, and re-create, then refreeze their history. Using this process, they can to an extent repair problems and imbalances in their present time. They can prophesy, but this does not involve predicting things that are absolutely inevitable. Rather, a prophecy is a warning. Its purpose is to identify dangerous

[72] *The New American Bible, Acts 10:25-26, 34, 44-48.*
[73] *The New American Bible, Acts 9, 26-31.*
[74] *Communion,* Whitley Strieber, Beech Tree Books, New York, 1987.

future situations that are inevitable given present conditions, so that those conditions can be changed. In this sense, the best of all prophets must always be wrong, because the dangers that they see are averted by their prophecies.[75]

Also if we consider time as being 'always there' as in quantum physics, then all events are happening all the time, at the same time. Our understanding of time or space is still limited to what our scientists search for. Its is like a searchlight in which we select what area we choose to study, not necessarily what may be really there behind the scenes. People of all manner of cultures are surly living in the present and past someplace, on earth and off, living their lives as if we don't exist yet, and to them we don't. We could be walking through their ghost lives as we walk down the street and don't even know it. I am sure the people in our future walk through us like ghosts but they use mental and/or a physical method to deliberately travel through time.

Imagine the world learning, growing, and spinning itself as it moves through space. At once creating one solid twisting worm through time with all the lives ever lived left behind us but still living on the worm—our lives only the latest if its creations on the moving earth. Then multiply this throughout the solar system, all planets moving and growing their own worms. If we were to try to visualize the world worms as being in the present now and solid at this time we probably wouldn't have any black vacuum space left, it would all be filled with solid earths and planets of different forms and times.

Thus the idea of time and evolution and growth through time and perhaps the cycle or turning of time can be ascribed to cultures reverting back to the tribal life. At some point, maybe all technological cultures choose the tribal way of life. Perhaps we all will some day because it seems to me that

---

[75] *The Secret School,* Whitley Strieber

an egalitarian culture is what Jesus and all the other moralist teachers were trying to tell us would be the most perfect way to live. Jesus tells us to love one anther, to share with each other, to honor one another just as the people living in an egalitarian culture might do, at least among themselves.

I don't think I have strayed from the subject too much because Jesus, as I have said before, must see time as vastly different than we do. He may also have use of it in ways we can't fathom. So Jesus may have come to earth many times and Jesus may know more than we do about our future and understand more about how to teach us to sit up and take notice. It is up to us to listen.

One night, I had a very strange memory about the future. I felt it was a memory rather than a dream just as dreams can sometimes be past memories. A couple hundred people were sitting in rows of seats on a shuttle to Mars. We were supposed to be tourists but we had secret plans to hijack the shuttle and stay and live on Mars. Somehow we had it all planned out to hide so we couldn't be found when it was time to go back to earth. I was walking down the isle and checking if people had their hidden supplies packed. They nodded that they were ready. The dream never did explain what we thought we would use for oxygen or how we would grow food. We must have had some kind of plan worked out. I only relate this dream because, if there is any truth to it, then it shows that in the near future we will still be ornery and fanatical and mixed up. We will still not be conserving earth's resources and may have spread our blighted emotions, technology, and war mentality to Mars. If this is true, I feel a great doom hanging over our heads and that of earth.

At a funeral tonight, I suddenly asked Jesus "if I was coming back to earth by choice, was it for the same reason that most of us come back, because we don't want to leave life?" Do we hold on to earth with our souls only because we loved our lives? Jesus said that I will choose to come back, after we take the time to travel around the universe which we can do in a moment of infinity if we choose. My purpose will be to live again and find my personal job, the one I will be born to accomplish. Jesus also told me that I will only come back one more time. He didn't say why. He didn't say if it was because humans will have grown in maturity or if, I shudder to remember the image, the world will not be fit for life. It is still a toss up, however the dice will fall, so goes the world. Only God knows.

Saturday during Mass Jesus appeared as The Sacred Heart and seemed to float high above and to the right of me. I needed to look up toward the alter to see him. He was very large and present and asked me to stay with his presence throughout certain parts of the mass, even during the priest's sermon. He told me one of the reasons was so that I would understand that he had been next to me during last weeks at mass also. It was then that he looked like a man. He said, "We are one and the same," meaning the man I saw and The Sacred Heart. This day, there was no doubt in my mind that it was Jesus. Interestingly, we were in Sacred Heart Church, which gave Jesus' presence a fine, hallowed symbolism that still sends chills through me. Jesus' smile resembled the icon painting but with the sun shinning around him. His eyes twinkled. When they did, his eyelids would squeeze together with wrinkles that I loved. His heart glowed so fierce I avoided looking in that direction and concentrated on Jesus face. He spoke of many things but once he referred to me as, "Always the practical one." I felt slightly hurt by this connotation because I thought it meant stubborn or hard headed. I answered by joking, "You don't mean that I am down to earth?" We both smiled at this.

When I got home I looked up the word "practical" The dictionary definition states its exact meaning as "useful and sensible." I hoped not too sensible. Perhaps I should try and be less practical, learn to play more?

One thing I learned was that when we gather, it can intensify Jesus presence. In fact, he told me that we would be surprised at the mental imaging and work we could do in small groups. We need to begin to pray in this way, use mental imagine as an addition to our regular prayers. Imagine if the idea could grow? We could eventually have Mosques, on Fridays, Synagogues on Saturdays, and Churches on Sundays all of us mentally imagining the blue earth between our hands as it gently turned.

An earth where we use mental energy to lesson the effects of storms, draught, or hurricanes. An earth where people connect people together hanging in the sky. An earth where people hang above the earth and hug each other.

I imagine a prayer where we float above the blue, fleecy sky of earth, hugging and pulling more and more people up to join us in a silver net made of light. But Jesus said there was more that must be added to my wistful prayer and that he will instruct me at a later time what to include in it. Something like quieting the weather? Calming earth deep inside? Really I don't know so I'll wait for Jesus.

I may have strayed a few times from the subject, but what I have written so far, Jesus agreed, is ok because I am floundering and questioning and striving for the answer. This is what he has encouraged me to do all along. But when I saw a photo of a hurricane in the newspaper, I felt a jolt of recognition. Could it be so simple? Is the weather unstable and unbalanced. Top heavy, so heavy that it will topple over into a pole shift? But what could our minds have to do with weather? In *Conversation with God*, God said that it is the people living on a planet who control or destabilize the weather. When I first read this I was amazed, but the more I thought about it, the more it made sense to me. Why not begin that control now?

It all has to do with balance? All my questions may be correct because we now stand on the brink overlooking a cliff and it won't take much to push off over the edge. Any event will do. The most vital element or problem may be so deep inside the earth we don't know it's there. Last week there was an earthquake five miles down towards the center of earth, an unheard of depth for an earthquake or so the news reported. This may be what causes the earth to eventually wobble itself out of alignment? The major danger is an H-bomb from a rogue nation. Could this set it off? Would it affect depths of earth?

The next major element to look at is that our technology is heating up the earth's atmosphere. The Ross ice sheet is on a slippery slide of water, precariously balanced and close to sliding into the sea. With the conditions gathered so far, who needs an asteroid but we could get one close enough to earth or near enough to set off the Antarctica slide. Remember in Whitley's Book - He gets warned about an asteroid coming with the change of equinox. It doesn't need to impact just come near enough to set up a disturbing vibration? Any of these scenarios could unbalance the earth's wobble towards the danger zone. If the Ross shelf goes into the sea, suddenly we would not just have a flood and tidal wave, we would have unbalance, and chaos, like what happened on Mars? The earth is a spinning top, change it's conditions too much and like a top spinning on a table, it could go out of control, so out of control that a hurricane will cover one whole side of the earth. As it spins, sucking downwards, further destabilizing the mantle below and wind on top, vast earthquakes will start a chain-reaction into explosions, further destabilizing earth? If any of this adds up, it will be curtains for mankind. By that time, of course, no one will be around to witness it.

Still all this is only speculation, all I have is a vision from Mary showing me an event of world wide proportion that I have not been able to define yet and a promise from Jesus that I need to. Jesus was right, I am too practical, I need to go out and play. I did. I took a few kids and my dog and we went for a walk on Belle Isle. The sky was cobalt overhead and didn't lighten up until I looked across to Canada. The short, stubby green trees hugged the ground forever, unable to catch one of the wispy clouds floating by. The wind cooled the water to mint green froth as it hit the rocks lining the shore. We walked, or ran, in beauty so breathtaking and far-reaching as to be unbelievable. Truly we are too infinitesimal to affect this grandeur. Truly the Titanic is unsinkable.

I wanted to visit the people who Courtney describes as working in the Galactic Federation. So Jesus took me to visit these highly evolved beings and I thanked them for helping earth. I didn't' stay long at all, just a few seconds because my mind hasn't been up to par lately because I have stopped taking my medicine and my body is still adjusting. So I could hardly focus while I was there and so was upset and asked Jesus if stopping my medicine was making my mind slow. He assured me that I will adjust. He added that we were going to visit many places through out the years. Then he told me, "Hold out your hands. I want to give you something."

I closed my eyes and held out my hands. Suddenly my hands got very heavy and so I opened them. There, between my two outstretched hands, hung the earth. Its blue oceans and fluffy clouds revolved as I watched with my mouth open, gaping at its beauty. Oh, its beauty was overwhelming. As I watched a wispy string of clouds stretched around its circumference above the deep cobalt ocean and other clouds of fluff gathered and dispersed. The continents peeked through in green splotches and tiny polka dots bound with ribbon. Until finally the heaviness outweighed my gawking curiosity and as I lowered my hands the earth disappeared. I will never forget this gift from Jesus. I will hold it always in my heart forever.

When we arrived at our next visit to Silver World, the people were in a huddled meeting. Suddenly government solders came out from the trees and shot the people as they prayed. Jesus explained that they were not killing them, but drugging and dragging the people off in a covered cart. They are conscripting the people into service for the government. They are being put on ships and taken to the moon base. Once there they are forced to work the mines and farms. The government has recently banned all such gatherings so they are criminals that are meeting and huddling that way. This was being done in secret for a while but word spread about what were happening and the people began doing their prayers in secret with lookout to give warning.

We moved a short time ahead - suddenly they were at war. There was a lot of fighting. The government still didn't kill many people because they wanted to send them to the moon. The people needed to kill those in power though. They didn't have the luxury of just drugging their enemies.

I watched as a Silver person amid the forest was on his hands and knees crying over a dead body that he had just killed. Jesus said their civilization had been stable for a long time and without a recent war. This was hard on the people. I watched as one group was surprised by attackers but fought back, fires were raging in some places, cities were emptied because the people were hiding in the forest. But why? I asked.

Jesus said that their government truly believes it is for the best, that it is the only way to save the people but many are in the thrall of power and want to keep their power base strong. They need a slot of manpower to keep and run a moon because it is a false environment but also serves as a perfect prison.

In the meantime, people need to hide and pray and use their mental abilities to hold off the blight. They are putting most of their effort into war and not enough effort into pushing back the blight. At this time, it is in a holding pattern, just enough to hold back its growth but not enough energy is diverted to it to clean it up.

"But they were successful!" I wanted to scream. If they had been allowed to keep praying, they may have eliminated the blight?

Those in power, they had the resources, money and government machinery in place to disregard the people's success. They said it was an illusion, and that the people who believe it were working for evil, were really killers of their future. But it is the people in power who are the killers. That was what started the continental war.

It is a large continent with one central power for government and only a few small nations on the fringe. So when the war began in earnest, the people were at a great disadvantage by surprise at the ruthful ness of the government.

Both sides believe their future depends on winning the war.

"Stop it," I kept wanting to yell at them, "Stop it." But I was only a ghost image, unable to even pluck a leaf off a tree. I begged Jesus please can't you stop them. We are doing all that we can, he assured me.

I can't believe they could be so ignorant. It worked! the blight was succeeding?

What's the matter with these silver people. As I said this, many silver bodies lay on the dew-wet, green bushes and leaves in the forest. Struck down by government army forces and waiting to be transported to life off planet. A life of servitude and slavery.

The people didn't know how to make bombs but they were learning and finally were attacking a few of the lift off points. I couldn't stand it. It was too stupid and ignorant and wasteful. My emotions were pumping adrenalin and fear and disgust. While they played at war, few were active at prayer—it was left to a few women and older people. I was horrified and worried. I can't bare it, I told Jesus and we left. I carried thoughts of Silver World with me through out that day.

SACRED AVENUES

Jesus and Mary took me on a visit tonight. We traveled through a vast white sphere. We kept going through this total white space, on and on. We went deeper and deeper into it, so deep into the whitish sameness that I was beginning to feel disoriented so Mary gave me a red rose to hold in front of myself. It was the only thing not white; we were in a total white-field, non-space with nothing seeming to move or stir. I couldn't see Jesus or Mary or myself either so the deep red rose glowed as if a beacon lighting my way.

Finally, after a long, long time, I began to perceive faint shadow rings dancing on the periphery of my vision. As we kept moving inward, the huge shadow rings glided past us intertwining and superimposing upon each other until they become slightly more visible in spots. A number of times along the way I almost lost my concentration, then almost totally at one point until Jesus suggested we wait for another day but I refused; by now I was intrigued and curious and determined to go on.

Then I began to see a spark here and there flaring just at the edge of vision. Then more flared up, brightening into tiny suns then disappearing in different colored puffs. We kept going forward past the spinning shadow rings which moving around us in wild gyrations now, until I was suddenly and completely surrounded by a million white beings. White against white, lights within lights, angels. Uncountable whitest of white angels moving forward and receding in vast numbers, clouds forming and evaporating everywhere I looked.

One angel floated up close to me and I noticed that the being closely resembled a human except for its glow of white light like radiance. The angel's words were strange, "We are amorphous," it said to me and disappeared back into the milieu. I knew what the word meant nevertheless looked it up later. Amorphous means formless. A unique definition for these glorious, flowing life forms, I am sure.

I understood that their purpose in life is to go to different worlds and help spread light and love. Hearing our prayers, they congregate in the empty space between words and thoughts using our prayers like highways to send love and healing on its way around the globe. They are what Jesus calls "Love Beings" Their joy is spiritual love, it is these angels who by spreading their spiritual light, keep the darkness at bay. They move as a spirit moves and did not have or need wings.

This angel took me further into their world or space because it wasn't solid like we think a world should be. As I went deeper, the area I floated in became more colorful until it was filled with dappled pinpoint mixtures of formless smoky, hues of light. We seemed to make a circuit around before coming back to where Jesus and Mary waited. I picked up on the notion that their color or nature of invisibility changed as they used up their energy traveling to the different worlds. They stay invisible to our physical earth minds unless our love grows very strong and we will ourselves to see them. They are lovely and joyful and constantly bask in God's presence and love.

Later that night, thinking about their beauty and invisibility, I wondered how they might have evolved or is it possible that some beings did not need to evolve, could they have been born as mature beings? The idea is almost inconceivable to our way of thinking but I couldn't imagine any kind of flesh they might have evolved from, and wondered if they had been forever insubstantial and made out of light. Why not? What do we know about the other myriad forms and diversity of life in God's universe.

We humans have a number of concepts of angels and try to categorize them into levels or hierarchies but in truth there are probably as many numerous kinds as we have ideas for. Some beings that we would consider angels are really people like ourselves come down to earth for various reasons. Some other beings are messengers for God, like the two angels who held my shoulders when they took me to an audience with God. Then some are like these cloud people who carry our prayers aloft for us. I also know that some beings that we would label as angels are not angels at all but people from other worlds and time, some our own ancestors, who remain invisible to us for their own reasons. Then there are the beings who help the adversary do his work against us, but let's hold on to the light and shy away from dark thoughts.

I have thought about the feelings we get from spiritual light and asked myself what gives us our sense of "the sacred." When I went to a small church-corner gathering on Chane they prayed and sang and held hands but still, I waited for the feeling of the sacredness but could only feel its absence. The closest I got to the feeling of holy was when the leader held his hands up towards the sunlight and prayed in silence. When he did this, I felt like he was seeing and talking to Jesus just as I do, and that he was wrapped in sacredness at that moment, but it was not shared with the congregation. On the whole, the service seemed incomplete, a sense of the holy was missing from the service. And this even though there were many people pulled in from the streets to join the later cookout, those who don't usually join any church service. I was proud to see so many from this derelict neighborhood worshiping, praying, and singing. I wondered if the problem could be inside myself, caused by my own expectations and my prior conditioning. Just what was I looking for, anyway?

I tried to think back over the times and places I have felt "the sacred" of Christ during a service and what elements were there at the time. Personally I have felt sacredness in numerous churches at various times. Certainly not at every mass in every church. Some churches I hardly seem to find it at all while at others I find it often. This is odd because some churches are popular and full while some empty but the best working churches are not necessarily the most sacred, for me. Does this seem strange?

What do I mean by the feeling of sacredness? Does it depend on my own personal mood? What elements seem necessary? At least a sense of quietude? The holy reaching into my soul and joining within it? These qualities and more. Perhaps its effect is more pronounced during our wakening, the time when Jesus seems to call each of us to his side, when we have found him again after being lost. During that time when Jesus is pulling us back into his heart we are so open that Jesus every whim and teaching seems everywhere. But as time has moved on, my own ability to feel the sacred has grown, so much so, that the sacred awe touches my psyche so deeply it becomes more than I can bare. I sob with the pain of delight.

Does it depend on who is doing the religious service and how well the priest or preacher conveys their own feelings to the group? Or does it rather depend on our own receptivity and love for Jesus? Certainly people are necessary for the feeling during a gathering, but at what point does it reduce to only a gathering instead of a possible joining in love with the holy? A peace march is a gathering but no one expects it to give people a sacred experience like we expect at a Sunday service. Although, for some people, perhaps a gathering of this nature does become a sacred experience. Since God is everywhere, why not the feeling of sacredness everywhere? Yes, I may be looking for too much in too little space, or not enough in all of it and my speculation gives us food for thought only.

I have felt this sacredness during my own personal meditation but I don't feel as if I could ever impart it to other people. This is a job for preachers and priests and other workers of the Devine. I have noticed that very often I come out of church after Sunday mass, feeling empty, as though it had all been a waste of my time. Yet there are those few times when the smiles and handclasps seem exceptionally beautiful, close, and loving. When strangers seem familiar and joined in oneness. When the holy seems to hover above the alter, when a few words in the sermon or gospel can send me into a spasm of love or sorrow for Christ, or a song brings tears to my heart even though I have heard it numerous times before but never in quite in the same way. Is that what we all wait for, the specific time when the Devine seems to step down and hug us. And does it depend on anything but ourselves, God, and the opportunity of place?

I have noticed that certain priests seem to radiate this sacredness but not necessarily because of the mass. A visitor priest helping with throats, was like that, I felt his holiness as it glowed through his face. Certain people who constantly help with the service at a church also seem to glow at times with Jesus love inside them. Just recognizing them can make my heart flutter for Jesus.

What does this sacredness have to do with the fruits of our labors? We can pull hundreds of people in, but how do they get a sense of sacred? Is it a matter of setting an example and making Jesus available to many people during a cultural ritual so Jesus can more easily facilitate in them a sense of his being? The feeling is personal and deep but perhaps the setting must also be open and prepare us to receive the Devine?

Just recently I read that Bible disks were being put into cereal boxes so people could put them on their computers. But my first thought while reading about this was, "It isn't owning the Bible that is important, but living it." Will anyone read their computer Bible? Will they then live by its precepts? Could this help Jesus touch their souls and give them a first feeling of his sacredness? This may be the purpose behind the Bible gift and who am I to dispute the possibility of its happening, but somehow I doubt the quality and method behind the gift. It seems too much like propaganda to me. God must always be a free choice, which is what he has given us.

I am going to search out this feeling for sacredness and take note of where and how I find it from now on because it seems vital for humanity's proper growth. A definition of the "Sacred verses profane" in Exploring Religion[76] Sacred is the same as holy according to Marcea Eliade. He says, "What I mean by sacred is really a sense of the Devine or a feeling of holiness emanating from God's entrance into a person." He adds that it is a rite of sacredness because it would depend on individual mood and feeling, and that there is probably not a place or event that would give everyone a sense of the holy at the same time?

---

[76] *Exploring Religion*, Roger Schmidt, Wadsworth, Inc, Belmont, California, 1980, p 73.

Jesus smiles at this because he intends for exactly this to happen one day. An awesome request of humanity, don't you think.

I went to church on Saturday because the service is smaller and more intimate and thought I might more easily find the sacred. Jesus promised to tell me when we got to the most sacred point of the mass. Although any feeling of sharing in the Devine during a religious service or any place, for that matter, is ok, when the priest began saying "Take this bread and eat it for this is my body which will be given up for you," Jesus said, as a few tears fell from my eyes, "This is the sacred." I sobbed as the priest said "Take this wine for this is my blood which was shed so that sins could be forgiven…" Of course I knew it was, as I wiped my eyes, I knew it before, I have always known that Jesus sacrifice is "the sacred." It is the greatest gift ever given to humankind, it changed history, our understanding of God, belief in the afterlife, the practice of religious ritual around the world, to say nothing of the disgraceful animal sacrifice it eventually replaced or stopped. Jesus asked us to commiserate how he gave his life for us and we have kept that remembrance for two thousand years. I had found what I came looking for—the sublime sacredness of Christ.

What about the deep feeling of sacredness I experience during meditation? It isn't directly related to Jesus sacrifice, but it does depend on my love for him, and Jesus often joins me during meditation using this quiet time to instruct me in how to use the new mental energy God gave me.

When we feel the sacredness well up within us we understand that God has entered into us completely, filling our mind, body, and spirit with presence. But we couldn't have this feeling, at this depth all the time and still function. We must remain content to have only smatterings of sacredness when and where we can stumble into its presence or could it always be there within and without us, waiting for us to notice? We are all joined in this body, mind, and spiritual existence.

God = mind because all existence is within his mind.

God = body=personality=psyche=we are physical beings swimming in the mind of God.

God = spirit=our soul can expand to the whole universe.

God = the universe.

We in the west will only allow Jesus to have the trinity, father, son and Holy Spirit, but we all share in it, we are all holy. Western psychology, as Amit Goswami, Ph. D. says in his book, *The Self-Aware Universe*, does not go far enough to include the soul or "cultivating the awakening of buddhi."[77] It stops at the mind/body duality. As he argues, much more eloquently than I can, in the opening chapters, the unquestioned materialism of the west has been a barrier to further spiritual progress. He quotes Mother Theresa's observation when she rightly said, "Americans are materially blessed but impoverished in spirit."

I hope to change this. Heaven will change it. I have begun teaching children how to touch their soul through meditation, I help them imagine their spirit helper (some neighborhood children are not Christian) and how their spirit will take them anywhere they wish to go. This doesn't seem like much but for children it is a beginning towards discourse with the spirit. This is what Jesus wants from all of us, to know and talk to him. It doesn't matter what name they call their spirit helper because Jesus is God and consequently always within the spiritual awareness of every person. I hope to begin teaching adults a similar method of meditation but many adults may find it harder than children to imagine their own spirit. As adults we can become afraid of leaving our bodies behind or loosing ourselves in the spirit.

It will be worthwhile for all of us to learn more about our spirit. Jesus tells me that we will be surprised how well our minds work as groups if we once learn to coordinate them together. This group mind may still not be measurable to us but its effects might just barely be, over time. When I think about what the average person or a group's mental energy can do

---

[77] *Self Aware Universe*, Amit Goswami, Ph. D.,Penguin Putnam Inc., New York, N.Y., 1993, p 236

about the future there is only one thing I can think of, setting aside some time for mental imaging like we set aside time for prayer and to begin teaching our young people now about meditation. More than that, I don't know what we can do? Would it be enough? So far we don't have enough concrete evidence that mental energy or even prayer works; although, many of us believe it does. Is it more examples we need or miracles?

What are we talking about when we refer to mental energy or prayer? Mind and its non-locality? And space time? Travel? We travel because we "know" we can. We know when we get there. Plus there are no hindrances to our being there because of non-locality of mind. Is it also because space is so vast and various that it can absorb a mistake without notice. Not so in a small system or area perhaps. It becomes harder to "know" you have traveled the closer you are to yourself? There are obstacles built up and magnified along the way? Simple leading to complex?

I am just guessing but this may also hold true for mental energy and prayer that can steady the earth's tremors and shudders, the obstacles to prayer reaching into the bowels of the earth may be so few as to be almost non-existent. This, of course, also holds true negatively, for our psyche traumas, our arrogant thoughts, and our inconsiderate life styles. We aren't just raping the earth physically but mentally, as well. We are giving and sharing with the earth our sick vibes.[78]

When we pray for the earth or attempt to visualize it, I think it is important to note that exact location or any specific location is not always necessary for viewing or imaging. When we visualize the damaged fissure deep inside the earth, we don't need to know its longitude and latitude and depth, in fact, we don't have any of this information. Visualizing its presence that it exists is enough. Then we can go on from there to pray for or visualize its release. This relives us of the need to be strict and precise and gives us the freedom to keep focused on the job at hand. Most of us

[78] *Making a new science,* James Click, Viking Penguin, NY, NY 10010, 1987

are not adepts at mind control, it is enough that we try and concentrate, and then let Jesus and the angels do the work.

This also holds true for pulling a person up to join you as you hug the earth. Focus on any specific type of features, wither facial features, race, or dress or some other item, just pull that person up to you. If the person resists strongly or even refuses, no matter, just go get someone else. Do not expect a person you know to admit or even understand they have been pulled up to hug the earth. Actually it is better to stay unanimous, just pick any human at random, this causes less strife and psyche trauma to your own expectations. Later when you get proficient, you can try with people you know. But if you expect too much, your disappointment may hinder your own abilities to focus on your meditation.

I am becoming afraid that it is too late for most of us. That my book is for the next generation of survivors who may be able to better take stock of their own nature and do something about it. If earth's survival in any way depends on togetherness or group mental powers to control the forces of nature, we have a very long way to go to the goal. The Bible hints that we should have this type of mental ability some day in the statement, "The lion will lay down with the lamb." Because who will lay them together if not us with our greater ability to control our surroundings? So there may be hope after all.

Mental energy and thought may always surround us. As I become more used to traveling, I find that whole packets of information impinging on my awareness at once when I enter an unknown place with Jesus. I automatically understand the scenario. I always did up to a point but never noticed it before but now this ability has grown stronger the more I travel. I still need to ask many questions but at least now I can pick up if a person is male or female or what is happening right away if not why it is happening.

My own methods are easy but you may find your own or read about a different method, that is certainly acceptable. When I sit down, I sort of defragment my mind. I let my mind wonder in and out of the past day and beyond. Sometimes I play with ideas, sometimes I daydream and hope a little because my life can be dreary at times, and we all need hope. Sometimes I spend a long time at this cleaning house process, sometimes not, but eventually I settle down to my real job and purpose once these scattered pieces are set to rest. This is when Jesus takes me somewhere, talks to me or I begin to meditate..

It is different in the early mornings, then I often get into a lotus position on the floor and feel the golden light penetrate and cover my whole body. I then try to send it out and share it with the world. I practice gathering the light into myself because it is too vast to fit all at once. It is all golden, all the universe of suns in a solid sheet of golden light like an ocean made of gold. Jesus is within this golden river of light. Jesus is the gold as God is the gold as we are the gold.

I see in the future that my simple gift to the children will spread around the world reaching even into the most poverty stricken areas, to the children in Mexico's slums, Romania's sewers, China's sweatshops, India's homeless, and Africa's ragged hoards. Many of these children can't buy a book but I will reach them anyway through meditation; eventually they will learn to use the mental energy, maybe sooner than others because their need is greater.

Here, children, is my gift to you: How to touch your soul.

Begin by breathing slowly, in and out, quite your mind, relax your body, close your eyes and go into the light. The light expands as you enter. This light is your spirit helper, a part of your soul. Tell your spirit helper where you want to go, your soul will take you there. When you come back, tell your spirit helper "Thank you." As you grow in spirit, learn to hug the people of earth. But Remember-oneness can't be imposed from without. It can only grow from the heart. You will keep growing in life until your soul fills the universe.

I am still growing, like a flower, God's flower. I keep growing in wisdom but I still need to learn to control myself better, I will. I am not without help as I develop. My own spirit helper watches over me during my training into becoming. This same training that you will have if you choose to walk towards the light. I was born with a natural mental ability that was almost burnt out of me at an early age. It has taken all these years of life and growth to begin replacing these gifts. Jesus has been training me but I realize I still have a long way to go-into forever.

GOD'S GIFT

In the last chapter of book I, God said he would show me something. I have waited all these months and it was definitely worth the wait. The next few pages complete the chapter God's Show. This gift is so superlative and grand that I don't know how to convey its essence. Its beauty is almost more than any mortal being can absorb and handle. I am wondrously awed by this eternal moment. It's so regal and imposing that it could only be given to me in stages of development. I will try and write these stages of how it was presented to me.

During meditation I was surrounded by a group of highly evolved beings. A great soft and penetrating light hovered between us in the form of a globe. One of the beings said to me "you have been given a great gift." I recognized its greatness but I questioned how I should use it and to what purpose. I even had to ask how I should carry it and was told to "carry it within yourself."

This I have done since it was given to me. Sometimes I perceive this light as a nugget within my body, at other times I see this light as infusing my whole self and radiating outward in waves. Jesus told me that as long as I always remember to send the golden light outwards when I use it to share with others, I will never need to worry about misusing its power.

The next stage of the gift was given to me when Jesus showed me how to use the light energy. He told me to hold a person's hands in mine to share God's golden light with them. I asked, "but what should I say?" Jesus replied that "It doesn't matter what you say, you don't need to say anything."

I need to explain the next development differently because it is a place or understanding of God's being. I see myself walking on golden ground. All around me is gold, everything in the room, everything in the world, has converted in substance into this golden type of matter. As I move further into the golden world I recognize that nothing is differentiated in type, everything is made of golden God Stuff and God light. From here to all parts of the Universe is God's substance and all parts are within this golden substance as if I were in an ocean composed of only God.

Often, because the total ocean is too much for me to handle, I revert to surface texture of God's ocean. This is when it becomes a golden light shinning on a water pond. Waves move outwards in all directions. Reducing it further, I see a golden drop of liquid fall into the surface of the pond. Here I find God's eternal moment. Here the drop ceases to fall, the waves remain in stasis, the air forgets to blow, the birds stop singing. My heart seems to stop in mid-beat and my breath whispers away into silence. All is stilled. Time stands on guard at the palace gate. All breezes cease while even traffic horns and tires forget to roll in this soundless fraction of eternity—then the drop of golden water fattens and stretches in an elongated taffy string as it splashes into the next wave. My breath expels marching to time's rhythm once more. The golden city dissolves into sparkles of light.

Another development came with Jesus sitting across from me in a lotus position.[79] I saw a million suns gather into one waterfall and pour downward into my soul. This golden flow, I understood, was to help me visualize that I was a fountain through which God's energy could flow. From this fount energy could flow outwards into the population as was needed. I felt its soft godliness fill me to bursting and then I let it flow beyond myself in a spectral galaxy of golden nodes that reached far away. With Jesus' nod, I then played with the light pouring out braiding it and twisting it rivulets and different shaped streamers as though each shape had different meaning and I were the weaver of patterns. I sent this flowing stream into Jerusalem where major decisions are being made about the future. I thought the leaders felt the light at one point but then later everything seemed to disrupt and shatter. I will try again another time.

---

[79] He said this position is not necessary if it is not comfortable or if my back bothers me, position is not important, comfort is.

The next stage was walking on God's golden universe again and again realizing everything was intertwined and continued flowing as if made of one substance. Then when I was about to leave Jesus said I was not finished. I looked around and saw beneath my feet lay a cloth like pattern of brocaded silk. This brocade was made out of red and different other colored threads running down its length in swirls and turns that represented life flowing throughout the universe.

The last step, so far, was when we entered the brocaded cloth, a symbol of the complexity and intertwining of reality, even further and it is what left me so breathless with wonder. Jesus took me down into and between the threads of the brocade of pastel threads that represented the flow of life. Suddenly the brocade and thread turned golden and converted into God's ocean. But as we followed a single thread, grown huge, it turned into a beautiful transparent flower like image, larger than life. The flower was a life, its soft transparent petals turning and swaying in a unique dance for this single life force. All of this being's life was represented by the flower petals moving and turning as if in a gentle breeze amid the brocaded threads that interwove within it. This life's past, and future and present circumstances moved within the current of golden time. I could see small fragments defraying at the flower's edge and Jesus reached over and smoothed the edge with his hand. The transparent flower shape now rippled as if greeting a master.

I felt like crying with delight. The flowers petal formations rose above my head swaying as if to the gentle waves of butterflies multiplied in flight. As we rose above the garden I saw births and deaths in flower form as inter-wrapped threads that rewound and rewove further down the brocade of life. Suddenly I realized we were in God's Kingdom. The same golden forest and sky that I had visited before had come alive with actual beings who lived and breathed and walked on multiple worlds. God's garden had become the cosmos and a reflection of each life living within it. Each swaying flower a perfect mirror reflection of treasured life, a pulsing throb of pastel roots and golden sky in one vast Kingdom of God.

I let out my breath as tears of joy swam in my eyes reflecting Jesus smile.

On our next visit to God's Kingdom, Jesus took me to my own flower of life. I saw small parts of my past as I touched the flower's rim and actually smoothed out a few frays along it as Jesus showed me to do. Jesus explained to me that it is vary hard to heal oneself. That it is far easier to see and send the golden energy into other people. Knowing this, Jesus is healing me himself, working from the inside out. It is a slow process and I am content and thankful for his help. When he was done last Sunday, he told me, "This day you are healed."

Since this time, I continue to learn much. Jesus is instructing me in how to use the energy and to gather it into myself. He has a purpose in mind for its use. A purpose that I don't know or understand at this point but I trust that I will learn eventually. You will also continue to learn. May God's love be with you.

EARTH SPEAKS

At this time, we humans are reaping excessive fortune—we have it all—a beautiful blue sky, fresh smelling spring weather, flowers wafting in gentle breezes, temperate seasons. This will begin to deteriorate more and more until at some future point, there will be only a remnant left of these qualities we now take for granted yet now are so dear.

A worse case scenario for saving earth: The last people remaining finally make the conscious effort to change from selfish humans into highly evolved beings. Or, the more likely road, a long steady increase of people praying, meditating, and stabilizing the earth. A small movement already begun, growing from a mustard seed, growing and gaining and pulling in more people as the necessity becomes more apparent. Regardless of which path we choose, we will experience disaster. These disasters are the birth pangs Jesus spoke of 2000 years ago. Birth pangs that will usher in the new age of mental development within mankind.

Jesus has said that the erratic weather patterns, a sample of the changes in store for us, have already begun and they will increase. I think we have all noticed a change in the weather during the last few years. It is getting more unstable and probably accounts for much of our peaked interest in the weather programs on TV and the Web. Amazingly, Jesus said I live in one of the more stable areas of the country, I assume he is referring to drought and storms. So far, this spring he is certainly right, we have had more rain than we need while much of the rest of the country remains hot and dry.

The immediate future frightens me so much I refuse to go there, but Jesus admits that along with the erratic and scattered disasters there will be normal times, as many peaks as valleys. The problem is that we will refuse to see the extent of the problem until it runs so deep it will be almost too late, we won't change our outlook and old-fashioned ideas soon enough to prevent the major traumas to earth or ourselves. We will learn the hard way because it will take a lot of punishment before people finally begin to realize that we are intertwined into the psyche of soul of the earth and therefore we must incorporate it's well-being into our decisions.

All this makes so much sense as to be unarguable. But few of us will take it seriously for a long while, though some people are beginning to demand less development, it still remains too few to make much of a dent. While prosperity runs so hot and great, no one is interested in long term consequences, no one cares to read ugly predictions. Or, I smile at this, perhaps Jesus will decide to produce a few miracles to wake people up. Will people finally read what Jesus has asked me to write down? He says that whatever is needed, I'll know what to do when the time comes. Actually, I don't see a problem with this, a miracle is easy for me to believe in and understand because I have felt Jesus' power flow through me once before when he saved a person from choking. But, needed or not, it will be for Jesus to decide when and if extraordinary means are necessary.

For now, I am trying to gather my thoughts and put all the positive aspects together into one drawer, the Hopi Indians, the eastern philosophers, the naturalists, green peace, prayers, laughter morality, kindness, and love all into a Yin Yang like balance to weigh against negative forces. I wonder if earth's balance may be also intertwined with the quantum principals of non-locality in time and space, as is all existence. Have we up-set this balance on earth? Are we talking out and not giving back, not sharing?

Dare we attribute feelings of sadness and loss to the earth. What about a tree? Could we think of a living tree hundreds of years old as without merit or a sense of being? Would we give it no attributes of biomass, or psyche? Or accord to it some essence, at least, of all the life that has scampered in and out and between the crack of its bark and green leafy heights all those years. Then if we can imagine giving a tree some psyche, can't we also imagine and remember to give honor to our huge, living earth with a semblance of aliveness? as much as any living body could have with and among its parts. Earth with rocks and core, wind patterns and storms, sunshine reflecting off its snow peaks and bio-thinking life spread over its surface. This earth on which we stand, at the very least, deserves respect, and at the other extreme deserves our awareness of mind sense, perhaps like an intelligent, integrated computer or soul. Couldn't it also have a sense of its own self-being? We may need to finally come to this consideration. How dare we think otherwise. We are the earth - we are each an extension of earth matter. To deny earth its soul is to deny our own. Is our mind collectively earth's mind?

The Gaia hypothesis is a scientific idea of the earth keeping itself in balance. Some people have taken this theory and given it an element of worship of the Earth Mother but this was not in Mr. Lovelock's original theory. The idea begun as a science concept that pushes science further than it has went before, far enough to cover the living globe as a system of interaction that balances itself. It supposes that a part of any balance system revolves or centers on the life that lives in it or on it. The merits or demerits of the theory are still being debated by scientists around the world, and dismissed by most.

Obviously, I don't intend to wait for science to catch up with the ideas presented in this book in order to write or believe them. So I can throw out suggestions with impunity and jump off cliffs if I choose. Actually, I had forgotten about this specific cliffhanger until Jesus reminded me in his odd way. It is so gratifying, this knowledge that Jesus always knows, I was happy to be done copying my notes from the notebook and closed it with a sigh of relief. But Jesus smiled and said, "You're not done, you will fill up the last few pages and more."

"What," I laughed, because I knew I was all written out, except for a few odds and ends. Then when I checked out one of my odds and ends, I knew I needed to write more notes but suddenly I found something else, a reference to Teilhard de Chardin's book *The Phenomena of Man*. I had forgotten all about him but shouldn't have because I was coming around to these same ideas on my own. Just as all roads lead to Rome, all ideas lead to God, the rest is only side trips. So here stands the tall cliff, one a few other people have dared jumpe off too: Humans are the earth's collective mind.

When you stop to think about it, because we are the earth, we may hold the self-expression for the earth within our own being. As the earth is made of star stuff, we are made of earth stuff. At the very least, perhaps we are its outward expression of itself. At one point this week I actually remembered Jesus as the Alpha and Omega but still didn't to connect to Chardin. Now I have just re-read his book and find our thinking similar. In fact, I imagine Jesus was with him as he wrote his book too. Here are a few excerpts from his book with comments:

> "…because we are evolution." Page 232.

> Either nature is closed to our demands for futurity, in which case thought, the fruit of millions of years of effort, is stifled, still-born in a self-abortive and absurd universe. Or else an opening exists—that of the super-soul above our souls ; but in that case the way out, if we are to agree to embark on it, must open out freely into limitless psychic spaces in a universe to which we can unhesitatingly entrust ourselves" Page 233

My comment-As I read this I suddenly saw that I had realized his dream-my travels beyond our small earth system satisfies this.

> We have said that life, by its very structure, having once been lifted to its stage of thought, cannot go on at all without requir-ing to ascend ever higher. This is enough for us to be assured of the two points of which our action has immediate need.
>
> The first is that there is for us, in the future, under some form or another, at least collective, not only survival but also *super-life*.

The second is that, to imagine, discover and reach this superior form of existence, we have only to think and to walk always further in the direction in which the lines passed by evolution take on their maximum coherence." Page 234.

My comment-Ah, to turn back the clock to the naive 50s and 60s once again where the future had to be better and science would be the vehicle to take us there.

The general gathering together in which, by correlated actions of the *without* and the *within* of the earth, the totality of thinking units and thinking forces are engaged—the aggregation in a single block of a mankind whose fragments weld together and interpenetrate before out eyes in spite of (indeed in proportion to) their efforts to separate—all this becomes intelligible from top to bottom as soon as we perceive it as the natural culmination of a cosmic processes of organization which has never varied since those remote ages when our planet was young." Pages 243-44

My comment-Believe it or not, I wrote my own within and without and thoughts about this, on a lower lever to be sure, before I read Chardin's. He calls this grouping "a gigantic psycho-biological operation, a sort of *mega-synthesis*…" Page 244

His statement about mankind, "It is in the last resort only definable as a mind." P 248 and refers to "…*a spirit of the earth*." Page 253

Mankind, the spirit of the earth, the synthesis of individuals and peoples, the paradoxical conciliation of the element with the whole, and of unity with multitude—all these are called Utopian and yet they are biologically necessary. And for them to be incarnated in the world all we may well need is to imagine our power of loving developing until it embraces the total of men and of the earth." Page 266

"…A sense of the universe, a sense of the *all*, the nostalgia which seizes us when confronted by nature, beauty, music— these seem to be an expectation and awareness of a Great Presence. The 'mystics and their commentators apart, how has psychology been able so consistently to ignore this fundamental vibration whose ring can be heard by every practiced ear at the basis, or rather at the summit, of every great emotion? Resonance to the All-the keynote of pure poetry and pure religion…" Chapter 12, Page 266

I love the phrase Omega Point that Chardin used. It seems to me that Chardin was saying that mankind evolves into earth mind or earth spirit and then into the universal Omega Point. It was no accident that he chose this phrase to reflect the ultimate Christ.

I think our interactions, our lives that run trampling around and across its outer skin may enhance its psyche or soul. Unlike Chardin, I needn't worry about being scientific. In Chardin's day science held the promise of great things to come. Now we are more sophisticated and realize although science has given us much we can recognize it has flaws. I see a future where science will play a smaller part in our world. We have learned, almost too late, that science and its technological child is what changed humankind's positive interaction with earth into a negative. We began using up too much too fast and our constant over-use has become rape and pillage. We emptied the water tables that took eons to fill, burnt up fossil fuel that took, thousands of years to acquire, slashed millions of acres of trees without concern for air quality. Fortunately, the system kept in balance amazingly well for eons in spite of people, which are probably due to our inability to literally remove anything from its system, everything goes back into the system at some point just as it would in a closed space ship, but this recycling unit must stay in working order. If we change the composition so greatly that it can't recycle itself, what then?

Earth shares our spiritual force and because of this, it is subject to disruption by the misuse of spiritual power or neglect from us. I am not saying to worship the Earth Mother or Sopha? All I am saying is what many spiritual groups have said all along, to respect the earth and the life that abounds on her. Where can you stand, set, or swim without life teaming in abundance? So much so, that it seems to me that earth must have some semblance of a spiritual awareness—to think less is to limit God. God gives life. Earth's life could have grown or evolved just as human life did. It could have a type of mind so different from ours that we could never know it, or it could be a collective of all our minds, or it could be alive in ways unfathomable to us.

Do you remember the Source in my first book? I still don't understand exactly what I saw except that it was majestic and seemed to be a cornucopia fount for life, all kinds of life, not only arms and legs and people and wings, but whole, round worlds tumbled out of its light as well as mountains and forests and elephants and ants. So if it is true that in some low sense, or high, earth does have awareness—we, all of us, have some making up to do, and its time to join in and repair the damage.

Ah, perhaps you didn't read a thing I said after I mentioned Gaia and the Earth Mother. The phrase caught and held you captive. Why are you afraid? Isn't there room in your philosophy to love the earth you stand on as well as God and saints and heaven. If a mature mother can find room to love all her children surly you can find room in your heart for many philosophies and earth's lifeblood may grow beyond philosophy. Your blood came from the earth's soil. The earth is within and without you. You are the earth, your mobility doesn't make you less so. Jesus likes this thought. Besides, how does loving earth detract from loving God? It all belongs together and is all part and parcel of God's creation just as you are a unique expression of earth matter. Perhaps The Source was the breath of God. Perhaps God gives as much credence to the life of an earth as to a man, or to a mountain as to a worm. I'll say it again, how dare we set limits for God. All things are possible with God, perhaps even an earth with a voice of its own.

Jesus tells me that the Catholic Church will not like this aspect of my book. But I don't know why not. We are more grown up now, aren't we? Grown up enough that we don't need to do battle over who worships who. It isn't who you worship— how could you worship anything that was un-God. No the real battle has always been, good against evil, right against wrong, lovers against haters, light against the dark. Jesus smiles at the simplicity of what I write here yet armies march onto battle for every contrived reason but the good.

Sometimes I think God should come and wipe the earth off—clean it up, then maybe next time we will learn—but didn't God try that once, or twice? And we still didn't learn. We'll maybe with Jesus to show us the way we will finally understand this next time what the problem is and fix it. Perhaps it will sink in deep and begin a positive change. He has given us indications of what to look for as we search out the problem but chooses not to get specific. We must fumble for an answer. I guess, if it came too easily we would dismiss it just as easily.

One clue I found was in the Chaos theory, "Simple systems give rise to complex behavior, and complex behavior gives rise to simple systems and most important, the laws of complexity hold universally, caring not at all for the details for a systems constitution atoms."[80] This means that small irrational vibrations or errors in a system can no longer be ignored. On the surface this chaos theory has nothing to do with earth's soul or its problems but chaos plays a large part in earth's weather patterns. The metaphor that the flight of a butterfly can cause a storm on the other side of the

---

[80] *Chaos: Making a New Science* by James Gleick, 1988, p. 304

globe is not only a beautiful image but has some truth to it, as well. Simple systems can affect complex ones, complex fluxations can cause simple ones. So if we do something small, like eradicate a small fish from the oceans, it could have huge effect on the larger system in which we live. We need to learn how to manage and watch out for the small stuff, not just the large.

When I was still questioning if the hurricane or vortex could be dust, and dirt and wind from asteroid impact that has hit sideways or glanced off the atmosphere, Jesus told me to watch the television weather program. I did. I soon realized that if it was an impact of some kind, we would be able to blame God, not ourselves because we cannot prevent it and would not be the cause of earth's destruction. Jesus has said we are causing earth's future problem, so, could I eliminate asteroid impact from my list? Not really because we could be thinning our atmosphere and thus creating a larger potential for disaster? Ozone holes, ultraviolet from sun seeping into holes are not the same as thinning our atmosphere so I don't think this is the case. We are changing the weather, but even so, Jesus agrees that the problem is larger than that. We could be doing something to our atmosphere that will make the glancing skim of an asteroid deadly to our survival? This is a possibility. Antarctica is ready to slide into the sea because we have added heat to the atmosphere? So far my list continues unscathed, I haven't eliminated anything.

The reason I like the Gaia theory is because I believe God allowed for the system to vary greatly and the balance to stretch as far as possible. There is probably a lot of room for give and take and yielding on a world system and it probably can absorb many mistakes. I questioned if our hydrogen bombs had the same effect as a small volcanic eruption ?

Jesus immediate and empathetic reply was, "No."

We'll darn, I'll just keep on guessing. I even wondered if our collective thoughts could have as destructive results as our actions do. Interestingly, Jesus didn't have a comment about this thought.

I know you still wonder about Jesus. Most of you don't believe me when I say Jesus is here, most people refuse to see him. Which makes me wonder, because I can see or hear him, what else do most of us refuse to acknowledge or see, what else slips by our consciousness because we have never imagined its possibility?

Then, Eureka! All this time, I had been looking in the wrong direction for the problem–as soon as I found it I knew it to be true. Bio, breath, biology-life is the answer. Or it is central to the answer.

Jesus said, "Now I can show you how to save earth."

I felt such joy—I immediately went outside and touched the damp earth in my back yard. I put my fingers through the grass and felt the black soil then the bark of a tree. It had just been raining and it smelled earthy and alive and a prolific source for life. I felt myself pulse with the earth as I stood upon its surface.

At present, it is late spring, the weather couldn't be more perfect here in Lower Michigan. It is cool and sunny after a small rain. My roses are in bloom and the grass is bright green. The soil is so abundant I need to keep pulling out elephant ears, and dandelions and wild grapes. Maple that started as shoots last year beside the fence is already as tall as I am. Weeds are even taller. Life is so profuse and wild. We can touch any spot on earth's surface and it teams with life, so much so, that it is impossible to believe that this could ever change so drastically as to become barren. Earth life is so voracious that it takes hold everywhere on every landscape, even inside volcanoes and hot springs.

We all know that some areas are in danger, that life may have been pushed back in some hot, dry areas, or where we have over planted but that land was fragile, the soil shallow. We presume that further changes will be gradual and that our technology will be able to cope with them. But I wonder. I suspect that the huge farms centered on profit motive will weigh heavily against the real purpose of the land, and that earth will loose that battle too, though farmers will give it a good try. Huge farms may turn out to be one more blow against earth, an earth that is already feeling spasms and tremors? An earth that may be choking and strangling. What can we do? We can't help growing and spreading our cities across the land, can we? We must continue.

I had been racking my brains earlier this morning while listening to the birds sing and suddenly it hit me, Jesus is referring to biology, life, the biological process of living, breathing, thinking, and existing, of souls inside all biological systems. I feel so stupid. Why didn't I see this before now.

But that doesn't answer everything. What still throws me is that we are doing it to ourselves and that heaven can detect it. How can we fight what we can't even detect? Unless Jesus wants us to combat the whole ecologic damage system we have caused and fix it all? Perhaps it all hangs together, of course it does. Species are dying out, to be sure, but this would not make earth barren some day, species can be replaced even if not us arrogant humans. No something else is happening.

Jesus told me last night that our problem is similar to Silver World's and that we will need to use our minds to solve it. If true, I feel that we are doomed. We humans find it hard to gather together on a large enough scale to be effective. The only thing we have ever joined together for was to watch "who shot JR" or some similar TV event. Surly Jesus knows this, in fact, he says heaven admires and delights in our complexity and diversity, But it is this same complexity that negates togetherness.

I still have not grasped what earth's ultimate problem is yet. Although Jesus has promised to tell me if I haven't grasped the answer soon, even so, I am afraid he won't give us factual information we expect and usually receive in our modern scientific modes of thinking. So I had to accept that even his answer might not be as complete as I would hope. Plus, we may need to invent a new branch of science just to detect the problem. It seems there is only dilemma after dilemma.

I often wonder if Jesus is enjoying my quandary, my search for the truth and earth's ultimate problem, and I think he is. But remember, this problem, whatever it is, is a long term one that will require a long-term solution to solve. So there is still time enough for play and whimsy like listening to the trees sing.[81]

I was doing exactly that while sitting by myself in my son's back yard, listening to the breeze whistle through the aspen trees when I suddenly got the notion, "Why not ask earth what it needs, or what is wrong?" I meditated and a few highly evolved people joined me (I am not highly evolved but only a student). Then a person of Indian decent (I don't know what tribe he was from) joined the group and someone in the far distance began to dance and chant. While the highly evolved Indian guide contemplated and tried to listen to the cry of earth's soul for all of us.

We were all sitting or standing on a grassy knoll of his choice with square, blue/purple rock mountains far off in the distance. We stilled our thoughts and tried to help him listen to the earth and the wind as it blew across the knoll. Soon we heard a soft whistling and our guide crunched up with all his muscles tightened as if in agony, then he almost fell to the side and began jerking in small quivers. We got a sense of great imbalance like a sea-saw. When he straightened up he looked very fearful and frightened and we perceived pictures of h-bombs, primed and waiting, as if it could erupt at any second. We all felt earth's fear at this point. Then we received a warning and visualization through the ocean depths and down to a deep fissure or crack in the earth before our guide was finally done. Suddenly, I felt emptied as we were left to contemplate earth's anger and fear before we disbanded.

I finally thought to ask, what does a thermonuclear bomb look like from the top? I have never seen a picture of one from the top. We are always shown hydrogen bombs that look like mushrooms as if some fairy garden had went berserk, not us. Would it look like the vision Mary showed me? It seems right. It seems likely. It seems damn eminent.

---

[81] This next part I was going to put in my third Travel Book but Jesus said to put it here in this one.

If we are looking for a nightmare, thermonuclear bombs will serve nicely. Actually, now that the United States and Russia have begun to defuse a few of them, it seems to have dulled our minds to the hoards of nuclear bombs still sitting in silos around the world, 36,000 in all, thousands of which are hair-triggered to alert status. Not included in this number are the bombs the political fringe have waiting for us, the fanatics who use dirty basements or warehouses instead of silos.

The picture Mary showed me could have been a warning, not an actual event because some nations are still testing nuclear bombs and the tests by these nations and the west years ago could have had a disastrous effect deep down inside the earth. In some way indefinable to our science, the test may have set up new vibrations within the earth's core that is causing, or threatening to cause great physical havoc and spiritual discord.

What to do. Jesus says, "Dismantle the bombs." Oddly enough, almost everyone agrees that this should be done but no one (read governments here) knows quite how to do it. We could and do write letters to congress but then again, what can one government do? Or who can plough through the red tape each government has set itself into?

Jesus is going to speak to us about the problems on earth and what we can do about them in the next and last chapter. He seems to be hinting that at some point a nuclear bomb is inevitable and that some serious damage from bomb tests has already occurred. It seems that all we can do is lesson their impact and retaliation potential, in other words, keep control of the situation when it happens. For a number of reasons, America is considered a target by many rogue nations. I can't think of any worse scenario than a nuclear bomb unless it is more of them. I am terrified of fire and always have been. H-bombs bring firestorms and conflagrations to large areas-areas so large that emergency teams can't even get through. Back in the 70's and 80's a few TV movies showed what could happen in a nuke war. The horror was actually understated because the reality would have been too graphic for television.

Somehow with the bomb tests or perhaps radioactive waste leaking down into the earth we have caused an addition or subtraction to life forms there. They may spread out and begin sterilizing the earth. This sounds preposterous but this is serious business; a magnitude worse than even an asteroid impact that would destroy civilization but leaves the earth intact to reproduce once again. This is where we came from, remember. To sterilize the globe and leave it un-habituated to all life in the future is unconsciousable. I do not understand what would do this, unless it is radioactivity of some sort that effects the DNA molecules, the building blocks of life, so that they cannot replicate. I am still playing guessing games here.

I keep begging God, "please no, anything but thermonuclear bombs— floods, hurricanes, tornados, earthquakes, heat waves, anything but nukes, anything. We can continue trying to keep the lid or turn bombs off, but in the end, prayer may be the only effective action we have left. So I continue to pray. Jesus has not instructed me how we can save the earth yet, he has told me that "My part will be easy." I don't know what he means by that, like you I must wait and see.

I must go back to Silver World soon. We have at least one more visit, Jesus says more than one, but I keep putting it off because I am afraid of what we will find when we get there. I have no prior information of their status. It could be anything from complete annihilation to complete recovery. Jesus knows but has not for-warned me about what is happening or has happened or will happen on Silver World, I must go and see for myself. I hesitate once again deciding to wait another night.

During morning meditation, Jesus suggested we travel to Silver World for our last visit in this series. I was a little startled by his request but readily agreed besides the cassette tape of chants had just clicked off and I still felt very comfortable in my lotus position on the mat.

Jesus told me as we neared a wooded section filled with women and children that I should go into the women's mind because I would find it interesting. It certainly was. The women, children, and senior adults, you'll remember, were left in small enclaves while the men went to fight the war against their government. As I went into the women's mind, I found she was thinking about the blight on the other continent. She was not only thinking about it but was actively folding a image of it's black soil and bleak deadness into odd shapes, she kept sending the images inward and outward, kneading and pounding on them as if she were reducing air bubbles in bread dough. With each fold she reduced the mental image in size; so instead of bread rising from leavening, it was like black bread being shrunk further and further into small tight knots. I suddenly realized that everyone in the wooded area was using the same set of images to reduce the blight that all of the women, children and adults were doing household chores all this while.

The women was not sitting in a spiritual circle with the other women while her mind folded and refolded the blight into itself but moving items around on a open wooden cart that was roughly made out of huge sticks tied together with twine, a type of grass cloth formed the sides and shelves. The cart seemed to hold pots and bowls and she was stacking the bowls after wiping them with a rag. The children were doing various other household jobs, sweeping and picking up sticks from their general living area. The oldest men and women were also doing their part. They were all folding and refolding as they worked.

Evidently, out of necessity, they had devised a new spiritual level that they could carry with them through out the day-they could fight the blight and join one another on a mental level that had been unknown before the war. Left to fight their own war for their world, the women and older people and children had evolved a new method of reducing the blight that was quick and very effective. Vast areas of naked land were being opened for recovery by the mental process of these women. The blight was shrinking further and further back to its point of origin. Soon they would be able to re-seed the continent with green trees and grasses and flowers.

Except for a few skirmishes, the war was now over, and the men were returning to the forest glens victorious but wounded. I watched as a few elders lifted a solder whose arm hung limp and useless against his side, limp over to one of the cots, more were being carried through the green trees. One group of men sat around a low table in the clearing talking about the new method the women had devised to get rid of the blight. They were amazed that the blight had been fought off so quickly in their absence. They would quickly learn this new technique themselves and begin the reseeding the other continent as soon as possible. First they had a lot of work to do recovering their own continent from the ravages of war.

There was much repair work to do in the cities and countrysides and Jesus took me on a quick tour of the war torn world. I saw that the city we had visited once before with its quaint buildings and large framed windows was burnt almost to the ground. No children played gliding games here now. Vast areas of forest were now barren and burnt as if a monster had eased its milk teeth by gnashing and chewing on bone. This even though most of the heavy fighting took place near the space ports for the moon base.

The war on the moon had also been fought and won but recovery would be slower on the moon. It would take a long while for all the men to return home from the moon because transportation was slow and inadequate. In the meantime a peaceful use would be found for what was lift of the moon caverns and mines.

All in all the people of Silver World had survived severe hardships during the war on two fronts but had risen to a new understanding of their own mental abilities and their place in the natural order of life. They would recover from their wounds and rebuild their world to incorporate their newfound strength and spiritual growth. I was pleased and happy for them and thankful to have met such beautiful people.

JESUS SPEAKS

I asked Jesus the pivotal question tonight. What can we do to save the earth?

You know what Jesus answered?

"Turn them off, turn them all off, Throw every bomb away."

"But that is so simple" I complained.

He smiled.

"I mean it's so simple that it can't be done. All the governments around the world have been trying to dismantle these hydrogen bombs for years, sort of, treaty after treaty and talk after talk, Russia and the United States have begun to dismantle bombs."

Jesus just nodded and repeated his statement, "Turn them off."

"But how? I said exasperated, how can we get rid of them?"

I remembered what Jesus said about how surprised we could be at group imagery and its effectiveness. I played with the idea that people could just use imagery and mind travel to go to a bombsite in a warehouse or silo and bombard the sight with mental energy. Don't worry what country or nation or group owns the bomb, in fact, it might be construed as treason if you did, so just go to any silo and focus. We could even imagine water flooding up to the top if we needed to, anything that works to keep our mind in tandem with the site. We may never know or have concrete evidence that our efforts bore fruit, but in this case, no news is good news. Perhaps if we kept going back over and over to focus at the same site, our mental energy would become more evident. We might imagine it rusting and breaking apart or caving in. It would be nice if we could do this. My imagination was running full steam ahead. But then we could ask a valid question—if it is so easy, and who said it was, why doesn't Jesus just use his own mind to dampen or flood these bombsites?

He can't!

It was people, by their own violation who choose, by voting or not voting, by putting the wrong people in power or by omission of that power who put the bombs in place. It must be people, collectively or otherwise, who take them away again. What we put into place, we must remove. What we do, we must undo. What we sow, we reap. Jesus would be violating God's decree of free choice if he removed the bombs.

"We'll we can't do it either."

Jesus agreed with me that it was not feasible at this time in our development to turn off the bombs mentally. "If you were more mature you could turn them off with the use of mental energy but you are not strong enough yet to do this," he told me. "You could try though, some people may have the ability."

Is there something else can we do? I don't think I can turn off a bomb with my mind, Believe me if I could I would, but I can't even turn these horrible radios off that race down the street booming rap music, I've tried. If I had any mental abilities at all, there would be a lot of radios turned into slag heaps right now.

"Yes you can," Jesus said.

I thought about the idea for a minute and how thoughtless and arrogant it is of people to blast their radios like they do. I love piece and quiet. Some people have begun turning them off. Some neighbors have turned their radios down lately. Probably for a number of reasons, complaints to the police being a major one. Then I suddenly realized what Jesus meant. The problem is people's actions not the radio's. We may not be able to use mental energy against physical radios but people emotions are a different story. Behavior is impressionable to emotions, words, and thoughts. We can use mental energy to affect people's attitudes and desires, increase their concern for other people. Love can turn people around. Expressions of love, however applied, can help people to grow and perhaps choose to stop venting their anger or hurting other people. To me loud angry swear words in this music is hurtful. After all, hatefulness and arrogance are actions people use when they are begging to be understood or liked. It is like Gandhi taught us. Keep giving and showing good manners and it will wear down the anger in people. They will stop being so aggressive towards other people.

"I don't know," this seems almost as impossible as mentally turning radios to slag. Some people will not listen no matter what words are spoken or feelings we share with them. Would they listen to the whisper of psychic hugs or feel our love penetrate their hearts?

Of course we must continue to march and write letters, to fight in every way possible just as many people are doing now. But sending out our mental energy and thoughts of caring to specific people who hold the reins might prove to be a vital part of this fight to turn off the bombs. Small groups would be more effective than individuals. We would need a photo of a person who must be reached, then hold this person's image in our minds and go to that person and give them a huge hug? Love them and request that they turn off the bombs, or just let them know they are loved. I have used this method to reach out to people and I believe it works.

Jesus said it will work. That eventually if we continue to use the power within our minds we could deflect destructive events. He suggested that we could even put an idealized image in our minds of the type of person who would likely build and send out a bomb and somehow our thoughts and hugs would arrive at the right person. Jesus advises that this method is slow but effective. It can work if enough people try hard to learn how to use the mental energy they get from God through meditation. According to Jesus, it will be important to continue directing our love and concern to the same people repeatedly. I would think that it is also import to not neglect the chain of command of the leaders.

On the negative side, Jesus added that we need to remember there are some people in the world who cannot be turned from the destructive path they have chosen. This mental energy will only work effectively with people who already feel a sense of guilt, people who still care about other people and the consequences of their actions. Some people are beyond reach and you can look around the world and see this to be true.

I know personally I have found this to be true. Many people in prisons seem beyond hearing a psychic whisper, also people so caught up in power's thrall that they have lost their sense of psyche. The leader of Yugoslavia is one such person. He can't be reached through prayer or mental energy and when I tried, heaven advised me that my efforts were useless.

"Do everything you can to get rid of these nuclear bombs," Jesus said to me, "Continue to fight on every front, pray and start groups for meditation. Send your thoughts to the leaders and drivers of nations."

But he asked us to remember—hate begets hate—we must not send destructive thoughts, only love and caring will be truly effective. We must remember that every person is worth loving and needs our concern and empathy.

Referring to my search to find the problem that plagues earth the most, Jesus said that I am wrong when I try and concentrate on one problem as if solving one problem will solve them all. He said we must turn off the bombs but he also explained that the status of the population is directly related to their threatened use of bombs to solve their problems. In Jesus words:

A happy, contented people wouldn't think of destroying each other with hydrogen bombs. Everything is interrelated-surly you know this by now, how tightly woven the fabric of existence is-like a brocaded cloth with many colors and patterns running through it. In order to stop one event we must change a thousand other events—this is basic and everyone knows that a social system is complex and diverse, but to feel it in your bones, your heart, and your souls is not so easy. This complexity is so grand and all consuming it can discourage your effort too.

Remember, I am here to help. All of heaven is concerned with the future of earth. You are not alone as you work out the different problems. And these problems are many and more serious than you can understand. Most of the predictions are potential and almost certain. You have the evidence before you of these potential disasters. The warming of the earth and change in its weather patterns are only surface manifestations of the more deeply underlying dangers. It is already too late to divert many of these disasters from occurring. This is why I told you to concentrate on turning off the bombs. Their destructive power lays further into the future and therefore you have a better chance of diverting the damage if you begin now. I repeat-It is too late to prevent many major disasters on the globe from occurring but some can still be diverted-namely a major nuclear war and the blight that threatens to turn earth into a dead and empty world.

You can lessen the impact of the coming disasters by recognizing and using your mental interaction with the earth and helping the earth throw off the ills it now faces. You are the earth and you must learn to give it as much love and attention as you would your own child for proper growth. In order to turn off the bombs, you must learn how to use your mental energy to good effect as well as physical abilities. When your mind and soul and body work in tandem, when you are balanced, your total environment is also balanced. This is the only way to save yourselves and your earth. If you truly loved one another, many of these disasters would not be in danger of occurring because earth as well as yourselves would be in balance.

Prayer is a step in the evolutionary process, mental energy, the mental energy God gave you is the next step and a vital one. Many people have already walked down this road—follow them. Their final step will be into heaven-a heaven alive with many people interacting throughout the universe.

I asked Jesus to explain to us what heaven detects is wrong with earth. He continues:

Heaven detects a problem on two levels, in earth's mental energy and also in its physical make up. We have caused a rift in both systems. They have become unbalanced. Mental energy is what pervades the universe, we might consider it like thoughts or thought vibrations. This thought energy is being stilled and held more in earth's gravity well than is usually the case. You could imagine earth's mental energy as knotted, tangled, and bound up so tight that it is not breathing, as if the fresh country air that should be blowing in from afar has been cut off. The psychic energy has been twisted and keeps twisting upon itself instead of loosing up and breathing.

We are not just taking about tragic, filled scenes or a skirmish of wars like people experienced in the past. This is like a neurotic grip of fear. This mental imagery of fear as a certainty, a picture of a future that is frightful to behold. So terrible that earth's breath is frozen in place and unable to move forward or backward, like a person in a catatonic state of dream. The future lays ahead by its known path and without change will not be turned from that path. Earth sits frozen in fear of the nuclear bombs that will certainly be used. The severity of their use will not only determine if humanity survives but also if earth itself does because without human intervention the lifeless hole will grow. Without human persistence and effort, the chemical-nuclear mix will not be halted. Without human creativity and resourcefulness earth cannot rescue itself from the brink, regardless that humanity was the original cause of the rift. Sickness and empty seas and land will be the result.

This grip of fear prevents the earth from keeping itself in balance. A balanced earth prevents major disasters from occurring. It is like an over blown system of mishaps that will keep sizzling and popping because the on and off switch is blown.

The physical problem is a direct consequence of the imbalance of mental energy being out of kilter. A mix of nuclear and chemical substances have seeped deep into the earth and will work itself upwards to begin spreading unless it is prevented by the energy matrix of balance.

Jesus is throwing concepts at me and I am trying to write them down in ways we can understand but I can hardly understand them myself. I also need to ask myself, and Jesus, if I am getting too dramatic with the imagery. He continues:

If the deep fissure of nuclear and chemical mix are allowed to fester and grow then at some point, it will become too late to stop it. At this point it can be halted just by tending to the earth and all its various life forms, by making earth healthy. The blight can be overcome with good mental imagery and mental vibrations. We have a few years to learn and practice this fact. It is a long-term problem, the solution of which can be matched to our ability to tame the weather. As we learn to use psychic energy to blend and unify the weather with our needs we will see the effectiveness of our efforts at work.[82]

Jesus said that all of Traveling in Space and Time, Part III will help complete the answer on how humans can save the earth from destruction. It will show how some people already use mental energy and other hidden abilities for the benefit of earth.

---

[82] Jesus does not say control the weather. He means for us to work with it as a friend not a foe.

As a final statement in this chapter, I asked Jesus about the other half of the prayer he began to tell me about. What is the next step?

Jesus told me we could all do the same thing I was teaching the children to do when they came to visit, go someplace with your mind. I told the children to go to Disney World but we adults can go when our psyche is needed. A prayer or meditation session may need a speaker to narrate and hold group's thoughts together. As the group mentally gathers together they can surround the earth like a net with their feelings of love and compassion. They can hug the earth or surround specific groups of trees or rocks or rivers or meadows or swamplands. The prayer can encircle every part with our mind and respect for earth. We are the mobile trees, we are their sisters and brothers upon the earth. Let our combined spirit bow our reverence to God and this system we call earth.

Part III

NOTEBOOK

It was Jesus who suggested that I leave this section of my notes in their original form; therefore, I have edited it as little as possible for readability. I don't know what the exact message is that Jesus wants you to read. He has stated that this third section will help us learn how to save the earth. I hesitantly took out some sections of self-pity and a few other items. This section three will read like a diary because I have kept dates intact. Sometimes, it will also read dumb and stupid because I wrote my thoughts as they rambled through my mind and had every intention of deleting or rearranging them, skip these sections when you choose.

When I began these notes I thought this book would be about three or four highly evolved people who I can sense or talk with mind-to-mind. I have put extensive notes about these people throughout this notebook but, even if I know their names, I have chosen not to use them for their own privacy. A list of symbols I used and what little information I started out with regarding each person is in the back of the book.

Also please understand that I edited these notes after the September 11, 2001 bombing of the World Trade Centers and was tempted to add explanations regarding this tragedy, but did not except in for a few footnotes. In hindsight, it is easy to see the writing on the wall. It is also hard to put any real sense of time to Jesus words but he did warn me that something was coming. I want to add that in the current notes that I am writing now, notes that will not be included in this book, I asked Jesus to please explain why he can't give me a more exact warning. He told me that if he was to give me an exact warning of when where or how it would set the event in the future place as fact, perhaps unalterable fact. The future is not fixed but fluid and mobile like an ocean current; this is why it is better for me to grope and search for meanings and explanations. The good news is that the future can be altered, That is the purpose of this book.

Note on the symbols I use for certain highly evolved people who I have met during mind travel and who may be included in this third section.

Z–One person who is so very old and highly evolved that at the point of death one day, she won't face death but only a slight transition between two different states of being. I don't know her name but regardless she has the right to remain anonymous. I don't know if she is recognized as great in her own country but hope to learn more about her one day.

Y–this person is male. He has given me permission to use his name and I will one day but, at this point, I choose not to reveal his name. Y tells me he has been watching me grow and evolve, just as he has been evolving ahead of me. At first, I did not know he has known me for so long a time, I presumed that I found him one night because he seemed receptive to becoming my friend. We are good friends even though my upbringing was so different from his. All his life he has evolved in the mental discipline of meditation while I have had almost none. I am considered by all to be a wild card therefore they watch my life with interest. Y tells me that I belong to their group now even though I have far to go with learning how to be.

X–This person is also a male but he remains mysterious by circumstance and choice. I don't know his name or who he is but I have tried to guess and often been wrong. Sometimes I think I hardly know him and other times I believe he is very close and familiar. I hope to solve the mystery of X one day.

W–The only thing I know or choose to say about this person at this time is that he resides somewhere out West in the United States. I believe we will learn more of each other in future years.

There are more people that I can hardly perceive at the present time and some who I have just touched mentally for a moment, but not too many. Jesus said there are not more than two handfuls of highly evolved people on our world at this time.

7/31/00

Did everyone get to paradise except me? Driving on the freeway on this beautiful, grand, country strip of freeway, everyone going somewhere, shopping in full malls on Hall Road, boating on the Great Lakes, traveling to friend's homes or relatives in other states, everyone on the go. Black people are moving up to middle class while white people keep rising into higher and higher wealth. Stores are full, jobs are plentiful, people are beautifully dressed, moving, dancing, happy. They all seem to be in a won-derful land of happiness, happiness greater than has ever been achieved on earth before. Even twenty or thirty years ago, prosperity on this scale was undreamed of except by a few.

As I look around, I wonder at my own state of affairs compared to this multitude of plenty. Is there something wrong with me? Assuredly there is, I and a number of other people who prosperity has passed and left behind, uncaught by the hook of plenty as if we were invisible. It could be argued that many people on the bottom have had problems that kept them where they are, drinking, substance abuse, children at a young age or too many of them. My own problem could be lack of industry? Or ambition? Lack of friends and lovers? Regardless, I and others seem to have missed the boat of earthly paradise.

I am not unhappy. Happiness seems to arrive for me in little delights rather than large ones and I realize that I am content most of the time. But is all this happiness paradise? I also perceive that something is wrong here. That this picture postcard is out of balance. Grossly unbalanced in the long term, grossly centered in self-happiness now, at all costs, and almost desperately so. Get everything now while its still available, never mind anyone born in the future, the next generation will need to take care of itself because this paradise is neglectful of those born even at this time into the wrong circumstances or odd situation. One fourth of the population of the world lives on less then one dollar a day, where is paradise for these people?

Can any true paradise neglect so many? "No." By definition paradise must include all people into its circumference or it is rotten in its fringe or core and fake. Also, a little thought helps us realize that this style of paradise is lopsided and unworkable for the total globe. If everyone on earth had this kind of prosperity, the ability to squander and spend and play and use up vast sources of energy, the whole structure of this unworkable paradise would fall down around our ankles and all of us would be caught wanting. How long can it take to run out of gas, raw materials, food, land, and water. The gold of the next century? It will be water.

No way could our life style be shared around the globe without killing it sooner than later. So what's the answer? Don't share it, stay in clumps of rich against poor. Make sure nothing is handed out except a bit here and a bit there. If this isn't the way we think, it's the way we act and actions speak loudly. That way we can insure our own future and never mind theirs. Instead of the roaring 20's we will have the roaring 2000's before chaos rears its head and life once again rises from the ashes. We must face a real fact, a person like Hitler or a new World War needs only a push and poverty serves just as well now as a lever as it ever did. It was and is probably the underlying cause of most wars. And all because someone forgot that we all need a share of paradise, not just a few. A world out of balance cannot stay pushing smoothly against its soft velvet curtain, storms and thunders will eventually shred it to bits, the crest of poverty must slam and stab against us, that is its nature.

So what, you may think, if it happens it happens. This is the fun time and who cares about tomorrow. When it all falls down, then we will deal with it. If we get nuked or crushed then we will rise again, pick up the pieces and put them back together again. This type of thinking is not thinking at all but avoidance of reality. Long term planning or care for the future could prevent great heights and crushes from happening and must if we are to ever achieve a true paradise. People living in a true paradise would not allow even one child to whimper in hunger or pain because their pain would reverberate around the world as an unfinished work of art yet to be done. The craft of paradise should be sustaining itself and keeping paradise available for all.

8/5/00

What does God see? God showed me a field of flowers, like fat water lilies laying on the water surface. All of these flowers seemed beautiful with only slightly torn or frayed edges here and there on each flower. Also, all these flowers flowed together as though moving down stream. If we ask God about justice for all, this may be why it comes so late, we are all beautiful to God. A truer picture of what God sees would be all one flower with intricacy related veins of people running through its petals. How could God destroy such beauty. How could you? Perhaps you can't, perhaps you could only destroy an underlying concept or layer and not the whole of it.

A better analogy or another way to recognize such beauty is to see ourselves as infants, children as God does. Look at any kindergartner room full of children and watch their interactions at play and learning, their different temperaments, abilities to pay attention, interactions with other children, and their constant tendency to keep and keep what the other child has. We try to teach these children tolerance and other qualities and we have not taught them to ourselves yet. Yet, if you speak of justice, how would you dish it out? Could you ever think to destroy these beautiful children for not learning their lesson quick enough? What if Susie and Johnny who have gathered most of the crayons and toys in their corner, refuse to share with the child who is timid and unable to hold on to any toys. A good teacher in these small cases can bring about a semblance of justice and equality, but not by destroying the room. Think of our whole world reduced to this Kindergarten Room as God looks down at us.

What is God to do? How should he bring justice? Will God do as Jesus suggests in the Bible, wait to pull the weeds out. What if God sees that it has gotten out of hand? That the children were not learning or that they were destroying the room and breaking up the toys? windows? Each other? Yes, what then? God is the teacher and will do what must be done—gently or sternly?

8/5/00

Our hearts determine what system we choose to live under. If our hearts and consciousness are selfish and infantile, then so will be the system that runs our world. Sometimes I think, "If only there was a true justice" but then who would be left standing? And I may not be among them. Economic justice alone might level three fourths of the population of the world down in size until they matched the quarter who live on less than a dollar a day? Wait, you say true justice would be each according to their own consciousness and ability to understand? Yet, most people deliberately refuse to understand or see the need for all people to share goods in a finite system. Although, thankfully, those who are truly young and exuberant and who are just starting their full lives, even evil seems to leave them more or less alone. Perhaps their love of life sends evil on its way. We should learn a lesson from this. But they will soon pick up our old habits and the system of greed we parents have chosen.

Also, when we think of justice, we should remember that there is one thing God will not or cannot do and that is to choose our course. God has given us the ability to choose the system in which we live. Individually, we can choose to follow God or not, but this choice does not eliminate God's reaction to our decision, his temperance or severity, relaxation of rules or punishment. During the diatribe of writing this night, Jesus has said nothing at all but God has smiled and frowned. It is enough to turn my knees to quivering.

8/15/00

What is prosperity? As I take a look at myself I suddenly realize that I am very prosperous. I have few needs that aren't fulfilled, the main one is lack of a companion. Real prosperity is acquiring what you need for equanimity not acquiring what you don't need. It is often hard to tell the difference and judgment must be made accordingly. When young and raising a family the needs are greater and also at different stages life. Youth needs experiences for education, teens need experience to spend and contrast people and items by interacting with one another and shopping and fulfilling their cravings. Eventually we should strive to outgrow these childish cravings. My philosophy of an ideal life would be low-key living with higher mental energy gradually replacing much physical effort. This coincides with most religious teaching and eastern thought so I am only restating the obvious.

I would like to see a more philosophic and balanced economic life style spread in the nation and thank those who are already poor because they are already half way there. Their gift is knowing how to live cheaply and still persevere in life. Probably, if a community could grow around such a philosophy it would need to be very tolerant of people who couldn't live up to its ideals, people who were at different stages of development and people of different religious practices; although I doubt if a community like this would be workable without strong belief in God. Sounds like we're back to monks in a monastery. This philosophy depends on large part on meditation and achieving the mental energy that replaces many of our wants and desires. In that sense religion and a strong belief in God or the ground of Being or Allah is vitally important but perhaps not absolute.

What about evil? Evil crops up in any group or community. The ideal way to discourage greed and selfishness is to direct our pity towards the person who is so immature that they need to be greedy. Depending on how greedy they feel they must be and presuming they don't hurt anyone, we must look on them with a tolerant attitude but let them know how we feel. Substance abuse is intolerable and needs to be shunned if necessary because it takes away from the healthful mental energy of the whole community as does any evil. Substance abuse of hard narcotics makes too strong demands on the mind of the person using it, so hard that they can't recover from its effects but should not detract from a community's ability to party and have drinks for pleasure. We must recognize, as God does that people are born and raised with difference needs and desires to fulfill themselves.

The highest form of human is a person who has fulfilled themselves and achieved their life's purpose then moved into the blissful state of being and becoming. None of this philosophy can be forced on other people although we could raise our children to adhere to many of its principals, they still must make their own choices.

This philosophy accepts the fact that mental energy impinges on us from all the earth and universe. And that we can only try our best in our small groups to gather this energy into a workable body of active value. Much negative energy still exists and must be closed off, evil or deliberate attacks on another human or life form would be an example of negative use of the mental energy of the group and should be smoothed out as soon as possible. It seems to me that many people won't be able to accept this philosophy at this time, that many of these people are those who have much, so have much to give away in order to live simply. Many are so filled with stuff that they have no need for mental energy to fill their lives. These people will fall by the wayside as the world progresses.

These ideals I have stated are the same as all the religions have been preaching for thousands of years. Some systems have been tried in various communities through out the years but did not persist. Why? Is it because human nature is inherently greedy? What does living simply mean? It means making honest decisions about what you need then choosing and acting on those decisions. It means to buy what you need to but to recycle older items when you can. It means to set aside a time for contemplation and ideally a place for quietude every day. It probably means living at a slower pace than much of the current society. It means downplaying the goal towards material status and increasing the goal towards workmanship and mental energy and the power it can give a person. It means using mental energy to enhance other people's ability to achieve their growth potential and goals. It means that vital needs should be met for all in community. It means tolerance towards other viewpoints.

Also anarchy never works so some type of democracy must be put in place or other social system that sets certain standards yet allows people the freedom of choice. It seems to me that the quickest way to achieve a philosophic community of this nature is pride of certain accomplishments, any accomplishments besides making money. Pride in creating works of art or writing, pride in achieving mental powers, pride in crafts, pride in workmanship, pride in people management, child rearing, physical gifts, pride in all abilities, pride in sharing, empathy, teaching and having time to ponder and listen to another person's sense of pride as they grow to maturity. Silly, who would want to listen to my simple philosophy? The same things have been said more eloquently by better and more knowledgeable people than me.

8/21/00

Usually people who are highly evolved prefer to stay underneath the currents of the population. Sometimes they must become well known for a short time for various reasons. Gandhi would be an example of this. Many choose to stay anomalous but may agree to become known now because it is the proper time. The time has come to open up what was hidden, what has always remained hidden from the general public so they may see and make a turn around for the betterment of their world.

We should try to remember that even though there are only a few people who I have met or perceive who are highly evolved, I know them for a purpose, the purpose of writing about them in this third section. I suspect there are numerous people who are not highly evolved yet but who are growing in spirituality and will eventually arrive into the highly evolved status. I have not been in a personal position to meet people of this caliber on a social bases because I don't get around socially. There may be many who talk about the state of the world and who are thinking about what to do about it but I don't meet them. I may have read their books. I know of people concerned with the state of the world but people I meet on a regular bases don't seem to be involved in this problem of economy verses ecology. True, there are many other concerns. Take your pick which one you will pull for. We are little people and don't have enough time or self-effort to pull for all of these charities or goals or world needs. What can a person do? I don't know either. Maybe Jesus will tell us, maybe he won't, often he makes me figure it out for myself.

Many people are learning to send their thoughts out to specific people but this alone does not make a person a highly evolved being. Although these people, like myself, are evolving, it takes a lot of self-control? Spirituality? Love? Wisdom? What does it take to be highly evolved? I can't answer that one because obviously it takes a like mind to understand, but at the very least, I have learned about a few abilities and methods; they have great mental powers at their disposal, powers they can choose to use when or if necessary. My information I have gathered by bits and pieces over the years and since I began writing this book. It's not much. I hope Jesus will help us understand better who they are and how we can emulate them. I want to know, don't you?

10/2/00

When God lifts the veil of darkness for me I am suddenly blinded by the sunlight from the total universe. It is as though a black veil with a million pen holes cover the stage and suddenly God opens the curtain to the light. The veil opens to an orange gold haze of luminosity that penetrates my skin like an x-ray. I feel the urge to bow down in wonder at this new manifestation of God's love. This golden blazing energy gathers in side my soul like a golden nugget. How can I contain it? I can't. It begins to sing as it turns, spinning faster and faster converting visual energy into kinetic energy within my heart. Truly I don't deserve this gift that resides within my breast. I can only share it with others, it's light shines forth like a galaxy, or at least it will when I learn how and why I have been given it for safe keeping, because keep it I must until Jesus releases its power from within my soul.

10/3/00

During church Sunday Y came to visit. He was curious about what I considered sacred. He didn't understand the pulling power of the Mass. He came in before the priest consecrated the host, so I told him to wait a few minutes before we got to the sacred part. I think the last time he visited with me at mass he perceived it as only a gathering for prayers. This time he watched through my emotions and mind and eyes to perceive what it was that I considered sacred. When the priest says the words "This is my body…" I no longer see a priest, I see Jesus as he was two thousand years ago agreeing to give up his life for us, agreeing to stay on earth and allow himself to be put through an agonizing death, agreeing to give up his body and blood so we could follow the percepts he gave us.

Just before he left, Y said, "I understand now," and he also invited me to join him one day during his own sacred rite. I would feel proud to do so but I wonder if my ability to concentrate is great enough for even ten minutes, long enough to witness some of his rite. I intend to try. I am looking forward to the invitation. Years ago I went to a Hara Krishna Service, which was nice with a lot of chanting and singing. Y's service, I am sure, will be much more profound.

I felt X all day Sunday. I felt his love for me and his concern and Monday too. Perhaps that is why I woke up feeling good this morning. I have been in a slight depression lately . His love brought me around. But I so wish he would visit and wrap his real arms around me. As I woke up I kept singing the song. "Don't worry, be happy" to myself. It still makes me smile at how absurd it is to worry all the time but I do anyway.

10/5/00

Evil is a force like a wind that we need to push against constantly as we go through life. Heaven serves as a counter force against it because it tries to give us what we need or supply us with what we think we lack. But evil entwines its way through our lives trying to annoy and then destroy. By allowing negative thoughts to take over I have allowed this evil force too much power over me so I was rethinking my life as regards to love and employment.

So Jesus asked me "What do you want to do." And I am astounded and begin to think and think and learning and thinking some more. He has thrown me a punch line. My immediate answer was easy and true, I want to continue writing but I also need to get employment that pays money. The next answer was long in coming especially since Jesus implied, as heaven often does, that what ever my answer was, it would be possible and heaven would help make it possible. This has been a part of my problem, expecting heaven to do all the work. I keep forgetting that I need to push against the negative force to accomplish anything just as I needed to push against the force to find heaven and learn how to travel with my mind. At least in this one area I pushed hard enough to find and accomplish my goals and only need to get the book published now.

Yes I would love the chance at a job like teaching as long as I could squeeze in time for writing. I need to get busy and feel like I am busy and writing is non-productive as far as feedback, acknowledgment or money goes. But what I want and like is often impossible to get. It is like that husband who would be my companion and provider so I could do all my writing and art and teaching. A dream that seems more and more over a lost horizon now. When ever I read of successful women writers or artists, they always had a husband to support them while they were struggling. This has been what I craved most in life but I forgot I needed to push against the evil force and get out there and fight first.

10/6/00

Jesus said I have used my "gift" twice. I don't know when or how or for what because I am still unsure of what heaven means by "gift". I know I had some very close calls where the other car stopped just inches from my own. Does that count? Maybe that is it. Not sure. Jesus has also showed me how to heal people, that is if I had the guts to try and know who. I am waiting for Jesus input here.

10/11/00

After struggling for a time I have come to realize that I am ready to reach out again into the mental realm. This is where my true friends are. I am ready to learn more about them. As far as my social life, I will try and improve it for the purpose of seeming normal but I seem to follow a different drummer. Social interaction may not be as import to me as it once was. This may be true for all of us as we grow older. I woke up in the middle of the night and thought this through. Y agrees with me. I feel him in the back ground, as I used to feel Jesus in the back ground, at the same time I feel his acceptance that it is time for me to move on. I also get the impression that not too long ago, he went through similar personal decisions and that, like all of life, it is a series of forwards and backwards and troughs and highs that finally carry us to our goal.

Interesting that I now compare him, or his method of teaching to Jesus. I still feel as though I have let him down because I am not able to concentrate well enough to visit and join him in a worship service. I have hesitated for that reason but I may be missing much; it may be that his style of training is what we are looking for to save earth and therefore will need to be spread widely through the population.

10/12/00

Father Thomas talked about marriage Sunday from the gospel. He said we all know that some marriages don't work out. I think most of us get this wrong. What God joins together is true but has anybody been joined together yet to become one? If a marriage is 'one' they could never be separated because their minds would also be joined into 'one.' Two peoples minds and hearts would be joined or touching even when they are apart, this is what 'joined together' means. A preacher joining together two people doesn't necessarily bond them together, even calling on God doesn't necessarily join them together as we suppose but it is a good imitation of what should be, a practice for the future when two people will be mentally joined together in the way of heaven. Is this only now becoming possible? I have often thought of this, that the message is for the future when this ideal pair of one will be possible. "When the two become one" is a phrase supposedly from Jesus in the Gospel of Thomas. In fact, it may be a warning of the end times but it has many interpretations.

Many of us are so caught up in our own concerns that we completely forget the threat over our heads. Why haven't I read anything in the newspaper about the bombs triggered and ready. Why has this threat suddenly been neglected or downplayed lately? It is as though when something doesn't get into the newspapers or news it no longer exists as a reality. Years ago I read about the children living in sewers in Romania. Do these children still live in those sewers? Who can say? They are forgotten by the news media. I suspect that the problem didn't go away just because it is no longer is a top story. What about the children living on the streets in Mexico, South America, India, where twenty million work in sweat shops? All these children still live on those streets but it is seldom reported. How could it be current, it would soon get boring and news is not suppose to be boring. The Detroit Free Press has a Children's First program that is wonderful and which tries to keep the reader alert to children's problems. But news creates or enhances the news by reporting it. We become aware of an event through the news, so as soon as the news has stopped reporting the event, our awareness drops off accordingly. The millions of ideas on the World Wide Web fight this single mindedness, which is one reason for its appeal. Yet, this same choice of millions of subjects threatens to overwhelm us with too much input.

10/13/00

I tried to meditate because I am more calm in the mornings, lately I get so antsy in the evening that it is hard for me to sit without moving my limbs. But, as always happens when I get close to Jesus in meditation and God's kingdom, I forget about myself because the universe takes precedence. This morning Jesus took me back down into the brocaded cloth. We stood and let the gold, red and green colored (symbolic) stripes flow past and around us. I saw large clumps, wrinkled in the cloth ahead. These were events and conflicts soon to happen on our world. I would have liked to smooth this huge knot out ahead of us but Jesus said not to do that.

He said, "Some things must be."

"But I will be able to change some things won't I?"

"Yes." He answered," there are a few small wrinkles up ahead that will be yours to change."

It is all much more complicated then I or you can possibly understand. The flow of cloth behind me was very wrinkled and contorted in some places and smoothed out in others, the same ahead. One of the knots ahead was the conflict in the Middle East, this was the one Jesus told me to leave alone because it must be allowed to run its course.

This cloth, rough textured and striped and flowing, is, of course, an illusion, a symbol of our world with life embedded between the weave. Then we would need to imagine layers upon layers of cloth like this stacked and filling up space to find an idea or approximate of reality. But even the movement of the cloth from front to back is an illusion. Every cloth and pattern or flower upon it is involved in the dance of life. Only God sees it all. It is almost as if God can't see the color of our skin because it is all gold from his point of view so why ask something so trite of God like who I am biologically or should I go to doctor? These little questions must seem silly to God. Yet many of us believe strongly that God is as interested in these little things as the big ones. I am such a minor event in the Universe, ready to disappear almost as soon as I popped up on the cloth.

Jesus said he was very proud of me and loved me deeply because I had reached the point of seeing the cloth and its flow and knots. I said I needed to leave now so I could write it down while it is fresh in my mind.

"Yes." Jesus said to me, "Write it down."

10/15/00

In church today Jesus helped me use the gift. I believe we only used a small portion of the gift's potential but it wasn't used for physical sickness but mental. As soon as I felt it work I knew this would be the purpose I would choose to use it for most of the time. There are all kinds of sickness, not just physical.

I saw this lady and my heart just went out to her and I sensed her inner turmoil and need. Her face was scarred and she was sitting with the homeless men and looked as if she had led a desperately hard life. I believe God sent her the strength to over come her sickness and pick herself up by her own bootstraps, to help her start over again. It probably doesn't mean that she won't falter at some point, but I hope it means that she will get over a huge mental slump.

I felt so good when it happened, I wanted to cry for joy and hope for her well-being. Jesus didn't point to someone and say to heal this person, it was spontaneous and sudden and love seemed to flow out of me. God sent a small burst of power through me and sent it to the other person. I did say a little more than usual, I said, "Peace of Christ," then added, "Today and every day." I think I said more so I could hold on to her hands a moment longer.

10/31/00

Last night I learned something from God. God's light or power and immensity are so great that Jesus needs to shield me from it. If it wasn't for Jesus I couldn't stand the golden flow of strong light storm when I am standing in God's realm, uncloaked. Jesus sort of stands within me as I gaze on God's immensity of light after the curtain, black with pinholes of lighted suns opens. What God gives me as his Gift is a minute aspect of his majesty and might. It is as if from the whole ocean that covers the world I were given a small cup of ocean to share with others. The whole of the ocean is behind the cup. If it were to all pour out it would overwhelm everyone.

11/1/00

I wrote this the morning before work on the day my house was broken into. This period of my life I call the 'in between time.' It should be a period between writing ideas and doing. Later, there will be much for me to do for heaven. The purpose of my work will be to show the way, to lead, to instruct how others can achieve heaven and then we can all save earth. Jesus had told me before that it was not time, that people weren't ready, they weren't afraid or worried enough yet. The time is not ripe yet. As it says in the Bible, "There is a time to reap and a time to sow."

At this time the book is written and only needs to be published and printed out and distributed. This will take a few years, all told. Then it will take more years for its awareness to seep into people's daily lives and become widely known. By then I hope to have completed this section of the book. At this point, I am just throwing information into it because I am really waiting for input from Jesus . He explained that there is no hurry and that I should go out and live and enjoy life. I will concentrate on my other writings and art work and hope to find someone to share my life with. This is still my dream. It will be accomplished this time. What I have been writing so far revolves around my own notes. It will eventually grow to include real actions we must take or real knowledge we need to save humanity and earth. There will come a time when I will need to gather some of God's immense light or power into my self each day for use. That time is not now. Now I try to live in God's love. It is all about love but the word has been reduced to such a cliché that it no longer has power to teach us. But this is always what heaven, Jesus, and God is about.

Mary gave me a white rose this morning to hold in my heart. Her message was peace. I feel much better now that I read what I wrote yesterday morning. I don't feel abandoned anymore.

I should say something about the barrier between the physical and the ethereal or heaven. I have always noticed it being there but spent so much time on understanding Jesus and that realm of heaven that I kept ignoring it. Yet it seems like a true edge between universes. Ours and the one Jesus is in. I believe it is in Jesus power to dissolve this edge at any junction. I don't know if it is within my power but maybe. I even suppose that its thickness varies according to ? I don't know what term I would use here. I have always thought that it was a barrier of choice, a choice of reality over illusion, or good as opposed to wrongness. I am not sure what else I can say about it. I know that from Jesus and Highly Evolved Beings I get the sense the non-locality of mind is a true state and it is our job to learn how to move within this immense universe, to learn how to maneuver, floating as it were, without sign posts, but finding those sign posts that are needed to grip and hold on while we investigate this new territory of the immensity of God.

I felt so bad I wasn't going to transcribe or write the notes from yesterday morning. Now I feel much better. I realize that Jesus didn't betray me because I am, more or less, done writing his books. [This statement was certainly wrong.] So although I need to get another computer, I can overcome its loss and I did not loose heaven just because I lost a computer. It helped me to re-read what I had written that morning. No one ever told me that my life would slide easily by. So I should stop expecting it to. If I need to change course, then do so. Besides I find that I like working but I also like the art I have been doing lately and my new writings in the mystery book and the young adult's book I intend to write. It seems I have much to do so just go on and try and enjoy life while I am doing it.

Thank you Jesus

11/2/00

The worst part about having my computer stolen is my loss of faith with heaven. I feel violated and that heaven didn't protect my home. I think it also nullifies my books. Jesus had told me in my first book that everything would be ok until I didn't need it any more and that all would be restored. It doesn't look like that is true. I may have misinterpreted what he said but I don't think so. He told me over and over that it was all true. This is where the violation comes in. A computer can be restored, a broken promise cannot. If one part of the book is not true, none of it is true? This was my biggest hurt of all last night that heaven may have let me down. I am ashamed I yelled at Tom but I was upset. Actually not as upset as I let on because my real upset was because of heaven not my computer. After I learned that my books were still there, I felt better, although some of what I wrote is probably lost, I have retained most of it. If the thief hasn't come back today that is. I'll go home and check my files of disks and make sure I have My Files from the computer. I think I do in the drawer.

11/12/00

This morning, Sunday, I woke up early and decided to meditate. I learned a lot after I finally allowed the ripple of every day surface worries to settle down. This always takes me about ten minutes. When I had calmed myself with even breathing and felt relaxed, I directed my gaze at Jesus and I suddenly laughed and he smiled because I realized how easy it was to direct my gaze at him and why. He is ubiquitous, as God is ubiquitous, He adds that all heaven also has that quality but this was too much for my understanding.

Then I reached out my hand to touch Jesus as we entered space. The barrier was there that always seems to separate us at first for an instant, like a short flash of quiet lightning that turned on and off just before contact or a crackling piece of saran wrap tearing open. As we stood there, with every direction a possibility, I compared it to a stairway in the stars. A stairway that led up in every direction that I turned or down in every direction; can you imagine a circular stairway with infinite directions on which a person can travel? This is what I saw as I went with Jesus . This time as we walked into the brocaded cloth it was like embracing a storm tossed sea. Everything was undulating and moving. Jesus said this was more in tune with reality, more true than the quiet view I saw in my last encounter. The movement was true because everything was winking into and out of existence all the time. Like Christmas lights twinkling, every life, every part, every thought and action was being born and dying over and over again. The dance never quiets or stops—it goes on forever.

With each visit I had reached a new understanding of the golden brocaded cloth of existence, and I now realized that this also was part of the dance of the universe, that the levels of understanding are also unending. Not only could we ascribe a layer to every world and type of world but the levels of understanding or possibilities within each layer was like sinking into a different ocean depth of knowledge with every movement. The complexity is awesome and unending. It can't be represented in it full multi-dimensional reality. Perhaps it could be compared somewhat to the movement of the expanding universe. The universe as it is represented like an expanding balloon but the balloon's surface is made of thick Swiss cheese with movement at a twirling pace up and down and around during the expansion. It is too complex for me.

Jesus says that my many examples of layers and definitions and symbols will help people someday understand the closeness of God and how to reach him. This depth of levels for understanding also applies to the Gift I received from God. I can't fathom its full usefulness or purpose at this time and may never understand completely. Partly it is the gift of writing and describing what I see, which includes the act of visualization but sometimes it includes the build up of power and strength that I will use someday to help people. This is also beyond my understanding, how and why God chooses to heal certain people as well as why use an intermediate person like myself. Does it have something to do with the belief system? Our belief in concrete events, of touch, of ability? Regardless I needn't worry at this time what the purpose of the gift is. I know only this, Jesus said numerous times "You will have what you need when you need it." He was referring to my use of the gift. So I wait with freighting anticipation that I will need to use it openly one day. But also I know that I will also use it as a quiet power that will flow at God's whim through myself as conduit to other people. This time is not now. Personally, I think now is the time of gathering in supplies for a large siege. These writings are the purpose of section three and Jesus' help and solution that will help us prevent world catastrophe.

11/21/00

Jesus told me at another time that I still needed to learn the difference between the truth and a lie. He meant that I needed to be able to discern when someone was lying to me from above. It is not easy to distinguish the truth when the statements make use your own mind. It takes a life time of learning how to guess when a human is talking and telling lies, so of course, it becomes doubly hard to know when you hear a lie inside your own head. It is even hard to believe that an evil person is out there sending lies out to people but I believe this to be true, most of the time. Usually I ignore these kinds of thoughts, they are not just negative but actually are lies; therefore, I can dismiss them as not worth my notice which is what most people do. Most people don't recognize evil when they bump into it. They just call it an adversity of life, hard luck, or fate. This may be the best attitude to take, see no evil/hear no evil.

We could look at the whole physical world as a lie on some level and most of the events that happen to us are less than the truth because they are always less than God? Or not enough of God. But if we all thought like that we would never get anything done. So this type of thinking must be wrong. We would all feel constrained by evil. Evil cannot constrain us, it can only tease and taunt. The problem is that so much of the taunts hit near enough to the truth to hurt deeply and seem so close to the truth as to be credible. I have been guilty of falling into the gullible hole too.

11/21/00

It is very important that I don't make the mistake of following the wrong path. My book depends on knowing where the truth lies. Jesus still tells me that, "The book is true." But I have to wonder because some things in it don't seem to be true. Or maybe I just haven't waited long enough to let them become true. We humans become impatient easily but heaven has a different sense of time. When my computer was stolen I thought that it was proof that my book wasn't true. but Jesus said I will come out of this, "Smelling like a rose." So I will wait and contemplate and keep writing. Secretly, I believe my enemies stole my computer but after reading what I have written they realized that they didn't have any reason to fear me. I do not write against anyone, I have never been against any one unless they hurt other people. So I watch and keep going along life's highway.

11/21/00

Interesting program tonight about adult brains choosing what to learn. choosing to learn by actively exercising or enriching the environment. I choose what I want to see. I mean out of a universe of choices I choose to see certain worlds with Jesus as opposed to seeing events going on in the city or our own world. I choose to see only what is in front of me most of the time. I believe this- that I have the ability to see further than physical vision would normally allow, that we all have this ability if we so choose. Most of us choose to only see narrow selected part of our physical environment. I could float over Detroit and see things happening if I wanted to, I have done this but I don't choose it often. This kind of sight takes training and trial and error but it is certainly possible. I don't usually choose to see this close to home.

I have agreed and chosen to enrich my brain with unusual and unique insight and events. Lately I have been very lax about this. Even about meditation. I think I needed my thyroid medication to feel better. I noticed that my thinking slowed down a bit. There are two kinds of thyroid hormones and heaven may not have helped with one of them. I also lost my appetite. This made me undernourished as well as tired. I noticed this in math class the other day, I couldn't seem to think clearly. Some protein helped. Does this also affect my travels with J? Don't know. I am ok now. Maybe it was an experiment on myself to see what would happen if I didn't take medicine. It helped me understand some people who do not think well and also understand other people who think superbly better than most of us in their own areas of expertise.

Medication and its various abilities is a case in point. It is a choice, an enrichment style and path that many choose to go down. It is totally opposite to the gadget-orientated life of most of American society. It is like the difference between a reader and a television watcher. By the way, I started watching more television lately, but I think I am just lonely for human speech.

My ability to see people stepping through time is a learned ability. Perhaps one that I agreed to explore? What about angels? Sometimes I see a blur of angels close by and far away. Once at her birthday party, Megan said, as she looked into the air, "I see angels." I will never forget this because it frightened me into thinking maybe she was in some kind of danger. People often see angels just before they die or have some other accident. Megan was just fine, so why did she see angels? Why did she say this during that specific time? Did she see angels around her other grandma who was very sick with cancer? or did she see angels near me? Don't know. She was only three at the time and has probably forgotten she seen angels by now. I hope to never forget to see angels.

11/25/00

I have been going through a crises for weeks. I have been alternately feeling sorry for myself and crying and yet trying to hold on to hope that I am doing something valid and valuable for humanity. I think the crises reached its peak yesterday. I woke up this morning and realized or re-asserted to myself that what I am doing is ok. Yesterday I saw the direction that my gift needed to go and this morning I realized why. My writing is going in the same direction. It is all about change in humanity. Humanity is changing, morphing, melting, stretching, dripping, and becoming, this is what I write about and what my art is about. I need to meet and inter-act with more people and friends, but I realize I am different. I sometimes scream and cry against being different. It is like have a defect or lack and screaming my anger at heaven doesn't do any good. But it is not a defect, just a different way of seeing and being. I no more fit out there shopping and going to dinner in the suburbs than I fit here in the center of Detroit, in the ghetto. Oh, well, maybe I have a poetic heart.

11/26/00

This morning I listened to the chant tape and seemed to float beneath God's gaze turning gently in the breeze. I was the center of a golden lotus flower floating on a golden river . At one point, it began to rain in golden drops that I absorbed into myself. My center still has the golden power. I have come to think of it as silent lightning because it is energy filled with light rather than light filled with energy. For some reason, even when I am deter-mined to bring my troubles here, I can't, I soon forget what impertinence they had and realize that they are not worth the bother. Most of our problems are too mundane for this golden place filled with love and light.

12/4/00

The other day after reading about the tragedy of the five children in the fire, all I could think of was their pain and screams. I begged Jesus to help me understand. He assured me that he came and got those children. He showed me the angels reaching into the flames and pulling the children out and taking their souls to heaven. This was a small tragedy that would be repeated a million times if they ever drop nuclear bombs. Could Jesus and the angels cope with that? Would Jesus pull us all up to heaven? the evil people as well as the good people? Today I was meditating and trying to imagine how Jesus could love all of us worldwide. Remember, he sees all the pain all the time. He can't dismiss it as easily as we can if we don't read about it or see it in the news. I had just read about the AIDs epidemic and other problems that plague our world. I tend to get over whelmed and dismiss large fractions of people as hopeless. Their numbers over whelm my imagination and so I dismiss them as uncountable and beyond my concern. I couldn't imagine how Jesus could actively love everyone on earth.

It was at this point that Jesus showed me himself as the Sacred Heart and he sent his own heart into mine so for a moment we shared the same empathy for the people of the world. I couldn't hardly stand it. There was so much hurt and pain weaved throughout it was like patches of dark pools and rivers and seas splashing and threatening to overtake islands still standing in daylight. Most of this running pain we don't choose to see.

So far in this third section, I have been writing my own thoughts and opinions. Now Jesus said he will begin to give me input for this book. This sharing of empathy and love was the beginning and will point the direction this section will go. I know from past experience that once he begins to help me, it goes quickly. I have been very lax and slow the last two months and need to get back in gear. Hope to continue the mystery book and the young people's book too.

12/8/00

This morning during meditation I had the strangest feeling that I was going home, to a home that I had been away from for many long years. It was a pleasant and peaceful feeling. A contentment that made me feel complete, as if a hunger was being fulfilled. I would have stayed in this state of grace for a while longer but someone knocked on my front door and broke the spell.

I also visited with Y again. I still have much to learn, my training is so very incomplete compared to his, I wonder if I will ever be ready to join him? For now, I have a lot of unfinished business to take care of and many books to write. He is patient, he has great self-control while I have almost none. How will we ever fit together, we are such opposites.

12/16/00

It's like the poem Footprints I was feeling very lonely, abandoned and sad on this bleak dreary day. I sat down to meditate and asked for Jesus help to make it through the day. This was when he was not only there for me but he also told me to open my eyes and he would be there in the room with me. When I opened my eyes Jesus was standing at my right side and his light rays shone and penetrated my body. The light rays gave me a since of fullness and love as if the emptiness in my life was gone and for a long while after the emptiness felt filled. Jesus said, "You will be filled" I believe this to be true. I thought to myself God knows what I need and Jesus knows what I need. So why worry. This was only one of those dreary days the kind that is hard on everyone. I was very thankful that I had Jesus help to get thought it.

12/17/00

I have been feeling so lonely and separate from the world I felt almost traumatized and frozen in place, unable to accomplish any work or art or writing. This morning even before I began to meditate and after I begged Jesus for help, I began to realize that I wasn't the only lonely person on the planet. In fact, I know a few other people who are almost as lonely at this time of year. I could call or write or somehow reach out and share myself. This would make me feel better. Then it suddenly hit me how I wanted to do this, I want to teach people how to meditate and travel for the purpose of helping the earth and other people and share with them a cause.

I felt ok then. I snapped out of my doldrums and felt almost back to normal. But I ask myself is evil the force that keeps pushing me down or pushing against me? Is it necessary or good by doing this? Does life take a combination of negative and positive forces swirling around like a tornado to make us learn? Is this negative force different than the evil one? Jesus says "Yes, this is true." But the evil one can use this negative force against us.

Life is a set of problems that we need to work out and think and learn from. Evil actively attacks our minds and persons and bodies. This is many times more detrimental than a negative force that hinders movement, I feel it like inertia, it is easier to do nothing than something like go places, meet people, travel.

Did anyone ever wonder how the sentiment changed so abruptly against Jesus. One day he was heralded as King and the next he was being persecuted? It was the evil one encouraging people to believe rumors and lies against him. Rumors, words face-to-face and whisper-to-whisper are the most destructive activities on the planet. It is the most potent weapon in evil's arsenal. Rumor plays on our fears and needs. Rumors have been instrumental in starting wars, hate against others, turning one group against another, making people shy away from love. Rumors are very alive, so much so that sometimes we don't even realize that we are contributing by listening. But even just listening can corrupt our thinking about a person. An idea once rooted is hard to pull out of its soft bed. This fact is deliberately used by evil to destabilize and disrupt harmony in our lives and in the world. It causes a rift to grow between groups and people of all nations. We must remember that Jesus is all conclusive. He taught togetherness and love for one another. Human to human. It takes a lot of guts to disregard rumors but we can.

What is the cause of hate in the world? It is seldom caused by actions but, instead, is caused by percepts and percepts are fed by fears, fear of loss, self-preservation, or personal need. Rumor can be more destructive to a person than picking up a gun and shooting. Rumors have set nation against nation, black against white, congregations against other groups. Everyplace we go there are rumors, work, church, shopping, visiting. It was a rumor that killed Christ. And Jesus knew who began the rumor. He knew all the while they were praising him. He knew how quickly they would change and turn against him because he understood our nature and the nature of the evil one who was working actively against him.

12/30/00

This morning I woke up at 4:30 almost crying. This whole holiday has been a low crisis for me because I have been so lonely. I compare my life to those I know in the suburbs, my families who have a lot of people around them. I have even neglected prayers, heaven, and Jesus with my loneliness and anger because I came so close to getting a boyfriend and then nothing. I was even silly enough to read my horoscope, something which I hardly never do, and it mocked me by saying "You have heaven that loves you but no love life" Had evil been watching over my shoulder? I cried all the more.

So in the morning I begged Jesus to forgive me. I know that I needed to rise above my own petty concerns and usually I can but lately I have been unable to gather my strength together. I keep asking why my life is the way it is while other people are out there spending money, and getting phone calls from friends, and invited to parties or dinners. I have none of these things. I keep dropping back into a hole, a hole of my own making by dumb choices in life. This state of mind may be why Jesus took me to where he did this morning.

It seemed almost like we left the usual universe because we went through a purplish, round, star-studded doorway into a deeper blackness beyond. Then I was suddenly confronted by human forms half lying on the ground. No I am not laying, they were merged together into almost a solid mass of flesh covering the ground. (I can hardly write this it is so horrible) It was a mass of flesh with torsos and hands and heads and arms reaching outward grabbing on to my clothing and Jesus being. All in various stages of decay or rot. It was red and purple and dark and dank and slimy feeling. If this place were named hell, it would be an apt title.

As I approached one body, it lifted its head and one arm to me and I prayed, to my horror, for it to disappear. It did disappear, by popping out of there. I went from half form to half form praying as they called out to me for help. I kept saying, "I pray for you." and sending my own emotions of love down to them. This seemed to help a few but most of the forms stayed welded together in contorted agony. I can't write any more for a while.

I was dismayed to find that Jesus ' presence and even my prayers didn't help much. Then I looked up at the horizon and as far as I could see, oh God I shudder at the memory, was this mass of human flesh tied and twisted together, melting and merging in slithering movements with the hum of agony filling the background. The flesh parts were unable to stand or rise up or away from another flesh person's being.

"I can't stand it," I cried out to Jesus and we left.

Back in my chair, still feeling the horror of what I had seen, I tried to make light of it by saying, "Of course it was only a symbol. It wasn't real." Then I remembered God's golden garden and asked, "What about God's flowers? We are all flowers to God. Then Jesus gave me an image of a vast field of beautiful flowers but at one extreme area the color was dead and the flowers were shrunk and wrinkled black almost to sticks. I saw this as if from a far off distance that part of the garden was withered and dead.

"But this too isn't real, is it?" It is only a symbol an illusion?"

"Everything is illusion," was Jesus ' only answer.

Later I wondered why Jesus had showed me this. Was it because I had been feeling so bad and he wanted to take me someplace where they were worse off or did he take me as a warning. Earlier Jesus had said, "There is no tomorrow."

Had this been a symbolic view of the pain humanity would go through after the bomb was dropped on cities. Since this is also an illusion, Jesus could see this event as a timeless ending of days and nights for our world. Standing at the event in time, no tomorrow. Or was this whole travel experience a reflection of my own pain and longing and needs. Is this why we went there because it was what was in my soul at the time?

I don't have any solid answers, only hints from Jesus . I thought of Mary and the hurricane she showed me and shuddered. But this is all far into the future, I told myself. For now there is time to go out and play, if only I could find someone to play with. But I need to stop worrying about myself. My own worries are trite and childish. It is time to grow up and keep pushing through the barrier set against me by life. Life cannot be lived without hope, I must hold enough hope to go on with the chores God has gave me.

12/31/00

A new year and I've asked Jesus to help me in a new direction. It isn't good to be wrapped up inside yourself too much. so I need to find a group to join so I can interact. I would like to join some groups concerned with the earth. I will keep writing this Jesus asked me to do, it is very important. I haven't been writing much since they stole my computer but when

Jesus said I would come out ahead and he was right. My art is going good since yesterday. No sense in waiting for a publisher, actually the refusal letter arrived a few days ago so I will need to publish the books myself. What about this book? I don't think I will get it done soon.

I feel like I have lost my mystical well being during these last two months. I don't want to loose my understanding of Jesus or heaven. I need to keep aware of Jesus love for me. Heaven hasn't lost me, I have drifted away from it. Y seems to have drifted away too. Yesterday, January third, after I felt much better and seemed back to my normal self, Y said to me, "You are back" And indeed, I did feel suddenly back. He has been very patient, just waiting for my return to normalcy and for me to climb out of this hole I have dug for myself.

12/31/00

In church this morning, I kept revisiting the horrors of melting, massed together flesh. Even though it is only an illusion (I hope) or symbol, the horror of the visit won't leave me. I am afraid and fearful that it could be true, at some place or time, a real hell. But I keep telling myself, "God wouldn't let that happen to us, either before or after death, would he?"

Jesus commented as I was thinking this, "They did it to themselves, it wasn't God who put them there." I shudder and cringe at the memory.

It is a new year, I am determined to get this book published and edited. Jesus says it is ok as it is. I now realized that I am afraid to continue this section, afraid of more revelations. So far I have mostly put my own comments in these notes. Jesus hasn't even started yet, except when we joined hearts and empathy. I have been afraid at the beginning of each book to venture on. But the fear leaves as soon as I begin. This time I feel hesitant because Jesus gave me a small dose of what is to come by sharing his heart with me during that one visit. He said it was a small sample of what I will experience during the writing of section or book three. I guess I am afraid of the intensity of Jesus love and empathy. Am I afraid of loosing control, of being over whelmed by the agony of feeling his heart pour out upon humanity and other worlds? I should try to remember that Jesus never gives us more than we can cope with. He has been patient with me long enough. Now I must once more become his instrument and write his message and warnings to mankind. I will begin tonight. Last night Jesus said I wasn't ready yet.

12/31/00

I now wonder if I misjudged the gift I have been given. Instead of healing, could it be that its main intent is my writing. Is that what Jesus meant when he said, "You used it twice already"? Two books were written but waiting to be edited. The gift may include healing, if necessary, and preventing accidents but its main purpose may be to get Jesus ' words out to the people. Some say that Jesus was a pessimist. Perhaps if we could see the fate of humanity after it leaves the earth in death we would be too. Jesus keeps telling me that it is important to keep writing, imperative even. I'll try Jesus .

I sat down for a moment to deep breath and meditate and the sun was shinning brightly through the window and landing on me. I said to myself, "It feels as good, like God's light." and Jesus suddenly spoke up and said, " It is." I laughed, of course it is.

1/4/01

Is this the beginning of the 'Thousand years spiritual rein of God'? This is why Jesus wants me to teach spirituality and mind travel? Even so, the warnings must be acted upon, the damage prevented, earth and humankind preserved to live in this future. America is only a small part on this planet. After America learns how to control wealth and use it wisely then the rest of the world can follow into a world where most needs are satisfied? Are we an example to be emulated? Not yet, because we haven't learned how to live spiritually within our power and wealth. Can the two ever go together? I don't know yet. Jesus will talk about it to me.

I am just beginning to realize and Jesus laughs as I suddenly figure it out, that the next 1,000 years may be the spiritual enlightenment that Revelation speaks of. Jesus has hinted about this before now. Jesus once told me we would become pious like in the Middle Ages. He told me that my life would change for the better, he said, "If I tell you, you won't believe me."

My life and emotions are reflected in my writings. This is the way it should be. How could I write about great joy if I don't experience some myself or the reverse, great pain? I think book three (section three)will reflect my feelings as I rise in status or emotional happiness or worth? This could be foreseen and planned by Jesus ? The danger and warnings are real but the last section of the book will be about how to prevent these catastrophes, how to live more spiritually, how humanity as a whole could accomplish its future for the betterment of all. Naturally there will always be vast numbers of people who will not ascribe to any change or spiritual awakening but the movement will be there, the beginning.

This new teaching by Jesus, I hope, will be a base for the beginning for the rise in spiritual growth, just as the spread of meditation in the west has been, just as Jesus name was the base of spiritual love and good works in the world.

I literally entered hell this morning with Jesus. I will never forget its horror. We must prevent it from becoming. We need to remember that history or the past is malleable as much as the future is. To change the future we must change the past, that is why we must worry about earth now and not wait until it is too late. When I entered hell with Jesus I also entered the depths of my own endurance, my own soul. Its almost as if Jesus stayed absent from my life so I could experience this depth of painful emotions. My pain may be a reflection of all humanity, since we are one in spirit if not flesh. In no way could I have ever imagined, in such vivid detail, the horror I was suddenly confronted with. Actually I had no prior hint that I was about to experience such abhorrence and turmoil on any earth. So I am afraid that in some time or place it is true and real even though I cry out that it cannot be. My body quakes that any human or other form of life or even someone I know could be there inside that turmoil.[I apologize that this section isn't complete. I don't know why myself. Perhaps I was referring to the mutilated body forms in had seen earlier.]

I read in the newspaper that some people in the world still have slaves and that they torture them in inhuman ways. I can't stand it that one human would do such things to another. We are supposed to be enlightened in this day and age. What or who causes these people to be so heartless? How do they grow? How were they nourished? We must somehow prevent and stop torture around the world and torture of the world by its people. Our misuse of our own people probably contributes to earth's trauma and death.

1/6/01

There was a Free Press news article about Clinton and how he declared a massive forest protection plan. I say, "Harrah" for his last attempts to fix things up, but the newspaper reported that many republicans are against it. Why? With Bush in office will the ecology get lower billing? Will money interest take over and come first? So far in energy Bush has already made some disastrous decisions. If Gore had won would it have changed the course of the future? Would earth have been better off? I heard that Gore lied about being ecology minded. Not sure I believe that because rumors are the stuff of evil but even if true, he would have needed to look good for a while and therefore push conservation and ecology. Woe to earth? And is this why Jesus said what he did? Was he making an off the wall quip about how we run the world?[83] Was he serious? He says he is serious. So we better get more serious too.[84]

1/6/01

I spoke with Y again today. We sat together for about five or ten minutes. Most of that time we were silent and just enjoyed each other's company. It isn't often that Y is available for just sitting and contemplating with me, so I asked him first if he was busy meditating. He said that he wasn't busy and that I could visit with him a while. One day, after I have learned more and am able to exist in mindfulness we will be together longer in spirit if not in body.

For now, I have too much unfinished business to take care of. He said he hoped it would be soon that we get together. By this I think he means a few years from now. It may be that he can see into the future more than I can and looks forward to our togetherness.

He is already with me when he chooses. He can zero in on my movements and share them but I can't do the same with him. Does this apply to X also? He is also able to block his psyche from mental interference from me or others. The only time I am with him is when he invites me in. This is ok by me. For some reason I don't mind loosing privacy with some people. It is as if we are two parts of the same whole, or opposite ends of a magnet. We will join one day. He is certainly the stronger and more capable. I think he really may be a Buddha or God who came to earth to save

---

[83] I don't mean to imply that President Bush will make all the wrong decisions, as it turned out he has make great, well thought out ones since the World Trade Centers were bombed.

[84] Jesus statement, "There is no tomorrow," was only a quick comment when President Bush won the election but Jesus didn't mean to imply to me that President Bush would be the cause of the disasters, only that they would begin during his presidency. This has turned out to be too true.

it. Perhaps my ignorance and weakness is the antipode to his attributes of strength and wisdom.

I still wait to join with X but have become as leery of him as he seems to be of me. Some person is working against me and I wonder if it is X or his opposite? Nevertheless X is part of my unfinished business.

1/7/01

The sermon today in church was about the Magi. The truth sticks out so vividly to me that I can't imagine anyone else not seeing it too. Perhaps they do but are afraid to think or speak of it. The belief was that "When a new star was born it portended a new king would be born. Obviously, new stars are seldom born, especially stars that stop and hover above the place of birth like the star did at Jesus birth. The stars are bringing new DNA and mental powers to earth by injecting earth population with a new strain of people and have been doing this for as long as earth has been populated.

If you don't believe me look up at the next satellite going by. Doesn't it look like a new star in the heavens, one that wasn't there years before. This was the advertisement for Jesus long ago, first the myth, next the expectation of his coming, third the new star in the heavens, fourth the new star hovering over one place on earth. It just means that the satellite at that time was governed by the watchers or angels.

I have known and suspected this for many years but now it is time to reveal the truth to everyone. Jesus came from space, or his seed did. He was also educated by heaven throughout his life and probably taken up to heaven to learn its ways before he began his ministry. He knew the universe then as we do today. But he could only tell us what we could understand. Besides, his real message was one of love and togetherness not scientific truths. Was he, even then, trying to prevent the catastrophe that he foresaw in the future/past? So his message is not knowledge so much as it is empathy and a striving towards oneness. All religions taught the same basic ideas and still do.

Odd, I considered not going to church this morning but it was Jesus who persuaded me to go. He wanted me to reveal the truth as I saw it in this gospel. That is what most of my books are about, revealing the wisdom of long held truths to the general public. As Jesus says, "It is time." The fact that Jesus might have been born out of heaven in no way detracts from the mystical element of his birth, life and death or religion in general. I used to ponder this dilemma for hours. But it is only our backward thinking that makes a dilemma out of it. Jesus exist as a physical and non-physical being (from our point of view) Most religions teach that we also have multiple existences, for example, souls, or anima. It is just that our scientific society believes that if you can't touch it or measure it, it doesn't exist. Well I won't step into that well again right now.

An interesting fact: We insist that there were three magi, we humans always use three as a magic number we delight in giving things three all the time, three books, three series, three parts, trinity, and right, left, center.

Odd but I am learning that writing is like art-it depends somewhat on my emotions. When I pour my emotions into my paintings they are better and this might also be true of my writings. This is why even my despair is valuable and my loneliness so that I can relate and understand Jesus message more aptly. Jesus has said my life is changing for the better and I believe he intends this new life to reflect in my writings about the next millennium. As a people we have opportunity to grow more mature, spiritual, and wise as we struggle to save earth.

1/10/01

Today I feel like heaven has set me down in the middle of a minefield all alone and told me to walk. Where are my resources? my help? my friends?

1/14/01

This morning during meditation I realized that I wasn't alone, as soon as I went high into space I saw many different people coming and going just as I was. This wasn't like Nexus because the people were almost invisible, wispy in form as, I suppose, I was. People were just there and then gone again. I knew that they were traveling just as I was but I don't know where they came from or where they were going. Some may have been from earth. Could it be possible that more people are learning to mind-travel? Or have they always known? The sky never seemed so crowded before. Or was I seeing the future?

Another thing I noticed was that my sense of time stretched like elastic while I was mind traveling. When I was done traveling no time had been used up by meditation tape. It was if time stood still for a moment. It may have been the sensation I felt as I lifted up. The meditation tape had played a gong or ringing sound that kept repeating itself and didn't stop for a long time. The sound actually seemed to lift me up into the sky and universe. I loved the sound and never wanted it to cease but eventually it did. I wonder what would have happened if I could have kept the sound going.

Later that morning I decided to review the gospel for this date since I didn't go to church this Sunday so I read the section of the last week's church paper but miss-read it somehow; Instead of 1 Corinthians, I read it as 2 Corinthians, but it was what I needed for that day. The writing by Paul, "Whether in the body or out of the body I do not know, God knows," gave me courage to stop questioning the veracity of my activities during my mental travels. I haven't been doing much of it because I am waiting for something, don't know what. Jesus tells me there is no hurry at this point and that we will get back into the substance of section three soon. For now, I have been working on my mystery book.

1/20/01

This morning after sitting quietly and thinking and meditating I realized that I wasn't ready to Put away childish things. Most of our compartments or needs in life are childish. Church services, friends, work, shopping, gathering together. We could broaden this category to countries, some are more childish than others, or less developed in mental habits. It is another way of saying there are higher orders of being and we are all at different levels or stages in this order. The most important thing is that we keep groping forward.

I went from this realization to the heights with Jesus. Heights so huge and beyond my understanding, I laughed at my own perplexity. And this perplexity persisted even though Jesus joined inside me and I within him. We became one as he expanded the idea of the development of life beyond earth into the heavens, into the galaxy, into many galaxies and finally into total universal states of being. This was not the end, universe after universe began penetrating our awareness. This was so far beyond my ability to comprehend that I had to laugh and beg off. I couldn't get it. But I was left with a joyous sense of moment. I felt so good I began to dance, I just couldn't help it. I wanted to dance.

Odd because this morning began with my thinking negative thoughts. I began to wonder if I was being pushed into a corner further than I realize. Or, I realized, I could use this same little upset and see it as positive. This was Jesus instruction to me. that the negative was weaved throughout the positive and both were joined in a grip whose bond was greater than anything we could imagine. I saw this as a weaving together into a tight wall of solid matter or like right and left hands inter weaving fingers together to make a fist or like beads of matter falling and flowing and circulating around each other and coming together in a banded net of light and dark pieces grown gray. This is the substance of the universal building blocks of everything. This is what Jesus showed me as filling all the universes—all minds , all matter, all non-matter. And the groping and bonding and dancing never sleeps or stops or ceases. God is truly playful. Perhaps instead of Brahma blinking the universe into being, he keeps laughing it into existence.

2/1/01

Hubble photos, photography, art faces made from large pictures, fractals, all add up to the moving and stirring dots of life around us in the matrix of our world. We visually misinterpret what we see all the time. We are all, individually or together, clouds of gas that only looks solid, six billion people around the globe like six billion dots that take on multiple patterns from a far distance, a solid mass of humanity circulating on this globe we call earth. Which brings me to my next step; I keep complaining about not having anyone to be with, a solid person, a companion, but I have had the angels near by and Jesus and Mary and lately higher evolved beings. How could I be lonely? I keep saying it is not enough, that I need real physical beings for love, comrade, and human companionship. But perhaps I am wrong to hunger for these things. True, we humans are gregarious but maybe I need to get over come this urge as my next step in maturity. Unfortunately, we can't recognize what our steps into maturity should be beforehand because its understanding is still beyond us. So, I don't mean that I should give up people but that I should realize that what I really want and need is as near as my next thought or his. As an example, Y is nearby often just as Jesus is near by, there is a difference. I love Y already because he has the strength of character I admire but I am not ready for him. Eventually we will get together but not yet. I also love X. He is mysterious and, so far, has stayed just beyond my reach.

The lesson may be that we can have each other to know but we can never touch in a physical sense. But Jesus has said that he and I will touch someday. I love a number of people and I believe we are soul mates. Does this mean that we can have a number of soul mates and spiritual lovers? I have never faced this possibility before. I have always been the kind of person who has only one man at a time but now I find that I can have many soul mates. Not sure how to think of this. If I carry this idea further it would not exclude women either, although it would never be sexual just close friendships. A few of the people I perceive who can speak with their minds are women and I don't know how I know this.

To sum up, I may wind up with many lovers just not the kind that I thought I'd have. Jesus always said that I would have many lovers, I keep repeating that I don't want many men, only one. But I may have been thinking backwards about this issue. Maybe it is like this: every person is different and every person has something different to offer or take from me. I need to learn that my lovers are close by and that we can touch minds when we choose. It is a new style of love in the world? That is the lesson, life can be lived on higher ground, a higher mental plane as well as on a physical one. Will this satisfy my hunger? Is my relationship with Jesus a forerunner to how I will feel about this kind of love? Jesus has filled me to the brim with love during certain visits, it is only later that my hunger returns.

Could all my lovers be like my relationship with Jesus? Could my life ever get so full of love that I never hunger again. I realize that to give love is to receive it, to send mental love is to contact a lover and get love back? Am I supposed to be a living example of mental love. Now I feel a sexual pull in every direction and a fulfilling promise everywhere.

2/3/01

During meditation today before church, I asked Jesus to take me on the next phase of my education as I climbed a tall stairway in the sky. At each step it was like an explosion outward in every direction, like star burst. My next step could have went in any direction, the choice was almost infinite. The stairway was infinitely long and twisted up into the deep far off universe. It was a silver, open staircase made of starlight. It rose to heights beyond my view. I took a step and found myself in God's golden garden with Jesus leading the way.

I was wrapped in a long golden transparent cloth that kept winding and winding around me. Then I realized that I was inside my own flower. My flower of life. I could walk in and out of the flower as it twisted and curled. Jesus motioned for me to walk forward. We walked into the future of this single life of the being I call Diane. It is but a moment in God's garden but made up of times stretched outward and squeezed together, events pouring from my mind, solid items coming into existence and turning back into ghosts in the blink of an eye or flooding slowly back into the matrix of my golden flow of life. I watch pieces of my future unfold in bits and pieces of scenes that I take note of for a moment before they winked out again.

I know that art and writing continue far into my future and that I remain close friends with Jesus. He remains close by until my life finally wears itself out. I see us travel together in the universe and that I will write about it. I tended to avoid any dark fields of future events that stay hidden behind folds or contortions in the flower. I preferred to stay and bask in the light and I felt wholly nourished within this life that I had agreed to live, it was complete. This felt good because often I have thought my life was so useless and uninspiring. During weak moments I thought perhaps shouldn't have been born because my life seemed so worthless. My golden flower proved me wrong.

2/5/01

When Jesus showed me my future I saw events as jumbled and only chose a few areas to take note of. It was hard to hold anything still long enough to recognize it, like pulling on a kite in a strong wind or a slippery fish. Potentially, I could have viewed my whole life and future but besides not wanting to know too much, I didn't know where to stop the flow. It resembled a filmstrip, no a pile of filmstrips that a kitten had played with because nothing seemed orientated in linear time. It was a jumbled mixture of events whose arrangement was unfathomable to me.

I couldn't see any one else's fate only as other lives touched on my own. I also didn't see dates or specific times. I had no reference to when or why an event had occurred. All I saw was a small sample of future events, and these seemed malleable, nothing seemed to be set. It was like touching the surface of water and trying to catch and hold your image as wave after wave pulls it away. It felt as though pushing on an event could change its character or form.

I seen a few details with specific events I choose to review. One event I watched was myself refusing to go on television because I was wrapped up in a mystic union with another person and I thought this union to be more important than a television appearance. I considered it to be a silly intrusion on my time. I also saw that my paintings were selling very good but I still felt disappointed because didn't consider my art to be anything great. I will probably never be a great artist and this lack will hound me forever. Selling my art was not a true measure of art. How did I pick up all this knowledge within the single images I viewed? I don't know but I seemed to grasp the whole of each situation at once. Will they become true? Maybe but who knows? As I said the whole effect seemed like a shimmering bowl of jello. I could have disturbed and changed events just by watching. It was too far beyond my grasp and I was happy to leave.

2/7/01

"Yes," Jesus will take me on travels that will be "Issues of the heart." So instead of facing this new mode of being, I run, I hide, I escape into my own importance and busyness. I tell myself I don't have time to dawdle in mysticism during this period, these few months in my life. How silly of me and shortsighted. But perhaps it is just a reaction to becoming too out of this world. Jesus said I will go with him and that I will be ready when he is ready to take me. Of course, I know this is true. Also I keep getting hints that I will have a companion soon. Will it be X? maybe. I already know that Y and I will join one day in the future but I need to get my book written and get other business finished first. I also need to keep maturing. We are together now but we aren't joined in one union. So far X is into subterfuge and role-playing. I can't believe or know the truth of anything he says or shows me. How can I deal with this issue? Are a lot of men involved? Plus, for some reason I can't forget these words, "You will come face to face with evil one day." They stick in my mind and continues to concerns me. But he also said that I will have what I need when I need it. Could X be evil? I don't think so. A bent towards role-playing is not evil. a lie to hurt or damage someone is. I remember that Jesus also told me once that evil is very short sighted and can't see morality or understand the rational behind it. The person of evil, any evil person, is flawed that way. Is X flawed in that way? Don't believe so but he does like to tease. Are we to be together like a wispy thought? Or in some other way? Am I to be with someone else? What do I need and want? Jesus help! Tired of being, need a change, rest and fresh outlook. "Soon," Jesus' answer flows out to me, "Soon."

2/10/01

I can see the hand of evil all around me, pushing a constant wind towards me as I stand tall against it. Most of this wind blows past but I can see its effect on the shutters and windows inside every mind I know. This force is so prevalent that I wonder if it is just a sample of the negativity that is all around us. But this is stronger and more persistent? Luckily I also see people's minds rebel against this evil or negativity.

Negativity is a necessary component of our world, if any world made of matter. Death is a sample of this negativity, matter decays. What I see pushing against me is different and selective. I used to think that evil pushed everyone evenly and that some people were better at avoiding its temptation. But now I know that evil is more selective, true it tempts everyone, but it hounds certain people unmercifully in its never-ending battle against God. Those who grow close to God or will do special work in God's name are destined to feel the brunt of evil's hammering taunts, blow by blow. Sometimes I feel on top and beyond this evil force and my life runs smooth but at other times I can watch its undercurrents.

Evil can be very sly and subtle as it uses people against each other. Hints, rumors, and psychic ideas inside our own heads are its ammunition. These methods are easily pushed and spread in any community and no one can ever find the source. And, yet, evil may not be anything more than a taunting voice inside my head. It exists but may do as Jesus does and send thoughts to receptive people without actually being there. Because remember that it doesn't really change matter to cause evil, it uses our minds, our hopes, our dreams, our needs, and our own yearnings against ourselves and others. This is its mode of activity. I have read that mystics in the past considered evil to be nothing but a jokester who plays games with peoples minds. So I should learn their lesson and laugh at evil's antics and plays. I should learn to float lightly above and through the days as a gentle breeze across the waters. This is what the eastern religions teach and mean by mindfulness. I hope to achieve this one-day.

2/10/01

I wasn't going to write this but Jesus said it might be pertinent to other notes. When I woke up this morning I had the startling sensation of falling. A huge slab of white cement was slanted in my direction, like a roof of a house. It had just fallen and I needed to stand up and scrape dust off myself. Naturally I was badly frightened but amazingly unhurt. Interestingly, I don't know if it was me who experienced this or not. I could have been feeling and seeing what some one else did during a quake. I also don't know when it happened. It could have been an event in the past or future or even in some past life. Also it could have been something that happened in my future. I sometimes dream of the future. This is scary. I felt as though it was a real event. It was very real, vivid and frightening.[85]

I had forgotten all about it until I was thinking about the big question in my life, should I move or not. I need help from Jesus for this decision. I was thinking that only he knows the future and perhaps there may be a reason that I should stay in this area. He said once that this area was stable compared to some other areas of the country. Yet I seem to keep getting pushed into moving out of here. There are not a lot of personal reasons for me to stay or go. Jesus said that when and if it is time for me to leave, I will know. So now I refuse to worry about it.

Jesus said for this book he will be giving me all the information I need in a short time like pouring it out to me in just a few settings. Each of these three books or sections have been different, each a surprise to me, each improved my growth tremendously.

2/13/01

I was sick with a cold today so I didn't go to work. Before I began my day of writing on the computer I wanted to dedicate and pray for the many people in China who are being abused. It hurts my soul so much that people mistreat and torture others. It is juvenile and must stop. I asked Jesus to help bring China's dictators down. If they encourage such behavior than they must go or change. I am sure my prayers aren't much but I believe Jesus watches that country with misgivings. I certainly don't

---

[85] As I edit these notes, it is October 1st, 2001, three weeks after the bombing of the World Trade Buildings in New York and this dream seems too relevant for comfort.

want the United States to ever face China but maybe their system will learn to be more tolerant one day. Life is hard enough without the horror of torture or other ugly behaviors against people. What's the matter with people? These thoughts were swirling in my head and making me angry so I decided to meditate in order to come to peace with myself.

I put the Buddhist tape of chants on. During meditation, I met Y. He asked me to join him in a walk. We walked down tree lined paths. I mentioned how important it is for people to be surrounded by beauty sometimes. He told me I was invited to visit this serene setting any time I wanted. I thanked him. He said he wanted to show me something so we kept walking. As we walked our paths crossed a few other people also strolling down the path. I thought maybe one or two were as I was, traveling. This pleased me but Y said only a very few people were able to do this wondering out of body. I also understood that this ability has been a Buddhist tradition throughout the ages but that only a few ever reached this level. A person had to study and learn self-control and struggle for a long time to achieve this ability. The science aspects weren't understood until just recently that it might be achieved by anyone who sets their mind to it because our minds are non-local although it still takes a lot of learning, practice and ideally a sense of equanimity.

We talked as we walked I apologized for my constant talking. I said I realize that I had so much more to learn just to get to his level. But he thanked me in return for opening up vast tunnels for our minds to travel in. I suddenly saw the image of open tunnels leading away in every direction and understood that some people were now traveling those tunnels into the universe. I was very pleased but still felt humbled to be around such mental steadfastness and equanimity as his own. He is a master while I am still a novice. I can only hope to achieve this level of well-being some day.

As we walked we came to what he wanted to show me. It was a small flame rising out of a metal plate set in the ground. Small bowls sat nearby. Another person sat near the bowls. I knelt and this person reached into a bowl and brought out something on his finger (ashes?) and put his finger up to my forehead just above and between the eyes. Y told that many people wore that same symbol of the third eye but that most didn't know what it really meant. He said that I had earned the honor. I felt very honored to receive this symbol. I tried to stay even minded but I need to admit that my pride got in the way. I felt very good to receive any type of symbol of respect from this great man. I am still such a beginner that I think the ability to travel was given to me by God because I had did little to achieve it. I don't think I deserve this respect but I accepted with the solemnity of the occasion.

We began walking again down the small paved paths between the trees. He spoke then and agreed that we will join or meet one day. He implied that he would be patient and wait for me to complete my own mission in life. I told him that I still needed to write this book. Then I asked Y if he minded if I wrote this visit down. He agreed that I could. I thought of my love for Jesus and felt a slight conflict. He said that Jesus could be with us when we joined in union. Also I learned that the flame I saw earlier was a symbol of God on earth.

I was still meditating and returned to my present position on the couch when I began to worry about finishing the book. I can't know all the people I mentioned I needed to learn about in the front of the book and despair of ever knowing them. Jesus assured me that I would learn all I needed to know about them eventually.

2/13/01

My calmness has evaporated. My neighbor Dorothy just told me on the phone that she is so full of cancer that chemo won't help but Jesus told me once that she would be ok. He has repeated this message over and over to me. Once he said that "You need to do it." I am so upset because I can't do anything. Does he mean that I should hug her and make her well? I can't.

I don't know what is the matter with me any more. I can't seem to feel deeply for anyone. I am afraid to love everyone, friend or lovers. I keep holding back. I kept laughing at Dorothy and saying "Oh she is just being a hypochondria I kept saying to her "You arn't really sick." But this was partly because Jesus told me she was ok. Cancer is cancer, it is not ok. I have a hard time believing that she has cancer. I keep saying no, no, because I didn't believe she was sick for so long. I wonder if evil did this to her for a joke, some joke, to discredit my book and Jesus.

I can't help her, no one can, only Jesus. I remember when they told me I had a great gift. He showed me how to heal but I can't, it doesn't work for me. If that gift isn't true, than nothing is true. Jesus says everything will be ok, "You'll see." So where is my faith. It went out the window with learning Dorothy had cancer. Also, how can she be helped if she believes it too. Doesn't it take a good mental belief in getting well to get well?

Now I worry if it was Jesus or not who told me that Dorothy would be ok. Was it Jesus telling me? I know it was, I know it when Jesus speaks. So I can only wait. I used to be so sure that it was Jesus speaking and saying that she was ok that I didn't worry about her. Even when her family worried I laughed and said it was nothing. But when Jesus says she will be ok, does he mean healthy in life or death?

I remember now, he showed me that she would loose a lot of weight and go through a lot of pain and trouble but that in the end she would come out of it ok.

Now I am afraid. I don't mind admitting it to the world and Jesus. I have known this woman for twenty-five years and we have had our differences but we remained neighbors and friends throughout. It comforts me that she lives across the street. She must stay around. God's golden light will penetrate her body and give her the strength to fight on. I know it.

Evil mocks me now but God will have his say. Now I understand how Jesus felt, why he cried when he heard Lazarus was dead. Jesus knew evil was taunting him because death cannot be overcome. Evil probably said, "What are you going to do now. He is already dead?" or something similar. At least, " Jesus wept." God help me but I can't even cry. I think I figured out that I need to take Jesus with me to visit Dorothy. I can't do anything on my own, this situation needs Jesus.

2/14/01

I sometimes think the world can be divided between the young and old. Young people are so full of life and so immature that they can't see evil for what it is and this is just as well. Middle age is where you begin to recognize the many problems in life but still, real evil doesn't enter into the picture. It takes a very mature person to see real evil and how it works. Notice all the many older philanthropists who began to feel very spiritual at an older age and began to go in spiritual directions and give money towards their different causes. They stand out because of their wealth but it happens to many older people. Then also there have been the saints and mystics of all religions who have attained wisdom and were able to speak of spiritual goals and the true face of evil. Some have been able to laugh at evil as childish pranks. This was because they had outgrown its ploys and perhaps they were secluded from the world, more than it is possible to be secluded today. I don't know if being secluded helps much, then evil attacks the mind instead of pushing people around it pushes you around. It is always at work. If it can't tempt you, it goes after those around you. It never rests but then, neither does Jesus. Heaven and the angels are always working. I have seen this in my own life every day. The battle is constant but because evil is immature and short sighted it will loose in the end. As Jesus says, "It is already doomed to failure." What I find so very sad is the many people work for evil because they believe they are doing something good. Jesus is all-inclusive. Those who are not inclusive have set themselves aside by preventing or destroying other people. Then again, Paul also destroyed other people before he became converted and we are still reading his words every Sunday in church.

2/15/01

I am worried that Dorothy's cancer is the leveler. Evil taunted me long ago that "this is the only book that will get published." He meant the book on the web now. I shrugged it off because I believed they would all get published. I didn't take into consideration that I would stop trying to publish them myself because Jesus told me Dorothy would be ok and she isn't. It isn't that people shouldn't get sick or die, it's that Jesus told me she was ok. Now I wonder if it was evil telling me that to throw me off. I believed it and now I don't know how to feel. Jesus said he will make it right, he will see to Dorothy but I don't know how. It has gotten too serious.

I don't even mind that I can't heal her like Jesus told me how to do. He explained that I just needed to hold someone's hands and believe they were well. Well it doesn't work I know because I didn't feel anything going out of me when I tried. I as the giver would need to feel the flow from God into the person being healed. I haven't felt anything. Once in church I felt a slight flow towards that women with the scars but it might have been just pity. Don't know.

My feelings don't seem to be working any more. When they gave me the gift I felt extremely golden for that moment. It lasted through out the day but then dissipated later. In church when I thought to let the golden light flow, a strong voice suddenly stated that "These people don't need it." And I felt turned off and have felt that way since. What does it mean? Many years ago when I broke up that clot in the young boys throat, I could feel a click when it happened. I suddenly moved something inside him and he became ok. I felt it work. So if I can help someone I expect to feel it work. I don't really want to go in this direction. People don't need healing so much as they need to grow up and become mature and wise. This is what is needed more than anything else in the world. I don't know how to give them this.

Where are my feelings. Is it because I don't have anyone to love? I keep dying inside every inch of every day because there is no one near to love. No man, no family, no children, no friends? This is wrong. I am exaggerating because it isn't true. All I need to do is reach out. Why is there no one for me to love? It just hasn't been all my fault. Something keeps pulling against me. I don't know how to fight it alone. When is Jesus going to help me find a lover?

I didn't write about what I saw during meditation the other day because I don't know how to think of it. So I won't write about it now. It was a vivid description of what Jesus looks like and how I will recognize him when I see him. He had the same eyes I am familiar with and his mouth had the crinkles at the corners and … It all began when Jesus asked me "What do I look like?" I answered "I don't know." So he showed me. This bothered me because it was so definite. I am not used to getting definite information from Jesus. Perhaps there was a reason that I should know at this time. Jesus has said that I would touch him in the flesh. If that is true, then he is here now, on earth, among us, or he soon will be. Think about that people.

2/18/01

Jesus tells me to write the whole truth about the different people. At this point most of the truth I know is speculation and guess work. I still have a lot to learn in order to write Jesus request. Plus I am not sure how much detail about people's lives I should put in. I don't think I want to give names away, I wouldn't without the person's permission anyway, but I believe it is important to describe the attributes and special abilities of certain people. The world needs to know what is possible to achieve. They need to be made aware of the advantages of further spiritual growth.

Interestingly, the trend in fantasy fiction foreordains this because fantasy is about power and the battle between good and evil. Remember SF was very big in the 70's and 80's. It foreshadowed the trend in science and technology. I think the trend towards fantasy tells us that people want power and abilities beyond the normal or what most humans have been able to achieve so far. A list of what a few have accomplished in their mind and psyches will play into this longing to increase in mental power which we will need to save the earth and ourselves. The leader of the Falon Gong in China promised them spiritual power and this may be why it stays so popular. If we want to think of it that way, Jesus is the ultimate wonder worker and he is still working and winning. Sunday the gospel was about spiritual growth that will be needed in the future.

1 Corinthians 15:54-55
"And when this which is corruptible clothes itself in incorruptibility and this which is mortal clothes itself with immortality, then the word that is written shall come about:

> Death is swallowed up in victory.
> Where O death is your victory?
> Where O death is your sting?"[86]

I have learned some things about X. I have learned how well he can play a role to perfection. In fact, that is what gave him away to me once, he was too perfect in the role he chose. I could see beyond his acting ability because he used a certain trait that he kept repeating over and over. He would never answer a question but always kept throwing questions my way. If he is in the character of an oriental person, he uses a camera extensively, a cliché, Actors do this

---

[86] *The New American Bible,* Revised New Testament, United States Catholic Conference, Washington, D. C. , 1970, 1986.

all the time, they over dramatize the role. Of course, I know to look for any wrong move in X and most people don't. One man had a bad eye and a large pimple that was all red and swollen in a prominent spot. The purpose was to keep sending my eye to the bad spot, it keeps you off track. This works with names too; at one time, I thought I could see a trend in the names X picked out. Before long, it became obvious to me that the person with the pimple was made up for the purpose of hiding who he really was, I don't think anyone else noticed. Maybe he wanted me to notice that he was made up? He might be a part of the group who knows I am writing this book. Other people play roles too. They are so good they are hard to spot and you could go nuts just looking for them so I don't try. They may be so good because they have been playing roles for a long time. They even incorporate these roles into their real lives, in fact, they make the character a part of their life. All the reasons and rationales for their behavior is speculation because I have no evidence to go on. But one of the first clues I ever had was seeing a bum or drunk hanging on a telephone pole but he didn't have the smell of a drunk. I know because I lived with a few drunks. This was a big give away. Even though the person was totally convincing at the time, later when I thought about it I realized that it had been an act. I may have noticed this because I was looking for a disguise. I was looking for angels. Angels too are walking around on earth as ordinary people. They have a certain quality that is different from people playing a part but they also fit into their part very well so well I probably miss them often.

X is so great at what he does I wonder if his leaking out the sides or his role of perfection wasn't done on purpose to clue me in to who he really is. It may be deliberate that I notice his many forms. I believe he has been instrumental in teaching other actors how to play their roles to perfection. I may be wrong in this. X is the ultimate in acting because he not only takes on difference character, he physically assumes a difference shape, mannerism, fragilities, mode of speech, etc. He literally becomes the character he is playing, so much so, I wonder if he could even drop the role in his own mind during the act. I have since learned that he can think about the role he is playing. I think he can become tall or short, fat or thin. His face can rearrange itself like rubber. He can even change the youthfulness or his hands, from soft, to clean, to hard, to calloused.

Who is he? Is he good or evil? I may never reveal the truth even if I learn it. Jesus told me he has been playing roles for a long time. When did he begin and when will he end? Don't know. Perhaps he will reveal this information to me at some point. Perhaps this information should remain hidden forever? It may be something that no one wants to know or believe. The most important question is, is he good or evil or both? Has he been corrupted over the long years or has he always been corrupted? Is his main concern with humanity's well being? Our frailty? Is his theme to help us? I can't tell from his actions because the role he plays may include attitudes that have ugly views. There must be an inner quality of character that will reveal his real purpose or I may be crazy and just think I see him?

One purpose of the role players could be to spread virtue or distress. It would be easy to change the circumstances of a person's life by having the character in the role start a rumor because evil isn't the only one who can use rumors to advantage. The right word in the right place can do wonders for a career or destroy one. There are a lot of reasons why a person might choose to wear a disguise in public and it is my own distress that I pick up on their disguise, they could even be working undercover or they could be angels or anything in between. Who knows.

2/19/01

Also the possibility exists that he X is playing a role-playing a role. By subtle hints and insinuations he could be purporting to be someone else that I know in disguise. Wow this could get so deep I'd never wade out of it. I can only trust Jesus to see me through. I have seen other people in disguise who still resemble themselves but are playing a different character.

This could be deliberate to make me think it is that person instead of an angel? This speculation may not be true because I can't find a reason for such deceit. Obviously some people not in the role-playing are aware of what they are doing and why. Jesus tells me that I will understand fully soon. At some point I will need to decide what can be revealed and what must be kept hidden.

I keep remembering a speech one person made a few years ago. He kept saying, "I was there, I was there." At the time, I thought, *I was there also.* we were referring to Jesus time. I wondered how many other people were there also and now here in this time. Also what odd circumstances had thrown many people together who had been 'there.' Surly it was God's work that so many of us who had been there during Jesus time are here now, in one city. Now I wonder how he was there.

I know I was re-born into this time, but where did he come from? I have to wonder if he and a few others have never left. Wild speculation I know but still I wonder. Remember in the Bible when Jesus says to the apostles "you will not taste death until I return" Was he talking to the people I refer to? Jesus loved me and I wasn't included in this decree. I may be the town crier who tells of things to come. the one who prepares the way of the Lord? Maybe. Maybe not. The last five pages are pure fantasy and speculation and wonder and questions. I don't think they should go into book unless I get more substantial evidence. [87]

2/19/01

Jesus took me through the Universe tonight. He said he had a lot of strange and wonderful things to show me for book three. He said that

---

[87] With Jesus request that I don't edit my book too much, I have decided to leave most of the information alone because I don't know what he wants the reader to know or for what purpose.

book three would consist of systems that work for one reason or another. and then he showed me a panorama of the universe moving around until it stopped at one specific place. It looked like a jewel in a king's crown. The ruby stones arraigned around a central glow. Closer inspection showed that these were worlds arraigned in perfect harmony that resembled a filigree of precious gems set by a jeweler of the utmost precision.

Jesus said they had actually moved the worlds in this sector. They were the finest engineers in this area of the universe and well known for this trait. Their system of worlds worked politically and technically. Their civilization was extremely long lasting and enduring. I immediately thought of Egypt. But their system is very mechanical and structured, everything is synchronized to run smooth. Nevertheless the population makes sure that the city stays at the correct pace. The only thing lacking for perfection, from my point of view is randomness. Most of the willy-nilly events have been eliminated because these people don't consider randomness a virtue. Life is of course random but these people in the society regulate it as much as possible. Jesus explained, "You would shudder at some of their rules of behavior." He added that these are necessary to keep their society running smoothly and I would think of their rules as inhumane and over cruel. It works and has worked for many millenniums. There is no crime or hunger or sense of want, or over population. The land is constantly rejuvenated to keep it a manageable and fertile. They live simply like the red bubble society we visited before but are much more regulated, they lack the wispy flotation and random choices that occurs inside the bubble population. Another difference is that these jeweled worlds are not perfect or totally lacking in evil. The people not only act human but also look human as well with some variations.

"Do they travel to other worlds in the strands of tunnels we saw?"

"Yes they are well known and considered the best engineers in the area and called on to help others often.

"Are all the worlds linked by the tunnels?"

"Most of them"

"Are they all good? I mean without war?"

"No, if they have a war they loose their tunnel or connection, that would be death to any world. None of the systems would dare fate that much."

"What would happen if they did?"

"The tunnel would actually shrivel up and disintegrate. Their link would be gone."

"God?"

"No, it is a natural process. It is a mental bridge of a kind that you wouldn't understand. If it isn't maintained it will collapse. It has physical stricture but is bonded by mind."

"I can't understand that."

"Yes, I know."

"You just showed me part of their world. Can we actually go to it?"

"Of course. It will be like one of your science fiction worlds with rolling roads and clean, perfect parks. It is a paradise to many, but you won't like the perfect arrangement or design. I'll show you."

Jesus took me there. First we stepped on a rolling road. I couldn't see any seams or mechanism that made it move only that it slowed down at the edges and small paths branched off in different directions. Jesus said that material goods were also delivered on rolling roads that ran in tunnels beneath the city.

"But it is a lot like a science fiction story."

Jesus smiled and explained that I should realize that human people everywhere build similar structures and utilize like ideas. They create similar strictures of behavior, thoughts, buildings, and patterns on almost every world. The big difference if often the age of the civilization because people mature in similar steps as well. On these worlds, technology and mechanical structures shape the cities in which people live. Flat roads and boxed high towers fit their idea of efficiency of space and therefore beauty as well.

We went and sat in a park. It was beautifully green with grass and trees and a fountain was spraying water upwards into a rainbow. It looked like the water disappeared into the sky. Colorful birds flew around - not many, just the right amount to give spots of color. Flowers were arraigned in orderly sets most often radiating out in concrete circulars from the center just like the arrangement of their worlds in space.

Jesus was right, it was very tame and perfect, pleasant and beautiful, but it wasn't my idea of paradise. The system might be long lived but I was glad I wasn't one of the people who lived in it; although, it would be far more outstanding then where I live now. I think I want the sense of growth that improvement of place can bring. These people seemed to have achieved perfection and have no further place in which to grow. I am probably wrong about this idea.

The people looked human but their skin had a gray tinge to it. Their features looked normal to me. They seemed very calm as they stepped around on the rolling walkway. I thought they were too calm for such a dangerous movement but they were used to it. To them it was an ordinary, every day way to travel in a city. I can imagine some one from another planet stepping on to our freeways; they would be horrified at our reckless speed but we are used to it.

2/25/01

I was amazed that even at the funeral Jesus spoke to me and said Dorothy was ok. He repeated this the next day also. I had been so disappointed when she died after Jesus told me she would be ok, that I was considering not completing these books. It seemed to me that if I was listening to the wrong person at this time who can say what other time it wasn't the right person or Jesus speaking, I thought it was. Ironically it was Jesus I asked to review the books for wrong information and he told me that they were ok. (If you ask why Jesus would use the phrase ok it is because he is among us, with us, within us and around us. We use the phrase, why shouldn't he. How did he speak to people who only know French or Italian or Latin? If you believe he ever appeared and spoke to people then you must also believe that he knew their language, perhaps from the inside out. I will try to write these books as accurately as possible. I do not tell lies although you are right to worry that I could be deceived, I worry about this myself. Yet some statements are so out of the ordinary and odd that they surly came from some one more enlightened than myself. For example, once Jesus said, "Facts put people to sleep." I might have thought the same thing but would have never stated it as a certainty.

2/28/01

Last Sunday I joked that I was giving up sex for lent. I wasn't kidding, I did. And maybe X decided to give sex up for lent too because Fat Tuesday we came together for a great night of sex. For some reason, perhaps lent, we were both in a sexual frame of mind. He began kissing me on the lips and neck then he worked down to my belly. All this time I was sitting in my chair squiring. I kissed him back and hugged and touched and let him tease me and play until I couldn't stand it any longer and went upstairs to bed so we could continue in privacy. (my dog and cat were in the dining room) He told me to undress and I hurriedly agreed and lay with him beneath the blanket. The rest of course is too hot to tell.

I could only see him in my mind's eye. His face would come and go and sometimes he looked like a shadow or I would see his narrow chest and then arms. He was old and mature and his face looked familiar. His face tried to change form but I refused to see a different person. I kept my mind focused on his dark hair and sharp features.

I think and hope it was X but which part of him was I with? Good or Bad?

At one point I said to myself, "This is all I'll ever get of him." A shadow lover. But later that night as we both lay panting with exertion and fulfillment he told me we would be together laying in bed physically one day soon. We are going to share some time together. It will be nice especially since we don't have high expectations, which often plague many relationships. But he lies a lot, so I don't know. He has said similar things to me before.

I felt so satisfied this night that I don't expect to see him again soon, at least not for sex.

This X is the same one who can change his face and perhaps body to look like anyone else. I have since wondered if he just takes over someone else's body, don't know. I am usually sure but only after he leaves. I know I have seen him but I can't tell when he is standing nearby. I think he puts up a shield to block awareness. At times I have penetrated this shield but it is hard. Jesus says he has been doing this for a long time and is very expert at it. I hope to ask him about it one day. If he is prohibited from physical sex or can't perform I'll accept that and we will just be very close companions. It will be his choice. I think I have changed my mind about this. I don't intend to let him rule me or mess up what I am writing. Need to be careful.

I hope he got as much satisfaction as I did that night. I am not writing about my personal love life for sensationalism or any other wrong reason. I want the reader to understand the ins and outs of the implications of the relationship I have with X. How two minds can unite in speech as well as body. Imagine, if you will, the further implications of this joining. If our minds can come together so intimately when we are not physically together, what will our mind and body could feel like when we actually come together in physical union. Imagine two bodies and two minds not only having sex but also mentally joining each other as they experience sex with each other. I am not sure how to express the delight we could feel. But I can't wait to try. While we couple sexually our minds may be sharing each other's pleasures and sensations of touch. The physical may be the pleasure I had last night ten times multiplied. This would depend on our ability to feel comfortable in each other's presence. This takes time and effort. We certainly feel comfortable in the presence of each other's shadow. So I am not worried, I look forward and anticipate our union. [88]

3/1/01

Jesus said my dad would be ok and he still has a few years left. After believing Dorothy would be ok and she died I tend to not trust what I am told any longer. is it Jesus or my misunderstanding. It must be me. So I can't trust my judgment? But when Jesus told me my dad would be ok I wanted to believe he would live and that is what Jesus meant by ok. Jesus also said "For a few more years." This was so definite I had to believe him. There is also the possibility that evil deliberately tries to undo the truths Jesus tells me and sometimes he wins. So truth can become untruth. Shows how worthless it is to know the future.[89]

3/3/01

I've been to two funerals in two weeks and my dad had a serious operation. I kept praying to Jesus that he would have a spiritual experience. Don't know if he did or not but he certainly needs one. He is so practical he hardly believes in God. It would be nice to know that he changed his mind. He is in his 70's and only has a few years left.

I thought about this at the funeral. It is amazing the millions of people who believe that Jesus will save them after death. We all believe Jesus will

---

[88] It seems that I might have been wrong about a union with him. He hasn't shown up and I may never see him again.

[89] Question – I believe Jesus wants me to keep the sex in this book because it will serve as a lure for people to increase their mental powers. But do we want people using mind for selfish desires? Is it worth the consorting of the good mind with bad? Jesus says, that yes because conflict is inevitable and change is needed.

come and get us, we need to. But so far the information he is giving me states it differently. He is implying that we need to wait until he returns then he will save all of us. There are exceptions like always, a few saints who are able to get to heaven. The bible also states this view. But when a human is confronted with death we need to know Jesus as a savior and he is near and loving. When someone close to us dies we need to know that they will go to heaven. We tell ourselves this even if we know the person never did much good in the world. I wonder if this feel good lie hurts us in the end because it prevents us from facing truths about our immaturity and lack of growth toward God. But a funeral is not a time to face truth. It is time to believe in Jesus and to realize we are all riding in the same sinking ship.

3/7/01

I have been neglecting Jesus lately. I feel guilty about it but he assures me that he understands and doesn't mind. The reason has been because I have been working a lot this school year and still writing and painting. I don't seem to have time for Jesus or even to set down and meditate lately. I also forget to pray for people, which I really feel guilty about. Need to do this at least during lent. starting tonight.

Jesus held me in his special way and assured me about this constant activity. I am reminded of the biblical statement "A time to reap, a time to sow." This has been my time to be busy and I am enjoying it. Jesus is letting me go for a while, running around and doing, working and creating. Last year I didn't work except for two days a week and couldn't find a job to fill in. I was poor but I had a lot of time to give to Jesus. My forced quietude and inactivity was very conductive to meditation. So even though I have been neglecting my spirituality lately, I have learned a valuable lesson. I learned that our busy lives with their constant phone interruptions and places in which to hurry to is detrimental to a meditate life. There is probably nothing wrong with busyness in our lives if we can keep it in balance, except that it takes effort to slow down for the few minutes of stillness we need once in a while. If we don't slow down we can't keep in touch with Jesus as easily. But in fact Jesus has assured me that I will once again be a mystic for him. I just had the sudden fear that I would loose my work and have no choice. "No." he smiled in the negative, don't worry way of his. He always says don't worry and means it literally no matter what happens in life. "Don't worry." This is probably because if we could rise above our lives and see the events unfolding as they really are, we would finally understand that we had no control over these events anyway.

There are times when I see life as acting a role I am playing. When I visit with Jesus I sometimes realize the shortness of life and the constant turmoil revolving on earth. But these evolutions of events are necessary to bring earth to completion, to finalize its growth into a world belonging to God's Kingdom.

I shudder to imagine what a world would be like that did not join God's Kingdom. Remember the movie "The Killing Fields" about Vietnam and how the little children were given rifles to hold over the people and the skulls and the torture, or the Nazi regime, they used children too, or the slave trade or the… But we could go on and on with examples forever. The Nazi regime almost made it world wide, the slave trade did. God may have stepped in to help us change events before they went so far we couldn't turn back. We don't know, but these events may have prevented worse horrors in the future. It may have been something earth needed to experience and grow out of. I hope so. We don't know what God has in mind as he moves our world towards its future. We don't even know if we could make any real changes, but how would we know? The changes we make are incorporated into Gods framework and list of necessary events. So we must keep trying to do the things we know to be necessary.

In some ways our world is more enlightened than it has ever seen before. Most of the world's countries believe in the worth of human life and respect a person's right or at least agrees that each and every person should have rights, even children. That doesn't mean that we practice these lofty goals but we at least have come to recognize them as true. The United Nation has certain policies that every country is supposed to follow. The countries that refuse to adhere to these humanitarian principals are recognized as backward regimes. Places like the Taliban, parts of China, Iraq, and others. They may change in time. I don't need to say more, others can say it better and more eloquently than I can.

3/7/01

I wonder if it would be safe to say that once you have touched another person's mind with your own, you are both in almost constant contact. It becomes so much easier to touch that person again. It is as if the person has joined you inside your head and any time you want to say hello the other mind is there as if waiting. That doesn't mean that you both will stay in contact or conversation, the other person may not want to hold the connection open at this time so you must gently retreat. This actually happens with Y. He is often into his own thing or meditating and doesn't want to be bothered. On the other hand, I am usually available at any time he wishes to contact me because I am not as spiritual minded or busy.

This mind-to-mind bonding needs to be thoroughly studied and investigated. I don't know if the links can be broken by one of the partners or how long the link would hold if there wasn't intermittent contact or even if just certain people can hold an open link. The reason I believe it is possible at all, besides experiencing it, is because we are all one on the same level of existence or layer even though we don't often recognize this fact while in the physical body.

It seems more and more true to me that we are all visiting on the globe we call earth and taking part in an experiment, a double blind experiment run by God. (Am I joking? And listen to this scientific way of thinking). We are all riding on a road full of flesh, layers rise and fall as each life is born or dies, its job done for the moment and maybe ready to punch in again?

As far as minds binding together, this same system may work for Jesus too. I suppose that Jesus is somewhere in the universe or even on earth now in physical form but as soon as you make real mental contact with him, you are united in that bond and it remains unsevered. This also means that you are both in instant contact with each other.

I feel good about what I have just written. It is as if I have shed my perplexity. It has rolled off me in layers, first one doubt then another slid past while I watched it go unconcerned. Jesus smiles at this sentence and I am pleased to have him so near. I revel in his presence now, at this minute, for this short time, doubts are lifted. Ha just wait, with my short memory, I'll be right back in the middle of complex mechanisms to prove the working model of the universe soon. And it is all so very simple, so simple as to be unbelievable. It is us, mind, that makes up the universe and we are thoughts rolling around or bounded by God.

3/8/01

Who is X? Which X am I talking about when I refer to X? I don't know but there is either two X's or two different characters types in one person. I don't mean evil or detrimental to people, in this instance, I mean childishly naive about spirituality and the depths of love a person can have for God. It may be like I quoted before from the other book, if there is an evil one, or evil X, he is perverted in some way and doesn't know how to make matters right. Evil may have as much at stake in preserving the earth as we do but divides people and himself against our own best interests. Could he be, in reality, two people at war inside himself. Aren't we all?

But the evil one has more power than most of us. Can anyone so utterly selfish be also good? We can only be on the right side to the extent we can loose our own selfishness. This is what Jesus meant when he told us to feed the hungry and love your enemy. He is trying to help us grow up towards our ideal. A measure of a person's, or country's, or nation's or world's maturity could be taken by how unselfish they are. In this respect the U S is not too bad? In this way the Catholic, Christian churches are correct, we must do good works. What a horrible phrase this has become. But mystics are also needed to keep us in touch with heaven and re-enlighten us during each new culture or age. Jesus Christ was the ultimate mystic, as was the Buddha, Mohammad and other great prophets.

3/9/01

Last night Jesus took me to an unusual place. We only stayed for a moment but we will go back soon. At first I didn't know if it was on a world or something else in space because it was all pink. Even thought it had no edges it resembled two pink couch cushions put together and we were floating between the fluffs. A smoky atmosphere swirled around but the smoke was pink too. Pink, everything was a rosy, swirling swimming breathing in and out pink. It was impossible to get any barring in this place because everything looked the same, a rosy blush of air that felt and looked like a slowly moving mist turning in a gentle breeze. The only difference I could see, and this was so astounding I didn't believe my eyes at first, were the body forms appearing and disappearing from time to time as they floated by. In one spot I'd see a torso, in another a pair of legs and feet, and then a head, all serenely poised as if gently laid down and tucked in for asleep. Then the sleeping body would float back into the swirling mist and disappear. These were sleepers on this world. Jesus said they were hibernating in a huge place set aside for that purpose. I will learn more when we go back.

3/11/01

When Jesus transformed in Luke 9:29 we aren't sure what his appearance means except that Jesus' looks changed.

Luke 9:29
While he was praying his face changed in appearance and his clothing became dazzling white.[90]

Remember after his death when he met the apostles on the road, at first they couldn't tell if it was Jesus until he began sharing communion with them. They didn't recognize his face. They couldn't tell who it was by looks alone and needed his actions to confirm who he was. This is strikingly odd. This same clue is in other parts of the New Testament. Mary at the tomb couldn't recognize Jesus either because Jesus was posing as a gardener. This is a strange way of writing; and even though the gospels were written long after Jesus death, we must still ask ourselves why, if they were so strange, these parts were left in? Perhaps they were left in tact because they were true and needed to be there as information for the future. Just because we don't plan far into the future doesn't mean that God doesn't.

Could it be that Jesus has been with us all along but unaware of himself? I don't believe this, do I? Or, he may have been lifted up and came back, numerous times? He could have experienced both staying and going. He may have stayed on earth to help us or he may keep coming back during every age?

The priest said in church that Jesus died for our sins. What does this mean? It is a phrase that is over worked and just slides off us like oil. But what sins are we talking about? The cardinal sins? Greed? Selfishness? Hate? Murder? It is these same sins that are destroying the earth. Jesus

---

[90] *The New American Bible*

came to show us the way to the Kingdom, to teach us how to life. How can this Kingdom come to earth if earth is no longer viable. Many believe we must grow God's Kingdom on earth. If so, we better begin now.

The phrase "Died for our sins" can be interpreted in various ways: A few people have speculated that Jesus was really the first Adam who came back and died to take away his and our first sin. We could think of the phrase as Jesus died for all our past sins. Or he died so we would not sin again, or he died because our sins overwhelmed and killed him, or he died to prevent more sinning. The phrase has become a cliché, it rolls right off us because we think, "Oh yah, he died for the things I do wrong." But exactly how did our sins kill Jesus? Why would Jesus die for *our* sins? He must have meant to prevent these same sins from reoccurring? Surly, he had a reason to die?

It is those same sins, sins of two thousand years ago that are destroying our souls now. These same sins are also destroying our world. They prevent spiritual growth and the ultimate human potential. Jesus wanted us to grow into God's Kingdom, whether on earth or beyond earth, we can't deny this. How can we do this unless we change from sinners into un-sinners? We need to grow ourselves better, grow a better society, and grow towards paradise. Jesus' words have been applicable during every age, our age is no exception. Now we live on the edge of the space age and his words apply vividly to this age as well.

A well-run world would not be facing the same disasters that we are now facing: Warming of earth caused by greed and self-centeredness and ignorance. War and possible nuclear destruction, caused by hate and narrow-mindedness. Ecological disasters, caused by selfishness and greed. Over population, caused by ignorance and not spreading wealth around. It has been proved that people who are educated have a higher standard of living and less need for a large family. Our over use of recourses, again caused by greed and selfishness.

Would it be wrong to say that Jesus died to save us from destroying ourselves as well as our earth? Did he die to save us? from ourselves? Some could possibly be saved without the earth, the Bible even states this by saying people will be lifted off, but wouldn't it be better to save all of us and the earth too? Jesus may have planned on the fact that we might destroy the earth one day, maybe all worlds come to this crises. B dare we give up on earth? Jesus went to make a place for us, was this because we would need it? Will our earth be gone? Remember what Jesus told me "There is only a slight chance of saving the earth." He means for us to get busy *now*.

While sitting in church Sunday, Jesus told me that I would write about this gospel and sermon. At the time I didn't think so but I just did.

3/24/01

I finally understand something about social connections and interests that X seems to know instinctively. The truth doesn't count, only perceptions count. Rumors floating around make the social perceptions more real. Even looks take a back seat to perceptions of a person's standing or ability. I have never been a very social person, so in a way the social niceties throw me off my stride. Certain ideas seem so sensible to me. Remember once Jesus said I was "His practical one," but that isn't how the world turns, we are not governed by sense or intelligence but by emotions, sex, and fears. Perhaps when we become more mature this will become less true.

Note - I worry that I might write words that the evil one tells me but Jesus assures me that we will not include any of these words in the book.

3/24/01

What a night. I had a blowout on the freeway at 12:00 am going about 70 mph. I felt the tire give and pop and flop so I was able to pull over to the side. Then I kept driving to a corner gas station. The man couldn't or wouldn't call a cab for me. He was closing up and perhaps he was foreign and didn't know how? I had called my son but he was so drunk that he couldn't' get out of bed. This was the only moment when I felt in danger, thinking I would be stranded alone on the highway. But I was in luck. An all night store was open across the street. The girl was nice enough to call a cab for me.

This experience wouldn't be noteworthy except that Jesus, or someone, knew before hand that I would have a blowout. So I ask why didn't Jesus prevent it from happening? Why just warn me ahead of time? Is it because certain events must run their course? Perhaps Jesus or heaven can move events sideways but not change or prevent them completely? This is how I was warned:

Earlier in the week I got money back from the doctor because he just gave me a prescription and no office visit. This was lucky because I usually only carry about five dollars on me at all times. That night I was going to throw the two twenties on the table before I left home for the party but a voice said, "You'd better not." I became worried. "What do you mean? Is someone going to come into the house even with the alarm on? No answer. This voice mocks but is often right, at least, right enough to tease and taunt. Earlier this same voice mocked me about spending money. It said, "You better hold on to it."

I asked why. The voice said, "You'll see." This voice is not my own, it is not the little warning voice we all have. This voice was vividly real. Telling me not to spend money was like saying my future was going to crash, my job. as if he were going to make sure of it. These worries were rolling around in my mind and finally Jesus said to me, "Don't worry, you can spend money."

This little event is trite but it shows what can happen when you are in touch with other beings and your mind is open to their words. This mocking voice also played up to my fears of being jobless and in poverty again. Remember it knows us inside and out the only difference from Jesus is that it can't understand our morals and stamina and love for others. It expects us to always choose to love ourselves more.

Back to the warning. It was Jesus who told me during the party to not drink too much. I was drinking and almost decided to have another glass of wine but Jesus warned me that I should not drink too much. So I switched to coffee. I did have another glass of punch but by then enough time had elapsed from the other drinks that it didn't hit me too badly. Jesus knew that I would have the blowout and wanted me to be able to handle it. But why not prevent it? Oh, well, I had a great time at the party with the other church members.

3/27/01

It was so tired today I went to sleep after work and slept till late. I won't have a problem sleeping tonight either. I have been so busy I can't get anything important done. And my mind has become corrupted with normalcy or in other words, everyday reality. I feel like I have dropped into a deep well and it is becoming darker and darker as I fall further away from the sun. I fear I am loosing my mystical point of view.

J just assured me that I am not. That it is only temporary, although I am afraid that the word temporary has different meanings for both of us. I have a lot of deadlines by the end of April so I will certainly be busy till then. I hope to finish this book by the end of summer and the mystery book too. For sure the mystery will be completed but this book may not be because I need to wait for Jesus to give me more input. Jesus has said at this point, there is no hurry. He also said that as our world continues to face dangers and threats, my book will become more and more important, more necessary, and believable.

Jesus is here with me now and I feel his love pour into me as he smiles. I feel so pleased by this because lately my busyness has caused me to neglect prayer and his close presence. Last

Night, as I was lying in bed, Jesus told me to pray. He meant it seriously. there must be something very wrong that he is worried about.

Maybe China? He calms my fears and mental strife. I love Jesus and promise to get this book done before too long.

3/29/01

Suspicions were running around in my head, too many things fit into a slot, some people were acting against me, some people didn't like me. It was horrible. I sat and meditated this morning before work and all the suspicion dropped away like rain after a storm. It seemed to me that Jesus actually glowed standing next to God and it was if the sun and sky had entered my house and given it a fresh breeze filled with flowers.

The relief was palpable. I felt clean and fresh and anxious to begin a new day. I carry God's glow and Jesus smile as I write this. It surrounds me like an invisible shield covering me. I suddenly realized this when I thought of evil's methods and how it tries to penetrate the shield. Jesus protects me from harm. This is what I said to Jesus this morning. "Why do I keep getting suspicious. I don't have any reason to think these kinds of thoughts. I know you are standing near by shielding me. I don't need to worry about anyone hurting me so I should not let my mind build up suspicions. I will not fall into evil's plot again. I will depend on your guardianship. to keep me safe. This is what you mean by "Don't worry, don't worry"

Notice that I need to repeat these same lessons over and over. I learn and believe what you say and then forget again and need to be reminded all over again. Jesus smiled at me. My love for him rose to unbound heights, my mind felt pure and uncluttered. Evil was gone.

A note on how evil operates: He whispers doubts into your mind, and most people believe these thoughts to be their own, they are not. After the doubt is instilled, evil pushes on it and nourishes it, trying to make it grow huge and over take your common sense. If you have this same problem, and I think most people with sensitive minds do, remember that evil always tries to divide people , to separate you out of a group or family or away from friends. Perhaps now in our modern times we all read too many murder mysteries or television plots which can sink into our minds to become real possibilities. A nudge from evil can inflame a simple idea into an act of revenge or hatefulness. I have decided to stop concerning myself with the possibilities. I will let Jesus take care of plots and sub plots while I travel down this stony road to heaven. Stop worrying about under currents.

Jesus told me this morning, "It will be over soon."[91] He did not explain what this meant. He said these same words again this afternoon. "It will be over soon." He did not elaborate this time either. What does he mean? He could mean that I would be or my problem will be over. Don't know but I think he was referring to me personally and not the big wide world?

3/31/01

This morning I was listening to the Buddhist Chants and relaxing with Jesus said he wanted to show me something. I was reminded of the beautiful lady from nexus who spoke to me yesterday as I listened to the chants. She said, "You will bridge two worlds." Jesus was near and his face let up with a smile as I felt perplexed at her words. To understand my perplexity you need to know my circumstances, I live and work at the bottom of the hierarchy of status in the United States. If anyone could be said to have little value, it is me, so her words seem out of place directed at me. What can I do? Perhaps it's a way to encourage me to keep pushing. Perhaps this is their hope. I apologized to Jesus that I am so imperfect and ineffectual but I promised to keep trying. This is often hard because I

---

[91] After the events of Sept 11,2001 I understand better what Jesus meant. What if the United States had retaliated immediately with bombs without gathering the consensus from the other countries? I could have been over.

don't get any return. I felt guilty because I haven't been meditating lately like I should. I will do better.

Just before Jesus took me to the place he wanted to show me, I went up into the blue sky and promised to bring a part of it back home with me. I want to fill the earth with feelings of joy and contentedness, but I need to feel them first.

Then Jesus smiled and suddenly in front of me in the star lit sky stood, what appeared to be a huge translucent ruby. It was cut in an oblong with the corners trimmed, an emerald cut. We walked into it. As we passed through the outer wall or skin it felt like stepping through red Jell-O or gelatin. It gave somewhat to the pressure of our hands like a rubber skin or bubble.

Inside it was much larger than as seen from the outside. We floated in an atmosphere of pearly red while I could see the night sky beyond with the stars blazing and shinning. Jesus said, "It is a warning beacon. It is a part of the tunnels that join worlds. As soon as someone steps into this section of relay or comes too close to earth, the color and other effects warn them that earth is extremely dangerous for travelers, even psychic ones. A few travelers choose to visit regardless. But most visitors to earth are there for a purpose. "Write about it," Jesus said. Then I realized its importance and the message it would give us. the need to change so that we too would be able to travel to the other worlds or receive visitors.

4/4/01

The more I think about it the more I believe the lady from Nexus serves as a catalyst for ideas that heaven wants me to use and write about. Both times she spoke abruptly and in a Koan type of world puzzle. I was left to figure out what her words meant. In the first instance she let me know vividly that she wasn't from earth. The second instance of enlightenment pertained to some truth that I haven't pulled out of the hat yet. It is knowledge that still eludes my grasp.

Jesus keeps repeating "You will understand soon." But soon never seems to get here. So what did she mean about bridges or joining two worlds? I thought I was writing about many worlds. I speculate are the people we call angels from a world close by? A companion world? A few theories have a dark (red dwarf or brown dwarf) sun out near the Oort cloud. Muller's Nemeses? There is still Sitchin's theory about planet X or Nibiru. Now some astronomer is talking about floating worlds. But we suppose a visible world must be near a sun for energy. So I don't know. To speak of two worlds implies a connection of some sort. Connected but vibrating at a different frequency?

When I meditate and listen to the Chants, I sometimes step into the sounds. In fact, the other day, Jesus told me to do so. He said, "Step into it." meaning the sound. I felt like I was vibrating with the sound, that the sound was a world in itself and I had joined into it.

4/5/01

A critic would say of me that my reduction of life as good verses evil is trite and too simplistic. I might agree except that I have taken the notion that we are all existing in the mind of God, therefore our God lies at the base of every action and reaction and thought. All else is a cover up a mask put on by matter, a mirage we call reality. Reality we describe as anything that most people can perceive or think. Those of us who step beyond realities boundaries are called eccentrics or worse. But ultimately, we all step out of its grasp at death or do we? We may keep hold of the grip of reality so strongly and tight that some of us never leave this world scene but keep existing in a shadow of earth? As ghosts who never choose to leave. Jesus nods agreement at these thoughts. Frightening.

4/10/01

The China situation worries me. I think it will be resolved but it shows a pattern for the future. Other nations are beginning to hate us because of our wealth and because it seems that no matter what we do we come out on top. How long can all the other nations stand for our superiority? While we rape the earth and use up its resources, they must grovel and beg for alms. No the nations may unsettle into another war?

Some leaders use religion to whip their people up, strip them of their egos and strengths and then send them to war against the infidels, America. I see this as very possible in the future. Of course, prayers, Jesus and all of heaven are working hard to prevent this from happening, but remember the evil one rules the world with our compliance and it may be evil that keeps increasing the wealth of this nation. And we keep reaping in the fruits of God's labor even though we now know for a fact that the earth needs to be protected right now. It is heating up, the trees are crying, water is drying up or flooding, the winds have turned, the sky is falling unless we prop it up with forethought.

I felt real stupid tonight. I haven't been praying much and I needed to ask Jesus all over again how to pray. I said a Lords Prayer. He reached for both my hands and held them and this was such a pleasant surprise at that time and good feeling that I began to feel love inside. Love that reached outwards. I imagined hugging the earth. I imagined sending love to the leaders who have been in the news lately. I imagined that they needed love to also that they are only afraid just like we all are afraid. This was when I perceived that the leaders in China are afraid of loosing their power. They want the people to dislike America. It serves their purpose.

We would be right to be afraid of China and India for that matter plus other populated countries and … the list could go around the world. Any war with a country with such a high population as China would be so horrible it would make the Israel-Palestine conflict look like child's play. Our machines would need to plow down vast numbers of innocent people. Oh thank God it isn't happening, it would be too horrible. By the way, when we think of our own feelings at the Oklahoma bombings we can understand the feelings in Palestine and Israel and the people's hatred for each other. We should take note of this and try harder to understand.

4/16/01

I went to get my hair colored today. Jesus wanted me to. He wanted me to meet the lady beautician, to come in contact with her views, which were so difference from mine. She seemed upset and asked if I was a Christian. I said of course. She asked me what I thought about aliens, with my background the first thought jumped into my mind was aliens from another planet, but she was referring to Mexicans. I stayed quiet as she added, "What do you think of a Mexican alien going out with your daughter?"

I agreed that it might be a problem but I was very cool to the idea of rejecting someone just because they were Mexican even in this country illegally. Then she said he was into the occult and her daughter had a baby with him. She did not explain what kind of occult but I picked up the idea of devil worship, drugs, bad music, because she also talked about evil. She talked about fortunetellers and horoscopes and how evil they are. I interjected that true evil can turn young peoples minds but also that many people who get their fortune told aren't evil but just ignorant of the harm it can do. She then quoted scripture that said fortune telling was evil, the devils work. I agreed that we all need to be diligent because evil was everywhere but that some evils were not as harmful as others.

She told me her daughter had been turned by this man. I told her that in time she would probably be ok as long as she didn't do something really stupid. Then she said she was having that young man sent back, deported, and he said he was going to kill her. All this time she was very angry and hurt and told me she was a born again Christian and that young man was evil and she would fight him to save her daughter.

This lady made sense in a way but to me she seemed fanatical and I usually avoid people like that. When she left to do someone else's hair, a voice, a very distinct voice, spoke to me, "She is one of mine." I thought there was a sense of pride and bragging in the voice. This made me unsure if it was Jesus who spoke or not. I was afraid it was not because of the voice's tone. I became afraid because I have been mistreated by beauticians before who messed up my hair and I still don't know if it was Jesus who spoke or not or if I could trust that lady.

Her actions seemed too drastic to me but I don't know what she meant by occult. What if this young boy was just telling fortunes to earn a living for him and the baby? What if he was ok but she didn't want him to be with her daughter? What if? what if? What if it was the evil one who she fought for? That she was a soldier in the coming war for his side, his kind of people? What if Jesus was telling me that he needed that kind of fighter to win the war? Does Jesus want me to fight too? How could I? I am so broad minded that I always see the other side of the story. I believe in life but life as long as we don't hurt some one else. Could this lady be pushed to kill or hurt in the name of God?

I said to the lady, "As long as a person don't hurt someone else, like a predator, they may be ok. Some people prey on others."

"Yes," she said, "My daughter is being preyed on by evil. I am fighting it."

But to me it seems that evil is so all-pervasive that it is impossible to fight it all or get rid of it. We must pick the worst evil to fight against.

Jesus told me that soon in the coming war he will need fighters like that, strong people willing to fight. He also told me to write tonight about her views and situations. He will give me more comments later.

Jesus wants me to write about this and understand, but what is it he wants me to understand? Perhaps my washy-washy attitude isn't behavior becoming a soldier in a war? At the moment I seem to be alone as I struggle to pick out the message that Jesus wants me to get. What is the message?

I'll meditate later and ask because I am not sure if that lady was right or wrong.

Now I know. Jesus tells me that that is the point! In a war, each side believes themselves to be on the right side, the winning side. So how will we know if we are on the right side or not? If we were to battle everything that had a tinge of evil in it, their wouldn't be much left to our society. "Yes," Jesus said, "It will get that difficult to know where the truth lies."

4/17/01

The music lifted me up. This morning while listening to the Buddhist chants I felt myself lifted up but this time I didn't go any place so much as the layers fell away from me. I then understood why prophets of old said there were levels to the hierocracy of God, seven levels I think. I didn't count or see the differences but I felt each layer fall away as I rose up through them. It was so strange that I wondered if what I was experiencing was true. Jesus stood in front of me and told me to lift up my arms, I did, and he put his hands around mine. There were blood scars in his hands. I felt like crying. He wanted to assure me that this gentleness and beauty was true.

I need his reassurance of late that this is what he wants us to be. Lately I have been wrapped up into myself a lot and I think part of the cause is the feeling of empathy that I am afraid will consume me if I reach out. The resulting fear has been a burial of my feelings to the point of hardness and self-centeredness. We all do tend to feel and react this way. I see that I need to move more away from myself and let my love out more as well as open up and allow love in.

Since yesterday I have been feeling so mixed up after meeting the born again Christian with strict views I actually woke up thinking of the problem. This is the problem that Jesus set out for us. In the coming war it will be hard to know who is on your side. I don't want division but we will get it.

I have been worried that gay people would war against straight people, wouldn't that be a mess, but now I am learning that it won't be so cut and dried. There are gay people on both sides of the war of good and evil. And the biggest problem for most of us is that there will be Christians on both sides. That is very frightening. How will we know the difference? Why should we Christians fight each other when both are fighting against evil? or so each group will perceive themselves to be. In the coming war or skirmish or troubles, each a better word than Armageddon, as the Bible says, it will be children against parents, neighbors against neighbors and churches against churches. Many of us won't know where to stand. Where should we stand?

I asked Jesus. "What will determine if we are on the right side? Your side, the side of heaven, where is it? I await your answer."

This battle will have many fronts. It is about saving earth as well as our souls. Help us Jesus towards solid ground. Help us love you.

Jesus has just answered me. He said that love is the determining factor. Love is the central theme.

"I am love."

My emotions surge at these words from Jesus. I love him so much, but I am still not sure I understand. As an example, and this is why Jesus wanted me to meet her. The beautician loves her daughter, is trying to save her from what she perceives as an evil person so she is having him deported. What is wrong here, if anything? Could or did this lady go against another person in the name of God? Could she kill for God? Would God ever ask for us to kill in his name? It is easy to be against people while using the name of God. We say, God only loves me, God is against sinners, God has a rod to wrap against their knuckles. Could this be Jesus' God? God of the Old Testament certainly knew how to punish. But in modern times, after Christ, we believe that we should leave just punishment to God because only God *knows*. I believe this.

If Jesus is love for all creation, empathy for the poor and sick, love for sinners, then God must be this too. Isn't Jesus a reflection of God? God or earth? Then some how we must make this knowledge our demarcation line. If the skirmish intensifies into war, Jesus and all of heaven are working to prevent such a war, we will need to ask ourselves all the time one simple question, "Where is the love." and like my problem with the lady beautician, the answer will not be obvious or simple. Only our heart will know which direction in which to turn. It is our hearts and souls that will choose sides I am afraid.

4/18/01

Something I haven't written about before is that I seem to look out from another person's eyes at times. I have assumed this person is X but I still don't know if this person is on God's side or not. I remember following him in and out of hospital rooms the night Dorothy died. This frightens me. I also saw through his eyes as he watched another man get dressed? Don't know because I only saw a small part of person. There have been many other instances of looking out of X's eyes. Too many to remember now.

Plus some people can send themselves into my thoughts. Suddenly I may see X's smile inside my head. I am not thinking of him or anyone familiar at the time. The vision is different than a thought, it is a contact of some kind, between two minds, if only for an instant. This person knew that I knew and that was what his smile was about. Good or bad, I don't know.

4/18/01

Jesus told me the other night "In a hundred years, they, meaning churches, will wonder how they could have missed the obvious." this is regarding to Jesus and heaven as from space.

Comment-Today a voice told me " I did it." Voice was referring to the broken phones at work. Still don't know if it was for or against me or even the truth.

4/20/01

I felt a little frantic this morning while I was meditating for just a few minutes before I left the house. I was thinking how hard it is for me to tell a truthful statement from a false one. I remembered the words, "I did it." A statement from I don't know who. Not Jesus surely. So I was feeling frantic.

"How can I tell the diff?" I asked. "What is the difference?" I kept asking this of Jesus and then I put my arms around him and hugged.

"This is the difference." Jesus said as he held me and I him. "This is the difference."

My emotions rose to new heights as he said that. I felt so beautiful and loved. And although I still worry that I am not loving people enough, not good enough, not working hard enough for Jesus, I still need to experience his love whether I deserve it or not. I have learned to be afraid to show love for people or even caring sometimes. I have been holding back for so long that it has become a habit not to show people that I care. I am not sure how to fix this.

I have felt Jesus looking out my eyes at times in the past and for much longer periods than I have experienced looking out from someone else's eyes. My view (invited?) lasts only an instant. I have felt Jesus linger and watch events play out, usually when someone was seriously mistreating me for no reason. Now, long after the feeling is past I wonder "Was it really Jesus watching those people through my eyes?" I hope so.

"Yes," it was Jesus watching our behavior. He just said so. Is he inside each and every one of us? Or just certain people?

4/22/01

Ever since the gospel today in church a scene keeps running through my mind and I can't let it go. I' vet heard this same gospel a hundred times but this time a sudden image popped into my head. It was so real. The gospel was about doubting Thomas. I suddenly saw Thomas with Jesus hands on the sides of his face and he was crying into them, sobbing. Jesus hands had blood on them. Thomas is kneeling while Jesus was standing . It was so vivid and real for a second I thought I was there watching.

I thought about it possibly being a movie scene I had watched once but I felt so close to Jesus side and felt so intimate about the scene that I believe it was real. I picked up the emotions along with the image, a shock of recognition from Thomas and a feeling of shame. So I speculate that perhaps I was standing there next to Jesus and Thomas? Then who was I? I think I was Mary a lover of Jesus and this is why I still love him. Women weren't considered apostles. I think I considered myself one and still do, a follower of Jesus.

4/23/01

The Buddhist chants are pointing to where? other places on earth? Off earth? Jesus wants me to write this. He told me that I have been given a gift that enables me to understand so that I can write about it. Most people need to go through rigorous training to learn before they can sense the true nature of the chants. Yet I have been told that they are for amateurs. What would a more learned person feel? Depending on the type of chant, I perceive and felt different things during a twenty-minute session. It is pleasurable to just sit and listen to the pure sounds. As I sat very comfortable on the couch, Jesus said "Follow the music."

This chant seemed like smoke rolling up into the atmosphere. I can still see this effect. It kept gathering like over a table in a room of card players.

The smoke kept twisting and churning upwards in a slow undulating movement towards a peak. It grew into a chimney made of rising smoke. Then the chant stopped for a time, there are planned pauses between chants. I was left suspended and hanging in the air above and next to the column of smoke that was still swirling and rising, waiting for the next chant to begin.

The next chant seemed to bring me down again, at first. It was liquid drops slipping into a small pool. The drops kept expanding and swelling as they plopped into the water ringing into waves moving away from each pounding plop. I expanded each time a drip met the surface. I rolled and contracted in ever widening circles and then again hung suspended in air, fat and plump with pregnant anticipation of falling to the surface once more, ready to explode in the silence of no-sound.

One chant exploded into a long line from top to bottom. I became a pulsation, a fractal rose caught on a line of disappearing infinity. As the chant changed the line began to open and close with the pulses. At this point Jesus joined me to teach me the path through the doorway. It was too all encompassing and open for my senses. Hanging in infinity, I collapsed back into myself and lost it. It was too much for me to take in. This portal conflicted with the ruby one? Jesus had showed me another time. I wondered why there were two portals, two ways off the earth? Did one lead to the other?

Suddenly writing this with Jesus very near I realize that all this has a purpose. It isn't just an exercise in movement. the purpose is to learn how to go beyond physical matter and leave the earth. The perplexing or frightening question is "why?"

4/26/01

Question-What does X want of me? It's as though he is standing up and shouting "Look at me." Or is he just mocking me?

4/28/01

I had a sudden intuition about the truth of X. He is the evil one or at least one X is. I remember when my thyroid was very hyper and I went to the doctors. As soon as a doctor would want to examine me I went berserk with nerves and shaking. I couldn't' understand why and put it off as part of my thyroid condition. It wasn't only that, it was being examined by doctors in space. X's slave workers. I can't remember this specifically at this time but I think it may be true that we are all being manipulated by him. He comes and picks us up like cattle and causes many of our illnesses. We don't understand this, we think they are natural, no, many are not natural. Probably half the population of earth has been effected by being abused or caused to mate or other behavior that we forget by morning. This all happens while we are sleeping. The only evidence I have is the dream memories of breaking a container in space once and a few other vague memories. This evil plays with us like we are his toys that he can break or crush at his whim. Our only protection is knowledge and Jesus. Heaven tries to put a shell around us.

He can go where he wants and be who he wants to be, he owns the earth or thinks he does. He plays with me but I know him. He is trying to loose my film, my clock is blinking so I might not wake up for church, etc. He tries to frustrate me in numerous ways. I don't have many answers at to how he does these things or even why. Why does he try and hinder my every effort? I can guess, because I refuse to follow him. He is so skilled at what he does it is almost impossible to know when he is near or who he is acting against. The only thing we can do is keep praying and asking Jesus to help us walk through life and avoid evil's whiles as much as possible. It does no good to worry because we are helpless as he plays with us. But why does he leave some people alone?

Jesus says we are not completely helpless. When we keep on the side of heaven, by doing so, we throw a kink in evil's path. I think I need to take out the part where Jesus changes into many people of all makes and models. Maybe it wasn't Jesus at all but the evil one? Or are there two, an evil X and a good X? Jesus asked that I write of this; therefore, it must be one of the truths that he wants the world to know, I'll need to leave it in.

Here is another truth: The beloved disciple of Jesus wasn't John, it was Mary. She has been almost written out of the Bible because she was a woman. Women were also looked down on during the many years that the Bible was being copied and transcribed. The transcribers slipped in new names and pronouns to reflect John as Jesus ' beloved. Even Leonardo de Vinci got it wrong when he painted The Last Supper.

Even during Jesus time the other apostles tried to exclude women. But we need to keep in mind Jesus rational, his course that taught togetherness and for every one to love each other. His message didn't exclude any type of person, even though the social melee at that time, like the present one, tried to exclude different types of individuals or groups. Women were treated a whores or as necessary reproductive or sexual bodies. They had little value until our own time. Jesus also included in his group tax collectors, sinners, perhaps even men who liked men, and probably a few sick, unclean people. Many people followed him and he tried to hold all of them into his arms. Just as he now encloses me in his arms when I become afraid.

I have always heard rumors and tales that Jesus had a twin. Now I am beginning to believe that the evil one posed as Jesus when he could to throw people off. I can say this-during spiritual meditation I have never felt like hugging the evil one. He stands aloft and his voice and manner is harsher than Jesus'. It is as though he is always cocky and angry about something.

I have witnessed Jesus angry but it had more depth and empathy in it. The other day I read a book of fiction but it involved young boy children used as prostates. I felt so bad, I looked up at Jesus who stood near by at that moment of need and I asked, "Is this true, do people really do this to children?"

Jesus didn't answer he just nodded and tears were in his eyes. It was almost unbearable to me as well. The abuse portrayed in the book was so psyche damaging to young people, I had to put it out of my mind for a while, and stop reading. Like most of us I can't dwell on a lot of things that go on in our world. Some of it is so seriously horrifying that we can't hold it in our awareness for too long. I choked up and tears dripped from my own eyes too. But only for a moment. Imagine how Jesus must feel all the time being a witness to the atrocities in the different societies on our earth, day after day. It is a wonder we are still around and Jesus has not slapped us down yet. Truly, Mary must beg him every day to stay his hand.

I feel hurt as I write this. I am a lucky one, I hardly ever cry except dry, silent tears of empathy. Oh Jesus help us grow up out of our ignorance.

4/30/01

We went someplace tonight that I find hard to understand completely. And I realize that it is important that I understand because both Jesus and Mary took me to see this place. This gave it added weight but I still failed to pick up the whole message. I can only share the little I could feel and know with you.

I had tried to meditate and go with Jesus early this morning but I couldn't' seem to concentrate so I gave it up. But I kept seeing a blue strip floating in deep space. It was like a ribbon winding around and seemed to be full of people and worlds or cities. My mind kept wanting to turn it into different islands or areas of land like I had read once in a science fiction story. Oddly enough, this is the first time this has happened, that I know of, to almost see something I had read about, an actual SF setting getting mixed up in my travels with Jesus. But the idea threw me off my stride and I gave up.

Tonight we went back. At first as often is the case, I needed to feel my motion through the universe because it gives me a feeling of going somewhere, so I imagined moving past stars and through the blackness of space. There have been times when Jesus and I would just suddenly appear someplace but often when I am out of practice because I have been too busy, I need a mental boost to get me going again.

After a few seconds of travel through space, we came to a sky blue area. I thought it may have been the same ribbon of a world or worlds that we tried to visit earlier but we entered it so fast I didn't see the outward shape clearly. we entered a bright blue sky that was only sky and nothing else. There was no clouds or anything else to differentiate anything except more blue. But the blue kept getting bluer and bluer. We traveled from a slight sky blue into a final royal deep blue that was almost black.

Here is where we found different forms. The forms all looked cream colored against the deep royal blue. One looked like a cream or white as I waived my arm through the blue fog. We were not in water or in wet fog that I could feel. All this time Jesus and Mary were silent. I kept thinking wondering how we came here. I watched the forms as they seemed to grow before our eyes. M held a rose up to show me. It was a real rose but it was white against blue. Then I realized that every bush and flower and leaf was real but just lacking in color. It all seemed to be growing out of the deepest blue possible before the foliage became black ground.

Then I suddenly saw a panorama of the graded levels of blue as if I were looking from above. What I saw next seems impossible, foliage growing as if from the underside like on a flat ribbon or Mobius strip on a blazing lighted surface. on top of the dark side.

We walked on this surface. The forms growing were almost black but ranged in difference shades of blue. The same rose, perhaps literally, was growing from its stem as black but it was surrounded by white light. The light was so bright it hurt the eyes. I kept getting the idea of mirror images, shadow-light. But I kept saying "I don't understand what you want me to see" You want me to see mirror images? and shadows?

Jesus said, "Yes" while Mary explained that this is a view of what life and objects really look like—opposites. This is the only place in the universe where this truth is apparent to the eye. Everything in the universe is made up of opposites, all life has a mirror image. Most often it is not revealed and stays in a shadow world. It can become manifest and does during insightful times.

This is what causes the rumors and ideas of twins when great men rise to the surface of societies, there is always a counter force, a shadow-light.

"Oh this is so hard to understand and see, I don't think I can get it right"

"Yes it is complex and not easy to follow"

"Did I pick up on some of what I was supposed to see?"

"You did ok." Jesus and Mary both smiled at me.

I got the feeling that the seed was planted and this was the purpose of our travel tonight. Perhaps I will learn more at another time.

5/6/01

The Sunday gospel for this week was comforting and revealing. I felt Jesus presence strongly as Father Thomas read the words, "My sheep hear my voice; I know them, and they follow me…No one can take them out of my hand.…The father and I are one." Jesus was right there beside me reassuring me as I heard those words, loving me, promising me that he will never let me fail. A quick view of the pain I had been through ran through my mind.

I said, "If God did it to strengthen me or straighten me out so I would belong to him, then I accept it. It was all worth it. If it was Jesus calling me, I accept the pain and problems and hurts. Again I remembered all the times Jesus stood near by when other's turned away, when he seemed to carry me through tongues of fire.

A great deal of what I have written in this notebook is about myself instead of what it should be about. I still don't know what it will be about or how to arrange it or where we will travel. Jesus tells me not to worry, that he knows and I will know how to arrange the book when I need to. Already I think of things I should take out of section two, unless Jesus specifically tells me to leave the items in.

Again on a personal level, I am ashamed to admit that I have been neglecting prayers again. I have not been sending my love outwards, I did this morning. I can't seem to find any love within myself sometimes. This would be frightening if true. But I still care about people in general and hurt for them. I think I burn out sometimes and then come back to myself or Jesus pulls me back to himself and I revive like during church service Sunday.

Jesus keeps telling me "They are afraid." He is referring to the people who deliberately put barriers in my path but he never gives me any specifics as to exactly who they are or what they are afraid of. This leaves the idea open too much speculation and probably mis-thoughts on my part. Could they be afraid of me, why? On the surface it doesn't look as if I could cause harm to anyone. I have wondered if they are afraid of my writing but I just write what Jesus tells me. I never get specific about what I think is going on in the background with certain people, I never use names. Most of my complaints are about groups or types of behavior that affect all of our well-being. What are they afraid of? Are they afraid that Jesus is watching? He is. He seemed to me to be surveying their antics during church today, I don't mean that the people who were in church but a certain group.

Jesus suddenly said, "I have not arrived yet," in a very firm, not to be ignored, voice.

I got the idea that he was almost smirking at this certain groups blundering around trying to hide themselves or sweep away their actions. And yet I don't know who he was referring too. It was as if he was standing above a crowded town square while people jostled and shoved one another like children arguing like children often do. The wisdom that poured off Jesus was staggering at this moment, his knowing, so all encompassing, threw me for a loop. Sometimes it catches me up short with a sudden panoramic view of it all that Jesus shares with me for that instant. I never fail to be amazed.

Another thing Jesus told me in church today, this day was one of those times when Jesus seemed to make up for all my doubts and worries, there wasn't a spread of doubt about who it was speaking. His authority was mind staggering, all encompassing. He told me that my children would belong to him one day. I felt assured that they would also fit into his hand one day. I had been thinking about how the world seems to be divided between God's people and those who follow the evil one. I hoped that my children, even though I hadn't raised them well, would follow Jesus before they died. Jesus assured me that eventually they would also be among his followers. So now I worry about what travails and pain they will need to endure to finally find Jesus in their lives. How will they finally feel the call to Jesus? I always find something to worry about. I remember the gospel where Jesus says, " I will not loose my own." It is almost as though we are born in one camp or another and each side does the job it was put on earth to do. Talk about undoing science.

When I told Jesus about the theme for my mystery book he laughed and said, "I like it." It is about the battle between good and evil and how we seem to be pawns in a game run by Gods. He didn't say it was true, he just said he liked the idea as though the theme teased him. The point of all this is that Jesus is here in spirit now, he does know and he does watch and he does enjoy our antics as we try to cover up our tracks before he arrives. We needn't bother.

I've thought about Jesus arrival. There are a number of ways for him to get here: He could be born again, the least desirable and probable. He could be here in adult form but not have awakened to his real self yet. He could be here among us as an adult and not come out to reveal himself yet. He could be traveling and on his way here and will arrive in full glory like it says in the bible. He could stage a number of these events for our benefit. However Jesus gets here or "arrives" we can be certain that God in on the way here with his accompaniment of worlds, cities, conveyances, and angels.

5/10/01

How can this be possible, all these little contrivances against me, and not for the first time. Took in my film and they lost it, couldn't find it for a week, I went there and they found it, after I pointed it out to them, but it wasn't processed. Took it to speedy that Saturday, he said it would take five working days. It got back the 8th but no one called me. He was supposed to call me when film came in. Girls said there should have been a star in red marker to show them to call. I specifically told the man I needed it in a hurry because of a grant. So twice my film was hijacked. How did he do it? At two different places and times, though they are next door to each other. This makes me all the more determined to get those grant papers in the mail. Most people would call it fate but I know better. Does he take on another person's mind and make them screw up? He must, he can't become all those people with different jobs and home life's, can he? So I never know when or where he will attack next. But Jesus says don't worry. He only can do so much, and why doesn't he want me to try and get a grant? Actually my chances are very slim as it is.

This is probably why my alarm got messed up too, him. I thought I felt him when he was installing the system. That is why I worried about him getting back in because he has the code. But it probably wasn't him, just a young boy doing a job and he took over for a minute? Can he take over anyone? Or just his own? Or those not aware of the possibility? Or am I crazy? But I know him, I have seen him before in various places, screwing people up royally. It doesn't make sense, does it? Be careful and don't see him where he is not, could become paranoid just watching for him to show. Take Jesus advise, don't worry and keep pushing. All he can do is try to push back, I don't need to let him get away with it.

Jesus told me before that "you will understand soon." Is this what he meant? That I would find the evil one in many people. I thought he was changing his face and pretending to be certain people but I may have been wrong. Instead he may just attack their mind for an instant and they do his bidding? Does he whisper to them to "just let it slide, you disserve a grant more than that person?" Somehow he may induce hate in a person. Easily done I have felt my own hate and the need to control myself. For that moment of hated thought, they screw up? To simplistic? Don't know. Hope I don't learn any more about him. Don't want to know. Enough of these junky thoughts.

Interesting article in the Free Press today about segregated kids. It said that without diversity, "Adults who never shared a laugh or a tear with a friend of another color, will leave their world no different than they inherited it: separate and unequal." Detroit is one of the most segregated places in the U S (Fifth) Many children don't ever see a person of different color except on television. Sad. As an example a young man I know says he had a hard life. He is still so young but he thinks his life is hard, wait a few years and he'll learn what hard can be. But the point is that so do other people his age. Almost every young adult thinks life is hard and unless they get a chance to intermingle with others of different races, they will think only their race has it hard. When I had the teenage kids to write poems for an assignment in class, I was shocked at how disastrous they thought their lives were. It didn't matter whether they were girls, boys, white, black, fat, dirty, poor, rich, almost all of them had an outlook as if their life was horrible in some way. I can't remember if I thought this way when I was their age, or I don't know if it is common for that age group but it doesn't seem right. These kids don't really tell their parents about their perceived bad life, they only speak in poems, writings or actions. I wonder what other teachers have found in students writing? Need to look into it. If we ask our children or grandchildren they just say "oh, everything is ok"

Need more white people to move back into Detroit. Wonder what would induce them to move back in? Something tells me I will soon learn, that the economy will hit bottom or something like that. I don't wish for a bad economy just that people should find a reason to move back into Detroit so it would become a more mixed population. I suppose it's a matter of class segregation, which will never be fixed, even the Bible tells us that.

5/13/01

We expect magic from Jesus. We are waiting for him to step down on earth and wave his magic wand to make everything well. Can he? If he did that he would be destroying our autonomy, our ability to make choices. No, we are the ones who need to change ourselves and our world. He can only push us on. As we grow more able to understand one another and be in touch with each other we also need to use that understanding to enhance our human growth. We have untapped powers in the human psyche, powers we never dreamed of. How else will the lion lay down with the lamb unless we set them together and hold them still with out minds?

5/15/01

Jesus said to get moving on the book. Mary showed me again a quick snap shot of the hurricane covering earth. Even though it needs to get done, it will still take a long time before it comes out. At least a year even if I publish it myself. So I promise I will have it ready for publication by the end of summer or earlier. Jesus still needs to show me a lot of stuff that will go in it, but he can do that while I write.

5/16/01

Yesterday morning I was trying to meditate before I left for Florida. I wasn't successful because I was too wound up, exactly what meditation is supposed to solve. My mind kept drifting off and at one point I saw an image of two people at the end of a driveway and edge of lawn setting out large black bags. It looked like an older man and large plump women. Then suddenly they were gone. I just considered it a fragment like most fragments that float in and out of our minds when we are relaxed.

At that point Jesus stood in my awareness and said, "We can't keep you home." He smiled as he said it.

At his words I realized that I had been traveling or my mind was drifting to other places as I involuntarily voyaged somewhere unknown. Thinking about it, I realized it had felt as if I had been floating above the people looking down and because it happens so often, I thought it was a made up image. Not true. I doubt that I was looking out from someone else's eyes because of the angle. I must have been just viewing a random scene while I free floated. These people didn't notice me so I must not have been physically there just my mind was.

The scene had no meaning to me and no purpose, no explanation from my past or present. It was just a simple moment in the couple's life that I happened to drift into. It's scene played out like a movie and I had as much involvement as I would in a movie. None.

This brings up the question, of how many times do we all see fragments of scenes and attribute them to imaginary dreams. We never consider them to be real images. Perhaps we should begin to take note of those sometimes-silly scenes that have no apparent meaning. Just playing out and running through our mind may be all the meaning they need. We may be there watching. We may be traveling and not even know it. It may be a latent power from our psyche. Often we get these scenes while we are drifting off to sleep half awake. This is the time when our minds are held less to the reality we have imposed on them during the day. It may be only at these times that we are able to overcome perceived reality to travel and view places far away.

This hidden ability may also include time travel. It looked to me as if the two people I saw had just gathered a large bag of leaves. Leaves that fall in the autumn not the spring when this happened. Although it may have been large black bags of grass clippings, don't know. The view of grass behind them was on a slight rise or hill and the road in front was dirt. I did not see enough to include a house or mailbox but I believe it was a rural scene. It didn't have the flavor of an urban setting.

I wonder if we all travel the world and don't even know it, every day. How wonderful. We only need to learn to give ourselves more control in order to stay a little longer than a quick visit. I speculate if our movies and TV programs play a large part in this ability. By making the world visible and common for all of us, it has also broadened our mental capacity with imagination. Yes, I am sure this is the case. The more we take in as stimulus the more we put out as knowledge. This delights me. I love to see us grow. This will also help with empathy and understanding our fellow humans who are different. We are on the road to homogeneity, for better or worse. This is why evil tries so hard to divert our course by separating us with hate and jealously.

Was it Monday or Tuesday I saw the picture of the Fatima statue in the newspaper and the large crowds attending it. It made me feel so little. Who am I to assume I speak with Mary. It is nothing like at Fatima. Just as I thought these words, Mary seemed to put her hand in front of me and gave me a beautiful red rose and a smile. What bothers me is that I accept her presence as normal. I don't shake or gasp in wonder because I realize I have a job to do for heaven and Mary's advise is part of that job. I need her words and encouragement to do the job right. Besides we are more sophisticated today, we are more able to accept a visitation as less a miracle and more a moment of mind in space. We now know the truth about the hard to understand reality of both time and space. So I don't consider Mary and Jesus presence so much as a miracle as much as a grand ability on their part to make themselves known to me and my struggle to recognize that they are with me and wish to communicate.

5/16/01

I' vet been thinking. It seems to me that we all have a good side and a bad side, trite and over worked concept but if we think about it as Jesus on our good side then he is always potentially with us if we choose the good side. Just the same we could think of our good side a like a blank movie screen and the prophet, or God, or guru that we most admire is the one who develops on the screen. The same could be said for our evil side, which is on the backside of the screen.

We don't need different screens for different people. All of heaven speaks for Jesus so it doesn't matter if it is actually Jesus who speaks at any moment but only a sense of his being. I could also be wrong because Jesus can be so many places at once. Even I can see out from another person's eyes once in a while. Imagine Jesus ability to see out of multiple eyes simultaneously. I even wonder if God is on both sides of the screen because he is the screen just as he is the universe.

5/23/01

So much to write about I don't know if I can write it. I went to Florida because my dad was sick. On the way back I left my purse at Krystal's restaurant. They are like White Castle up here. When I found it missing I wasn't sure at which exit we left it. I tried to call but the operator hung up, and the police didn't give me much help, they said to call the nearest Krystal, which was long distance. I didn't know which Krystal I left it at or the name of the city. I was in a quandary of confusion. How could I get my purse back? Then I walked into a small Exxon station and asked if I could use the phone. [92] When I explained why I needed to use the phone that I lost my purse, the shopkeeper and owner or manager made a number of

---

[92] Exxon Station at 4621 Bill Gardiner Parkway, Locus Grove, Georgia

calls for me until they located where I had left my purse. It turns out that the manager of Krystal's in Tifton was holding my purse until I went back to pick it up, two hours back down the highway. I was very thankful to all the people who helped me find my purse because it would have been staggeringly hard to replace what was in it. I had a disk copy of all my books with me for safekeeping.

I believe that Jesus sent me into that small gas station far off the highway. When I walked in I noticed the shopkeeper had a red circle on his forehead, which meant he was a Hindu. I think we had an instant mental rapport and this is why he agreed to help me so readily. As spiritual people we help each other when needed. He couldn't make the phone calls on his own but his manager or owner who agreed to allow the calls. I was so thankful. It is amazing how one person can meet a complete stranger who is in tune with God or a higher spirituality and their minds click for a moment. I never did learn their names but names are not necessary for recognition in the spiritual realm.

This reminds me how I kept seeing angels while I rode down the street but I didn't pay attention. Perhaps they were trying to tell me that I had left my purse, if so, I didn't hear the message, I just kept thinking of other things. It was left to Jesus to finally direct me to the right place for help.

5/25/01

I have been thinking of Y. His job is to accelerate the spiritual awakening of the people in the world. At least, those who are willing and able to tune their minds to a higher realm. There will always be people who refuse enlightenment. I am so proud to know him.

5/29/01

This is all crazy speculation. I am seeing Xs everywhere. I know this is really stretching what we believe in but I have been supposing and playing with an idea that won't go away. It fits many facts even though it sounds crazy. It is that the original apostles are still around and have always been around as immortals. They have been playing with our culture and sending us ideas from behind the scenes. The Bible says that they will stay until Jesus return and at the end of Luke ? The apostles said that Jesus didn't say his beloved would live forever but they took it to mean she would. In other words the apostles took the idea seriously that they would live until Jesus returned, but they also thought he might return soon because who could believe deep down that they could out live other people. So much has been rewritten and translated wrong in the bible over the years that I find it surprising that these little snippets of outlandish ideas were left in. Maybe they were so outlandish that no one dared to take them out or change them. This wasn't the case with changing Jesus' beloved, it was easy to change the name of Mary into John.

I don't really believe the twelve apostles are running around playing with our lives, do I? Fun and game. If they were still around, and I think X is one of them, imagine their thinking. At first they probably were very faithful to Jesus words. but as time went on it would have been easy to play God as they increased their powers. Anyone who lives two thousand years would accumulate powers. They could manipulate people in the name of Jesus. After all those years how could they help feeling a little superior to all the rest of humanity? But perhaps Jesus slaps them down to size once in a while. He does me. Or they may just keep plodding along waiting for Jesus to return but he never did. When Jesus does return, they may die like the rest of us or leave with Jesus and most of humanity? A promise they have been waiting for two thousand years for Jesus to keep. Now I come along and purport to talk to Jesus and travel with him. They at first think it is another false alarm? There have been many. So they test me and learn that I am sincere although this doesn't prove anything. If any of this is true, my question is are they hopeful of Jesus return or afraid? What have they done during all those two thousand years? Was it for or against Jesus? Jesus just told me that they all remained faithful. So now I wonder if they are tired and want to end their long vigil of work.

Is any of this true? I don't know. There have been very great prophets who didn't live forever or did they? A future science , where Jesus or his advisors or support help may have came from, might be able to change a person's DNA to everlasting life. Of course, Peter died on the cross, upside down. But how do we know that after a short coma-death he didn't get up and walk out of his grave. It would not take long to realize that you need to stay hidden. Or would it have been good advertisement to not hide? Ah here is the crack in the armor of the idea. Seems like an apostle would have shouted the miracle if there was one. So none of this must be true. It could also be that their deaths were worth more than their living bodies. Or maybe it was only rebirth in the flesh and they remembered who they were?

Jesus told me I would understand soon, maybe I am beginning to.

I think I knew one person who staged their own death but he was certainly no follower of Jesus that I could understand so I conclude that if any of this is true, their are also people working for the other side who are immortal too. Maybe this all isn't as silly as it sounds. If you start stepping out of your usual reality you must expect to confront weird ideas and beliefs.

Is it X who keeps trying to discredit me? or is it only a person who prefers not to believe what I am saying? They may be so used to hiding that they don't want their cover blown away.

Jesus said, "Blow it off." He also told me once that X is so used to changing covers or illusions that he is expert at it. I wonder if he even knows who he really is? I am still in the dark and don't know anything. I need to understand soon. I know one X is a great illusionist when it comes to character but is he the only one? Could he just be a good actor? Then I've met a few of them.

5/31/01

I get the impression that it is very important for humanity to learn to use their minds better, to grow the ability to perceive other worlds as well as grow in empathy for all people of every world. I actually feel a pressure from Jesus to continue because of this need for mankind to reach outwards. If Jesus is sure of its importance, than who am I to doubt? I will push to get this book out there for all our sakes.

6/1/01

Tonight we went for a visit to Cotton world for a few minutes. It was my choice, I actually felt lonely and wanted to meet the people again, and I still don't know their names but is that important. Of all the world's I have visited this one feels the most like home. It's aromas and colors and textures and quiet friendliness gives me such a feeling of hominess that I've seldom felt in my own home.

I got huge hugs from the adults and children who where in the home when we arrived and then I sat at the dark wood table and watched a young adult get up on the family mound and speak about their history. They have helped many worlds and places over the years and they are proud of their service to diverse peoples in the universe.

I did not understand any specific things that he was talking about because I wasn't familiar with their history and other places. I didn't mind, it was pleasant sitting there listening to the drone of his voice as it arose and lowered in pitch. Besides I wouldn't' have had any reference to the different worlds he was talking about. Very soon after we arrived we left. We walked out the door in the tree and the sun was shinning and the tree's leaves were very green. It was just after a harvest and all the cotton had already been raked and gathered up. It looked like a wonderland.

Surprisingly I saw a tree down in Florida that resembled the trees on Cotton world. It was in the center of Devil's Den, a camping and swimming resort. It stood majestically just at the cave mouth where the divers go down into the caves. This tree was just amazing the way its branches spread out all around and its width was enormous. I've never seen one like it before on earth, but then I haven't been many places. The owners of Devil's Den knew the value of this tree too, it was in the center of a walkway as you go into the office. I was so happy that we went in to the office that day, I loved that tree at first sight. We asked how much to get in and couldn't afford to go but luckily the day before, ignorant that there was a cost to enter, we went swimming in the man made pools. We, my daughter-in-law, brother and myself just walked in. I thought Florida was such a nice state to have such beautiful places to swim free. Ha. (Later I went to a county owned river to swim that was nice too, while I visited my father who was sick.)

6/2/01

I am beginning to understand. I know and see so much that I don't write about. I don't want anyone to read certain information pertaining to specific people who have a right to their privacy so I try not to reveal names unless they or Jesus tells me to do so. He has told me to write it all but he did not say to include names or reveal certain people who are in hiding.

They are different although one of the most obvious differences is their long lives. It makes all the difference in character, behavior, ability, and outlook. Not for them the same standards and morals that we have grown throughout the centuries (perhaps through their contrivance). They don't need to worry about escaping death, death makes all the difference. It overlays all our thinking and behavior and drives our cultures. Our whole civilization could be described a culture of death. Everything leads to the fact that our lives are short and disposable: Fiction, laws, attitudes, fears, hopes, politics, greed, religions etc. all have their base on the fact of our final death.

I have called some of these people angels but they are not true angels though they have abilities beyond the human. They have been watching us for such a long time that they know us inside out and backwards and therefore can anticipate our thoughts and behavior to certain stimulants and events. This makes it extremely easy for them to turn us one way or another in whatever direction they want us to believe at the moment. The catch is that they are not all of the same stripe, some would turn us forward and others backwards. They are not Gods so they have limits but they can outmaneuver us when they choose.

Most of all they lay low staying hidden from view. I think you could find them mostly in the lower classes because this population is so invisible. But of course, since money is the current exchange mode and necessary for existence, they have that too, as much as they need, but probably they attribute much less to wealth or power than we do. They may have provided a few great men to our history but on the whole, I think, they prefer to mix among the crowded lives of everyday humans.

Here is the point, humans who attain the same attitude towards life, wealth, and power become more like these psudo-angels. Even some of their abilities and magical deeds can grow within a human who has accepted this kind of philosophy. This is one of the reasons all the great religions produce prophets and other great people, they all finally come this philosophy of life, even though, or in spite of the fact of death. Christian's await life after death while Buddhists await rebirth, it all adds up to the same thing, life, death, and life. In short the universe is a garden of life, change, rebirth, change of life into many different forms.

The lady from Nexus's words may have also had a figurative meaning when she said, "You will join two worlds." Christian and Buddhist beliefs are like two different worlds but whose underlying purposes may be the same. In fact we could look at Jesus words as being Buddhist. So much so, that many people have speculated that Jesus may have traveled to the East when he was growing up. East and West could somehow join the concepts of love.

6/3/01

It felt a little odd today in church when I suddenly thought of Y, I had been thinking of him and lot lately pertaining to my writing, and Y suddenly said, "I am here." This pleased me but startled me nevertheless. I hadn't asked him to visit today, I assume he was there because he wanted to observe the mass. I liked his presence for the few moments he stayed with us.

Perhaps you are wondering if there is a conflict about Y being there in Jesus church. There is no conflict. Even if Jesus wasn't Buddhist to begin with, it may be that older and wiser religions grow into Buddhists beliefs eventually anyhow. While mass was going on I thought about the words Jesus gave us for the Bible and couldn't find much that wasn't Buddhist. A lot of people have noticed this. Jesus is like Buddha. Both Jesus and Buddha taught humanity, both teachings were changed over the years into religious dogma, both teachers were religious rebels. I am telling you this because I think Y is attaining Buddha-hood, of course, that has been his direction all his life. But it is one thing to strive towards a goal and quite another to reach it.

I am not saying that he has reached full enlightenment, I don't know and you would need to ask him, he says not. I only suppose that he is gaining abilities that most of us don't understand. This is as it should be. I feel like such a child when he is near, almost as much of a child as when I am close to Jesus. This childish feeling isn't intended but I recognize my own limited spirituality and reflect this feeling when I am with higher spiritual beings. I also recognize that I am only a voice that is my job, to see and report.

Another reason I mentioned Y at this time is because he was with me for a short time while I was painting too. I kept struggling to paint myself meditating like my last painting but no matter what I did I couldn't do it. I wanted the whole painting calm, serine, and quiet. It turned out anything but. When I was near the drawing that would satisfy me. I felt Y's presence and agreement for a moment. When I looked at what I had drawn, it was just the opposite of calmness. It was a person meditating, all right, but the person was nearly starved, deep circles were under her eyes and the background was spotty and violent. Then I realized why. This was just what I wanted. It was a reflection of the torture going on right now and in the past in Tibet with the Buddhists monks and the Falon Gong sect in China. I have been upset about these people lately but it took a nudge from Y to push it out of me on to the canvas. Now I hope I can paint it well. I am not a real great artist but I love to express myself in paint, so I keep trying.

This brings up another question. I perceive you might ask. Where is Jesus when Y comes to visit? I have asked this myself. During church Jesus was there with me and he was at the alter when the priest said communion. Jesus is always with me but I don't always perceive him. But just as many humans can gather in one room, so can many minds gather together. I have experienced this once or twice but it only confuses me because I am such a novice at mental gathering. I now suspect that mental traveling has been going on for a very long time but only now is it coming out into the open, especially in the west. We'll Jesus told me to do it. He has instructed me to tell it all. I think Jesus means that it is time for all of this information to come out because the earth is in such danger that only a great number of people using both mental and physical strengths can help. He wants us to recognize the real power within spirituality.

Here is an odd thing that happens when you talk to someone mind to mind, and Jesus tells me that each person tends to do this. When you talk to someone mind to mind, you give them a spot in space that belongs to them. In other words, when Jesus first began talking to me, I saw and recognized his voice on my front/right. Later I changed this because the evil one took over his spot on purpose to confuse me. When I talk to Y he is on my right/side a little towards the back. When I talk to others they may have the left or front or even back. For some reason having to do with our need to know where a speaker is in space, we give attributes of place to each specific person but we can change these places as we choose. These set places are arbitrary and fictional, they don't exist except in our minds. The voice does exist but not in the spot we assign it to. Unless it is like Jesus is when he has actually appeared to me, then I can assume he really is there and has taken up that space, but he doesn't always appear in that area of the room.

6/3/01

I have been thinking a lot of Tibet lately. I've just read their history. It was one of the highest spiritualized nations on earth at one time. Why was it destroyed? We know materialized nations and empires rise and fall as Rome did but we can usually ascribe the reason to conquest. But this was a great spiritual realm that should have been allowed to exist in isolation. What lesson should we draw from.

Tibet's almost complete obliteration, even though they were not secular because even the common people strove towards a higher spirituality, may serve to teach us that no wall is high enough. High mountains didn't stop China from running over this land. What can give safety to any people bent towards a spiritual way of life? Or any non-military nation? The only true safety would seem to be to spread spiritual beliefs around the world until it reaches a homogenous force of empathy and tolerance for one another.

This reminds me of the Sufi religion or philosophy, or a few main points that I remember about it. They have no center of worship and are disbursed all around the world. Also they can live and participate in all areas of life because their beliefs don't exclude any other. Another way to spread spirituality out is like the Christian churches do in America. There are so many small churches that it is like foam on the top of the water. These small-scattered enclaves of worship would be hard to displace with any mighty conquest. Finally, the best idea and most rewarding for the world are for all religions to interact together. After all every religion comes from the same source of spirituality, we are all one in spirit, genes, birthplace.

6/5/01

Jesus specifically insisted that I write this. In church Sunday the priest kept saying that Jesus didn't know he was to die. But he did. He only hinted of this to his disciples that he was to die but he knew. He had also pushed and prodded events until the final betrayal. Don't forget that he also knew he would suffer tremendously. His beloved knew. He didn't tell her but she was so close to Jesus that she picked up on his emotions. She was also afraid that he was deliberately walking into a trap or cauldron of evil. She begged him to stop, to reconsider. She was there in the garden. She kissed him first. Her lips tasted the salt and sweat of fear on his cheek. The taste clung to her lips long after.

While I was writing this Jesus stood nearby and assured me that it was all true.

He had made his decision and refused to back down. None of this was said or needed to be said. Fate was set. Worry and distress had only cut through his shield for a few moments. He arose to meet his fate as soon as the solders arrived. At any point in the proceedings of slaughter he may have been able to put a stop to it by calling on heaven to intervene, maybe not. He did not and I still cry to this day that his death not be in vain. Yes, I was there too.

6/6/01

God opened up a door in heaven and pouring golden light down on me during church Sunday because I had been feeling so bad I was afraid my heart had turn to stone. When the door opened, God's golden light flowed down on the gathering of people. I realized that all over the globe God was listening to people as they prayed and sang in churches this morning. It makes a beautiful picture. In fact, we give God the whole weekend. The Jews worship him on Saturday, Christians on Sunday, and Moslems on Friday. Imagine a million calls from earth to our God, wonderful.

6/8/01

I was thinking before meditation about the difference religions and how they should all be one-But I'll get to that in a minute. First I want to explain about the Buddha Chants this morning. I put the tape in the middle and soon began to see and experience rain falling upwards and then a quiet pause. the next sounds pulled every breeze into vast clouds that gathered on each side with a funnel of golden light in the middle almost like a doorway. Then the movement pulled everything into a central column of spiraling movement as I lifted higher and higher and higher up the funnel.

The next range of sounds had me free floating in space like an astronaut. The stars and the deep blackness of space near earth was all around me as I lay with my arms stretched out-I just free floated. Then an opening began to appear with glimpses of sunlight and a blue sky or colors of rainbows and flowers. It was as if they were inviting me to enter, then like an eye, they closed up again when I didn't accept the invitation.

I hung there suspended for a long time until I heard a loud clang, the cassette had turned off. My soul carried this peace throughout the day. I feel so solemn and full of quietude it's hard to keep writing but I must.

Last night I was supposed to be meditating but I kept drifting off, usually when this happens I try to drift myself back. I kept drifting off during some chants too but was able to keep returning to my center. We'll finally I gave up and just sat back thinking. I was thinking of all the religions. I had recently looked up information in my Dictionary of World Religions. I looked up Sufi to double check whether they can incorporate other religions into their own belief system. They can. In fact the Sufi religion is almost a joining of Christian and Buddhist beliefs. This is beautiful. Hindu allows other Gods into their religion. We'll I suddenly laughed and told Jesus "I am not much of a Catholic am I?" and he smiled back at me agreeing. I practice the Catholic religion by going to mass most Sundays but other than that I am not sure how catholic I am because I don't like rules. I know I am a Christian but I also believe I am a Buddhist, Sufi, Jew, Hindu, and perhaps more.

Jesus agrees with my attempt to incorporate all these religions into one belief in my personal life. I have for a long time. I seems to me that most of the difference between religions is ritual practice that evolved around them. Most have as their base a belief in something greater than ourselves, if not God, then the universe. Most religions show us how to experience the love and spirituality of humankind and we do need this.

I am not an expert in religions so I am unable to list the differences and likenesses. I only know that I personally don't find any conflict. I can use a method from each of them and delight in its truth. I am not talking about the practice of religion but the feeling of spirituality at their base.

If Jesus brought the Buddhist Religion to the west two thousand years ago he would have reformed it to fit the life styles of the Jewish people of his day. He may have let go of some ideas he didn't like or thought they wouldn't work in his home territory. During all the time the Buddha religion also evolved and grew as did other religions. Today we have a globalization of better and worse religions ideas that have evolved over the centuries.

Personally I just pick and choose what beliefs and esoteric knowledge helps me change and grow because I believe that is the way into God's universe. I have found much to love in every religion I have read about and sampled. I stay with the Catholic religion because I find it comfortable. Here is an odd note. A number of kids I talked to say they are not Catholic but Christians. I try to tell them that Catholic is Christian too. I don't know where they are picking up this idea that Catholic is not Christian.

You might ask, "But if you're a Christian and love Jesus how can you also worship Buddha or a Hindu God." My answer is, and Jesus smiles at this as I write, "Jesus is no kindergarten child who says "me, me, me" You must love only me." No, he is a God or at least a highly evolved being who puts the people of the world before his own cares or glorification. What's more, he sends us on the same road as he walked so we could follow in his footsteps and acquire the same mental powers.

Send your love up to heaven. Do you think it matters in what name you send it? If God is love does it matter if love is called Jesus or Christ or Buddha or Brahma or Vishnu or the Prophet Mohammad? The list could go on forever. Beyond our small world of matter, names do not count, only the essence of character has substance and validity.

When I began my spiritual road I used to feel a conflict between God and Jesus, I would think and worry that God would feel lift out if I prayed to Jesus more. How silly and childish. I know that now because a mature faith is just that, mature. It does not include jealousy or conflict or hatreds or narrow mindedness. The more mature I become the more I can include the whole world and universe into my worship and oneness of being. It's like the Sufi tale of the elephant. You have all heard the story. A man tries to describe what he saw and each blind man who checks him out only feels one section of the elephant. Yet it was all one elephant. This is the moral of the story. It is all one God.

6/9/01

I have arouse into heaven on a pillar during meditation, this same pillar that is called the center of the world in many mythologies or world tree, or nave. Originally, there may have been a bases of fact to these symbols. It is also possible that original events were reinforced throughout history. It is true the idea could be explained as the need for imagery and to symbolically touch the vault of heaven, which was always strikingly overhead. It is also true that to accept that as the whole explanation, we shortchange the intelligence of our ancestors. They were not stupid. Jacob may have meant a symbolic ladder that the angels climbed up and down on but he could as well have been describing a specific method or means that put the angels on earth. Remember I have seen angels I have noticed angelic beings and other portraying themselves as humans. In fact, except for their long life span, there may be no physical difference between us and them.

Jesus asked me to write about physical verses spiritual to assure all of us that both should form the base of the cosmos in our beliefs. This is hard for us because we tend to believe in either one or the other but we must remember both interact and are valid. We must always remember that even if we ascribe some kind of Star Trek to the angels and heaven, the spiritual is truly a part of it all. I remember the time Jesus has told me that he feels like a real solid person when I can only perceive him as an ethereal person.

When Jesus comes back will he still be mostly spiritual? He expects us to be more spiritual by the time he arrives. You will need to be ready for him but you need to do this for yourself. Would Jesus ever disrupt your needs and wants to serve his won purpose? Would he suddenly rip your soul asunder? Would he force you to love him? Could he force you to be more spiritual and loving?

I know most Christians believe Jesus will take them in spite of their sins. I am not talking about trite sins here but a souls direction in life. If your soul is going in the wrong direction, I doubt if even Jesus could turn it around quickly, he needs time to teach you through experience that what you prefer to do is follow him. I may be wrong here and did not ask Jesus. This is what Jesus has been doing through two thousand years, calling us to follow him.

I need to admit that when the beautiful Lady first told me that it was all true, I wondered if she was from the evil one because I was afraid that I was being led down the wrong path. It was a bitter pill to swallow after believing all my life in religion as only spiritual. I am not even sure what we mean by spiritual. I think we mean things we can't see that are above us and superior. We can't see mind. We don't understand how spirituality works because we still don't understand how the mind works or all that it could become. If Jesus sends his mind to me in the form of a visit, is that spiritual? I believe so. If Jesus arrives on earth again with his physical form but a spiritual mind that could enclose everyone on earth, will he then be spiritual or both? So this would be an example of the spiritual and physical event mixed together. Our small minds or abilities may only see one part or another and not both. I only state this as a descriptive example but Jesus smiled so I guess it does set out some truth and understanding. My ignorance is probably the reason why I was picked to write these notes. All of you should feel superior to it.

6/9/01

I can't sleep tonight, my head hurts and my bedroom is too noisy. The sound of the city at night sounds like a fan or furnace running on high. the hum of the city turns into a roar at times. This night it is so loud that it bothers me greatly. The day is noisy too but tolerable. I keep getting tortured every day with loud music and vibrations because so many young men live in my neighborhood. I hate to hear the swearing in the rap music all the time. It actually hurts my psyche. I speculate that my ears have become more sensitive since I have increased in spirituality. I seem to pick up sounds so much more easily now. Well, get to the point.

The reason I came downstairs and am writing is because laying in bed I saw a line of people carrying their mattresses and other items of ownership on their backs. I thought they looked oriental, not sure. They are in trouble with nowhere to go and be welcomed. I asked Jesus and he said they are in China but he didn't tell me why they must leave. No doubt a war of some kind. Is there nothing I can do for them? I asked Jesus. Then I thought to send out angels to give them hugs. It won't feed them but the spiritual hugs may pick up their spirits. The reason I am writing this is because I feel so ashamed of myself. All I can think about is my own pain and intolerance for loud music and my worry about how I could move away from the constant parties and noise. But as I write this I remember that the last two evenings have been quiet for some reason. What a relief. Here I have seen a long line of people with no home or food or water just walking to some destination they know not where or even if they will be welcome when they get there. They must be heading towards a refugee camp someplace. I hope they find food and shelter. I have a home, food in my refrigerator which is more full than usual and I am ashamed of that too. Usually it is half empty. Here I am worrying about noise and those people are worried about survival. This puts my own concerns into perspective and trite.

This is cute. Now I remember that Jesus told me earlier that I wasn't done writing. I said I was because I had put the tablet up and was tired and ready to go to bed. Now here I am writing just as he predicted. Maybe now I can to go sleep.

6/11/01

There is so much to write about I don't know where to begin and I've forgotten most of it. I wanted to write this down Sunday but didn't so now

I need to try and remember. I remember Y visiting in church again, just before the concentration of the host. just before the words were repeated about Jesus giving up his life for us. This part of the mass always chokes me up. Y was there and I reached out my hand to touch his but of course there was no hand there. Just before that part I had told him that most of the mass was ritual built up over the years. He said he understood completely.

I am sure most religions consist of more ritual than substance. But it's all-important to us. I asked why he had joined me in church again. He said he liked to see the church service through my eyes, my understanding of it. Yes, I agreed, much better than trying to read a dry book on the subject of the Catholic Church. But I warned him that I wasn't much of a Catholic. He said, "I know." And smiled.

Then we talked about Jesus being a Buddha. I could tell that he believed it as a truth, that he felt Jesus and he shared close spiritual ties. I smiled at that. I believe he studies all religions that he is searching for their essences, the nugget that drives them. He may study them through many people's eyes, how fascinating.

I imagine God as he poured forth his truth in different times and to various peoples throughout history, serving up diverse aspects of himself, different modes of belief, different ways to worship, different descriptions and different images and symbols. I imagined the many manifestations of God spread though time and the complexity of the idea all together was mind-boggling.

I am not sure if Y believes in an actual God, the Universe as Being, or Oneness. Then why not God as the Universe too and in only a few religions does he becomes a being like ourselves. I remembered God pouring golden light down on me the last Sunday and pictured his golden world and how easily he could have produced a son on earth for our benefit. Aren't we all sons and daughters? A son who deliberately step by step laid down his life for humans everywhere, so that we could see and believe. The Bible says he died for forgiveness of sins but it is the same thing, we must believe in order to ask that our sins be forgiven.

Also in the car on the way to church Jesus told me I would have something to write about from church. He was right. In the scripture Jesus talks about the Holy Sprit and that it is apart from himself but that it speaks truth.

John 16:12-13

I have much more to tell you but you cannot bare it now. But when he comes, the spirit of truth, he will guide you to all truth...."[93]

And I wondered if it is the Holy Sprit who has been speaking to me about these truths I write about. But isn't it Jesus? Of course it is because it is Jesus who speaks. Wasn't it Jesus death that released his spirit so it could speak. While we are in the flesh on earth our likeness to God, our spirit or soul and our bodies are bound together in a tight union. It is only at death that they can separate. We are all made up of a trinity of god, soul, and body.

Jesus being more superior, more Godlike, more Buddha like, more higher evolved, could direct his Holy Spirit and still does. His spirit speaks for all of heaven. So when I wonder if it is Jesus or a representative of heaven speaking I should realize that it makes no difference because all of heaven speaks the truth and is with God.

On a new note, I was beginning to believe that I wouldn't die, that Jesus would come and pick me up. Now I've been told that Jesus won't get here before that time. I have been told that I would live a very long life. I wonder and dread that it will be a long life as lonely as the past 20 years have been. I certainly don't mind dying. I already know Jesus will take me through the U. with a golden flower in my hair someday. I love him so deeply. I love Y too and X and the kids around here and in school and my family and all the suffering and abused people and all the distressed people and all the lonely people of the world. I frown that I am unable to show my love in physical ways. I can't really hug everyone but with the angels help, I try to hug many. In fact, my lonely type of personality is somewhat

---

[93] *The New American Bible*

necessary for writing and thinking and listening to Jesus. I find it hard to sometimes converse or use small talk with people let alone hug them. I think this is why I liked taking care of senior citizens. I could hug them easily. Kids are spontaneous huggers and I like that and the people in church hug me sometimes too. I am fine, but sometimes I just don't recognize how fine I am. Tonight I set beside my backyard pond I've built up over many years with rocks I've found. It is only a hole that needs running water from the hose to become a pond, but it has weeds and grass and flowers and dark woodsy smell and bird chirping and pheasants calling to each other and a tree canopy overhead. I allowed the trees to grow huge over the years for shade. I love to sit and listen to the water trickle over the leaves and rocks and the birds singing. I love the green all around me. I avoid the ugly garage and telephone pole wire and the other harsh noises from the street, the ice cream jingle bells truck, and children calling out as they play.

This night there is no loud rap music playing to invade my green corner, I find the rap music actually painful at times. Yes, this evening my corner of the world is perfect. I must apologize for even thinking I don't have enough. God forgive me for my selfishness. With Jesus and the angels near by my little corner has become a shrine.

And this reminds me of the Sufi fable: The Shrine

Nasrudin left his father's shrine where he lived all his life and was traveling through the mountains when his donkey suddenly lay down and died. Overcome with grief for his many years companion, he buried his friend and raised a simple mound over its grave, then silently meditated beneath the high mountains. Before long, people taking the mountain observed the Mulla weeping over his profound loss. They thought that a great man must be buried there to cause such grief for so long. Soon a rich man chanced by and ordered a dome be put on the spot. Other pilgrims planted crops whose produce helped keep up the shrine. The fame of the Silent Morning Dervish reached all across the land, even to Nasrudin's father. He came to ask his son what happened. When his son told him, he exclaimed, "Why that is just how my own shrine was built more than thirty years ago, after my own donkey died. [94]

I paraphrased the story so much I took some of the enjoyment out of it. I took the story from the book, *Caravan of Dreams* by Idries Shah. It is listed in the footnotes and Bibliography in case you want to read a better and longer version of the story.

6/2/01

This is twice that I saw the World Tree. Today sitting in my back yard with my eyes closed I saw it again. It grows wherever we plant it in the mind. It helps us lift up to the stars. Jesus says it is only a construct made with the mind of the observer. I bypassed the tree when I traveled with him to the stars. It seems that ever since the chant grew it in my mind, it is there when I close my eyes and become calm and relaxed. As if it breathes and heaves its mighty girth and height up into the sky for me. As if the tree is proud in its majesty, its beauty so grand. I imagine its roots clinging to earth and enwrapping it like eagle claws. That earth's soil and soul that feeds on it. I think it will always be with me now and that perhaps it represents every tree on earth and entwines our souls within them. After all, we are a united part and substance of earth, we too are grown from its soil.

---

[94] *Caravan of Dreams*, Idries Shah, The Shrine, Penguin books Inc., Maryland, 1972, pp 111-2

6/14/01

Jesus told me to go in the house and get my notebook. He wants me to write something tonight. Don't know what yet. I tried to meditate but couldn't. Jesus said, "You don't need to meditate." But I find that it brings me peace and lately my emotions have been upside down. I need to center myself, to breath peace inside. I feel much better.

He assures me that my notes are more or less the way I will print them. I haven't looked far back into my notes and even forget what is in there. My notes are very immediate. At this moment Jesus is pouring love out to me. I feel his calmness and understanding, his eyes twinkle with his own inner knowledge. He has just reached out and hugged me. The last few days I wasn't capable of being or feeling so close to Jesus because I'd been wrapped up in my own sorrows. I just fall into a hole sometimes and need to clime out. Jesus waits patiently until I reach for his hand to lift me out.

I haven't been traveling with Jesus very often. This third book is going to be deficient in travels. Oh, I feel such over overwhelming acceptance flow out of Jesus. He assures me that the book won't be deficient. I need to remember that it is his book even more than mine and he will see that it gets completed.

I had to go to the bank this evening. It reminded me of another evening I went to the bank. It was dark and as I came away from the ATM machine, a small black man jumped in front of me with a gun. He told me to give him my money. I don't remember what money I had at the time but it wasn't much. I was extremely poor at that time. He pointed the gun at me and said, "I'll shoot."

I told him that I couldn't give him any money. For some reason I felt calm and unafraid during the encounter. Then he yelled, "Give me the damn money," and then pointed the gun at the back car window where my son and foster child were looking out. When I still didn't give him any money, he pointed the gun at me again and pulled the trigger. It clicked but wouldn't go off. He looked at the gun with surprise as if he couldn't understand why it didn't go off. He pulled the trigger again twice but the gun still didn't shoot.

By this time the man was shaking so badly he could hardly hold on to the gun. I thought he was going to collapse. I still felt calm and unafraid because I knew Jesus was with me. I even tried to send love to this pathetic man. Finally the man pleaded with me to give him something. "Please, I got to have a fix."

I took out a $10.00 dollar bill and gave it to him and he ran away into the dark.

As soon as I sat down back in the car, the reaction set in. I began to shake almost as much as the man had. I was almost crying and kept telling the kids it was ok, that we were on our way to the police station. But I couldn't find the police station. I drove down Gratiot and couldn't find it for a while because I was so shook up. I knew it was on the corner but couldn't see it at first so I doubled back. Finally when I found it and we went in and reported the hold up, the police understood my inability to find the station as if it happens often to people under stress. By the time I talked to the police and gave them a description I felt better and drove home.

But I often wondered why Jesus saved us that night. I could feel Jesus at my side and this was long before I accepted that he would actually talk to me. But I did pray and meditate at this time in my life. Jesus was one of the reasons I became a foster mother. So I knew I wasn't doing anything great, I wasn't a valuable person. I could never understand why Jesus saved me that night or my children. Perhaps one of my children would do something great one day and the trauma of my death would hinder that? Perhaps I would do something for God one day? I speculated for a while and then forgot the incident until tonight. Now I can answer my own question. I believe Jesus wanted me alive so I could write this book. That it would take someone who had been through what I have, the change of life into the city? the men I married and never respected because they drank, the crazy useless anger. Who can say what makes a life or what makes a person have a specific quality in order to accomplish a certain job. For some reason as topsy-turvy as my life has been, Jesus knew I would grow the quality he needed and I still thank him for his encouragement. I love you Jesus. I guess that bank hold up was what Jesus wanted me to write about tonight because I feel dried out of words.

6/15/01

While reading the library book *Images and Symbols* [95] by Marcea Eliade, I came across a lot of information about the various religions that I had forgotten. It's been a long time, ten to twenty years, since I read a great deal about religions. Also he grouped the information in interesting ways. But of course, much of what he considers symbols are my solid ground. I try to walk in both shoes and therefore see images and symbols differently. I was reading his reference to the Buddha's first seven steps and their symbols. When he describes time as reversible for the Buddha I inadvertently think of Jesus as he is now and perhaps as he was on earth. I sincerely believe that Jesus was Buddha or a Buddha who "Knows not only the past but the future. He can travel through time backwards and forwards." The parallel to rebirth is fascinating. "Brahmanic initiation, as quoted in book by Paul Mus was regarded as a second birth, he said that a person had to be re-born. Jesus says the same thing in the gospels a number of times. The birth of Buddha is linked to the Cosmic Egg or Golden Embryo, the Father or Master of Creation. This relationship resembles Jesus relationship to his Father, the Creator. To the Buddha all time is the present tense. Compare this idea with what science has learned about time. The Buddha has also

---

[95] *Images and Symbols*_[Harper Collins, Marcea Eliade, Mythos paperback edition, translated by Philip Mairet, originally published in France Libraire Gallimard 1952, Mythos 1991, Princton University Press, Princton New Jersey, pp 76-77.

transcended space therefore the Buddha exists everywhere in space/time as does Jesus, as does God, as do we if we should attain to these heights.

Except for Sufism, I know little about the Muslim religion but this I do know, if it is true that an angel spoke to Mohammed and of course it is true, then this religion too at its base agrees with the same cosmological ideas of all other main religions. I know this because all of those in heaven know the same underlying truth. In this sense heaven and angels are the opposite of Star Trek. They are all of the same mind or philosophy. It is like saying that if we really knew God, we could never do anything against his will, although we can't forget evil as a real force in there too.

So why do we have so many ways to practice and believe in the same truth? Because it needs to be said over and over again to diverse peoples around the world. We forget, the message gets old and ritualized, it becomes changed through time. Strange as it may seem, the phrase, "The more things stay the same, the more they change," fits religions as well as history. Interestingly, much of spirituality and mysticism hasn't changed. I have read the same messages before in many religions. In fact, not too many of the ideas in this book are new. Most are a repeat of other thinkers, other ideas brought to faith. Each era of our understanding of Jesus does not give us more than we can understand. He stays within the perimeter of the probable and possible for our benefit or the full truth would be beyond our understanding unless we already had achieved it.

Interestingly, none of this recent information has come from Jesus yet he endorses it with his continued presence and smile. Y said to me "No one will dispute that Jesus is Buddha." He must have meant those of the Buddhist faith because many Christians would disagree, though I don't know why. The final dream is the transcendence of the profane. To quote Marcea, Yoga is a means of turning a person into the "Glorious Man with perfect health, absolute mastery of his body and his psyche-mental life, capable of self-concentration, conscious of himself."

This is certainly a definition of Jesus and Buddha. It is hard for us to realize what a man like this could accomplish. It would take many life times for most of us to come close to this perfection. So how did X do it? How does his shadow do it? Or is he a special breed of man. A face changer? There are hints through mythology of face changers in some religions. Today we usually ascribe a person with such powers as an angel or devil. So I began my book asking who is X and I don't intend to end it without him. I must remember that his control of illusion is so great, I may know him, and I look for him in everyone, and not be aware of it. He may be able to send an illusion to me. Ah, what a trap I've crated for myself. I have a special name for X, I call him Peter Pan.

I tried to meditate earlier but couldn't. I haven't been lately because it just needs to relax and Jesus is there to speak with. But tonight I couldn't sleep so I got up and after eating I decided to try meditating again. this time I closed my eyes and stepped into the Cosmos. As I breathe in and out the cosmos absorbed into me as if my skin were porous. I was feeling enrapture of the deep, wrapped within the myriad worlds and suns and colors and events and wonders of it all. It seemed that I belonged, that I fit perfectly. It amazes me that I continually experience new delights often during meditation. I wonder is this how it should be? or is Jesus training me so I can write about it? Is he moving me step by step up the ladder of being and joy?

6/20/01

This morning I took a moment before I left for work to sit and visit with Jesus. We went to the beautiful meadow. This is the place where I have often went to sit and visit with Jesus. We walk down through the wild flowers until we get to the lake and there we take a wooden boat for a ride. I love the smell of fresh flowers and damp earth. The water is sparkling clear with cattails growing on the shore. I can hear the water lap up against the boat, the oars slap the water and the hollow sound of wood against wood when we put the oars up and just drift. Jesus is aware of my fondness for water and rocks. But this morning Jesus told me something that surprised me about this meadow.

He said, "It will all be yours."

"You mean I'll own it?"

"You will come here after you leave earth. This will be your home."

"Oh, you mean that I'll exist in it and own the pleasure and experience I derive from it. But where or what is it. I thought it was a figment of my imagination."

"It is New Earth."

I paused at this solemn thought, then asked, "Will I be with you?"

"You have been with me and will be again."

Tonight we went back and Jesus hugged me. Usually I hug him but this night he hugged me. Then I sat there and prayed for the people I know who need prayers. Can't sleep, I keep thinking of the junkyard growing on my street and next to my house. I know why and who, it is a little annoyance caused by the evil one who is trying to chase me out of my home. The reason is simple because I would become more vulnerable to his antics because I wouldn't have a place to live or would need to keep working very hard just to pay rent. I am not the only one evil attacks in odd ways. He is working on many people in my neighborhood. He is very subtle as he plays with people's minds but most the time he hits barriers because they want to be kind and good. Most people don't believe in him, this keeps him invisible. He hates me because he knows I can see him and recognize him. He is the same one who instigated the hate against Jesus two thousand years ago. He is the same one who overwhelms you with annoyances until you break. He is the same one who whispers against other people in your life.

Can he be doing so many things to so many people at the same time? Yes. Remember he has all the powers of the angels, the only difference is that he is trite and little minded, so much so, that he can't understand any mind higher than his own. He can't understand spirituality-it throws him off his stride. He fights anyone who would become more than he is-anyone growing towards a higher evolution because he will not or cannot evolve.

6/23/01

I took a few minutes before I began my busy Saturday to listen to the Buddhists chants. This lifted me up into the World Tree and then flower petals began to fall and I with them. Each petal or leaf turned into a world that expanded if I went towards it. Then the air was filled with flower worlds and the ground lay profuse like a field of poppies on and on forever. I stood among the flowers world feeling diminished beneath a blue sky and then delicate butterflies swarmed around me in a spiral and lifted me up and up their tiny wings giving my body flight until we reached the top of the universe or world and then they spread out as I did creating a dome over the world. Then I dissolved and dissipated and scattered in the wind. Such a lovely and beautiful moment. But that's when I lost it and fell back into the usual type of random thoughts. But Jesus had been with me during meditation and vision and he encouraged me to take a few minutes and write down where the chants took me.

6/26/01

This morning I went with Jesus back to Silver World. This time it didn't feel as though I was there so much as mentally viewing different areas. Jesus was summing up our many visits for a purpose. First he showed me the dead continent. Even from above it didn't look huge. It had few mountains and they were not high. Mostly I saw smudges and large areas of yellow, green, and brown. Then Jesus showed me the same area where I had visited before during the severe blight. I noticed that we had been on the edge of the rot. It was still a blighted area where we stood but a close look at the sparse vegetation in the area showed dark, dry green and brown. It all resembled scrub land that was old, like an old person loosing their hair. The plants looked wispy and lifeless. The edges of the rot was growing backwards although this wasn't apparent to my view. Jesus said the people were making headway section by section but it would take years to undo the damage. No one would be able to live there for a few generations yet. Jesus also showed me a quick overview of population. They happy and productive now that the war was over. I saw gliders in the air and more lively and colorful activity.

There was a purpose in going back this morning, a message for earth. Jesus said that the method the people used against the blight on Silver World would also work on earth. My first thought was that earth doesn't have a severe problem like they do but then I realized that we seem to be growing one. Jesus must be referring to a possible future blight unless we fix our environment now. I shuddered as I imagined earth dying and growing in a dead blight but like most people, the possible consequences and seriousness didn't sink in for long. We don't have a problem yet.

Jesus keeps saying love is what is needed on earth. Our own earth is crying for love just as millions of people also cry out for love. Love is the answer. Most of us agree with that statement but it is too simplistic; so I hesitate to write the word love because the word has become so watered down and general that it is almost useless at explaining anything. It lacks oomph. Even though we all agree that it is true, the world does need love, it isn't enough to just say it. So I ask myself how else could we express the needs of a desperate earth?

If I think about what the people of Silver World actually did, they sent care, concern, and feelings of tenderness and hope to specific areas that were dying, then it becomes obvious what we on earth need to do. We need to act out our love by sending thoughts to those we love and the earth's trees and animals and fauna.

"Is this right? Is this what we will need to do some day?" I asked Jesus His answer to my question was, "Yes."

It is hard to envision right now during the lushness of this rainy, summer in June, that we could ever be in such danger of a blight like I saw on Silver World. But then I read about the environmental concerns and all the changes taking place: the warming of the earth, the melting glaciers, the loss of forest, the changing migration habits, the lack of water in many areas, the poverty of large numbers of people, diseases, fires. Remember that Revelation said that one third of the earth will burn. Don't we have a lot of forest fires now?

Jesus has said before that we are at a turning point, a cusp of dangerous change. We need to stop, reverse these severe changes to the environment in the near future or we will get a runaway situation on earth that will have gone too far to change.

Ideally we need to have large groups to send out their feelings, to hug trees, hug the earth, enclose it in their arms, hug people, hug the ground and the sea and the rocks of earth. To reach out to all humans on earth and bring empathy and togetherness to one and all. Then we need, and I know this idea is almost impossible to envision at this time, to slow down our growth and consumption of everything; utilities, food, meat, land, housing, travel. We almost have to consume to keep the economy going. This is where we are today but if we continue in this direction we will short change the longevity of ourselves, our earth, and our children. Our extreme short sightedness, our "I want it now" attitude, is killing the next generation and the next. We want cheap gas now, never mind twenty years into the future, never mind what gas does to the air, never mind how it is non-renewable, never mind that each new automobile uses up plastic and pollutes the environment, never mind that many more roads are needed for the autos and more land is paved over and more people move further and further out. All this is just one small symptom of how and why we must begin to change.

If this cry goes unheeded for long, it will become so drastic that we will be forced to change by circumstances and by then it may be too late, that is if we escape a major war. So far consumerism, by spreading itself around the western world has helped to keep peace by catering to our wants and whims but as these products become more scarce and effect our environment more harshly, the stress will build up more between countries. The US will be lucky if it escapes retaliation. It is like a very rich neighbor who is tolerated during good times but jealously hated during rough or bad times. We are the kings at the top of the hill, more rich and more visible. The rest of the world will one day look at us with hate while we keep playing our fun games and continue to use up the earth's resources. We forget they own those resources too. In short, we need to learn balance. Balance our wants against our needs and the needs of the other people on earth. This idea is not new, all the environmentalists are saying the same thing. Jesus hasn't dictated these words to me verbatim but he nods approval at their tone and message. After all that is the message and purpose of this book, to save the earth and its peoples.

6/26/01

Sitting out side in front of my pond this evening, Jesus told me about the new world. He said it is not a copy of earth as far as the exact mountains and rivers. But the atmosphere, fauna, and animal life is the same. We sat near a small waterfall where water was trickling down playing water music, just as my pond was doing at the moment and I said, "I love this waterfall."

Jesus said, "You have one similar in front of you in your yard."

"I know but here you are sitting here with me.:" I meant that as we sat on the grass I could see him clearly next to me. This is not the case sitting in my back yard. So at this point I was in two worlds at once. On one world sitting on a glider and on the other sitting in the tall grass beside a water fall and deep pond leading into a brook. There were mosquitoes there too.

I laughed, "Are you sure this isn't earth?"

"No, it's not earth. Only people with certain mental abilities will be able to come here.

I became afraid at these words, "But if we need all that much mental ability, many people will be excluded." I was thinking of large groups who adore Jesus but who are still very narrow minded. They are not able or willing to change their type of thinking. Perhaps their only problem is immaturity; I notice that young people go through stages of belief. We all grow more broad-minded as we mature.

Jesus said, "Everyone has the same potential to improve their mind's ability. It is a valid choice, but for some it requires a longer and deeper step than for others."

This must be the same as sending love to others? "What will happen to the people who can't come to the new earth."

"They will need to fix up the old one. Earth can be saved. There can be two earths for humanity."

"Won't we do the same thing to the new pristine earth that we did to the old one?"

"No because you will be able to hold each other's minds. You will be able to hold and know your children and keep them under restraint with your minds. You will need to learn how to do this but you will. This also applies to the plants in the gardens and animals. There will still be storms, bad weather with dry and wet spells. It will not be perfect and was never meant to be. Even with your nimble and useful mental abilities, you will not be perfect and will still have a long way to grow.

"What about life span?"

"Yes, you will still have death but because of your greater mental powers and attitudes you will be extremely long lived and will choose when to die."

"Won't we over populate this new earth too eventually?

"No, you will mentally control the number of births. Every new human will be loved and cherished and raised with the principals of the group."

"What about war?

"Could you harm someone if you felt each blow as though you were hitting yourself? There will be no wars. On this world each of you would gladly lay down your own life to save another in distress and you will know their distress and feel it. Accidents will be very rare but possible. As you mature even these possibilities may change."

"It sounds like you are describing a utopian paradise, a sort of dream. How do we know it isn't only my wishful thinking?

"You don't."

"Earth could never be that beautiful, it is already too corrupted with confusion and hate.

"People on earth will begin to grow to this ideal if people want to live. Traumas are coming to earth, have already begun. If you would save earth you will need to begin using your mental powers that you have so far neglected. It is the only way. You will need to appease the earth, its people, turn it back from its course of destruction.

6/27/01

I can't figure out what X is up to. He seems to delight in confronting me with his made-up presence. He always looks different and actually speaks to me but I still don't know it is him until he leaves. I met him in Kmart and he spoke and when I began to look more interested he waived his hands in a funny way as if he were gay to throw me off the scent and push me away. He uses little movements to try to draw your attention away from who he is. He might chew on something or have a crumb on his lip or a pimple, something that draws your attention to a specific spot. He also seems capable of setting up an aura around himself that prohibits me from knowing it is him. Now that I know that he exists, I search for him on every strange face and some not so strange. Since I am always looking, I should be able to spot him. How does he know where I am? We are linked somehow mentally? So he can always be at the same place I am if he chooses to do so. But the biggest question is why? Why is he hounding me? And, how does he get around so fast?

Is he slowing himself to me because I am writing this book and it has him in it? Is he supplying me with the information I need? I think this may be the case. I was hoping we could be lovers one day but this seems out of the question because he seems to take the opposite track to this idea. I have learned one thing at least, he is not just looking out of someone else's eyes, he truly does have a body, of his choice, and face that he can change at will. Or is it all done by illusion?

Think about how we see and how we believe that "seeing is believing." Few of us question what we see. Why should we? If we assume that he is an angel then these slight of hand tricks and seeming obsequiousness is normal. At least for an angel. But because we don't think beyond our ordinary assumptions we can easily be fooled. That is how he can be so many places at one time. Take a large gathering and put him in it and assume he has a beard. He walks around speaking and shaking hands. But he has another character and place to be at the same time. So he slips away, goes into his other character and place, then slips back into his bearded form. No one has noticed him gone. Even though if you were to ask if he is there, people would say that he was there all the time. He could be on the other side of the crowd so who would think he wasn't there? Even if he has center stage, it may be only for a short time and his disappearance wouldn't be noticed between speeches. Again this quality wouldn't seem so strange in an angel. But his is not an angel. In fact, he is the person of who Jesus once said to me, "He doesn't know what he is."

I still can't figure out if there are two X's, one good and one evil. I have never been afraid of him, in fact, I seem drawn to him after he leaves and I realize who it was. He has deliberately put obstacles in my way, at times. (Just a minute ago he said, "I will take your notes." And when I thought of the back up disk, he said, "I'll take that too.) Could this have been another attempt on his part to show me what he can do? Believe me, he can do and be anyone he wants to be and has a hundred characters set up with histories and the necessary papers and other pertinent information ready at his fingertips. This is all a guess on my part but I believe it to be true.

What if there was an army of such people interacting in our society? I would hate to think what would happen.

"It is not true." Jesus said. and I thanked him with a sigh of relief.

6/30/01

I am frightened and worried. Jesus said something last evening that I woke up thinking about. I have been lonely and would like family to visit once in a while but I am ok. If I had too much company, how would I ever get any writing done? Well back to Jesus' comment. I had put the reading book down and was just smiling relaxed and thinking I should turn on the water in my pond when Jesus said, " You should enjoy it while you can.?

I didn't think too much of this statement. I wondered if he meant that the neighbors would turn up their music. But a little while later Jesus said something else.

He said "Something is going to happen soon, within a few years (or months)."

I said, "I don't want anything to happen."

He answered "You don't have anything to do with it."

Most of the time I am content even though I write about my loneliness or upset moods, it is just to get them out of my system or put myself on display as an example, but earlier just before Jesus statement, I had been thinking of past words by someone? evil? Speaking of my family by saying, "They'll all be back.." This is impossible under the present circumstances. I can't in any imagination conceive of my children moving back here. My children are all happy now. I even called my oldest son and he was having a get-together in his garage. I smile at their good fortune. But it is their fortune I was now worried about. Evil is always taunting me about my family and that I will need to move or they will.

But now I am worried about Jesus words. Is something going to change drastically? Something bad? Was Jesus referring to America or only that something would happen to my family or myself? If it is America the first thing I thought about was a hydrogen bomb. But that would be hard to accomplish, it's a long way over the ocean to America. No doubt some countries may want to, especially since President Bush talked about putting up a shield, that won't work. Except for these dire thoughts I couldn't think of anything else Jesus could be referring to. Obviously he doesn't want me to know the full situation. And I should probably be thankful, I have enough to think about now, like how to get my books completed and published. Besides, who knows, maybe Jesus was referring to something good that is going to happen. I tend to take everything in a bad light.

6/30/01

It's reasonably quiet and breezy tonight as I set near my idyllic pond. The trees rustle in the wind and the shouts of people seem far off. I thought of the trees today as I left Belle Isle after a few hours at the beach. They were so green and waving beneath the strong sun light as if to absorb all they could at this feast of energy. I imagined the millions, or trillions or uncountable number of trees on our planet and how their roots reach down deep into the soil through the earth worms and dirt granules rubbing against tiny feeder roots and all of it interacting chemically, ripening, enriching, growing, moving. I wondered if there could be more interaction than we give credit for, more than a chemical feedback, more like a joining of every tree to its earthen soil and the soil filling every nook and cranny of earth. Trees are more one with the earth than we are because it may be their business to stand tall and hold it all together. Trees are such slow living forms of life, hundreds and thousands of years old, they have seen it all. Could there be some kind of psyche connection between all the trees on earth or their biomass. I am beginning to believe so. I've never read or heard it put this way before except when the Indian on the west coast sent his emotions to me after communicated with the trees.

I don't think I mean that they can talk and think like we do because they are without brains, although what is a brain except chemicals making neurons interact. I am more on the road trying to understand their psychic communication that can't be detected by us because it is multiple by nature. It may be that all trees feel as one large group o that one tree can't communicate to us. They all reach down sensors into the earth as well as high into the sky, they may sense more about the earth than we can perceive. Perhaps there is such a thing as treeness, a tree as a single life form with a trillion parts. I feel enclosed and comforted by these thoughts. I sense the truth of them and also that my learning of this fact has the proper timing to include it in my book. If we cut down a single tree there is hardly a dent in the biomass, but when we cut down orchards and lay waste to huge areas, the sore may be felt around the globe.

This makes me wonder about all the fires we have in the United States each year. They are increasing tremendously. Every year more and more forests are killed by fire. Sure some fire is an advantage to younger plants but like anything else, too much becomes detrimental and dangerous. We are doing it. We are doing it to the trees as well as our selves. By heating up the earth we are affecting all life upon it. The trees are fearful. I know you think it is silly of me to feel the fear of trees. But as soon as I had that thought, sitting here beneath and surrounded by trees and wild grape and bamboo and raspberry bushes, the feeling of fear increased as if the trees psyche were trying to reach out and communicate their warning and fright. Silly or not, I believe it to be true.

So what does Jesus say? When I asked him he said, "It is time that you should write it." He did not elaborate.

6/30/01

I just realized tonight that I love Y deeply. I told him so and he smiled. I surprised myself with the strong feeling I had for him. I wondered when it began, when did my feelings grow so strong that I suddenly poured forth with them. I find I love him like I love Jesus, almost as much and it is a similar kind of relationship we share but not as mystical. After all Y is here on this planet. Is Jesus too? After I told Y I loved him, we walked for a short time and then sat down. He asked me if I wanted help to go into a deep meditation.

I thought about it for a minute but then answered, "No, I am afraid of getting lost."

He said, "Then you are not ready."

"One day soon I will be, that is a promise."

Later I asked Jesus, "What do you think about this? I am flabbergasted."

Jesus smiled and said, "Yes, it is well."

It seems as though he had been waiting for me to love Y or is it that Y is so mature he has almost reached the title of Buddha. Has he become so similar to Jesus that I would naturally love him? Reasonable assumption, regardless, I don't intend to write more on the subject because it is private. But, of course I love him, everyone does who would know him. Jesus also said that I would write more about this at another time. Odd how we can spread love around. As much as I love Jesus sometimes, I would wonder how I had room to love someone else at the same time. But it's not odd at all, we mothers can love many children. I can love many people with different intensities and depth of feelings. Nothing odd about it at all.

7/4/01

This is an interesting dilemma. Earlier this evening I thought about work tomorrow and the fact that all my notes are copied already, I hoped there would be something to keep me busy. Then Jesus said, "You'll have something to write."

I thought about it but had to disagree because it was late and nothing happened to take note of today. I just couldn't see myself writing tonight. We'll maybe I'd meditate later and this would get me thinking. I continued reading a mystery novel.

In the novel two suspects say they did it, that they heard voices telling them to do it. They were obviously delusional and wanted to be found guilty. They were a pair of very sick people. I suddenly wondered if I was delusional. Jesus speaks to me, angels speak to me, Mary speaks to me, sometimes, even God speaks to me. Am I delusional? I asked myself , is it so deeply ingrained in me that I believe in its falseness; it's totally, its untruth? How would I know? It certainly seems real to me when Jesus speaks. Some events with him still reverberate in my mind as the most real events I have ever experienced. How would I know?

And then I laughed. Can a delusion speak or warn of a delusion? Can a delusion tell me beforehand what I will do? How I will write? Can a delusion speak for itself or predict what action I will follow later in the evening? My head felt so dull and tired earlier when Jesus spoke those words that I was sure I would not have anything to write about tonight. I was mistaken. Here I am writing. How did Jesus know that I would hit on a word that involved me writing two pages. No problem for a person like Jesus, on that point, at least we can all agree.

7/4/01

Jesus tells me that we have a few more places to go. He implied that it would be wonderful and that I would like it very much. My first thought was that perhaps we would go to Jupiter but I think that the forms there would be too strange for me to understand and I am not sure what message they would bring to this book. Perhaps this visit will be different altogether from what I envision it may be. Perhaps Jesus will show me depths of his love that I have not reached before, perhaps I can't imagine where he will take me next. I can only wait until he invites me to go with him. How beautiful is my anticipation and love for Jesus Christ.

7/8/01

This morning before church, though tired and dragged out, I woke up early. It was Jesus who suggested that I meditate and use the Buddhist chants. For some reason I haven't been able to meditate easily lately. I am too restless a lot at night, so morning meditation is better for me.

This morning as soon as I sat down and relaxed with the chants on, X joined me. He wore a black suite and I asked him why? It took me a moment to recognize that it was X. I was startled and dismayed at first to have a third party join my private moments with Jesus. But after a second of unbalance, I adjusted to X's presence.

At first he tried to throw me off my stride by teasing and playing with me, he sent a snake at me and I petted it and wrapped it around me and then sent it on its way. Then when a breeze blew in butterflies, he sent in bats to gulp them up. But finally, I put a red rose between us with sharp thorns, a symbol of beauty and danger. This seemed to settle our differences. Even so, it felt strange and awkward to have him with me so I didn't get very deep into meditation until the end.

I purposely used mental constructs and images for his benefit and showed him the World Tree. He flowed up with me until we reached the top and then stayed floating as the chants took us up higher. The sound of the chants brought in flowers, butterflies and other swirling life around us. I thought of it as a creation chant, as if it were viewing God as he created beauty. Finally we floated down with all the blossoms and birds and butterflies and came back to the meadow. I smiled at my own romanticism then grew curious because this is where Jesus took over my mental images.

He stood off at the end of the path and then he brought the sun down to us, a golden orange globe from the sky and it set behind him. Jesus enclosed the sun with his whole self and waited for us. We walked down the path and entered the glowing, red sun. Just before we entered, everything turned into a golden, lighted entranceway. At this point, suddenly, the vision was complete and done. I got up and turned off the tape player and my living room was once more silent.

I wonder now what the message or symbol was that Jesus was trying to convey. Was it a prediction about the end of the earth? I don't' think so because even though it was a setting sun, the sky stayed blue. The sun was a red and swollen, molten like the sun had been heated up from constant motion, yet it was also awesomely beautiful.

I told Y he could visit me whenever he wanted and he said I could do the same. But, as I explained to him, I don't have much sustaining power, I can only stay a few minutes at a time and besides I don't want to disturb his meditation.

"I am meditating now," he told me and smiled.

I thought it was amazing how he can go all over the world at a whim, "And other worlds," he interjected into my thoughts, playing with me. He is so mature and wise and well trained. I think next he may learn how to actually teleport his body, that is if he doesn't know how already. I think X has already learned this trick? I think I will learn how to do this, some day

too. But I am an infant playing with an adult mine field, I still have much
to learn.

7/9/01

Tonight I am sitting at my pond swatting away flies. I know that some
people can ignore them during meditation but I don't even try. Y said that
you need to become invisible to them and they will leave you alone.
Sounds impossible to me. They aren't too bad, not so bad I can't tolerate
them. I forgot about them when I went with Jesus this moment. He took
me to a wild running brook that was musically flowing across the rocks.

"You know I love nature wild and untamed, don't you. Not for me the
organized flower arrangement and perfect grass, although some arrangements can be very beautiful, it isn't my first choice."

We walked through the meadow and I reached down and touched a bush
of wild roses. I cut my finger on a thorn and watched the blood bead up.

"You don't need to bleed here." Jesus said.

I thought of myself sitting before my pond at the same time I was walking with Jesus in the meadow but Jesus said that isn't what he meant.

He explained that he meant that humans that live here don't need to
bleed. They can stop the flow of blood if they choose. It is usual to allow it
to flow for a minute to clean the wound. "You also don't need to let a
thorn cut you if you are prepared. He gave me an example, if a person is
walking through a large patch of thorn bushes they can protect themselves
by creating a shield around their body.

"Would you give them this magic?"

"No, they need to have the mental compactly and ability before they
come here. No one is allowed to live here unless they have certain mental
abilities already in place that can nurture and grow.

"But isn't this earth?

"Yes, the new earth."

"What about children being born?

"They will be asked if they choose to be here"

"That seems odd but I like the idea.

We walked further over a hill of boulders and I recognized the small valley setting. "I've been here before"

"Yes, many times" Jesus answered.

We then went up into a very high mountain and watched the sun set. It was mild but very beautiful.

Jesus explained that there were diverse types of fauna like on earth, new earth has frozen poles too but the weather system is not so extreme. "But don't worry, it is wild enough for you.

I smiled.

'What about earth, the real earth? Will you show me what will happen to it? Then I stopped and changed my mind. "Never mind, I don't want to know. But I thought you told me once that earth could be like the new earth? How? All I could imagine was billions of people crowding themselves out and pollution raining all over the continents.

"Yes, some disastrous events will happen before humans finally change the direction that earth is going. "

"Then we will change it?"

"It will be your choice. You will make the decision. I don't choose which way mankind will go. After the disaster, with the right choice, earth could be vitally alive again.

" I would rather be here"

"Yes."

I watched a flock of birds fly across the sky and looked around at the far off landscape once more before we left.

7/11/01

Sometimes an event is so wonderful it shows the heights that our society can attain. I am referring to the Right Whale that is swimming off the coast of Cape Cod with a fishing line imbedded in its mouth. Our concern for this whale and backing of the scientist's efforts to free it says a lot about us and our potential. We are all concerned and praying for the best. This ability to focus our concern isn't only in the West or U S. It also applies to other nations. I remember the sick feeling I got when I learned about the elephant that stepped on a land mind. the elephant cried and I cried too when I read about it. I wasn't the only one. Thousands of people all around the world cried and prayed and sent money for that elephant. God Bless us. We are looking up, following heaven's decrees at last. It takes a great civilization to show such concern for non-human life, at least, when it is pointed out to us in the news. We still have millions of people starving and hurting every day but they become old news fast.

Although a part of the rise in consciousness is probably helped by the way news travels around the world at the speed of light and also because of high living standards and education. Leisure now gives us time to contemplate the feelings of other life besides our own. I am proud of us when we show such love. Even if we can't save the whale, we cared, we tried.

Jesus said that something else will shortly show up that will bring out our concern too. I'd like to thank the groups who are sending funds to help the Right Whale.

7/11/01

We are changing, constantly changing and evolving. What may seem a backward step is in reality a lesson that pushes us onwards, ever onwards. This is Jesus message tonight. Mary is with us and Jesus and Mary took me into space. We went where the stars are so close together there is no darkness. Instead, a million rainbows, auroras of silken curtains surrounded us. We floated, bathed in light, milk white and this turned into a blend of colors but they were constantly changing and moving. Even when the whitest of white was changing and flowing I could perceive its movement. I could look far out, very far away and see the darkness of space again.

We went further inside until the flow grew like chrysanthemum petals constantly renewing itself or a fountain of pure silver star light moving up and outward, never creasing its outward flow. Over and over the flower flowed out, growing large then expanding. The point would ever flow and expand again and again.

Jesus said that this was the Mind of God, that we were inside the Source, God's continuous thoughts and imagery. Thought elements, sheets of flowering ideas, creative nodes of if's and then's and causes and effects flowing forever everywhere, expanding infinitely.

God's creative thoughts never cease, according to Jesus. The movement continues into unfathomable reaches. If I put out my finger and imagine the tip penetrating the universe at that point, I couldn't count the worlds, universes, substances, times, reckonings, ideas, that go on and on forever.

"Nothing stays the same, all matter and events roll onwards towards God's goal.

This is the message Jesus and Mary wants me to convey tonight. The constant creativeness and movement of the universe. It never began, never stops, and never ends. It goes on forever. My mind cannot grasp a fraction of its totality. It has no totality, only movement and change. Only unending beginnings. Like a river that has no source, like a snake biting its own tail, like riding on a mobius strip, like the circumference of a circle, like a balloon that keeps expanding and expanding infinitely, no beginning and no end, only change.

We are changing and growing. We will never be completed. We will keep growing unceasingly because God will never cease. This is the message tonight, great change is coming, small changes are always coming, but we must not be afraid. Change is our birthright and our promise.

7/11/01

How many times has Jesus implied, or told me straight out that I would do a certain thing? not because he told me to, or ordered me to, or it was right. No, I would do it because that is what I did. The writing, the poem, the play, the book all completed for the most trite of reasons. The reason is that that is what I did and what the future has recorded that I did. Even tonight Jesus told me I would write, and it's now one am in the morning and I got up to write a poem and now this. And the sad part is that it all pours out from my loneliness and pain. So here is the idea, both heaven and hell cause me pain because, because pain is what caused me to write what you would read in the future. It all falls into one singularity, my life is empty so that yours will be filled? Does this make sense?

No, not even to me but it is more true than truth, more real than I am, more painful then you will feel reading this someday.

I hear a laughs and words that say, "Its almost over."

"What" I ask, "the pain or life or both."

7/13/01

This is a warning

I am really afraid now, I keep remembering what Jesus said about "Something is coming." When I watched the television movie about the biological weapon, a virus I suddenly knew or was afraid that this is what is coming. Not a nuke, a bio-virus. Many events and changes may be coming but this one stuck out tonight.

So instead of building an anti-missile shield we better put more effort into protecting people from bio-weapons. The movie wasn't very good but the idea is real. I wonder if someone else is getting the same idea, someone with the means to enact or the urge to disburse a bio-weapon within the United States. No, this information is already known to all.

Jesus said to warn you. This means that it can be prevented. I know from books I've read that the U S is always checking. Dogs check for drugs all the time, can they also check for a virus or bacteria? A person could wear a virus on their clothing or shoes or carry it in medicine pills. How could we prevent this? It would be easy. All it takes is a very sick mind with a dedication to harm the US.

I remember once when I thought I could heal people, even though I was given a gift and shown how to use it, I was afraid to use it because I felt uncertain. An angel told me that one day I would use the gift and that I will know how when the time comes. Is this what the angel meant? Don't know. This is a warning. I don't feel like writing this. I don't want to know. The verse at the end of the movie was true. "Not if, but when."

It is odd, but on the map of target areas and places where the infection was greatest and spreading, Detroit wasn't in the red. Odd because it is also an international fly zone. Detroit will be spared in the real life attack too. Why do I think I know this? I don't know, I just do. No one specifically told me this. Jesus did not tell me. I just believe it to be true. I don't know how virulent or extensive the whole attack could be. I am only using my own intuition to know it will not hit Detroit.

We all know everything because we are part of God and God knows and sees all. Remember King's book, "The Stand." I do. I remember it well. I don't believe we will ever get anything that bad, just bad enough to hurt.

When I think of the horror that might attack us, I feel very ashamed of my selfish outbursts and worries. My own problems melt away and pale next to the real possibility of a bio-terrorism. If true, why keep pushing, why hope or pray? The answer is because it is possibly not true? This is only a warning? and we can prevent a warning from happening, our government is always on the alert.

This is all badly written because I am tired and upset. Somehow it all fits like a square peg in a square hole. We can only hope the virus catches only a few people. With this fear, everything takes on a new light. I feel like running out to the suburbs and visiting my family and hugging everyone.

My book is about the earth heating up. That's disaster enough isn't it? It's as if the earth and its peoples are inside a box that keeps squeezing and getting smaller everywhere and in whatever direction we turn there is danger.

Jesus has said, "You are doing it to yourselves."

I agree. We have ourselves standing on a cliff edge and any major event can shove us off. It is all of our own making, it is grown from selfish motives. Maybe the purpose of my book isn't to prevent disaster, instead, maybe it's to show us how we should have lived, when it's all over. If nothing else, we will have learned what our priorities should have been. The potential is so horrifying that it fills my mind tonight; yet, by tomorrow I'll forget and go about the daily chores of living. Isn't that the real horror?

7/19/01

This is so beautiful that I keep reviewing it in my mind. Last night I woke up standing in front of a golden yellow opening in the sky. Such love was pouring out of the opening I felt like crying in happiness. The sky beckoned me and called to me. I hungered to walk into this opening in the horizon and did. But I couldn't exactly reach it because I went back to sleep. But before I did, I knew that I would paint this feeling and view somehow, that I would spend the rest of my life trying to capture its essence on canvas and that I will never quite succeed.

Tonight, Jesus took me into this same sky. I even thrill as I write this. We slowly walked towards it because the total effect of its impact would have overwhelmed me if we had arrived too suddenly. As I got closer and closer, I felt an aura emanating from its core. I realized that I wasn't only thrilled by the vivid gold mixed with pale and bright yellows but by something in the air. There was some quality that I couldn't describe at first. I only know that I felt invigorated and happy. Yes happy. As if all pleasure surrounded me, as if a cloak of delight enwrapped me in its embrace, as if…

It was a heady feeling just to take one step after another. I would lift one foot and then another realizing at each step that I walked further and further into its penetrating aura. Then I realized what I was stepping towards, I was walking in life's essence. The essence of God giving life to every being, every plant, every thing in existence. No wonder I felt rejuvenated. I was inside the Fountain of Youth. Bathing in it, breathing it in through my pores, absorbing it, loving in it, crying in it.

And then I took a small amount of it in my hand and put it into the center of my Dad who lay in the hospital in Florida. He just had surgery that day and his prognoses was not good. This golden nugget infused his body with a golden light as I watched. I left but I felt good that maybe this life essence from God helped him.

All this time Jesus was with me and I suddenly understood that this was where the gift I had received before came from. That this gift was not given lightly and it was to be used sparingly but I would use it again some day. Jesus told me that I would go back again and again to gather up this gift, this wonderful gift of life, this font of flowering sunshine. This was a fountain pouring out the sun, a fountain that never rests, a sun that never sets or rises, an overflowing cornconupia of golden life.

I felt my own center fill with this gift before we left and Jesus told me to write about our trip. He told me before that we would go to some wonderful places. My imagination couldn't have begun to know where Jesus would take me. I am so thrilled and humbled by this visit. Thank you Jesus, thank you.

7/22/01

I have found it, or rather it has been given to me, what mankind has searched for throughout its existence: The fountain of youth, the alchemist's gold, the philosopher's stone, Shanghai La, El Dorado, the pot of gold at the end of the rainbow. Yes, I have walked in the fountain of life.

Again this morning I was allowed to hold and carry a tiny grain of this golden loving substance belonging to God. Actually I carried the mental idea of a grain of golden substance or nugget because this helps me visualize it. I carried it to my sick father who has been diagnosed with cancer. The life substance glowed with aliveness as if a part of the sun were inside ready to shrink and burn off the unwanted extra cells. I don't think of it as a magic cure-all, its not, rather it is a life giving substance that brings back vitality? Only a guess.

Before I gathered a portion of the substance to take to my dad, I asked Jesus if I had permission. He replied, "You don't need to ask for permission. You have been given it as a gift" It was for me to use, God's life essence, the same essence that pours freely always and everywhere throughout the universe.

At Jesus invitation, I stepped into the richness and let the living substance seep into and throughout my body. I suddenly realized now, as I write this, the many implications of this living substance. It implies vigorous life but in the act of infusing life it also infuses youth because the two are entwined.

The legends of eternal youth are to be found here. This is the Source. I don't hope for eternal youth and have not been granted it. As with any great gift, if not used wisely, it could turn into a curse; eternal youth if taken too far could become unending life, perhaps a life of agony. I am thankful that I don't hunger for eternal youth. I have had enough of life on earth to last me a long while. I don't need eternal life, only vitality, health, energy, and mental well-being. This life will end I expect at God's own time for it or when Jesus picks me up. Hopefully during this lifetime.

There was an article in the paper today about the Promise Keepers. (a group of religious men) and how their numbers have went down from 40,000 to 7,000 (still a substantial number) When the group first began and I read about it in the newspaper, a voice said to me, "I did it." I was confused as to how owned the voice, was it Jesus or the evil one. At that time I couldn't tell or wasn't certain. I was in a quandary as to who spoke and for what purpose. I kept asking myself who and why. I couldn't say for sure but something seemed out of place with the group from the beginning. In one sense it was wonderful to see so many men grouped for the purpose of spiritual answers to their lives. One minute I would be proud to read about such a large gathering and the next I would feel uneasy and worried.

Now looking back, hindsight is always easy. I am more understanding of what made me feel uneasy. On the surface it seemed a great movement, and was, the problem was in its potential for propaganda. The group was too harmonious, too middle class, too white, too male, too ready and willing to listen to speakers and accept what they decreed. I think after Hitler's Nazis we need to be ever vigilant about such large gatherings for specific purposes. After all, Hitler's was kind of a religious movement too, cloaked as a drive to human perfection. It can happen here. If evil was the source of that voice, then it could have developed into an idea that could have swept over middle America just as the religious right tried to do.

7/24/01

A lot happened this morning during meditation. I turned on the chants and it took a while for me to feel within their sounds and I am not sure I ever did this morning. I was with Jesus and still worried about my dad. He said I should go into God's sky opening and bring out more golden life essence for him. I did and I tried to talk to my dad as he lay in the hospital. I tried to tell him what I was doing and how I was praying and trying to help him by bringing him this golden substance. That it would fight his cancer cell by cell because it came from God's fountain. I told him my name and that I was sorry I couldn't come down for a visit. I didn't know if he heard me. Jesus said that he did not. He is not spiritual at all and I don't even know if he believes in God. I hope he has changed his mind since his sickness.

When I finished talking to my dad, Jesus told me to go into God's fountain myself. I walked in and asked Jesus why he wanted me to enter. He said, "You need it." I kept walking but it was becoming intense and I told Jesus I couldn't walk any further. He told me that he would walk with me. So we continued into God's life giving substance. Jesus said that I should let it penetrate my whole body. I felt and saw my body as from a distance that it was so old and worthless, it didn't belong here and was nothing but a tarnish within the gold. But I did as Jesus told me. I opened my mouth and let the golden substance flow into me and felt it pour and pump through out my whole body system. I became a golden glowing human within brighter and silvery streams of golden water. I was inside a silver sparkling water fall cascading down around me. Everywhere was the gentle movement downward of silver and golden substance. I felt no pressure of down ness, just the view looked like an everywhere fountain. Somehow I knew I was far from the center of the fountain, if there was a center. I felt that I was still inside the diffused edge but I could go no further. Its intensity prohibited me.

We left and I felt the golden substance dissipate gradually from my system. A small nugget or grain of life essence remained within my body. I could sense it if I choose. I understood that this substance is dispersed throughout the universe, like a fog and that I had gathered it up into my arms to carry and into my self in a more intense form. As if I were more able to enter deeper I perhaps could have invigorated myself more thoroughly.

We then went to visit the old elderly women who I mentioned at the beginning of these notes. She is one of the few people who are both in heaven and on earth at the same time. Jesus asked her if we could visit. Somehow I know that she granted us an audience. That was the way I thought about it. For some reason I knelt before her on the floor before her presence. This seemed to come naturally and I can't remember if she was also kneeling on the floor or sitting in a chair. I felt as though I owed her obsolesce and great respect. Her body was so old and her face a mask of tiny wrinkles but strangely did not seem old. She even showed me herself as a young lady. I understood that looks were not important to her any longer, that most things that concern us seemed trite to her and not worthy of bother.

Her mind is so spiritually great that she can determine at what exact point in existence she will choose to leave this earth. At present, her continual, living thoughts are useful and valuable to all of us for a reason I did not understand or was not explained to me. I realized that she was so far beyond our spiritual understanding that any explanation would belittle her true purpose for staying alive. I also understood that the concerns that most of us humans fight for and strive for have no importance to her. She is truly beyond it all.

This one point worried me and I asked her if the health of the world was still important to her. I was thinking of the warming of earth, which has been on my mind lately.

She smiled

Jesus said, "She can keep trees alive and more just by her thoughts alone, and does.

Then I had a slight understanding of why she was still here and the work her spiritual mind was capable of. I nodded in great respect to her before we left.

I asked Jesus to tell me her name because I may need to know it one day. I couldn't tell her nationality or religion from her stance or the cloths she wore. I think she was beyond religious or cultural attributes that we usually think are so important. Because of her great spirituality I wondered if she might be Hindu but I don't really know.

"You will learn her name when she chooses to die," Jesus told me.

I am very ignorant of different cultures and can only wait until she chooses to reveal herself to learn her name. We are much better off that she lives. Earth needs her because she is helping hold it together. But I speculate that she must be a famous person and I thank her for her continued love and care she gives to the earth. We need more great people like her.

I would like to clarify for you my style of meditation and my writing. A lot of the events I write about last only a few seconds, at other times my mind wonders and I don't hold the vision or control it very well. Just ask Y how true this is. Sometimes I dramatize the events which makes them seem longer or more visually appealing than they actually are. I tell you this so when you begin to meditate and go on your own journey into heaven's realms, you won't dismiss events that seem too short or that quickly flow through your awareness. Don't expect more that you get. There will be times when the visions will be so intense and full of there ness that you will need to wake up from it as if from a different world but at other times it will be fleeting and seem to have little import. Grab it all because it is all God, all heaven, all Jesus' teachings. Grab it all.

7/24/01

Tonight I sat and meditated again. I had been thinking about Jesus words when he said that "I needed it." He was referring to God's substance. So I wanted to go into the fountain again. Jesus was there with me and so was X. Was it his dark side?

Jesus said "He wants to go with us."

I said, "No" Not because I felt jealous or selfish but because I was afraid he would put obstacles in my path or hinder my pleasure in some way. For some reason I felt angry with X.

Jesus assured me that he would not hinder me so I agreed to his presence.

He entered with us. He followed behind me. We stepped or floated into a large gold misty fog. The feeling was so good I eventually took X's hand as we traveled within and he walked by my side. As we went further it seemed more vivid. It was never glaring or garish, just soft and light. I stopped and let God's substance flow throughout my body and bath in every pore and, at the same time, wondered how X was doing beside me.

Then Jesus suddenly said, "Go in further."

I tried but couldn't seem to push against the thickness of the cascade flowing around and through us. I tried again and suddenly I did go in further. I gasped as I became a part of the whole. I was no longer there as a person in a human body but as a solid gold light. I can't describe it. The substance of God's fountain became myself. I felt God's substance so intensely and emotionally, I cried. Even as I left I cried. When we came to the edge of the sky I didn't want to leave. I still felt the beauty of the gold in my eyes and it seemed to me that I would loose the golden glow inside me if I left. I felt such life inside me I hesitated until Jesus took my hand and led me away to my favorite meadow.

There on the grass flowered hill with the lake in the distance I cried for my loss. X sat next to me and seemed perplexed by my intense reaction. I understood that he hadn't went in as deep as I had into the fountain. His experience was less than mine because I have built up my ability to perceive over the years. He was still a novice in that respect which made it more difficult for him.

But this time, after I left, there was a difference, I felt as thought I were still filled with God's light, that I had kept a greater portion upon leaving. though I still cried at its loss. Jesus nodded his agreement.

Later when I opened my eyes and told Jesus that I didn't want to write about this event. Perhaps because X had went with us, but I think it was too precious for me, still too raw and beautiful.

"You'll forget." Jesus suggested.

So I agreed to write it. After all, this is my job, to experience and report. Besides I would never disappoint Jesus. I still feel so good that I want to tell everyone I know. Especially I want to tell Y but maybe he already knows.

7/30/01

This morning I decided to listen to the chants for a few minutes and Y joined me. We visited and I told him I loved him again. I thought it was amazing the type of love I have for him and others. I would describe it as expansive because that is how it feels, as though my love expands us and makes us grow more together at the same time it incorporates more and more people and place. The universe becomes our love nest. And this love has few of the attributes of selfishness or self-involvement. It is very beautiful and I enjoyed our visit immensely. I won't write about what we talked about because that is private.

Then I remembered that I needed to think of my dad and encourage the cancer cells to stop growing. So I wanted to go back into God's fountain of life. Y said he would like to go with me and he did. We walked further and further into the flowing air around us and breathed in the glowing substance for a while then left. I apologized to Y because I was too self-conscious knowing he was with me to go in deeper. His words implied that he had felt the life giving water too and he understood my dilemma. I am so used to being with Jesus that when other people would share our space, I am thrown off my stride. I hope Y will choose to go with me again. Please do. I will ask him to join me and I won't be so self-conscious. I realize, as I write this, that he has probably been with me before without my knowing it. I joked that he could be following me but "You can't do that if you are invited, can you." It was a private joke and I only include it to show the kind of relationship we have together. It is similar to the relationship I have with Jesus. I have invited Y to visit anytime he chooses with or without my knowledge. We love each other and are becoming one.

In church yesterday, I was thinking of God's gift to me and worried about how I should use it when Jesus told me, "You haven't accepted it yet." I think he meant I haven't accepted the conditions that surround the gift yet, whatever they are. I don't know.

He added, "It is the greatest gift heaven can bestow on a human."

I thought I had accepted it? But I also suddenly realized why I hold back, it is because I am afraid and worried how to use it. I don't want to need to use it or even think about what all its ramifications imply. Yes, that is what held me back and still does, how and when to use it. For example, do I have the right , if I had the ability, to help my father who has cancer just because I know him when there are so many other people suffering the same fate. We are not talking about prayer here, of course I can pray and try to shrink cells with my mind, but what if I had the gift of God's life giving substance? Would that make my touch gold? Would that make me a healer? Would that make hoards of people stand at my door waiting for my hand? Would that be fare? No. If that is what God's life substance means than I don't know if I want it. If it means longer life for me or health, then maybe. What more could it mean? I don't know and refuse to think. What is Jesus asking of me by giving me this gift?

This life giving substance from God has more power than we can conceive of in your young minds. This also plays on my fears and most especially the fear that I could come to enjoy the power it bestowed too much. So yes I am hesitant and afraid. After this long spew of thoughts I smiled at Jesus and answered his unspoken question, "Do you accept the gift?"

"Yes, you know I do because I already did one day, it is already decreed that I had accepted."

Jesus smiled knowingly.

Then it was time for the priest to bless the bread and wine for communion and I realized once again very vividly the extent of the sacrifice Jesus gave us with his life. He could have lived forever, he had been given the greatest gift of life and he chooses to give up that gift on the cross. He did this for us. Most of us through the centuries have been ignorant to the thousands and thousands of potential earth years he gave up on the cross. Luckily, for us, as it turned out, God gave him life forever anyway. When God gives such life, a wooden cross cannot infringe or take it away.

7/30/01

I understand more about X now. I remember once when he saw me sitting and waiting for him he was momentarily startled either by the fact that it was me or my dress or? But it was dark there in the show and before he thought I noticed him, he faced in the opposite direction and I could almost see his bones and features rearrange themselves. His shoulders too grew taller. It was a new image that faced me, only slightly changed but enough to see a difference. He kept his eyes watery and half closed as if he had been taking dope, I asked him a few times if he had because during the time I was with him I was flamboosled into believing he was really who he said he was. Our souls are mirrored in our eyes so if someone needs to disguise themselves, the eyes are the first place to change.

I have learned more. Just as Y uses his spiritual gift to study religions and beliefs and people's attitudes to that belief, X uses his gift to study people and cultures from within, literally. He becomes a person of that culture.

One other thing I have learned about X is that he is very old, so old that when he pretended he had a bike that he rode, Jesus told me that he was too old to ride it for long and that I could out ride him any day. We never did go bike riding because he disappeared in that mode of character from my life, like he disappeared from every mode. He always does that, pops into my life in odd moments and then pops out again.

I also believe X is trying to live longer and is perhaps worried about it. In every mode of character he portrays he has talked about longevity and diet and exercise. I can't imagine why. Is he afraid of dying? Or is it that he enjoys life so much? If you think about it, with his ability to become anyone he chooses even within different cultures. If that is his intent, then the amount of raw learning potentials is almost unlimited. We live in such a huge, complex world with divergent cultures and peoples that his work could be never ending. X could spend many life times studying earth and its peoples and never get to the end, and perhaps he has tried.

This brings up the speculation or idea that God has bestowed specific gifts on certain people for a purpose. To accentuate those abilities and make them visual and a valued part of his promise. God may want us to learn and see what our potential is. These gifts are specific, possible within the human condition, and are promised to us if we accept them. How can we not?

7/31/01

The rich need help as much as the poor. God know that which is why he sent prophets out to other cities and towns. Jesus knew that too. Every time I go out to Hall Road to visit a friend and go to the show, culture shock grips my guts and makes me sick. The difference is so vast compared to my Detroit neighborhood, as to be mind-boggling. Thousands of people are out enjoying life, not just driving as you would see on Detroit streets, but going to movies, eating at fine restraints and fast food joints, shopping at malls and K Marts, and Wal-marts and Targets and Meyers and specialty shops. The huge parking lots are congested with people parked for the purpose of spending money. and the selection of places to spend that money is staggering.

I always drive away with a sense of amazement mixed in with envy and fear. Fear for the mindlessness of it all, the total disregard many people have for the state of the world and its future. How dare we so garishly continue such a disfiguring life style. Disfiguring to our mind, souls, bodies, lives, other people's lives, other countries well-being, our earth. We take from the trees, soil, un-renewable resources, and future. We give information, technology, money, air pollution, and heat back, so much heat that earth may become like Venus in the near future. Common sense tells us this is not right, that this is selfish.

If you could spread our extremely rich life style to most humans on earth, the earth would die within a few years, choked to death and withered. If you eat a Arby's beef sandwich, a sandwich loaded with enough beef to feed a city block in the developing world or many children in ours for $2.00 and a coupon, you are depriving many people nourishment, not only of protein but you are contributing to the beef cattle industry which costs more than rice, wheat, or soybeans.

All the supermarkets, and shows abundant Wal-Marts are using up energy for air conditioning or heat, people are using gas to get there, then throwing away used items and packages for trash pick-up and .... actually I don't know or understand all the ramifications of our life style and I have never been part of the environmental movement before. Like many of you, I thought it went too far when a dam couldn't be built because of a few small fish. Now after Jesus involvement in this book and a lot of reading into the subject, I realize that I was wrong. We all need to become environmentalists or we'll die.

Did I mention my own moment of envy? Can you imagine the envy that people may have in other countries? Can you also imagine how their hate might grow in proportion to our wealth? Can you imagine the extent that some countries may go to stop us? Never mind hate, what about idealism? Some misguided souls out there may try to stop us because they want to save the planet or their traditions from the influence of our over wrought culture. Notice that I didn't say how anyone could stop us because the methods are many and numerous and probably beyond even my imagination. The point is that we are wrong, if we don't know that we better learn it fast.

The end? except for another travel experience with J? I can't think of anything more awesome than Gods fountain of life? How can even Jesus top that?

Well not quite the end. I remember carrying gold light from God's fountain to my dad and placing it in his body. I remember thinking with my mind that the substance would shrink cancer, cell by cell. It may have, but it was too little too late. He died this morning.

Now I wonder if I misconstrued the purpose of the golden substance from God's fountain. Instead of healing a body, its purpose may be to spread spiritual awareness. Perhaps I gave him a spiritual gift, perhaps the golden substance helped him find God at the end, and perhaps it gave life after death?

Jesus is agreeing with me as I write this. This puts a new light on my acceptance or non-acceptance of the spiritual gift. Who could not accept a gift from God? The knowledge that it is spiritual life rather than healing life takes away my fear that I will need to use it one day to heal sick people. That is not its purpose, and I should have known this long ago. I remember the angels showing me how to use God's golden light after they poured it into me from a cup in heaven, how it should spread to cover the ground I walked on and the surrounding environment. As I watched I saw the street and curb turn gold, the bushes and homes and people walking by in the vision. Nothing turned hard, like in the Midas fable, it was all soft with a gold that no one could see but still penetrated all substances as it spread. I would like to be able to send God's golden substance all over the cities and countries of the earth, if I could. I have neglected to use this gift so far. According to Jesus I have not actually accepted it yet. I am still ignorant of how to use it or when and if I have it? Is it that I should not loose it after I leave God's presence?

Oh, oh, Jesus nods "Yes."

8/5/01

It happened yesterday but I am not writing it until today. I was asked to write a eulogy for my dad's funeral service the night before the funeral. I though about it and then wrote remembrances from my childhood and the gifts that dad gave me- playfulness and the love of knowledge. At the end of the eulogy I wrote a note about my concern about dad's spiritual relationship with God and that I believed he knew God at the end. I based this on the gifts of light from God's fountain that I took to him while he lay dying. I had miss-perceived the nature of the gifts from God, his fountain of youth. I thought its purpose was to try and heal dad. I was wrong. The real purpose, and more lasting purpose, was to heal his soul. The gift of life helped usher him into heaven.

As I sat thinking these thoughts and writing my final version of the eulogy, Dad's voice spoke to me and said, "It worked." Then the voice was gone. I felt surprised and pleased. There was one other time that I heard dad's voice from afar and that was once when I forgot his birthday. I heard him call out, perhaps in his sleep, "Diane." It was very loud and strong. He lived in Florida at the time and I never told anyone about it but I never forgot to send him a birthday present after that either.

I don't expect to hear from him ever again, nor do I want to. May he rest in peace. I don't think we stay around too long after death, unless there is unfinished business that we might attend to. Those who call the dead to their side are wrong in their pursuit. The dead are better left alone so they can ascend to heaven if able or called. I believe he is now or soon will be in heaven. But I will hold in my heart forever his words and that I may have helped give him the most precious gift of all, the gift of life.

8/7/01

I am back from Florida and the funeral. It feels good to be home but I didn't feel comfortable home until I sat and meditated this morning. I turned the chants on because they help me focus. As soon as I sat down I saw gold as if a golden cloud layer and then I went further in below the clouds. The sky was blue with grass and rocks tinged with gold. There was a small golden pond in front of me. Jesus told me to go down into it. I did. I descended the slope and walked into the golden water as it rose high and higher and then immersed my whole head and body. I felt cool, refreshed and tingly all over. Then I looked to the side and saw that the pond was a part of a long stream that flowed from God's fountain. The fountain's aura seemed far off into the distance. The haze of atmosphere was also tinged with gold. I felt soft and the air was soft and the water was soft and silky as it would feel at night on earth. But it was time to step out.

I climbed out and began walking but I noticed that every place I stepped I left a golden footprint. I was delighted and told Jesus so. He suggested that I step into my neighborhood and house to leave footprints. So I did. I stood in the middle of my yard and walked up and down, then I stood in the yard next to me with the junk and old cars and then I walked down the sidewalk a little ways and walked on the empty lot next door. I also noticed before that gold was also dripping from my hands and fingers and hair and spotting on the sidewalk. But now it was fading and the golden footprints were smaller. I was drying off, loosing the effect of emersion. I felt lonely.

Jesus suddenly said. "You can do this again" I smiled and opened my eyes on the couch.

I remembered the golden substance I had brought to my dad and the fact that it worked so well for him. I hope my few footprints give off a spiritual aura for a while to help the people in my neighborhood. Note- this was only a visualization of Jesus wishes. He wants me to spread God's spirit around but first I need to acquire it.

A number of days ago I was standing and admiring a large, majestic and beautiful old tree. A voice said to me, "The tree is aware of your admiration." I was surprised and felt pleased. This is a wonderful state of hope because if the trees can perceive somehow our admiration of them, changing our world for the better just became easier. Just by loving and admiring trees we can help them. Our minds send waves of happiness outward. The colliery of this is that we also send our anger and stress. Maybe we need another happy song like "Don't worry, be happy."

8/9/01

It is import to know when to quit when to end a book. I've decided that this is the final statement for this book. Jesus will take me one more place as a final statement. I don't mean that I will stop writing or traveling with him, just that my notes from now on will go into a new tablet. I've written all my experiences with Jesus in a tablet first before I copy the word on the computer. For some reason this fits the method and style of my notes. I leave the decision or place for our last visit to Jesus.

What a visit. How can I tell you where I went tonight without sounding silly? or weird? It was so odd, almost as if I stepped into a Star Trek rerun. When I said that to Jesus he laughed.

Where I went tonight, I still can't believe it was just a few steps away from my lawn chairs into a huge ship sitting in what I'll call N space. It was not really a ship Jesus told me more like a conveyance, a convenience to the group to use while they help prevent the earth from being destroyed. They have work stations set up for their use in many places on our planet. Many people are involved in saving earth.

I mean, right here. It covered at least a city block and I walked right through my garage to enter and then when I was inside everything looked ghostly. I could see my world super imposed into the ships. I refer to it as ship because that is easer for me but remember it is not a ship. Cars were driving through it from Theodore and Moran. More about this later. But there was sunlight and blue sky and clouds even though it was evening in my back yard. Like a glass ship. No not a glass or ship, a conveyance.

Jesus said they bring a chosen space with them. A number of people with the big eyes were walking around inside. This was their work area, where they try to convince us to change our behavior to do something different for earth's benefit. They move it around a lot. I asked Jesus if he needed it to get around.

He told me, "No." Then added that he will use a similar conveyance when he comes down to earth in his official capacity. "Or do you think I should just float down as a man?" He asked me, jokingly?

I answered that I didn't care how he got here, "Just do it."

He said, "People need to be more ready."

I looked around as we spoke at the near invisible walls. I had walked right through the burnt garage in back of me when I strolled in the ship with Jesus. Amazing. Amazing that the future beings and Jesus are so close to me in reality or N space? Amazing that for this night this ship landed here, in my back yard and lot, right through three fourths of my garage. Amazing and a grand ending for this book. I love you Jesus and I truly believe that we are never alone.

I still feel so delighted and surprised. This was every science fiction reader's dream to walk within a real ship. Well, sort of a ship, one that brought its own sky and weather. Oh I love you Jesus. He invited me to come back and look at it more closely one day soon because I was interrupted by a phone call. Later, I am going back outside and search for it.

I did, of course, I couldn't find it. I walked to the back of my garage. Nothing. I knew I was inside it but I wasn't because I couldn't see any difference.

I asked Jesus, "Is it really true, is it really here?"

"Yes, to everything." He was pleased by my reaction of amazement and joy. I think the only way to visit it was with Jesus. I would need to sit back down and let Jesus take me there. Fascinating, as Spock would say.

8/10/01

The ship is still here and may be here for a while. I think the people of the future like me. I even think they watching my cat who got out last night. Silly I know. But their love goes with any of us who are willing to work for a better earth. After all they are the people who will live in our polluted sky and seas. This is most of what they do, encourage those who try to try harder. I really believe that circumstances have changed this date of his arrival. As he told me ,"People need to be ready." So just get ready, all of us, lets change our lives and world so we will be ready for Jesus.

EPILOGUE

I ended this book and began a new one a month before the World Trade Centers were bombed, September 11, 2001. After this event I suddenly realized why Jesus requested that I keep my notes in tact in the last section, Part III. Jesus' words now hit home, right in the guts, their prophetic wisdom now stood out starkly against my doubts. So much so, that it became hard for me to edit the changes I did make because my emotions were still wrapped around the events in New York. The world turned upside down that day; I began to label everything as before or after. Our world has changed mightily since September 2001, and may never be the same again.

Jesus warned me it was coming but not when; if I had known exactly when and how, and tried to tell people, who would have believed me? No one, to be sure. Jesus still warns me that more terrorist's attacks will hit America. But again, I don't know when or how and even now, no one would believe any warning I could make; so I remain silent. I will say this, Jesus has told me that my next book will also reveal coming events and warnings about our world and society. I will get it out to you as soon as possible. I hope after reading this book that you can look at the needs of our world in a different light, I know I do. May the spirit of God be with you.

APPENDIX

Poetry

I wrote this poetry while writing this book. I put them here so they would-n't interrupt the flow of the book.

Night-fears

Though I dream
fear grips my guts
fear cements my smile in place
my fears reflect many true facts
I am afraid the ice will be too sharp
afraid the day will make me asleep
afraid the night will push me awake
I am afraid the sky is falling
and I alone amid the ruins
will stand as I stood in life - singled out alone
a forever witness to mankind's plight
while the old moon burns bright holes
onto cold earthen rocks
after the sun's red beams
have died
and I remain
with the last tear left to cry

My life

A single stone upturned
my plight
rolled to sea scrub smooth
barren and cold cast formed
removed from the field of play
then heated upon a spit
until I finally cracked in places here and there
halved and turned and halved once more
yet I stayed silly proud
at each step down the tortured lane
I dared brag at other stones that went grinding by
As my body ground itself to sand
"My dream stayed big, stayed whole" I cried
"I kept - in place - my soul" and died.

Untitled Poem

As if my heart had frozen in place
feelings held in stasis
tears uncried unshed
robotic thoughts swirl within the mind
pretending pretending I am alive
that my heart beats
that ruby blood pumps and runs
that sorrow swells upon my soul
It's a lie
that only heaven knows

every uncried tear-waits for me
every angry thought circles my self
every break of heart beats only for my own lonely
body wrapped naked in empty white sheets
crying time beats try
to live the lie of alive me

but I am not alive I know
heaven says even this
this stupid poem of pain and need
they know before I wrote
and laughed or cried
but caused my plight because
it was decreed
what I wrote this night

Poem - Golden Heart

Evil can't walk here
in this golden sea
its stillborn soul cannot
reach this height
its little mindedness
heaves it back to jumping size
while God at every door
opens to my sight
and every sun dreams
my next step walking

Here is a poem I wrote in 1994

God of Light

God must really be something
if He's more than the spectrum of light
He'd go from X-rays to microns to infrared
to beyond infinity, out of sight
He is the equation of e=mc2
and can step over the barrier of night
of photons at 86,000 miles per year of light
He can walk backwards or forward in time
as often as He would please
between the quarks of an atom
to the end of time or its beginning
then make a big bang of matter stuff
to shape our earthen ball of dirt
and give us life from dust to dust
and show us the way to His kingdom
when of life we've had enough

BIBLIOGRAPHY

Courtney Brown, Ph. D., *Cosmic Voyage*: Penguin Books USA Inc., New York, N. Y., 1996, pp 129-137

Chidester, David, *Word and Light: Seeing, Hearing, and Religious Discourse*: Chicago, Illinois: University of Illinois Press, 1992.

Conway, D. J., *Flying Without a Broom: Astral Projection and the Astral World*: St. Paul, Minnesota: Llewellyn Publishers, 1995.

Davenport, Marc. *Visitors from Time:* Newberg, O.R.: Wild Flower Press, 1992.

Davies, P. C. W., and Brown, J. R., eds., *The Ghost in the Atom*: New York, N. Y.: Cambridge University Press, 1986.

Dossey, Larry M. D., *Space, Time & Medicine*: Boulder, Colorado: Shambhala Publications, Inc., 1982.

Ferguson, Kitty, *The Fire in the Equation: Science, Religion, and the Search for God: Grand Rapids, Michigan: Eerdmons Publishing Company, 1994.*

Ferris, Timothy, *The Whole Shebang*: New York, N. Y.: Simon & Schuster, Inc., 1998.

Grabbe, Lester L., *Priests, Prophets, Diviners, Sages: A Socio-Historical Study of Religious Specialists in Ancient Israel*: Valley Forge, Pennsylvania: Trinity Press International, 1995.

Gribbin, John, *Timewarps*: New York, N. Y.: Delacorte Press, 1979.

Grosso, Michael, *The Millennium Myth: Love and Death at the End of Time: Wheaten, Illinois: Quest books, 1995.*

Gwswami, Ph., D., Amit. *Self Aware Universe: How consciousness creates the material world*: New York, N. Y.: Penguin Putnam, 1993.

Harkness, Georgia, *Mysticism: Its Meaning & Message*: Nashville, N. Y., Abengdon Press, 1973.

Herbert, Nick, Ph., D.. *Faster than Light: Supraliminal Loopholes In Physics*: New York, N. Y.: Penguin Books USA, 1988.

Rondall, John L., *Psychokinesis: A study of ParanormalFforces Through the Ages*: London, England, WCiB 3PA, Souvenir Press Ltd., 1982.

Shah, Idries, *Caravan of Dreams*: Baltimore, Maryland, Penguin Books, Inc., 1974.

Sitchin, Zecharia, *Devine Encounters*: New York, N. Y., Avon Books, 1996.

Smith, Huston, *Forgotten Truth: The Primordial Tradition*: New York, N. Y., Harper & Row, Publishers, 1976.

Spoto, Donald, *The Hidden Jesus: A New Life*, New York, N. Y., St. Martin Press, 1998.

Strieber, Whitley, *The Secret School*: New York, Harper Collins, 1997.

Tyhurman, Robert A. F., *The Tibetan Book of the Dead*: New York, Bantam Books, 1998.
Velikovsky, Immanuel, *Worlds in Collision*: Garden City, N. Y., Doubleday & Company, 1950.

About the Author

I have written nonfiction and fiction novels, children's stories, articles and short stories and I publish a monthly, neighborhood newspaper. I am also a painter, illustrator, and sculptor and have a Bachelor of Fine Arts Degree from Wayne State University.

INDEX

0-595-20526-7

Made in the USA
Monee, IL
04 February 2021